THE ZERO HOUR

GLASNOST
AND
SOVIET
CINEMA
IN
TRANSITION

Andrew Horton
and Michael Brashinsky

PRINCETON UNIVERSITY PRESS · PRINCETON, NEW JERSEY

Copyright © 1992 by Princeton University Press
Published by Princeton University Press, 41 William Street,
Princeton, New Jersey 08540
In the United Kingdom: Princeton University Press, Oxford

Library of Congress Cataloging-in-Publication Data
Horton, Andrew.
The zero hour : glasnost and Soviet cinema
in transition / Andrew Horton and Michael Brashinsky
p.   cm.
Filmography:
Includes bibliographical references and index.
ISBN 0-691-06937-9 (cl) — ISBN 0-691-01920-7 (pbk.)
1. Motion pictures—Soviet Union.
2. Soviet Union—Popular culture.   3.Glasnost.
I. Brashinsky, Michael, 1965– .   II. Title.
PN1993.5.R9H63   1992
384'.8'0947—dc20   91-47875

This book has been composed in Linotron Trump Medieval

Princeton University Press books are printed on acid-free paper,
and meet the guidelines for permanence and durability of the
Committee on Production Guidelines for Book Longevity of the
Council on Library Resources

Printed in the United States of America

1   3   5   7   9   10   8   6   4   2

1   3   5   7   9   10   8   6   4   2
(Pbk.)

*To my father, who did not live till glasnost;
to my mother; and to all my relatives and friends in
the Soviet Union who have not lost hope yet,
and to those who already have.*

MICHAEL BRASHINSKY

▼

For Caroline.

ANDREW HORTON

▼

Interviewer: What do you think about
cooperative toilets?

Leonid: One must think about
one's soul.

—*God's Tramp* (*Bich bozhii,* 1989)

▼

Contents

Illustrations

Acknowledgments

WE OFFER special gratitude to our editor, Joanna Hitchcock of Princeton University Press, for her imagination, generosity, and good humor in believing in the timeliness of this project and helping see it through with dispatch. Valerie Jablow, her assistant, has also helped make this project a pleasure, especially on endless long-distance phone calls. Finally, our thanks to Jane Lincoln Taylor, our copyeditor, who worked with us with the kind of patience, professionalism, and respect that any author would be happy to receive.

MICHAEL BRASHINSKY: I wish to express my deep gratitude and appreciation to all those friends and colleagues who have helped me at different stages of the research, writing, and editing of this book.

In particular, I thank, in the Soviet Union, Sergei Dobrotvorsky of the Modern Culture division of the Leningrad State Institute of Theater, Music, and Film; Peter Shepotinnik, head of the Foreign Department of *Iskusstvo kino* magazine; and my mother, Tamara Brashinsky, who was greatly supportive of me, both overseas and in the United States. In this country, I thank Eileen and Evan Lottman in New York; Moira Ratchford of the American Committee on U.S.-Soviet Relations; Emily Bernard, for her helpful stylistic reading; my inestimably helpful and tolerant coauthor; and finally, my wife, Allison, who let me work on the text even on our honeymoon and made joyful the final, least pleasant stage of work on the manuscript.

ANDREW HORTON: Time and money for this project would not have been available without the encouragement of Loyola University of New Orleans and its travel grant support (1988); grants from the University of New Orleans Graduate Research Council in 1989, as well as its Distinguished Research Professorship award; IREX senior scholar travel funds (summer 1989, fall 1989); the joint Soviet-American Cinema Studies Conference in Moscow, November 1989 (supported by IREX), Louisiana Endowment for the Humanities minigrants for the transportation of Soviet filmmakers to and the screening of Soviet films in New Orleans; and IFEX, for allowing me to see prints I would not otherwise have seen.

I wish to single out, in Moscow, the support and kind help of Yuri Khodjaev, Director of Sovinterfest; Oleg A. Rudnev, Chairman of Sovexportfilm, and Oleg Sulkin, its Vice Chairman; Valery Kichin, Editor-in-Chief of *Soviet Film*; and filmmaker Alexey Simonov, who helped open doors that led to films and other filmmakers. I offer special thanks to Peter Shepotinnik, Olga Reizen, and Sergei Lavrentiev in Moscow for spending too much of their nonexistent free time reading the manuscript, making suggestions, finding tapes of hard-to-get films, and offering continual encouragement. Thanks are also due to Alexander Kiselev and Marina Drozdova, critics and screenwriters. I am grateful for the help of Maya Turovskaya, Alexander Doroshevich, Marianna Schaternikova, and Nina Tsyrkun of the Film Arts Academy. The support of Andrei Dementyev, Kiril Razlogov, Felix and Natasha Andreev, Andrei Andreev, Jeannette and Vitaly Poplavsky, Asya Suleeva (in Alma-Ata), and Margarita Kasimova (in Dushanbe) has also been invaluable. I offer my appreciation to all the Soviet filmmakers I have interviewed, including Vasily Pichul, Rashid Nugmanov, Nijole Adomenaite, Boris Gorlov, Yuri Mamin, and Alla Surikova. I owe much to the following people in the United States for conversations and for their reading of parts of the manuscript: Vance Kepley, Jr., Anna Lawton, Moira Ratchford, Vida Johnson, Sam and Natasha Ramer, Donna Seifer, Svetlana Boym, David Wills, John Mosier, Elizabeth Weis, and Vlada Petric, among many. And a hug for Odette, my understanding wife, who stayed "home alone" with Sam and Caroline while I watched films in Moscow, Leningrad, and Tashkent.

All translations from Russian are by the authors, unless otherwise specified. In transliterating Russian titles, the authors were guided primarily by the rules of phonetic likeness, not by any particular academic system.

THE ZERO HOUR

INTRODUCTION

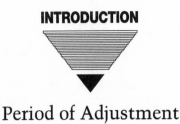

Period of Adjustment

I don't think that miracles ever confound a realist.
—FYODOR DOSTOEVSKY, *The Brothers Karamazov*

THERE WAS a joke in Moscow a few years ago that Mikhail Gorbachev's policy of *perestroika* (restructuring), begun in 1985, might finally turn into *perestrelka*—a cross fire. By August 1991 the joke suddenly had become a frightening reality. But just as swiftly, the fears of a new repressive coup gave way to an unprecedented democratic movement spearheaded by Boris Yeltsin, the elected president of the Russian republic, which swept away much of the socialist past, including the Soviet Union itself and the Communist party.

This book concerns the nature and changing role of Soviet cinema during the transitional period of 1985–1991, in which *glasnost* (openness) finally led to substantial cultural and political perestroika. Our work traces the development, the dimensions, and the dangers and cinematic rewards of these changes in Soviet culture and cinema. The first joint Soviet-American critical study of recent Soviet cinema, it is meant to be a report from the front, exploring the territory of perestroika as well as the new forces that have created a literal and metaphorical perestrelka among republics, ethnic groups, competing political parties, film studios, and independent film and video makers. David Bordwell has explained that film critics and scholars tend to be either pluralists or partisans (*Making Meaning*, 24). We are both. In our attempt to begin the process of mapping recent Soviet cinema, we are pluralists—literally so, in that each of us brings a quite different critical background to the project. And we are partisans to the degree that this book would not exist if we did not feel that, during the second half of the 1980s, Soviet cinema became one of the most interesting cinemas—aesthetically as well as in a sociopolitical and cultural context—in the world.

Soviet cinema since the beginning of glasnost has been in a complex and often contradictory state of flux; its future is still unknown. The fate of perestroika is equally unpredictable. The very word *perestroika* engenders a state of change, for it derives from the verb meaning "to reconstruct, to restructure." Thus the changes in Soviet politics, culture, and cinema under Gorbachev since 1985 must be viewed as a process, not a result. This period is only a transition, a period of adjustment. We should note that perestroika was an official political policy imposed "from above." The first reaction to the new freedom was an embarrassing silence. It seems that to be free in a cage is far easier than to be free on one's own. After this moment of silence, a range of questions showered the nation. "How can such a huge country be maintained if the economy needs to be scrapped and reformulated, since there is nothing left to 'reconstruct'?" was heard at one extreme, and "Is it possible for freedom to be allowed by the leader of the Communist party, however democratic he is?" on the other. Finally the basic philosophical questions emerged: "What is freedom?" "What is meant by a period of transition?"

Many filmmakers have expressed a grim answer. "We're close to civil war," director Stanislav Govorukhin stated at a discussion at "New Thinking and Cinema," a symposium organized by the Soviet Filmmakers' Union at its headquarters, Dom Kino, in Moscow in July 1989. "I've talked to thousands of people and nobody believes in perestroika." The following year, he presented his perspective in a popular and disturbing feature documentary about crime in the Soviet Union and the numbing difficulties of daily life for the average Soviet citizen, We Cannot Live This Way (Tak zhit' nel'zya). The film is a strongly worded diatribe against the Communist party, with a favorable nod toward the ousted Russian monarchy. While long lines queued for the film in June 1990, by August Govorukhin himself felt the film was already outdated, "because our life changes so quickly over here" (Horton, interview, Montreal, 26 August 1990).[1]

Despite the confusion, the questions initiated by glasnost raise excitement and hope to a level familiar to any traveler starting off for an unknown land. That Govorukhin could make such a brutally honest film suggests that hope exists. Such hope was unimaginable in 1977, when Mira and Antonin Liehm wrote of Soviet film of the 1970s, "The vicious circle of descriptive realism remained unbroken even by the genres of comedy, adventure, and suspense" (Most Important Art, 323). Valentin Tolstykh, a philosopher who has served as an executive secretary of the Filmmakers' Union, captures this double attitude in the title of his recent work in progress: Pessimistic Reflections of an Optimist. Director Alexander Mitta (The Crew [Ekipazh]) expressed the paradoxical spirit of the times in even stronger terms. "There is a paralysis of freedom," he

---

[1] All quotations are from personal interviews unless otherwise indicated.

observed. "We had a medieval culture, and now we are switching over to a democratic one, though we are still very far from the real values of a democratic society" ("New Thinking and Cinema"). Such a paralysis is largely a question of language—new and old, borrowed and invented, examined and celebrated. Tolstykh is quick to point out that because politics has determined the shape of language in the Soviet Union for the past seventy years, in this period of adjustment we have the task of inventing a new language, a different vocabulary. "The danger, however, is that instead of cleansing our language, cinematic and verbal, we wind up with a new conformism, a bourgeois art" (Horton, interview, Moscow, July 1989).

If much of Soviet cinema since the 1930s has reflected totalitarian impulses through socialist-realist models, the new Soviet cinema has begun to take on the responsibility of encouraging a polyphony of divergent voices. The promise of the new Soviet cinema is that it is becoming more fully connected to its own cultures and to an active interaction with other cultures around the world. Perhaps one of the greatest sins committed by the party against Soviet culture during the eras of Stalin and Brezhnev was that of isolating Soviet intellectual life from the international cultural mainstream. While cutting off the branch of the tree and putting it into a flowerpot, the leaders suggested "you're the wood, the real wood, and the only wood." Glasnost, however, has initiated a period of replanting that will be both hopeful and painful. It is difficult to be a seventy-year-old baby, but better late than never. What is particularly valuable in this period of glasnost is a new openness to world culture that is swiftly dissolving the vastly restricted worldview of previous Soviet culture.

"A plurality of consciousnesses, with equal rights and each with its own world, combine, but are not merged in the unity of event." These words might sound like an academic paraphrase of one of Gorbachev's speeches, though they were written even before he was born. The author is Russian literary theoretician Mikhail Bakhtin, writing about Dostoevsky's complex "modern" novels (*Problems of Dostoevsky's Poetics*, 6). What we wish to explore is the scope of what Bakhtin saw as polyphony, a plurality of consciousnesses (this is what makes Dostoevsky a modern author, as opposed to a "monologic," classical author) that is becoming, to varying degrees, a reality in Soviet cinema and culture today.

Michael Ryan has detailed the dangers of a rigid, centralized form of Marxism that turns polyphony into a monologue in *Marxism and Deconstruction*. Using the deconstructive critical strategies of Jacques Derrida and others, Ryan points out how the Soviet system has tended to canonize particular texts, thus "fixing" meaning as if there were no alternative point of view. Even Lenin himself, Ryan explains, used Marx's writings for his own ends in texts such as *State and Revolution* to produce "a reductive reading of fragmentary and heterogeneous texts by Marx and Engels" (160).

Because cinema is so closely bound to politics in the Soviet Union, Gorbachev's support for greater openness at the official level, which Ryan advocates at the cultural level (his book was published before glasnost, in 1982), is all the more crucial. "The deconstructive argument applies here: no text is a transparent medium for the communication of theoretical ideas, meaning or a truth, which preexists and is 'expressed' in the material practice of the text" (163). The task for filmmakers and those of us who observe filmmakers is "to keep the question open" (193).

To a great degree many (but certainly not all) Soviet filmmakers are living up to this challenge. This suggests that Soviet cinema, more than ever, is worthy of international attention, as it in turn has become more aware of and sensitive to a broader community of cinematic discourse. This positive sign indicates that the "renaissance of activity" can further clarify the "crisis of definition" in a rapidly changing Marxist culture today (Nelson and Grossberg, *Marxism*), and also in the larger context of shifting forms and practices of socialism worldwide.

Beyond these levels there looms yet another threat. "The world is close to global catastrophe, and that is an anthropologically caused catastrophe," cautioned Soviet philosopher Boris Grushin ("New Thinking and Cinema"). Film can exert a significant influence in such a state of crisis. Grushin continued, "We are living in a culture that we cannot live in at all, neither physically, socially, or spiritually. . . . We have *no language.*" The description of this search for a new polyphonic language expressed on film is our objective as well.

OLD ICONS, NEW IMAGES

Consider three images taken from the recent Soviet screen:

A bearded man in his thirties is attending a dance class at an institute of culture and is asked along with the rest of the class to do a Russian dance. He refuses and, drunk, shouts out, "There's no culture, no culture here!" He proceeds to do a wild, improvised dance "of the world" to a rousing Jewish folk tune as the camera swirls with him in a dizzying 360-degree panning shot.

A plain-looking, middle-aged woman in a drab dress, in a cramped, working-class kitchen, makes breakfast for herself. We watch every detail as she spreads butter on her bread, pours herself milk, and puts a light-rock tape in the cassette player that had belonged to her teenage son who recently committed suicide, in large part because of his mother's harsh judgment of him and his girlfriend. The scene is totally mundane and seemingly without "drama." The camera continues to observe this woman, who has shown little emotion throughout the film. Suddenly she begins to weep on camera, at first slowly and then with terrifying, uncontrollable sobbing. This is not acting: the documentary camera has caught a telling moment of "real life" as we discover the pain of a mother whose tears, we sense, reflect her loss, her guilt, her reaction against her environment.

An attractive, naked young woman with streaked hair straddles a young man who looks a bit like an unshaven contemporary James Dean as they make love in his bare student dormitory. Later, at the seashore, he asks her what she believes in. "Communism, of course," she says with shatteringly ironic sarcasm.

All three scenes come from Soviet films made since Gorbachev introduced sweeping changes in Soviet politics and society in April 1985 under the banner of glasnost and perestroika. It is highly unlikely that any of these new images—a critique of the collapse of Russian culture; a documentary depiction of teen suicide caused, in large part, by pressures brought on by an impersonal Communist system; and a graphic depiction of human sexuality spiked with a sarcastic commentary on the ruling dogma—could have been shot, let alone shown, before glasnost.

Our first scene is from a 1989 family tragicomedy by Vladimir Prokhorov and Alexander Alexandrov, *Assuage My Sorrows* (*Utoli moya pechali*). The second is from a 1987 Estonian documentary by Mark Soosaar, *A Life without . . .* (*Zhizn' bez . . .*), which addresses the rising problem of teenage suicide. The final image is from Vasily Pichul's film *Little Vera* (*Malen'kaya Vera*), which became the most popular Soviet film of 1988. It was seen by more than fifty million viewers, won awards at international film festivals (Montreal, Chicago, Venice), and gained a large following abroad. Taken together, these remarkable films suggest that glasnost has initiated a startling new era for Soviet filmmakers.

In this volume we aim to place these new images in a more meaningful perspective by combining Soviet and American critical approaches to this pressing subject. Yet we begin not with the new films but with the concept of the icon and the image in Russian culture. The thousand-year history of the Orthodox faith in Russia and its much longer history in the nations that made up the Byzantine Empire is testimony to the centrality of the icon to religious belief and practice. Two factors account for the particular importance of the painted image. First is the belief (opposed by the iconoclasts) that the icon embodies the spirit of the figure represented, thereby making the image itself sacred.

The difference between photography—the capturing of physical reality—and iconography needs to be emphasized. "The artist of Old Russia did not attempt to represent real phenomena," writes Leningrad art historian Irina Kyzlasova. "Instead he aimed to depict their essence and highlight their irrational qualities." Furthermore, the icon was structured in such a way that it "demanded lengthy contemplation and drew the viewer into the work itself" (*Russian Icons*, 5). This play between visualization and representation of that which cannot be seen has clearly been handed down, consciously and unconsciously, to film artists supposedly raised on the materialism of communism.

The second important aspect of the icon tradition is the simple reality that most of the followers of the faith at any given point were illiterate. Their religious education thus consisted of viewing, in church and at home, icons, murals, and mosaics depicting scenes from the life of Christ and the saints.

W.J.T. Mitchell, building on such diverse theories of images as semiotics, Ernst Gombrich's concern for nature and convention in iconology, and Nelson Goodman's grammar of imaging, points to our contemporary complex understanding of any form of image:

> The commonplace of modern studies of images, in fact, is that they must be understood as a kind of language; instead of providing a transparent window on the world, images are now regarded as the sort of sign that presents a deceptive appearance of naturalness and transparence concealing an opaque, distorting, arbitrary mechanism of representation, a process of ideological mystification. (*Iconology*, 8)

In this light, our study of cinema under glasnost is an effort to identify and explore the process of "ideological mystification" of the past and the current efforts by Soviet filmmakers to use images to demystify the reality behind them. That the traditional heritage of icon painting has interacted with Soviet cinema in often subtle ways is unquestioned. Annette Michelson, for instance, has demonstrated how Dziga Vertov's *Three Songs of Lenin* (*Tri pesni o Lenine*, 1934) is constructed in accordance with the principles of Orthodox triptych painting in Russian churches.[2]

Visual images and those who produce them have always carried special significance in Russian history. It is no coincidence that one of the most important Soviet films to appear between 1945 and 1985, Andrei Tarkovsky's *Andrei Rublev* (1967), was dedicated to the outstanding fifteenth-century icon painter of that name. The film is a historical epic, but Soviet audiences understood that the artist's conflict with his times had clear modern implications.

---

[2] Speech given at the conference of the Society for Cinema Studies, held at New York University in July 1985.

It is also no accident that, beginning with Stalin's dictatorship, the portraits of Communist Big Brothers and Fathers—Stalin, Marx, Engels, and Lenin—served as actual icons in social rituals glorifying "the bright socialist future," an image the entire propaganda machine worked to promote. As Soviet critic Mikhail Yampolsky put it in 1989: "Visual images in our society still keep the meaning of the semisacred symbols. The fact that, starting in the 1950s, the change of the state and party leadership has been accompanied by the disappearance of the previous leaders' pictures, makes a strong case for this point" ("Emergence of Faces," 29).

Against such a large canvas, the period of glasnost, in which film-makers are freer than ever under the Soviet system to express themselves, should be judged as another chapter in a long artistic, cultural, and spiritual discourse rather than as a sudden break into a new dimension. For centuries such a tradition has valued the visual arts because they represent the spirit as well as the flesh, the unseen as well as the seen. This dialectic between the spirit and the material world, finally, points up the thousand-year history of seeing the allegorical or meta-phorical in the "real," and vice versa. It is still characteristic of Soviet art under glasnost, though one of the goals of some Soviet filmmakers, as we shall see, is to attack such an "overdetermined" sense of the image.[3]

What unites these attitudes, however, whether they tend to be imag-istic or realistic, is the search for moral and religious values. Even the titles of many films of recent years suggest the desire for transcendence, spiritual renewal, religious redemption: *Repentance, Little Vera* (*vera* means "faith" in Russian), *Assuage My Sorrows, Higher Judgment, Save and Protect, Assa* (reportedly the first word uttered by Moses after the flood). The cry of such films is the opposite of a song by the American rock group Talking Heads, "Stop Making Sense"; it is "Start Making Sense," a sense that goes beyond the chaos of the present and the past.

One episode at the 1989 International Moscow Film Festival looked like a scene from a comedy of errors. During a special discussion with the members of eighty-seven Soviet film clubs, Americans were asked repeatedly, "Who is the spiritual leader of American cinema? Woody

---

[3] Of course, the word has maintained its importance in Russia and in the other cultures incorporated in the Soviet Union. But the visual still has a powerful influence on the faithful. This has not been the case in the Western world, where the power of *logos* has created a strong sense of logocentrism. Only now, with the kind of televi-sion production favored by the fast, imagistic music-video montages of MTV and of advertising, and with illiteracy growing at an alarming rate in the United States, can Americans begin to say that the power of *logos* has come under attack. Yet much of television is still a medium of "talking heads," and a medium primarily for the trans-mission of words.

Allen or Steven Spielberg?" The Americans had to explain that such a question is not one Americans would ask. Who is the most popular or the most artistically challenging or the most experimental might be debated, but "spiritual" would not enter the discussion.

For many Soviet people today, however, the question remains urgent. When most Soviet film buffs list Andrei Tarkovsky as their spiritual leader, their sense of the spirit and cinema begins to come into focus. "Religion" per se is not necessarily implied by "spirituality," though certainly crosses and religious lore appear and reappear in Tarkovsky's works. "Spiritual" cinema in the Soviet sense of the term denotes an artistic rather than a commercial orientation, a personal philosophy and vision rather than entertainment craft and skill, and a concern with serious matters of the human mind and spirit as opposed to a materialist focus. Another element implied but not stated is the sense that the filmmaker must experience a certain amount of suffering in realizing his or her projects. Tarkovsky's lonely exile and continual personal struggle to express his vision in a handful of films scattered over some twenty-five years is obviously a central example.

There is another moment in *Assuage My Sorrows* worth mentioning here. A young beauty in her late teens is naked and about to make love with Boris, the bearded, middle-aged, married man who appeared in our first "image." He watches her as she hangs on the wall an old Orthodox icon given to her by her aging landlady. "What are you doing?" he asks with impatience and curiosity. "Putting the icon in its place," she replies simply. Old icons, new images.

OUR HEARTS DEMAND CHANGE

These words, "Our hearts demand change," are taken from the closing scene of *Assa* (1988; cowritten and directed by Sergei Solovyev). A story about troubled youth, frustrated love, and the corrupting influence of an older, self-made "Soviet Mafia" millionaire, the film ends with a rock concert. The popular Soviet-Korean rock singer Victor Tsoy (who died in a car crash in August 1990) cries out to a large crowd waving candles in the dark as they sing with him, "Our hearts demand change. . . . We are longing for change." Tsoy's call captures much of the spirit of Soviet cinema since glasnost.

In a positive sense, glasnost has been an opportunity for filmmakers to explore, experiment, and expand the horizons of cinema after years of highly structured conditions under the influence of Stalinist socialist realism. Elem Klimov, the filmmaker elected to head the Soviet Filmmakers' Union in 1986, put it well: "It's the lifelong dream of the lunatic to run the asylum" (Aufderheide, "Tiptoeing"). Of course, the real "lunatics," many would argue, have been those who enforced a sense of socialist "normality." Now, however, is the time for Soviet filmmakers to take charge. It is a challenge many have embraced eagerly. Without question, more than ever before in the Soviet Union, filmmakers are beginning, if not to determine, at least to have a large voice in determining their future.

But glasnost has also opened new conflicts and old wounds, generating a great deal of confusion as well. With a sudden rush of freedom and no familiar patterns to guide them in handling that freedom, some have felt at a loss. "Our talented writers have a problem: what should they write now that nothing is really forbidden?" asked Sovexportfilm director Oleg Rudnev (Horton, interview, Moscow, July 1989). Andrei Plakhov, a former *Pravda* film critic and head of the Filmmakers' Union's Conflict Commission, which has managed to take more than a hundred censored films "off the shelf," notes that many of the best-known directors have been slow to function under glasnost because they appear to be "afraid of making a false move" ("Soviet Cinema").

Others have been even more blunt about the past record of Soviet cinema. "Filmmaking in this country has played its role in developing totalitarianism, not democracy. It has helped produce passive and obedient people rather than free and reasoning citizens." This sharply worded analysis came from Soviet writer Arkady Vaksberg in a discussion of the role of cinema under glasnost held at the Tashkent Film Festival in May 1988.[4] In part, such strong self-criticism has to do with the ongoing reaction against Stalin and his cult of personality. But these remarks also suggest something of the push for change that all aspects of Soviet life have undergone since 1985.

Change has been long overdue in cinema. In the 1920s, such talented filmmakers as Lev Kuleshov, Sergei Eisenstein, Alexander Dovzhenko, Dziga Vertov (Denis Kaufman), and Vsevolod Pudovkin transformed film into a vibrant art form. But as Jay Leyda has documented in *Kino*, cinema under Stalin became both bureaucratic and propagandistic. These shackles have been difficult to shake off, though among the hum-

---

[4] Vaksberg, a leading Soviet writer and social critic, led an open meeting attended by more than a hundred Soviet and foreign filmmakers and critics on the topic "Socialism, Democracy, and Cinema." His opening statement reflected the wide degree of openness that has begun to appear under glasnost. He commented: "We should all feel ashamed that after seventy years of socialism in the Soviet Union, we are just now beginning to learn about democracy. Anyway, better late than never." He then posed the question that framed the discussion: "How is it possible to have democracy within a single-party state?" He concluded by challenging filmmakers to accept the task of helping bring about democratic change.

drum socialist epics and simplistic comedies of the 1930s through the 1950s and of the 1970s, the challenging works of such auteurs as Andrei Tarkovsky, Sergei Paradjanov, Andrei Konchalovsky, and Tengiz Abuladze have stood out at foreign festivals and in art-cinema houses abroad. Before turning to more specific concerns, however, we wish to offer five overviews that may be useful.

SOCIALIST REALISM: THE MODEL OF THE PAST

One of the key challenges to Soviet cinema is the task of dismantling the burdensome formulas established during the Stalinist period. Katerina Clark has outlined in *The Soviet Novel* a "prototypical plot" for Soviet narratives. Clearly, what was approved for literature applies even more intensely to cinema. In this sense, what has come to be known as "socialist realism" is not realism at all, but a highly allegorical form of narrative in which "reality" has been tailored to celebrate the stated glories and goals of the party. As Clark notes, "After 1932 (at least) the Stalinist writer was no longer the creator of original texts; he became the teller of tales already prefigured in Party lore. Consequently, his function is rather like that of the chroniclers of the Middle Ages" (159). Edward J. Brown comments even more bluntly, in *Russian Literature since the Revolution*, "All forms of literature are quite frankly and directly used by the Soviet government for political purposes" (1); the possibility of "nonpolitical" literature has not been officially admitted.

Given the expected political function of the arts in Soviet culture, what is the prototypical plot on which both novels and films had to model themselves in the past? According to Clark, the formula is quite simple. Using Alexander Fadeev's revised version of *The Young Guard* (1951; originally published in 1945) as her point of reference, Clark, influenced by Vladimir Propp's study of narrative patterns in Russian folk tales (*Theory and History of Folklore*), suggests that typical socialist-realist novels generally possess most of the following elements in the order given:

> A hero sets out consciously to achieve his goal, which involves *social integration* and a *collective* rather than *individual* identity for himself. He is inspired by the *challenge* of overcoming the obstacles that bar him from realizing those aims: those "spontaneous," i.e., arbitrary and self willed, aspects of himself and forces in the world around him. . . . The hero is assisted in his quest by an older and more "conscious" figure who has made just such a successful quest before him. (Clark, *Soviet Novel*, 167)

What the hero then undergoes is a rite of passage similar to those practiced in traditional cultures. The climax of the novel is the moment at which, under the guidance of the older and more "conscious" figure, the young hero attains "consciousness," an understanding of his historical role from a Communist point of view. He is then capable of carrying through his goal to its completion, as in *The Young Guard*, whose hero sacrifices his life as a partisan fighting the Germans in World War II. In such a case, the heroic example of the hero's death becomes a symbolic victory over oppressive forces.

This cumbersome ideological framework precludes any substantial deviation from the basic formula. It also suggests that the pressures of political ideology necessitate a constant interaction between "reality" and "allegory" (the mythological), in order to assure that the narrative is read or seen "correctly." To those outside the Soviet Union, the gap between the real and the allegorical in these narratives appears wide. However, we should realize that to those raised on socialist principles, "the changes back and forth within a novel from the realistic to the symbolic are not as radical as they appear to be to the Western reader" (Clark, *Soviet Novel*, 176).

In cinema, the classic example of a sociomythical film is *Chapayev*, made in 1934 by Sergei Vasilyev and Georgi Vasilyev. Based on a novel by Dmitri Furmanov concerning his experiences during the Soviet civil war as the party leader of "Chapayev's" Red Cavalry, *Chapayev*, which combines lively action sequences reminiscent of any good Hollywood war film with rough folk humor, became one of the most popular Soviet films of all time. In a letter to workers in the Soviet film industry in 1935, Stalin, who spoke of the film as his favorite, commented, "Soviet power expects new successes from you, new films that, like *Chapayev*, will glorify the greatness of the historical deeds in the struggle for workers' and peasants' power in the Soviet Union" (Taylor and Christie, *Film Factory*, 348).

Chapayev brightly illustrates the changes in mythological attitudes from the revolutionary 1920s to the period of Stalinist conservatism in the 1930s. The dominant principle of Soviet ideology had always been "collectivism," a spirit portrayed in such films as Eisenstein's *October* (*Oktyabr'*, 1927) as a "collective hero"; the masses themselves were the protagonists. However, under Stalin, one of the hallmarks of Soviet cinema in the 1930s was the opposite. These films glorified the model Soviet individual hero, as in *Chapayev*. The Stalinist mythology redirected the enthusiasm of the struggle against the "old world" toward the cultivation of the idea of "complete and ultimately triumphant socialism." This mythology pierced all the layers of life and culture as well as all the levels of any particular artwork. It was closer to the traditional mythology, too. The wily peasant partisan Chapayev represents the archetype of a "cultural hero" and of a "trickster" as well, with his warrior's courage mixed with his slyness, sharpness, and rough folk wit. The scheme of *Chapayev's* plot and even the composition of certain frames (the right and the left, for instance, as the traditional opposition of masculine and feminine) also strongly correspond to myth.

After all, the origin of the character himself is mythological: nobody knows what the real Chapayev contributed to the victories of the Soviet state, and his literary and cinematic "re-creation" was historically justified by the murder of the actual civil war heroes. Stalin needed to fill the empty spaces left after he executed his victims, and he did so with the help of art. Inventing new historical figures was the simplest and most effective way.

As Sergei Dobrotvorsky, a young Soviet filmmaker and critic, puts it ironically, socialist realism was "the highest stage of the Russian avant-garde, which passed to the 'life-making' level." He adds, "Paraphrasing Lenin, we could state that it is modernism that 'won in one country.' In fact, any avant-garde tends to the total replacement of life, to the supplanting of reality. But it succeeded only in the USSR, where fictitious 'improved' life was accomplished by means of art. The results were certainly horrible" ("Most Avant-Garde").

The fight against these results, which meant simply lies for the audience, and the nets and tenets of sterilized canons and rules for filmmakers, is still in progress. The development of this fight, its victories, and its failures are the focus of this volume.

THE DIALOGUE BETWEEN FILM AND LITERATURE

The new Soviet cinema, like any normal cultural organism, is necessarily in dialogue with itself and with the traditions of Russian (pre-1917) and Soviet (post-1917) film and literature. Paradoxically, this is more true of literature than of film. Russian literature has been the mainstay of national culture through the ages, and its spiritual and philosophical heritage was always of the greatest importance in Soviet filmmaking.

Adaptation, the most obvious form of dialogue between film and literature, has been one of the most popular types of Soviet film. But while it is more or less common for any major film industry to search for adaptations, what is unusual about Soviet cinema, particularly for American audiences, is that classical Russian writers have been favored more constantly by filmmakers than have been contemporary writers. Since one of the first masterpieces of the Soviet screen, Pudovkin's *Mother* (*Mat'*, 1926), based on a novel by Maxim Gorky, Russian authors, especially

Chekhov, Dostoevsky, and Tolstoy, have been considered the best "screenwriters" of the Soviet cinema. At times, this has caused protests from critics and filmmakers who have defended film from such a literary invasion. But even perestroika, bringing an explosion of new topics, did not break this tradition.

However, while literature and cinema share a bloodline in the Soviet Union, several significant differences have evolved. The first has to do with the greater degree of control the state has been able to exert over the filmmaking process as compared to literary production. Because literary pursuits are primarily an individual affair, the Soviet state has never been able to extend total control over the creation of literature. The well-known tradition of circulating unpublished manuscripts, *samizdat*, has always served as a major way in which intellectuals and artists have been able to maintain a balancing alternative perspective on the official culture. (Many of Solzhenitsyn's books first appeared in this manner.) Such an underground system has been impossible in filmmaking. The requirements of money, equipment, a multitude of personnel, and distribution to theaters have meant that filmmakers have had to work within the system in order to be seen and heard. It is in this sense that Vaksberg's charge concerning the totalitarianism of Soviet cinema takes on added meaning.

Yet, even though filmmakers have labored under far more levels of control within and without their studios, significant films have always managed to appear. In particular, one of the benefits of glasnost has been the unshelving of all the films either made but not released or released and then censored for one reason or another.

Alexander Askoldov's *Commissar* (*Komissar*, 1967) is a significant example. Shelved for twenty years, this powerful narrative told in stark black-and-white photography the story of a party unit commander during the Soviet civil war who goes into hiding with a Jewish provincial family after she discovers she is pregnant. The film has now played to crowded theaters and critical acclaim at home and abroad. The release of such films suggests that even during the restrictive years, Soviet cinema was never so completely monologic as it has traditionally been considered. But the impossibility of any form of distribution for such films, unlike the possibility of piecemeal publishing in literary journals (*Novy mir*, for instance) or through samizdat has meant that daring filmmakers have suffered more than their literary contemporaries. *Commissar* in fact was the first and last film made by Askoldov, whose career was ended by the suppression of his debut film. Ironically, however, the advent of video has begun to make samizdat a reality for filmmakers as well; black-market video copies float much more freely through Soviet culture than film prints ever could.

A second contrast between Soviet filmmaking and literature has been the development of strong national cinemas in the various republics. Almost all commentators on Soviet literature begin their studies by stating that Soviet literature as it has developed is primarily Russian literature, reflecting the tradition of the dominant culture in a nation made up of a hundred nationalities.

Certainly Russian films account for the bulk of the roughly 150 films produced each year up to 1988. But to a much larger degree than in literature, Soviet cinema produces vigorous films in republics around the entire nation. In a multilingual, multicultural country, film has the power to reach large groups of people who may not have the degree of literacy needed to read books and journals. Film by its nature has allowed filmmakers in the various republics to have direct access to means of expression and forms of communication that transcend the limitations of written languages. While films are sometimes subtitled from one language to another (thus requiring audience literacy), the dominant form of translation remains that of dubbing (rerecording the voice track in another language) and, less frequently, voice-over translation (each line added in another language after the line is delivered by an actor). This practice has helped ensure that minority republics have been able to evolve distinct national voices of their own on film.

But the impressive quality of many of these productions arises from another twist of cinematic fate. During World War II, the film industry was shifted from Moscow and Leningrad to various provincial cities, so that production could continue at local studios. This unexpected boost in regional production has had a long-term beneficial effect on studios such as the ones in the south-central Asian cities of Tashkent, the capital of Uzbekistan, and Alma-Ata, the capital of Kazakhstan, which could not possibly have happened in literature.

Finally, literature and cinema have begun to cross paths with increasing frequency as writers become filmmakers and vice versa. The flow between the two mediums has always existed, but it appears to have grown in recent years. Such a dialogue between the two mediums becomes particularly rich in the hands of a writer such as Chingiz Aitmatov, who has for years been president of the Kirghiz Filmmakers' Union. Cinematic and literary influences, Russian and international, local and universal, are reflected in a work such as *The Day Lasts More than a Hundred Years*. Influenced by Gabriel García Márquez's "magic realism" in *One Hundred Years of Solitude*, Aitmatov's tale of a Kazakh worker who attempts to bury an old friend according to Muslim traditions celebrates local folklore while blending it with a science-fiction subplot involving missiles and mind-control caps worn by "slaves." (The film *Mankurt* [1990] was made from one narrative strand within the novel.) This "pastiche" approach to literature, which combines humor, satire, and sympathy for a simple protagonist while echoing universal themes, is a clear case of polyphony in practice: a multitude of voices are allowed to speak and interact with each other without drowning out or canceling each other.

As a man of literature and film, Aitmatov takes an approach that mirrors that of many Soviet filmmakers today, who are using their newly gained freedom to explore a multiplicity of "languages."

GENDER IN GLASNOST CINEMA:
BEYOND THE VALLEY OF *FATHERS AND SONS*

In our study of contemporary Soviet film, gender continually arose as a significant issue. We have therefore paid attention to the perestroika of male-female relations, identities, and shifting roles.

In male terms, the increasingly complex relationships between fathers and sons in recent narratives, particularly as they involve the reevaluation of the past, are worth examining. Turgenev's 1861 novel *Fathers and Sons* is thus still relevant to an exploration of the shape and texture of the times as (re)presented from the perspective of a male (Bazarov). Stalin was frequently seen not only as the prime exponent of the cult of personality, but as the father figure for Mother Russia (or the Soviet motherland). The interesting gender split of such a phallocentric evocation is apparent. In this vein, recent post-Freudian interpretations of the Oedipal situation are useful to our understanding of the collective disinterment of Stalin.

Peter Blos, in *Son and Father: Before and beyond the Oedipus Complex*, suggests that the interaction between father and son is much more complicated than Freud indicated. In particular, Blos suggests that while the emphasis is usually placed on the mother-son relationship in the pre-Oedipal stage, a similar close bonding between father and son is significant as well. What happens during the Oedipal phase is that the son learns to deal with all the stages incorporated in his emerging sense of self. Furthermore, the male adolescent goes through another phase in which the father becomes the most important parent in shaping the boy's young adulthood. In that period, what the son needs is the "blessing" of the father in order to mature. Blos explains, "At the termination of adolescence a new stage in the life of the growing son appears, when the father's affirmation of the manhood attained by the son, conveyed in what we might call the father's blessings of the youth's impatient appropriation of adult prerogatives and entitlements, reaches a critical urgency" (11). We shall explore in chapter 1 how this father-son transaction—the granting or denial of the blessing, which Blos calls "that protective magical spell"—characterizes many of the important film narratives concerning the Soviet past.

Such an investigation will not be strictly psychohistorical, but will, as Laura Mulvey has pointed out, help illuminate how history and narrative are shaped by particular "conceptual topologies" that are gender-related (*Visual and Other Pleasures*, 163). Such a mapping of "historical" films in light of male development under patriarchy will be contrasted with how women and "woman" are articulated on the glasnost screen, the subject of chapter 3.

PERESTROIKA AND CHANGING PERSPECTIVES

Glasnost and perestroika are equally important to our study, but the two terms should not be confused. Glasnost was relatively easy to implement. Perestroika, however, entails substantial sacrifice and dislocation. In its total sense, glasnost means an openness of opinion, of speech, and of information; it delivers ideas and has nothing to do with a material product. This is one of the reasons Gorbachev met with relatively little resistance in announcing glasnost, while the actual restructuring or perestroika, which is supposedly the result of open give-and-take, has been much more difficult to realize. Yet filmmaking, one of the main battlefields of glasnost, is also one of the areas of production in which perestroika is seen in action.

First and foremost, perestroika has given filmmakers much greater control over their own studios and productions. It has required studios since 1989 to be self-sufficient and cost-effective, reforming the very structure of the filmmaking industry. Furthermore, perestroika has led to a blossoming of coproductions on a variety of levels and has allowed modest forms of independent production (cooperatives) to be formed. The latest feature from Vasily Pichul, the creator of *Little Vera*, *Dark Nights in Sochi* (*V gorode Sochi tiomnye nochi*, 1989), for instance, was made by an independent cooperative, established especially for this purpose, with no state investment at all. Pichul certainly experienced much more creative flexibility; he also presumably discovered many more financial limitations dictated by his own pocket. *Dark Nights* never matched the success of *Little Vera*, either in terms of artistic quality or in commercial success and public recognition, but it proved that there is unquestionably a future for independent productions.

The Soviet "indies" so far are full of excitement and expectation, though they already know the feeling of sobering up after a feast of freedom. As Andrei Dementyev, a film critic and executive of several independent film cooperatives, one in Moscow, another in Kiev, put it, "The independent studios are certainly interested in art movies, but they are not going to sacrifice money interest to it" (Brashinsky, interview, New Orleans, April 1990). The plans of Dementyev's studios include collaborations with underground filmmakers and young official "art makers," as well as coproductions with France and the production of low-budget entertainment movies, one of which is to be a post-Armageddon Soviet equivalent of the American film *Blade Runner* (1982). The first production of the Moscow-based cooperative was *Mirages* (*Miragy*, 1989), a forty-minute video illustration of the music of a free-jazz group, Three O, directed by the leaders of the Moscow film underground ("parallel cinema") movement, Igor Aleinikov and Gleb Aleinikov. "It certainly won't make any money, but it was fun to work with those guys," Dementyev commented. The Aleinikovs, in their turn, complained that nothing was ready for shooting during the production period, including the budget, and it by no means looked like a "real business" to them (Brashinsky, interview, New Orleans, May 1990). "Nobody knows what to do with money or anything else; no one knows how to run a business," admitted Dementyev, who hires the crew himself and rents the equipment and facilities from a major studio. "But we are learning without teachers and textbooks."

Every month sees the formation of a multitude of new independent production companies. By early 1991, there were more than two hundred operating throughout the Soviet Union, a shift that in effect signaled the end of the studio era as it was known in the past. To a large degree, such a shift toward independent production was a movement away from the importance of the director-centered cinema and toward a producer-driven system such as exists in Hollywood today. As in the case of American cinema, the director often becomes a producer as well, in order to package his or her own film. Nevertheless, Soviet cinema has entered the age of the producer.

The studio structure itself has changed so radically during the five years of perestroika that most filmmakers are unprepared to work under the new conditions. In the past, as in all fields of productive activity in the Soviet Union, the employees of a studio, from the set workers to the directors and screenwriters, had guaranteed state salaries that were in no way related to their actual work. The studio staff was paid even in the periods between movies. The new model of cinema, initiated by the Sixth Congress of Filmmakers in 1986, offered to dissolve the vast studios and to dismiss their staff. Today, the major studios, such as Mosfilm and Gorky Studio in Moscow, and Lenfilm in Leningrad, provide only a general trademark for productions executed by much smaller units, called "creative units"—small, independent studios under the "dome" of a larger one. A creative unit is somewhere between a major studio system and an independent company. It rents all facilities from the big studio, which has no creative control over the production and serves basically as a storehouse for the unit. It also hires the staff and cast, including the director and scriptwriter, from outside the unit; the unit has no permanent production staff except the administration and the artistic board. Artistic boards usually consist of prominent directors, screenwriters, film critics, and script editors, led by the most prominent one, and it is they, no one else, who make plans for the unit and buy the scripts to be produced. Only one state body has a voice in the final cut: Goslit, the Soviet equivalent of the Motion Picture Association of America, which provides censorship and ratings, but its role in the artistic process has become more problematic under glasnost. The ultimate achievement of the unit system is that the unit itself can distribute its productions, receiving the major share of the gross.

As many Soviet filmmakers excitedly agree, it is much better to be led by colleagues than by officials who have no idea what movies are about. However, a controversy has broken out concerning the financial aspects of the "new model." Complaints have been heard from those filmmakers who find themselves confused by the new sociopolitical situation. During the previous decades they might have waited until the confusion ended, but under the new circumstances they are not paid for time between projects or time spent conceiving new ideas.

Another financial aspect of perestroika in the studios has been the injection of a market mentality totally alien to the majority of Soviet filmmakers. Complaints were heard that the studios' glasnost added up to a sellout, as market concerns dominated artistic or spiritual ones. However, the shoots of a healthy market consciousness have begun to appear. Thus, the creative unit Ladya (Boat), which emerged from the Gorky Studio in Moscow, produced a big hit, *The King of Crime* (*Vory v zakone* [*Thieves in Law*]) in 1988, a film of questionable artistic merit that will be discussed below. Yet the film, distributed by the unit itself, earned a huge gross, allowing the unit to put several "serious" pictures and a new commercial feature into production.

Independent cooperatives have also begun to find their legs. At a January 1991 press conference in Moscow at Dom Kino, the Soviet Filmmakers' Union headquarters, representatives of Katarsis (Catharsis) spoke of their twenty-six productions in two years. The press conference was held for the premiere screenings of two productions made by top filmmakers—one from Lithuania, Algimantas Puipa's *Ticket to the Taj Mahal* (*Bilet do Taj Mahala*), and the other from Georgia, *Coming Closer* (*Priblizheniye*) by Alexander Rekhviashvili—and involved "executives" who represented not only Russia but also Kazakhstan and other republics. "We want to make films people will see," said this eclectic thirty-something group of screenwriters, directors, and critics turned producers, sounding more like a new independent Hollywood outfit than a socialist unit from the past.

Testing (and tasting) the new circumstances takes time and a lot of effort. But as filmmakers have explored new territory and learned from their mistakes, the number of films produced has increased considerably. Until about 1988, Soviet filmmakers produced approximately 150 feature films, 100 made-for-television films, and 1,000 nonfeatures (including documentaries, educational films, and animations) each year in more than thirty-five studios scattered throughout the country. By 1989–1990, however, the number of feature films shot had jumped to about 300, and in 1991 more than 400 were made.

Yet a major problem—distribution—has made the flowering of independent expression all but meaningless. By early 1991, very few Soviet-made films were playing in theaters. Cheap American, French, Italian, and Indian imports—action films and romantic comedies—have crowded Soviet productions off the screen. In Moscow during January 1991, only *one* Soviet film was playing, in a few theaters, a poor imitation of Hollywood's film noir with tinges of soft porn: *Fools Die on Friday* (*Duraki umirayut po pyatnitsam*), a Soviet-Bulgarian coproduction.

The decentralization of filmmaking applies to the breakup of the official union of filmmakers as well. In June 1990, the Filmmakers' Union dissolved itself, forming instead a loose confederation of filmmakers from the various republics. Furthermore, by late 1990, filmmaking had become so diversified that legal battles had begun over which had the right to represent Soviet films abroad for sales and rental: Sovexportfilm, which had always been the sales arm of Soviet cinema, or each individual company ("Soviets Struggle for Rights," 1). Experts hold that both have the right; anyone can and will sell what he or she wishes, but many will continue to work through Sovexportfilm simply because of its contacts and experience. By early 1991, Mosfilm, the largest Soviet studio, was distributing its own films, leaving Sovexportfilm with a serious identity crisis, as worried executives tried to redefine their goals and possibilities in such a radically altered market.

Until late 1990, cinematography was under the overall direction of Goskino (the State Committee for Cinematography), which was made up of several divisions. These included the export and foreign-distribution office (Sovexportfilm), the office of international coproduction (Sovinfilm), the film-festival division (Sovinterfest), the film archives (Gosfilmofond), and the two educational branches, the traditional film school (VGIK) and the newer two-year program (Higher Courses for Scriptwriters and Directors), both located in Moscow. By late 1990, however, the whole organization was in the process of being dismantled, thereby turning the media situation into a free-for-all.

With the election of film director Elem Klimov (*Rasputin* [*Agonia*], *Farewell, Come and See*), who had the personal support of Gorbachev, as the head of the Soviet Filmmakers' Union in May 1986, a clear change occurred in how films are made and distributed in the Soviet Union. (Andrei Smirnov replaced Klimov as head of the union from 1988 to 1990.) A charismatic spokesperson for Soviet cinema at home and abroad, Klimov unmistakably shook up the filmmaking bureaucracy. Declaring that "cinema must always be dedicated to truth," Klimov brought filmmakers into every level of the decision-making process in the Soviet Union during his tenure.

The results are visible. Films have since explored a wide range of subjects: the problems of youth today, the effects of Chernobyl, prostitution, drug addiction, the Mafia-like embezzlement scams of Soviet white-collar workers. New talent has also been encouraged. Younger voices and voices outside the major studios in Moscow and Leningrad have now begun to find means of expression, especially through imaginative financing from coproductions between film and television studios, or between studios and other sources such as cultural organizations, specific industries, and city committees. Forgotten and forbidden films have been released for discussion and distribution, and international film contacts have been made, including those made through the American-Soviet Film Initiative (ASFI).

The effect of such restructuring has been to shatter many of the old bureaucratic institutions. As Oleg Rudnev, director of Sovexportfilm, noted, "We are now speaking like normal people. . . . We used to lie a lot in the Soviet Union, and it resulted in false films, false literature, false art. Now, with glasnost, we can speak normally, openly" (Horton, interview, Moscow, July 1989).

But after years of having to work under a cumbersome system, many filmmakers find it difficult to become innovative leaders and administrators. Victor Demin, secretary of the Critics' Committee of the Soviet Filmmakers' Union, admits, "We've solved problems and we've created three for every one we've solved" (Aufderheide, "Tiptoeing," 19).

One problem that has emerged is the general public's lack of interest in the more experimental films being made. According to director Alexey Simonov, "Filmmakers will make what they want first! Then we'll find out if audiences want to see these films" (Horton, interview, Moscow, July 1988). Another concern expressed by Soviet filmmakers is what to write about after years of being limited to certain approved topics and approaches. It is not, however, simply a matter of what subject to choose. It is also the issue of how direct or complete a filmmaker can be with a topic that may be sensitive without landing in serious trouble. No one doubts that glasnost exists. But it is often extremely difficult to know how far one may go in a given direction. This uncertainty is a challenge to some and an inhibiting factor to others: the paralysis of freedom. A number of films thus steer a middle course. Roman Balayan's *Police Spy* (*Filior*, 1987) manages to be critical of a state police system under the czar that resembles the KGB, yet carefully locates its criticism in a prerevolutionary setting so that the film cannot be seen as a direct critique of the present ruling party.

Everything in the Soviet film industry is shifting. Such a state of "unfinalizedness" (to use Bakhtin's term) suggests that the end of the beginning is not yet in sight. What is apparent is that Soviet cinema is headed in the direction of the more flexible filmmaking systems already in place in such socialist countries as Hungary, Poland, and Yugoslavia.

Yugoslavia may prove especially instructive for Soviet filmmakers. The Yugoslav film industry is a highly diversified collection of production companies that primarily work on a cost-effective basis, allocating production costs among box-office revenues, State Cultural Committee funding, and other sources, such as television (a large number of coproductions) and foreign coinvestment funds.

Such a decentralized self-management model, which emphasizes the importance of the artist in the artistic process, is truly between a rigid Stalinist system and an open-market Hollywood structure. If the Soviet cinema after glasnost does evolve more clearly in this direction, not only will the filmmakers have taken over the asylum, as Klimov put it, but they will have moved much closer to becoming semi-independent freelance artists like their counterparts in the nonsocialist world.

GLASNOST, FILM, AND THE WEST

The climate of excitement and experimentation ushered in by glasnost has meant an intensity of dialogue about film and on the screen unrivaled in the Soviet Union since the 1920s. Yet there is a clear difference: while the early filmmakers were using lessons learned from the West—D. W. Griffith's works above all—to construct a "Soviet" cinema in marked contrast to Western models, many (though certainly not all) contemporary filmmakers have attempted to steer a middle course between Soviet and Western influences in order to produce a more universal or international film style.

Jay Leyda captures this shift well in the conclusion to *Kino*:

> Long ago, when I first saw Soviet films in New York, the quality that struck me first was that they looked quite unlike other films in the last months of the silent film. It was even less possible to compare the really extraordinary films (*October* and *Earth*, for example) with the biggest American films. (403)

But by the end of World War II, Leyda notes, Soviet films had become more international in style. Even in the early postwar period, Soviet filmmakers were analyzing popular foreign films captured from the Nazis to see what made them appealing, and then applying such lessons to their own work. A typical example is the most popular Soviet film outside the Soviet Union, Vladimir Men'shov's *Moscow Does Not Believe in Tears* (*Moskva slezam ne verit*, 1979), which won the 1980 Academy Award for Best Foreign Film. In tone, style, and narrative approach, this story of three women, covering twenty-five years, owes more to the Hollywood tradition of following the lives of a few individuals, building on melodrama and comic elements, than on Eisenstein's efforts to construct through montage a "collective hero," or Dovzhenko's success in capturing a lyrical regional folk imagery in a work such as *Earth* (*Zemlya*, 1930).

Perhaps the ultimate form of the Soviet "international" film is the coproduction. Nikita Mikhalkov's *Dark Eyes* (*Ochi chernyie*, 1987), based on some of Chekhov's short stories, starring Marcello Mastroianni, and shot in Italy and the Soviet Union with international financing, typifies such films. Increasingly such productions aim to capture local color (but not too much), to shoot primarily in foreign rather than native languages, and to assemble international casts to ensure box-office appeal. In this sense we see Soviet cinema beginning to join ranks with a major movement in world cinema that is reflected in the large number of awards heaped on a film such as Bernardo Bertolucci's *Last Emperor* (1987), which was shot in English in China by an Italian director, using a multinational cast. Clearly such a trend is a mixed blessing. While these international films enable foreign filmmakers to break into the world film market, they are also compromised vehicles: much of what used to make national cinemas exciting has to be toned down, simplified, and streamlined so as not to confuse or confound the global audience. Nevertheless, the vast majority of Soviet filmmakers would doubtless drop their projects to direct such a film as *The Russia House*, which was filmed in the Soviet Union, with an all-star American cast, by an Australian, Fred Schepisi.

The Mikhalkov-Bertolucci formula, however, coexists with other, less-compromised coproductions. Pavel Loungine's *Taxi Blues* (1990), shot in Moscow in Russian with Russian actors, and coproduced by the Lenfilm Studio and several French companies, captured the Best Director Award at Cannes and received a relatively broad release in the United States.

On the other hand, the 1990 American production *Banya* (the Russian word means "bath") was coproduced by a Boston-based independent company, Zerkalo Films, and a Soviet independent producer, Andrei Ustinov, and was shot in the Soviet Union by an American director,

Chris Schmidt, with a mixed cast; most of the dialogue is in English, but 30 percent is in subtitled Russian. *Variety* called *Banya* "a comedy about four Russians with a love for American blues music and the American woman who comes into their lives" (Kimmel, "Yanks," 15). The filmmakers counted on laughs in both countries. It seems safe to predict that more "mixed productions" of this sort will be made in the future.

Under glasnost, no single trend dominates. For such popular genres as comedy, suspense, and melodrama, perestroika has meant a broadening of subject matter (more scenes of nudity and lovemaking than ever before, for example) rather than a change in form and structure. Yet it is with the better directors that a deepening of influences first charted in the 1920s can be seen, resulting once again in films that, while influenced by Hollywood to the degree that every cinema must necessarily be influenced by this dominant world cinema, nevertheless appear on the screen as definitely distinct and different from Hollywood products.

We have already mentioned the international influence of coproductions and the newly emerging "international" film. Glasnost has also meant an expansion of distribution for foreign films, especially from Hollywood. Thus each year brings an even greater influx of old and new American productions, often packaged as minifestivals and tours, such as Robert Redford's 1988 tour with many of his films. A movie-schedule billboard in Moscow during May 1988, for instance, revealed that the public had a chance not only to see many of Redford's films, including *All the President's Men* (1976), which deals with the uncovering of the Watergate scandal—democracy in action, cleaning up a corrupt government—but also *Tootsie* (1982), *Roxanne* (1987), *Salvador* (1986), and *One Flew over the Cuckoo's Nest* (1975). The increase in film distribution and videotape circulation means that the Soviet Union will soon be receiving the latest films from around the world on a schedule as up-to-date as that of any Western nation.

International dialogue about film has been aided by the development of several filmmakers' exchange organizations and programs, especially the ASFI, founded by Mark Gerzon, a Californian, and Elem Klimov of the Soviet Filmmakers' Union in December 1986 (Sullivan, "Hollywood Peaceniks," 18). This exchange has led to several meetings on both sides of the Atlantic, including a March 1987 conference in Hollywood to discuss the cold war stereotypes each country has produced, from *Rambo* to its Soviet equivalents, ending with a joint pledge to end such simpleminded, conflict-oriented practices.[5] Similar Soviet-American

---

[5] Certainly a Hollywood film such as Walter Hill's *Red Heat* goes a long way toward reversing the anti-Soviet *Rambo* trend. Arnold Schwarzenegger's sympathetic portrayal of a Soviet cop who goes to Chicago to bust a Russian drug-ring leader with the

exchanges among film-studies scholars have begun to take place as well.[6] And in October 1989, the most ambitious Soviet-American film conference to date, sponsored by the George Gund Foundation, was held in Cleveland under the title "Soviet Cinema Today: Literary and Cultural Aspects."[7]

MARGINAL POINTERS:
WHAT TO LOOK FOR ON OUR JOURNEY

As does any guidebook, this overview of Soviet cinema under glasnost needs certain explanations and qualifications. Since no book-length study of the subject yet exists in any language, we have tried to make our subject understandable even to those who are not experts on Soviet culture and cinema, and who do not have access to the films discussed. Furthermore, both as a frame of reference and as an international context for Soviet film seen in its larger perspective, we make numerous comparisons and contrasts to Hollywood and Western European cinemas.

Next, we make no claim to being complete in our coverage or evaluations. Naturally, by limiting ourselves to the first five years of glasnost, we have left more than enough material for many more specialized studies. The excitement, and the danger, of observing a process that is still very much in progress, changing by the moment, is obvious. Our study is for this reason meant to be suggestive rather than exhaustive, pointing to what we see as major trends, important shifts, and representative works. We have left out or only briefly discussed adaptations of major literary works, war epics, and ballet, dance, and opera films. We have not had the space to do justice to the importance of Soviet animation, which, in the hands of such talented filmmakers as Yuri Norstein, has produced

---

help of an American counterpart (James Belushi) manages to entertain while conveying positive information about Soviets and Soviet life today through the use of humor.

[6] The Society for Cinema Studies, the largest group of film scholars in the United States, has been working with another American organization, the International Research and Exchanges Board (IREX), to establish joint film-studies projects with the major Soviet institution for film studies, the All-Union Research Institute of Cinema Art. The first official meeting of Soviet and American film scholars was held in Moscow from 29 October to 8 November 1989. It focused on Soviet and American cinema in the 1980s, and has opened up possibilities for exchanges and joint projects in the future.

[7] The Cleveland conference brought together more than two dozen filmmakers, writers, philosophers, producers, and archivists from both nations. Such continuing cross-fertilization is clearly in the best interests of filmmakers in the Soviet Union and the United States, and should lead to even more joint projects, exchanges, and influences.

works worthy of lasting praise. Neither wholly a cinema history nor a work of pure film criticism per se, our study is intended to bridge both, offering what we hope is a balanced perspective.

In this spirit we have consciously tried to avoid what we see as the faults of previous studies of national cinemas. As Thomas Elsaesser notes in his recent work *New German Cinema: A History*, too many books on the national cinemas have either focused on individual directors and specific themes and genres or shown an obsessive desire to catalogue long lists of films and filmmakers; what is overlooked is the reader's need to understand the texts themselves and the contexts in which they exist. Like Elsaesser, we wish to provide a general "framework for understanding in a historical perspective" (1).

In examining the period of perestroika, therefore, we cast a glance back to events and films of the past ten or fifteen years, to see how often trends that have borne fruit in recent years were planted under previous administrations. We join those who question many of the cherished myths of Soviet cinema, such as the concept that little that was honest or challenging was done before perestroika.

Our attention to context as well as to individual films leads us to what Robert C. Allen and Douglas Gomery describe as the four levels of context to be considered in a film history. In *Film History: Theory and Practice*, they speak of the aesthetic, technological, economic, and social dimensions of cinema (37–38). Needless to say, all four of these areas cannot, nor should they, be given equal weight in each chapter and in considering each film. Nevertheless, a genuine effort has been made to see glasnost and Soviet film not only in terms of the films and filmmakers themselves, but in terms of the shifting modes of production and distribution at home and abroad, and as they reflect and interact with Soviet culture and life.

In another five or ten or fifty years, film scholars and cultural critics may see this initial period quite differently. But from our perspective on the front line, we have tried to make a distinction between films that are important because of their subject matter and those that have rewritten the language of Soviet cinema, as well as those that have managed to do both. Although we are particularly interested in Soviet film discourse as it affects its primary audience, the Soviet people themselves, we have also paid attention to which films could have a life of their own outside the Soviet Union.

Thus we have given far more attention to popular films than has been the case in previous studies of Soviet film. The tendency, both in the Soviet Union and abroad, has been to write primarily about poetic and prophetic auteurs such as Andrei Tarkovsky and to ignore the films that have sold millions of tickets. Our detailing of many popular films is in part meant to help balance such a lopsided view of Soviet film. But we are also indicating what is becoming increasingly true of Soviet cinema: the need for filmmakers, even "artists," to connect with a broader moviegoing public than in the past, for economic as well as ideological reasons. As the filmmakers have been given more self-determination, they have also been asked to come closer to being self-supporting. Thus a film such as *Little Vera*, which has won critical praise as well as an extremely large Soviet audience, does in fact merit special consideration as being representative of what the Soviet filmmakers are calling the "new model" of Soviet film.

The observations we have made about Soviet film of the glasnost period are arranged in the following manner.

Part 1 treats the examination of the past as it relates to the present and future, and the evolving sense of relations between fathers and sons, women and men, youth and older generations. In the first chapter we discuss the reevaluation of the socialist, and in particular the Stalinist, past, for without such a revisionist view, no healthy future is possible. As a common saying in Moscow goes, only the Soviet Union has an unstable past. Critic Marina Drozdova notes about this preoccupation with the past, "Who could have thought of such a close interconnection between the aristocratic Proust and the offspring of Bolsheviks?" ("Midseasonal Anarchists").

Chapters 2 (on youth and youth culture today) and 3 (on women behind the camera and onscreen) reflect the swiftly changing nature of life for youth and women in the Soviet Union in the 1980s and 1990s, as well as their changing presentation on film. This is especially true as many more young people and women have begun to enter filmmaking, a profession that was in the past almost exclusively the domain of middle-aged men, and doing so without the usual formal training from the state film schools.

Part 2 focuses on concerns of film language as it is changing under perestroika. Chapter 4 concerns the new documentaries, which are, by almost universal agreement, years ahead of most feature narrative films in coverage and topicality as well as in their ability to reach large national audiences quickly and effectively.

The new importance of genres in winning general audiences and exploring cinematic territory new to Soviet filmmakers is addressed in chapter 5. As the box office becomes a determining factor in the production of most films, how filmmakers connect with viewers will be a much more pressing question. One Soviet director put it this way: "In most countries, you make either films that are high art or films for the general public—for people to enjoy. But in the political situation that existed here for so long, the vast majority of films were of neither type. They were made to please the people in Goskino (the State Committee on Cinema) and nobody watched them" (Lardner, "Moment"). Now the significance of genre has become much more pronounced.

In chapter 6 we explore how comedy and satire have become particularly effective means of criticizing the stagnating elements in Soviet Communist reality.

Part 3 of our study surveys the emerging importance of national and ethnic cinemas as centralized direction from Moscow rapidly fades. We address the complex issue of whether it is still possible to speak of Soviet cinema at all, rather than of the cinema of each republic (Lithuania, Kazakhstan, Georgia, and so forth).

Our final section is neither a conclusion nor a new beginning, but something in the middle. We end with a dialogue between ourselves, exploring some of the differences in our views of the potential of the cinema of glasnost in a rapidly changing world.

"I think the absolute best filmmaking would be for the deaf and dumb," said the late Sergei Paradjanov, a strongly individualistic director who spent more years in prison for his beliefs than he did making films and who died in August 1990 (Williamson, "In the Soviet Orbit," 60).

Beyond all the changes of perestroika and glasnost we return at last to the nature and power of cinema itself. Paradjanov is right. Though few can attain such heights, Soviet cinema of these times has done much to break through to many who could not be reached before, at home and, increasingly, abroad.

A final image strikes us as living up to Paradjanov's wish. There is much in these pages about the troubled present, the shocking past, and the uncertain future. But a 1991 Ukrainian-German "mixed" production, directed by an Armenian, Karen Gevorkian, and shot on the far western shores of Siberia—the Sea of Okhotsk, opposite Alaska—transcends the immediacy of history, past and present, Communist and royalist, and with a simple, direct camera style takes us into the realm of myth and ritual. *Piebald Dog Running along the Shore (Pegii pes, beguschii kraem morya)*, adapted from a well-known story by the popular Kirghiz author Chinghiz Aitmatov, concerns the premature coming-of-age of Kirisk, a boy of about eight, of the Nivkh tribe that lives by the sea.

The film (and the story) documents tribal life untouched by the twentieth century. In painstaking detail and with a nonprofessional tribal cast, the film evokes the simple existence of a hunting and fishing community, an existence both brutal and beautiful in its elemental contact with nature. More powerfully than the much-praised American film

Dances with Wolves, Piebald Dog places us among the Nivkh people, using little dialogue. The film experience is almost purely of the visual and of the sounds of singing and of nature—wind, rain, animals.

Piebald Dog traces Kirisk's fishing trip with his father, grandfather, and uncle, a trip that ends in the deaths of all but Kirisk as each of the others—grandfather, uncle, and finally the father—goes overboard after a long storm in order to leave the scarce food and water for those who remain. After his father rolls into the dark water at night, Kirisk is absolutely alone. His anguish when he awakes to realize the horror of what has happened would deeply move Paradjanov's "deaf and dumb" audience. But neither Aitmatov's story nor Gevorkian's film, which took a year on location to shoot, leaves us with grief alone.

The final scene is of Kirisk's return. Barely alive when the boat reaches the shore at last, he manages to crawl out and stand, sighting his village in the distance. There are tears on his battered face, but a smile as well. He has come home. He has survived. Words are not necessary, but the voice-over of Kirisk's final message succeeds in leaving us far beyond the shores of glasnost in a land where survival itself is to be celebrated. Kirisk speaks—or prays—to the piebald dog, an animal spirit and protector:

> Piebald Dog, running along the seashore,
> I'm returning to you alone—
> Without Grandad Organ,
> Without my father, Emrayin,
> Without Uncle Mylgun.
> Where are they, just ask me,
> But first give me a drink of water.

Kirisk has been through more than a young boy should. But the sacrifices of his male relatives ensure that he has received their blessing and will therefore survive. In that sense, these stirring images on film suggest he is not alone.

GLASNOST:
BACK
TO
THE
PRESENT

Back to the Present: (Re)presenting the Soviet Past in Feature Films

Four out of every three are the enemy of the people!
—Varlam Aravidze, the dictator, in *Repentance*

"LET'S GO": UNPREPARED FOR DEMOCRACY

At a campfire in a frozen landscape, a middle-aged drifter sits across the fire from a teenage boy he has followed for several days, thinking he is his son. The unshaven bum discovers, however, that the boy is not his son, not his link with the past, not a connection with his previous life of order and regulation. But the boy comforts the crying man, saying "Call me by my real name." A new relationship has begun. "Let's go," says the boy as they walk off together through the dreary landscape.

This scene, from the conclusion of Nikolai Skuibin's 1988 film *BOMZH* (an acronym for the phrase for a homeless person, with the connotation of "drifter"), is our starting point. For Soviet citizens and filmmakers alike, looking into the future from the present is necessarily a process of coming to grips with the socialist past. This chapter is concerned with those feature narrative films that have attempted to call the past—Stalinist and otherwise—by its "real name."

"Our lack of tolerance is worse than our lack of soap." With these words, spoken in 1989, author Victor Listov, who scripted the feature documentary *Solovki Regime* (*Vlast' solovetskaya*, 1988), captured much of the friction between the past and the present in the Soviet Union today. "There were periods when we had sugar, but no period when we had tolerance," he said at the IREX–Film Arts Academy Conference on Media, held in Moscow, October-November 1989. The current obsession with investigating the past is, as Listov suggests, very much an effort to come to grips with a record of intolerance shaped and fostered under socialism, especially under Stalin.

What Khrushchev began in 1956 in his secret speech to the Twentieth Party Congress, the first official attack on Stalin's cult of personality, has become a battle cry under Gorbachev. "There can be no *perestroika* in culture and history without lifting the oppressive burden of Stalinism from Soviet life," writes Soviet expert Padma Desai (*Perestroika in Perspective*, 71). The first five years of glasnost suggest that de-Stalinization and a reconsideration of the past have indeed been priorities in the arts as well as in politics.

In chapter 4, we will examine the key role that the new documentary has played in treating the Soviet past. Our task here is to explore how the feature narrative film has begun to add to the national dialogue in its (re)presentation of the socialist-communist past. The treatment of earlier Soviet events on the screen traditionally meant the glorification and mythologizing of the Revolution (before World War II), and, after the war, the depiction of Soviet victory under the harshest conditions. Beginning with Khrushchev's "thaw," a new tradition of presenting war as hell began, implicating fate and human nature rather than the party and socialism.

Soviet cinema from its inception has wrestled with how to wed the ideology of socialism to the capabilities of cinema. Whether in the documentary championed by Vertov or in the fiction film (including reconstructed history, as in Eisenstein's *October* or Pudovkin's *End of St. Petersburg*), the Soviet task in cinema, in Vertov's words, has been to work with "the language of the communist deciphering . . . the visible" (Taylor and Christie, *Film Factory*, 203).

But the issue is more complex. Over the past seventy years the major thrust of Soviet cinema has changed from documenting the unfolding glory of the young Revolution to investigating the shortcomings of a stagnating socialism. In no single area has this shift been more apparent than in the reconsideration and, in many cases, the *first* wave of investigation of the Stalinist period. But we will also consider how Brezhnev's era of stagnation has also captured filmmakers' attention. Literature, journals, and the press have been in the forefront of what has become a massive effort of revisionist history and self-evaluation. Yet cinema under glasnost has clearly begun playing a major role.

Finally, the rewriting of history on the screen is also the rewriting and expansion of the language of Soviet film, the ways and means of presenting that (re)vision. "We were simply not prepared for democracy," commented Elem Klimov at the IREX conference in Moscow in October-November 1989. His candid remarks echo those of the mayor of Moscow, Gavriil Popov: "In my opinion, the forms of democracy being established in these countries [Eastern Europe and the Soviet Union] are exceptionally contradictory and in a very short time they will lead to serious internal conflict" ("Dangers of Democracy," 27). The current intense investigation of the past is, therefore, an exercise not only in deconstruction—primarily but not exclusively with a Stalinist focus— but in reconstruction (and thus perestroika) as well.

Since 1985, filmmakers have been using the new freedoms to push the aesthetic and ideological boundaries of Soviet cinema further than ever before, to the degree that "Soviet" is, in a number of cases, an inadequate term for the emerging forms of filmmaking. In this sense both film- makers and audiences feel how directly any film about the past is linked to the present. The difficulty filmmakers and citizens alike have experi- enced in getting back to the present is, as Klimov suggested, one of being caught unprepared; thus, as Popov makes clear, they are unable to "cre- ate an effective economy" in sync with the radical populism of the times (27). Once again, perestroika is a period of transition.

SHELF-KNOWLEDGE:
RE-PRESENTING THE FORBIDDEN CINEMA

Certainly the strongest early signal of change given by the Soviet filmmaking community to the Soviet public at large in 1986, as the Filmmakers' Union was reorganized, was to create a Conflict Commis- sion, which had the power to review and recommend the "unshelving" of works previously banned. Under the liberal leadership of critic Andrei Plakhov, the commission managed to clear the shelves and closets of all officially blacklisted films—more than a hundred (Horton, interviews, Montreal, August 1989 and August 1990; Plakhov, "Soviet Cinema into the Nineties").

In Plakhov's eyes, the most significant works in this process of shelf- knowledge have been Kira Muratova's films, Yuri Ilienko's *Spring for the Thirsty (Rodnik dlya zhazhduschikh*, 1965), Andrei Konchalovsky's *Asya's Happiness (Asino schastye*, 1967) and Alexander Askoldov's *Commissar*. The commission has had to act on behalf of contemporary films as well. Plakhov cites the scandal over the use of profanity and male frontal nudity in Muratova's *Weakness Syndrome (Astenicheskii sindrom*, 1989), which took place in early 1990. The film was finally released, an indication that once the censored shelf was emptied, no new shelf for glasnost films could be created.

The release of these films was more than a victory for glasnost against censorship. It reminded filmmakers everywhere that high-quality and challenging cinema was being done long before Gorbachev, thus re- affirming the belief that, in a sense, *glasnost* is a meaningless term for artists: to be an artist is to be free to explore and express one's personal vision. Glasnost, of course, offers the artist more security and less fear from persecution and detention, but it is not a guarantee of the quality or significance of speech, filmmaking, or art.

Commissar made the greatest impression on Soviet audiences in its wide release and on the film audiences of other countries, even beyond the film-festival circuit. Askoldov won the right to show his film when, at the 1987 Moscow International Film Festival, he protested that glasnost had indeed not been fully implemented, as proved by the continued suppression of his film. Those who were in Moscow that summer remember the dramatic speed with which the film suddenly appeared: it was shown the following day at Dom Kino to a widely enthusiastic full house.

Askoldov received immediate recognition and was invited to numerous festivals, winning four awards at the Berlin Festival alone. But more important, he came to represent all filmmakers who suffered for their visions before glasnost became official. The film was shelved in 1967, reportedly because it is the story of a pregnant commissar who must stop fighting for a few months during the civil war of the 1920s in order to have her child (a strong antiwar theme) and, even more controversial at the time, because the family she stays with is Jewish, so the "Jewish question" is addressed. Askoldov never again worked in film.

Soviet critic Maya Turovskaya best sums up the Soviet reaction to the film when she notes that *Commissar*, "for all the unmistakable signs that it was made in the sixties, has not aged a bit precisely because, like the author of the original story [Vasily Grossman, a respected writer whose literary work eventually made him an outcast], the director keeps a perfect balance [between the historical events and the personal story]" (*"Commissar"*). We can be even more specific. The film seems ahead of its time, and thus this stirring black-and-white feature is a bright example for contemporary directors in the Soviet Union because of its several types of balance.

First, this film of strong emotions displays a remarkable lack of sentimentality. Askoldov opens the film with the commissar, Klavdia Vavilova (memorably played by Nonna Mordyukova), cold-bloodedly executing a deserter who escaped to see his wife. The commissar moves from this seemingly heartless commitment to her post and to the Revolution through the full range of human emotion. The climax of the film is, of course, the birth of the commissar's child. Being a woman, a mother, an emotional human being is not what she has been programmed for. Thus, in a carefully constructed montage sequence, the birth is represented by the sound track, on which we hear Vavilova's cries and panting, while on the screen we see memories of her past in war and of her love for a young officer, the father of the child. The two parallel but opposite strands come together with the birth of the child and the death of the officer in battle. We feel, therefore, that the birth does not cancel out the memories of her lover, or of her duty to the Revolution, or of war. But the birth does mean her baptism into a new sense of herself and the potential of the human spirit. Sentimentality is also avoided in the sharpness of the ending, which matches the shock of the opening. A narrative that began in a cold-blooded official execution ends with the commissar giving her child to the Jewish family and leaving them to follow her squad and continue the Revolution. The moment passes swiftly, and the audience is left torn: is the commissar a bad mother but a good Communist, or is she somewhere in between, affected by her contact with the family of Yefim Magazanik (played by the versatile Rolan Bykov, who subsequently became a director), but unable to alter her life fully enough to embrace both realms? Askoldov and Grossman draw no conclusions.

Second, there is the careful balance between the protagonist, Vavilova, who in bulk as well as rank commands each image onscreen, and the elflike, small-town Jewish tinker. (The original story is titled "In the Town of Berdichev.") Challenging the patriarchal structure of Soviet official policy, Askoldov's film, though far from being matriarchal, does investigate the importance of women, both in the Revolution and at home. It ponders the concept and representation of women in cinema, which would place it ahead of most films made under glasnost. Although it is titled *Commissar* and is most immediately centered on Vavilova, it is Magazanik, the tinker, father, and husband, who bears the weight of the narrative.

In the figure of Magazanik we observe a discourse on gender, and are also introduced to the religious and cultural issue of the Jews under the Soviets. The timeliness of the topic could not be more profound. Glasnost has opened the floodgates to long-ignored or repressed expressions of anti-Semitism by right-wing nationalist groups as well as by individuals. As Askoldov remarked, the film still makes audiences uncomfortable, for Magazanik is portrayed sympathetically (but not sentimentally) as a husband struggling to support his family and maintain a strong relationship with his wife; consider the scene when he washes his wife's feet, looks up, and says simply, "I love you." He is also presented as a father who tries to influence his children but who is definitely not a tyrannical father figure—rather, he is something of a "wise fool" who ultimately plays the clown. This is captured in a scene in which he leads the family in a dance of life as the sounds of war close in on them. The music is that of traditional Jewish dances; the camera captures the swirling intensity of the moment and lingers on Bykov's sad, wise, tragically smiling face. This is the face not of a patriarch, but of a suffering human being who happens to be poor, Jewish, male, and living in the Soviet Union. Askoldov ends the film with a flash-forward to the rounding-up and extermination of Jews during World War II, thus projecting their suffering into the future (which is now the past), but suggesting the eternal nature of the narrative. It leaves us with little hope for Magazanik's family (despite the "balancing" image of the dance), or for Vavilova's child, who has been incorporated into the Jewish family and will share its fate.

A final dimension of balance in *Commissar* is the tension between public and private, personal and party, individual and Communist. Given that the role of Soviet cinema as defined from the 1920s on was to serve the public good and the Revolution, a film that is firmly rooted in the world of private life and the individual, and a woman at that, is clearly miles away from stark socialist realism. Two-thirds of the film occurs within the confines of Magazanik's home: watching children play, giving birth, talking, dancing, living. The outside world is depicted as violent, bustling (the market scene), and chaotic (the ending). The only peace is found in the midst of family life, and the most memorable line is given to Magazanik's wife, Maria (played with quiet intensity by Raisa Nedashkovskaya), who fulfills the role of companion and guide to Vavilova, leading her through childbirth. Maria explains, "War is easy: boom, boom. It's raising a family that's difficult." We laugh and nod in agreement at the same time. History sweeps over this family as it has and will over so many others. But Askoldov's camera allows us to see that joy and laughter and love are possible in the midst of history's darkest hours. The film's critique of Communist doctrine is not overt. Askoldov implies a more universal condemnation of rigid dogmas that lead one to make choices that elevate a cause above one's own happiness and flesh and blood. It is enough to realize that the film is set during a period of civil war, the worst fate that can happen to any people.

One other unshelved work bears mentioning. In August 1990 at the Montreal World Film Festival, the late Ukrainian director Vladimir Denisenko's 1968 film *Conscience (Sovest')* received its world premiere, presented by his filmmaker son, Alexander Denisenko. The film is testimony to the powerful independence of the filmmaking coming from Kiev and elsewhere in the Ukraine. Set during World War II, the film appears to be another antiwar movie centered on the Nazi extermination of an entire village, shot in a horrifyingly graphic series of sequences. It is noteworthy, however, not just because of the highly stylized black-and-white framing and composition, but because the partisans who are the protagonists are not Soviet Communists, but rather Ukrainian nationalists, members of the Ukrainian Partisan Army. Little wonder that the film was destroyed and that one print survived only because it was cut into segments and stored in various places, only to surface again in 1990. Screened during the festival's Tribute to a Cinema of Freedom, the film was well received. It was seen as presenting not so much a universal statement, as had *Commissar*, but more of a clearly partisan, nationalist perspective that could now be shown in the Soviet Union.

To a surprising degree, the "shelved" films helped establish immediately the true limits of openness for contemporary filmmakers.

THE DIRECTOR'S FILM AND STALINISM: ABULADZE'S *REPENTANCE* AND THE CRITIQUE OF PATRIARCHY IN THE MOTHERLAND

Increasingly, Soviet feature narrative cinema can be seen as falling into two camps: commercial films and "directors' cinema" or the "difficult films": auteurist cinema focusing on the filmmaker as artist with a personal vision to express.

Traditional wisdom has held that "genius" directors such as Tarkovsky who represent a poetic and prophetic vision did not need to worry about finding a wide audience or concern themselves with making money. State film funding and production provided a cushion between art and the box office. What many of the most interesting films made in the past five years have demonstrated, however (in the Soviet Union and elsewhere), is that it is possible to blur the distinction between these two camps. For example, *The Cold Summer of '53* (*Holodnoye leto '53-go*, 1987) was extremely commercial but has the aesthetic and intellectual integrity of an auteurist work.

Furthermore, although we focus on films made under glasnost that deconstruct the past, we must acknowledge that a critique of the myths of the past has been under way since Khrushchev's "thaw" in the late 1950s. Alexei Gherman's *My Friend Ivan Lapshin* (*Moy droug Ivan Lapshin*, 1984), based on a work by the director's father, Yuri Gherman, is the tale of an idealistic police investigator in provincial Russia in the mid-1930s. While he tries to carry out the difficult task of rounding up "criminals," as defined by Stalinist doctrine, his potential romance with a local actress is turning sour. In terms of technique, this black-and-white and sepia film mixes documentarylike footage of the times, as well as old photographs, with staged flashbacks of 1930s provincial life. What results is a study of characters who try to maintain their socialist idealism in the face of corruption.

The celebrated Georgian filmmaker Tengiz Abuladze, director of such works as *Magdan's Donkey* (*Lurdja Magdany*, 1955, codirected with

Revaz Chheidze), *Someone Else's Children* (*Chuzhyie deti,* 1958), *The Necklace for My Beloved* (*Ozherelye dlya moei liubimoi,* 1972), and *The Wishing Tree* (*Drevo zhelaniya,* 1977), captured the Soviet public's attention with *Repentance* (*Pokayaniye,* 1984, released in 1986), which presented Stalin's terror through a highly symbolic, allegorical, and at times surrealistic "comic tragedy" or "phantasmagoria" (as Abuladze has characterized his work). No simple plot summary will suffice. The "story" concerns three generations in an imaginary city ruled by a tyrant, Varlam Aravidze (whose name in Georgian means "no one"). We see, in the film's opening, that his body reappeared after it was buried several times. We learn of the horrors committed under his administration, and we discover that a woman, Ketevan Barateli (played by Zeinab Botsvadze), removed the body from the tomb because she felt that such a scoundrel should never have received the honor of a burial. During her trial, we see how Varlam's life affected his relatives as well as the citizens of the city. In the final shot, the body is flung by his son, who had protected the corpse throughout the film, off a cliff to be devoured by vultures.

Repentance is an important transitional film. Not only is it a document of changing times on the brink of glasnost, but it has already become a classic work of Georgian and Soviet cinematic art, despite a script that is needlessly verbose and convoluted. This shortcoming may explain why the film was not popular with Soviet youth.

Written in 1981, the script is a clear example of a Soviet film project that almost did not get made. Its very existence turns on two factors: it is the product of the Georgian studio in Tbilisi, with its proud tradition of being the strongest national cinema outside Russia for many years, and it received the unflagging support of one of Gorbachev's closest advisors, Eduard Shevardnadze, Politburo member, former foreign minister, and at that time the party chief of Georgia. As many noted, *Repentance* became a social event and not just a film. Over thirty million Soviet people lined up eagerly for tickets and debated the film hotly for months afterward.

Repentance is significant for its debunking of Stalinism for at least four reasons. First, it is meant to be a metaphorical, allegorical, Aesopian fable. In terms of characterization and plot, the film centers on the mythical mayor, Varlam Aravidze (played with gusto and tact by Avtandil Makharadze), who in looks as well as in concept embodies Stalin, Hitler, Mussolini, and, most specifically, Stalin's master henchman, the chief of the NKVD (now called the KGB), Lavrenty Beria. We are meant, as in many of Abuladze's other movies, to take the film on a generalized, allegorical, mythical level that transcends the historical and specific. Even the country and time are unidentified, though the film was, appropriately enough, filmed in Stalin's and Beria's homeland, Georgia, by a Georgian filmmaker. Thus the black-humored opening sequences, in which the body of the recently deceased Varlam mysteriously reappears each time it is buried, cannot help being read as a metaphor for the Stalinist past, which cannot easily be laid to rest.

Second, Abuladze has purposely constructed a widely polyphonic film that mixes extreme opposites in style and genre, ranging from slapstick to melodrama and tragedy. The whole film radiates out from Varlam himself in a disjointed series of often abrupt transitions between past and present. Varlam's contradictory moods and personas are reflected in a similar diversity of scenes as they affect those around him, especially his family. Dressed in Mussolini's black shirt and leather, wearing Beria's delicate pince-nez, which at one instant illuminate his piercing eyes and at another hide them according to the angle of the light, with Stalin's close-cropped hair and Hitler's mustache, Varlam plays at being clown, lover, leader, dictator, patron of the arts, and vulnerable child. Here the Georgian tradition of folktale and comedy in a surrealist, phantasmagoric vein appears similar to Latin American "magic realism" with a sociopolitical punch, as rendered by Gabriel García Márquez in *One Hundred Years of Solitude*. Rather than simply emphasizing past dictators and their reigns of terror—Stalin heads the Soviet list, of course—Abuladze suggests the complexity of totalitarianism, which involves seduction and perhaps misguided idealism, as well as greed, pride, insecurity, paranoia, corruption, and lust for power. As in Tofik Shakhverdiev's documentary *Is Stalin with Us? (Stalin s nami?* 1989), the deconstruction of the past in this film, made just as glasnost was coming into being, is remarkably sophisticated in its effort to capture, tease out, and represent Stalinism from a number of perspectives. Both films assume the complex existence of the past within the present, which makes the burying of tyranny particularly difficult, if not impossible.

Repentance views human suffering through the downfall of a family. The film examines Varlam's status-seeking, bureaucratic-minded son, Abel (also played by Makharadze), whose cool, managerial calculating in the Brezhnev manner (typical of the stagnation period) appears in many ways even worse than Varlam's mercurial behavior. It is also about Varlam's idealistic, troubled grandson, Tornike. Viewed from the diverse perspectives of three generations of men in one family, Abuladze's film offers both hope and despair. The plot concerns the trial of Ketevan Barateli, who fully admits that she is the one who disinterred Varlam. During the trial, the cumulative effect of the revelations of Varlam's atrocities finally leads his grandson to despair. As an American pop song of the 1970s, "Sunny," plays on his stereo, he takes the hunting rifle given him by his grandfather and commits suicide. Abel breaks down when he discovers the body of his son, crying out "What have you done, you monster?" His answer is to dig up his father one last time and fling the body from a cliff to be eaten by the vultures, as we see the modern skyline of Tbilisi in the background. To bury a corpse is to give respect to the dead, the angry Ketevan Barateli tells the court; to disinter it is to place Varlam where he belongs: in disgraced oblivion.

Abuladze's general exposure of totalitarianism and of Stalinism in particular may be seen as a critique of patriarchy as well. What we view in *Repentance* is a male-centered universe that does not allow boys to become adults. Varlam is not only a powerful fool, he is a child, given to tantrums and cravings in typical pre-Oedipal patterns. When these instant desires are fulfilled, he changes by 180 degrees within minutes. With no blessings being bestowed, no maturation occurs for either Varlam or his son, or, finally, his grandson.

Three scenes near the end of the film are illustrative. While the trial is still on, the grandson, Tornike, dreams about a surrealistic conversation with Varlam, a speaking corpse. Soon after, in the empty courtroom, Tornike confronts his father. He accuses Abel of lying and of being guilty of many of the same crimes as Varlam. Abel's defense is that "those were complicated times. . . . Difficult to explain." This exchange ends as Tornike storms out, shouting "I hate you." The third scene is Abel's dream during the trial. He sees himself confessing to a hidden "priest" who is eating a large fish. The "priest" succeeds in getting Abel to confess that he is afraid and feels a deep void in himself. Abel realizes, "I preach atheism and wear a cross: perhaps that is why my life is such a mess." At that point Varlam reveals himself as the "priest" and laughs at his son, handing him the bones of the fish.

On the immediate narrative level of the film, fathers have denied their sons the blessings needed to mature, to grow into complete men. On a metaphorical level as well, we observe the process of exorcising the Stalinist era as one of mass psychoanalysis from the male point of view. In chapter 3 we will explore how complex the relationship between Mother Russia (the female perspective) and the myth of Communist patriarchy (Father Lenin and Stalin) has become. But here we note that Stalin's distortion of socialism denied both men and women the blessings of the supposed fruits of mature communism.

The nature of the image and role of the father is also of critical importance to American cinema of the 1970s and 1980s. Robin Wood observes that the theme of "the restoration of the Father . . . constitutes—and logically enough—the dominant project, ad infinitum and post nauseam, of the contemporary Hollywood cinema" (*Hollywood from Vietnam to Reagan*, 174). Particularly in the most popular films of this period, those of Spielberg and Lucas, this theme, or as Woods labels it, this "thematic metasystem embracing all the available genres," emerges. The film *E.T.* explores the difficulty of white suburban family life without father; the father has left, and E.T. replaces the missing patriarch. The *Star Wars* trilogy builds to Luke Skywalker's confrontation with his father, Darth Vader, an Oedipal confusion resolved only partially by the presence of Alec Guinness as a spiritual, E.T.-like father substitute. In either case the field of representation is strongly male, with the women represented as absentminded mothers, as in *E.T.*, or tough and tender women like Princess Leia who, as Wood comments, appears to serve only as "a matter of narrative convenience" (175).

Restoration versus deconstruction of the father: such a perspective suggests how different are the approaches that Hollywood and Moscow have taken in cinematic (re)presentation in the 1970s and 1980s.

One more level of interest in *Repentance* is the spiritual Orthodox Christian dimension, suggested by the title. Like a parable from the Bible, the film generalizes human behavior. In discussing Stalinism in Aesopian terms, Abuladze has established a dialectic between Varlam and materialism on the one hand, and culture, art, and the realm of the spiritual on the other. On the plane of Christian fable, the film has a different narrative and thematic trajectory. From this perspective, the narrative drive of the film hinges on Ketevan, the woman on trial for disinterring Varlam. Not only does this give *Repentance* a female point of view, but much of the film is narrated in flashback, which ensures that about half the film is seen through Ketevan's eyes as a child, through a prism of innocence that contrasts strongly with Varlam's stunted male childishness.

The socialist-spiritual split is expressed through Varlam's attraction to and fear of Ketevan's father, the religious painter Sandro Barateli, and his hauntingly beautiful wife, Nino. Ketevan's rebellion against Varlam's burial is, therefore, personal and ideological. Varlam destroyed her father (in prison camps) and seduced her mother. While the Georgian Orthodox religion is treated as simply a repository of the people's culture, we cannot neglect the clearly Christian implications of this spirituality. "Repentance" is a term primarily charged with religious meaning and possibility. Structurally and thematically, the film begins and ends with religious suggestions. The film has a circular structure; we open and close with Ketevan decorating wedding cakes that have a model of a Georgian church on top. The time is the present.

In the closing scene, an old peasant woman carrying a small suitcase comes to Ketevan's window and asks whether this street is the one that leads to the temple. Ketevan explains that it is Varlam Street and that there is no church on it; a subplot of the film is Varlam's destruction of the beautiful ancient church after he used it as a laboratory, a scene that Soviet audiences see as mirroring the party's destruction of churches throughout the country. (One of Moscow's cathedrals was ruined to build a swimming pool.) The old woman shrugs and replies, "What good is a street that doesn't lead to a church?" as she turns and walks into the distance, her back to the camera. The final shot is of Ketevan's sad, understanding, thoughtful face.

The deconstruction of Varlam's patriarchal socialist materialism is complete. Abuladze suggests no simplistic victory of a female, artistic, spiritual force over the destructive elements represented by Varlam. But in Ketevan's steadfast protest and Abel's final repentance in disposing of his father's corpse after his son's suicide, the possibility of renewal and hope is present.

The film's enthusiastic reception suggests that *Repentance* was a major step in coming to terms with the Stalinist past, and that it pointed the way toward a form of catharsis. Varlamism and Stalinism did not disappear with the symbolic gesture of tossing the body to birds of prey (although the controversy over relocating Lenin's body from Red Square seems almost to have been influenced by Abuladze's film). But such an artistic and metaphorical representation does suggest that the healing process must involve the spirit—repentance—as well as the head.

PAST PRESENT, PRESENT PAST: DIRECTORS' FILMS
FROM ABSURDISM TO SURREALISM

Walter Benjamin was fond of saying, "There is no document of culture which is not also a record of barbarism." Recent Soviet cinema is now free to document the barbarism of the system, and of those who created and supported it. A spectrum of approaches has been explored in various "directors' films." These range from docudramas and fictional documentaries to surrealist and satirical allegories.

In terms of the further development of Soviet film language, these various efforts offer new possibilities for erasing or blurring the traditional lines between the genres, and between the documentary and the fiction film. Consider the use of actual documentary footage within a fictional documentary. *Defense Counsel Sedov* (*Zaschitnik Sedov*, 1989), for instance, is an intense first film by Yevgeny Tsymbal, written by Maria Zvereva, about a lawyer who takes on the dangerous and thankless task of defending four provincial agronomists falsely accused of an agricultural crime in 1949. In this narrative, less than sixty minutes long, we observe an average (and typically corrupt) lawyer move from passivity to activism as he states, "I'm fulfilling professional duties according to Soviet law."

The most immediate technique employed by many such "past-present" works to capture the atmosphere of the past is to shoot in black and white or sepia. The sepia tones of Tsymbal's film immediately force us into another era and add to the texture of oppression and the sense of reduced expectations and possibilities. Furthermore, this stirring debut film, which ends as a courtroom farce, skillfully blends in actual newsreel footage throughout. In one scene, while the solicitor is taking a train to the provincial town where the agronomists are being held, he looks out the window. What he sees is actually newsreel footage from the period, complete with sound. Period documentary clips add a certain degree of authenticity to a narrative, even while we are aware that such a combination is itself a construct. But usually such footage is from familiar scenes of our collective viewing memory. Think, for instance, of how the brief civil-rights montage sequence, complete with highlights of Martin Luther King's speeches, is used as a bridge in Taylor Hackford's *Everybody's All American* (1989), or how familiar scenes from the Democratic Convention riots in Chicago in 1968 and the Vietnam veterans' protest at the Miami Republican Convention in 1972 are interwoven on TV screens in Oliver Stone's narrative in *Born on the Fourth of July* (1990) to increase our sense of realism. Such interplay between documentary and recreated fiction is familiar to us, at times to the point of being a cliché.

What is noteworthy in the scene from *Defense Counsel Sedov*, however, is that the footage is not meant to be a bridge or an incorporated part of the actual fiction, as in Stone's film, for instance. Instead, the obvious abruptness with which the narrative is interrupted by the newsreel footage calls attention to itself. And it does so as an intrusion of one form, documentary, into another, recreated period drama. On a metaphorical level, such a suture is a suggestion of the intrusion of the times into the lives of individuals. Instead of attempting to create a seamless sense of realism, which is a major characteristic of the classic American cinema, including *Born on the Fourth of July*, *Defense Counsel Sedov* forces the viewer to consider the implications of mixing these elements in one narrative. (Such intellectual dialectics again bring us back to Eisenstein's formulations for Soviet art.)

Alexander Kaidanovsky's *Kerosene Seller's Wife* (*Zhena kerosinschika*, 1989) moves us beyond the level of documentary fiction and into the realm of a darkly etched allegory of the bizarre. Based on his own script, Kaidanovsky's film turns history into a collage of Christian and Greco-Western myth to create a nightmarish (re)vision of the Stalinist period.

Clearly, something of a new "Leningrad school" has emerged under glasnost as a number of talented young directors, such as Kaidanovsky, Oleg Teptsov (*Mr. Designer* [*Gospodin oformitel'*, 1989]), Sergei Selyanov and Nikolai Makarov (*The Name Day* [*Den' angela*, 1988]), Valery Ogorodnikov (*Prishvin's Paper Eyes* [*Bumazhnye glaza Prishvina*, 1989]), and Sergei Ovcharov (*It* [*Ono*, 1989]), have forsaken realist cinema in any classical mode—Hollywood or otherwise—in favor of producing highly personal visions expressed in allegorical, satirical, surrealistic, and, as Anna Lawton has noted, "grotesque" forms ("Soviet Cinema Four Years Later"). These directors are in a direct line with the "cinema of the prophets" practiced by Tarkovsky.

Kerosene Seller's Wife concerns the cold winter of 1953. The year Stalin died is represented in this surrealistic tale through a Cain-and-Abel fable of twin brothers (both played by Alexander Baluev) and one woman. To outline the story would be difficult at best, given the convoluted narrative. But what is significant in this recasting of the past is the framing of the times as a Christian (Roman Catholic as well as Orthodox) allegory. "Victory is the refuge of the scoundrel," intones a priest. The apparent victor is Cain, the "successful" brother, a Communist official of high rank who, in his quest for power, committed a crime for which his brother took the blame and suffered every imaginable disgrace, ending up as a kerosene seller. The kerosene seller appears to be a "holy fool" (*yurodivy;* see chapter 6) because of his unjust suffering and stoic resistance to political and social forces. As such, he is the bridge between the bizarre reality of Stalinist Russia and the surrealist intrusion of visions throughout the film.

Christian symbolism and tradition permeate the film. Images of dead angels, "magical" happenings, and grotesque events (at one point the Communist brother's face bloats, expands, and explodes, as in David Kronenberg's films) push toward transcendence, only to find history to be a nightmare from which the protagonists cannot escape. "I'm convinced that without hope for a miracle," the priest says near the end, "life would become a sad reality."

Overall, like many glasnost films concerned with the past, *Kerosene Seller's Wife* proved too ambitious, too self-indulgent, to reach more than a small following of critics and viewers. Brecht believed in the "alienation effect" of drama, and yet the truth is that his Mother Courage, for instance, is a sympathetic and heroic woman, and that *The Threepenny Opera* engages its viewers at the same time as they are forced to rethink history and politics. The deluge of dark images, disconnected and enigmatic, in films such as Kaidanovsky's work alienate without first engaging, thus leaving those in the audience bewildered and depressed.

For there are no miracles to save this holy fool in Kaidanovsky's tale. At the film's end, the Communist brother leaps to his death in a freezing river, shouting "Long live Marxism-Leninism," while another character remains in an insane asylum surrounded by idiots. That Kaidanovsky's camera roams over the faces of these real-life victims leaves us uneasy and disturbed. Once again the line between documentary and fiction has been shifted. It is one thing to read of such dark scenes in novels by Dostoevsky (whose elaborate psychological nightmares mixed with Russian Orthodox imagery this film resembles) and quite another to be confronted with the immediacy of images of real idiots smiling their unknowing smiles to a searching, intruding camera. Dostoevsky at least had a narrator through whom to filter the images of "reality" he presented.

A hymn plays over these images as the film nears its end. Is this music a kind of hope or merely a juxtaposition? Kaidanovsky leaves it to us to decide. The final image is of the kerosene seller alone, having lost everything, including his wife, pounding exploding caps with a brick and making warlike explosions with his voice, seemingly oblivious to the church bells pealing. From whose point of view has the film been told? Perhaps it is a tale told by the holy fool himself; after all, even in his silence at the end, he is outside the asylum, though locked in his own memories of the violence and betrayal that have been his history and that of millions like him.

Valery Ogorodnikov provides a stronger narrative base than Kaidanovsky in his imaginative *Prishvin's Paper Eyes* in order to bring the audience through a chilling vision of the Stalinist period. The surrealist blending of documentary, fiction, past, and present that makes up this work is framed within the context of a character, Prishvin, who is filming a docudrama about the first years of Soviet television during the late 1940s and early 1950s. As the characters become involved with the hatred, corruption, and perversity of the period, the contemporary actors themselves begin to suffer and overidentify with the characters. The film becomes a cathartic dark night of the Soviet soul, so harsh at times that it is especially painful for the non-Soviet viewer.

But two sequences remain in one's mind long after the film has finished. The first is a montage sequence in which documentary footage is edited for a special effect. In one brief sequence we see one of the countless "happy" dance troupes that performed a national folk dance on early Soviet television for the viewing masses. The strong melodic beat of the song continues as images from the Stalinist period flash by. Images of Hitler and Nazi rallies are then added to the montage to chilling effect. And finally Ogorodnikov intensifies the beat as he crosscuts from a constantly repeated segment showing a smiling Stalin pointing his finger to shots taken from Odessa Steps sequence in Eisenstein's film *Battleship Potemkin* (*Bronenosets "Potemkin," * 1925). It is one of the single most stirring images in glasnost cinema.

Eisenstein and others of his generation saw montage as the essence of their avant-garde and Marxist revolutionary fervor. As applied to the memorable Odessa Steps sequence, the conflict between frames built sympathy for the slaughtered innocent citizens, the children and mothers dead at the hands of czarist troops.

The scene has been quoted by so many filmmakers everywhere that to make reference to it once more is to risk cliché. Yet the power of Ogorodnikov's editing is that he follows Eisenstein's principles of dialectical cutting to turn the Revolution, at least as practiced by Stalin, on its head. This time there are no czarist troops ascending the staircase; rather, there is a smugly smiling Stalin pointing, as if to accuse, to name, to condemn. As the music builds, the screen bleeds red when we finally reach the frames of the baby carriage rolling and the bullet passing through the woman's eyeglasses.

Stalin is the murderer this time. Ogorodnikov adheres to Eisenstein's concept of montage of space: Stalin points his finger from right to left as the *Potemkin* shots move from left to right. The darkly surrealist effect of this editing, however, goes even further. We realize that the film's narrative uses two different forms and time periods—the documentary footage of Stalin and the recreated documentary fiction of Eisenstein— in order to play them off against each other. Recent critical attention to Eisenstein in France focuses on the ways in which montage may actually help its viewers understand the degree to which history and reality are constructs. Jacques Aumont writes that we see from Eisenstein that "history is also nothing but stories, the contents of a series of narrative representations" (*Montage Eisenstein*, 22), a remark that echoes Hayden White's emphasis on viewing historical writings as largely subjective.

Ogorodnikov's editing exemplifies this principle. Prishvin is trying determinedly to go beyond the "paper eyes" (false eyes worn by news announcers so that they appear to be looking at the camera while reading) of the times to present a closer look at how those times were carefully constructed and controlling narratives. Both character and director build on material supplied by the past to provide ironic insights. Framed by the world of early television, this sequence in Ogorodnikov's film has a stronger effect on audiences than does *Kerosene Seller's Wife*, for it is motivated as part of the realm of image-manipulation and ideological control.

A final sequence pulls the audience beyond the sense of nausea and depression about the Stalinist past. A large statue of Stalin is hoisted above Leningrad by a helicopter and flown over the city and out into the vast countryside. Fellini begins *La dolce vita* (1960) with a flying Christ hovering by helicopter over Rome; Ogorodnikov ends with the statue and all that it signifies being removed. But there is more. The statue falls through space and zooms toward the ear of a female victim of Stalin's crimes lying murdered on the earth. As we enter the darkness of her eye, the film ends.

David Lynch's *Blue Velvet* (1986), one of the most admired off-Hollywood films of the 1980s, uses a similar device: the whole narrative exists within the "ear" entered in the opening sequence. But while Lynch partially comforts the audience by exiting the "ear" at the end of the film, *Prishvin's Paper Eyes* leaves us literally in the dark space that Soviet history has become, still locked inside the body of a victim of the Revolution.

It takes us to extremes of cinema invention and film language in a satirical adaptation of a nineteenth-century novel, *The History of a Town*, by Mikhail Saltykov-Shchedrin. Here writer-director Sergei Ovcharov, who made *The Left-hander* (*Levsha*, 1988) the year before, follows the spirit of Saltykov-Shchedrin's work, yet manages to update it to fit the history of the Revolution.

"It" is life, history itself, which flows through one town clearly representing the whole nation. Such a structure allows Ovcharov the freedom to play with the simultaneous development of cinematic and photographic technology as it parallels sociopolitical developments. Thus the film begins with tinny sound and a jerky black-and-white image set in the preczarist past as we watch what seems to be rare medieval footage of Russian tribes gathering to express their desire to have a leader, a czar. By the time the film evolves to the Stalinist period, the film itself has a glossy 1930s look and the sound has become much more refined.

The well-known actor and director Rolan Bykov, the Jewish tinker Magazanik in *Commissar*, plays the Stalin figure and many of the other "town rulers," and part of the satirical pleasure is that we watch him evolve as well, from one role to another, with changing face and costume, but with a similar sense of "it," the oppressive force of the powers that be, looming over the nation.

Such an updated adaptation of a literary work suggests how the socialist past can be expressed in yet another imaginative manner. We realize the effectiveness of literary satire in the hands of a talented filmmaker. At least half the pleasure of this work is the close aesthetic control of humor, seen in the acting, set design, sound track, framing, and manipulation of images and colors.

The film picks up in pace as well as technology as it enters recent history and the present, zooming past a headless "Brezhnev," into an ecological disaster and a sense of mass suicide, for one more nightmarish vision of the future. The humor of the beginning ("our little town was famous for hard-boiled eggs") gives way to a sci-fi horror. The blue-tinted and then pink-tinted screen shows a bulldozer plowing under rubble and human bodies alike, and punk music plays, as if history has become some bizarre music video.

One other scene merits discussion before we end our look at the Stalinist past. "Stalin" eyes a young, beautiful woman married to a young man. As was the custom, she and her husband are rounded up in the middle of the night and brought by car to the leader. There is no humor or satire in these moments, stunningly photographed by Valery Fedosov. When the young man is brought before "Stalin," seated at his desk, he attacks the leader and gets in a few well-placed blows before he is dragged off.

What follows should be a seduction scene. Certainly the woman is brought for "Stalin" to enjoy. She is beautiful, young, and frightened. She strips and climbs into the bed conveniently placed by the leader's desk. "Stalin" climbs in too, but instead of making love, he begins to read. Soon he is asleep with his eyes open. The camera lingers on the young woman's face. There is relief and terror. No, she has not been raped this time, but there is in her tearful glance the knowledge that this man controls her life as well as that of everyone else in her town. It is a measure of Ovcharov's accomplishment that the humor and bitter satire of much of the film is balanced by such well-executed moments of pathos.

"It," we quickly realize, is not without gender. The "it" of history, pre-Soviet and Soviet, is (re)presented as male and as a series of incidents in which curses rather than blessings are inflicted on women and men alike. If "it" is neuter, this is because of the historical castration of bodies and spirits, the filmmaker suggests.

ON (RE)PLAYING THE PAST

What can we make of such a concentrated burst of attention on the Stalinist past? Soviet critic Pyotr Smirnov points out a real danger in (re)presenting the Stalinist period. He remarks that films that simply present and destroy images of Stalinism run the risk of merely being part of a current trend. In a sense, nothing could be easier today than making a film against Stalin. It is a bit like making a movie against rape or against the molestation of children. Speaking of the Soviet people, Smirnov notes: "Formerly they worshipped the icons (of Stalin), now they spit on them. But this does not prevent an icon remaining an icon. If anything, a desecrated icon can evoke pity and—who knows—perhaps a wish to clean it of spittle" ("What Next?" 15).

Smirnov is correct about the simplistic evocation of Stalinism in many glasnost films. *Kerosene Seller's Wife* and other works must answer such charges of ambivalence. There is even the possibility of a kind of reverse nostalgia: while some films present an anti-Stalinist message, the style of shooting, characterization, and evocation of the past actually present an attractive image of a "simpler" time.

But the best of them—and this list would include *It, Prishvin's Paper Eyes,* and *Defense Counsel Sedov*—do (re)present the past in such a way that we become aware of the process and subjectivity of history as it is made, manipulated, and hidden from view, often in a mode similar to that of making a film.

By late 1990 and early 1991, however, reconsideration of the socialist past had disappeared almost entirely from Soviet screens. Audiences voted for escapist entertainment with their tickets. Those filmmakers who did continue to evoke the past, particularly the Stalinist heritage, risked pushing the historical discourse beyond absurdity into incoherence, or past familiarity into the valley of clichés.

Considering the latter, the respected Georgian director Alexander Rekhviashvili (see chapter 7) presents both Stalin and Lenin in his absurdist "director's film" *Coming Closer* (1991), yet with a by-now overworked sense of critical iconology. One sequence of scenes takes place in a ruined Georgian village in the center of which stands a bronze statue of Comrade Lenin pointing into the distance, as if to a brighter future. The statue in a ruined wasteland has an initially arresting quality, but Rekhviashvili's constant repetition of the shot throughout the film becomes an embarrassing and boring exercise in emphasizing the obvious. Another sequence, in a Georgian high-school classroom, shows us, from time to time, a large plaster bust of Stalin, back to the camera, hidden in the classroom closet by the frustrated teacher. Rekhviashvili makes it clear that no learning takes place in this school, either about culture or about the worn-out ideology of communism. He ends this strand of his film with the teacher removing Stalin from the closet, placing him on the front desk, and sitting before the bust in contemplation. Many at the January 1991 premiere of the film, at Dom Kino in Moscow, however, had already left by the time this tired imagery appeared on the screen.

Sergei Solovyev, whose *Assa* is discussed in the next chapter, pushes his discourse on the Stalinist past into the realm of campy, surrealist incoherence in *Black Rose Stands for Sorrow, Red Rose Stands for Love (Chernaya roza—emblema pechali, krasnaya roza—emblema liubvi,* 1989). Although Solovyev has (de)constructed his film in such a manner as to defy simple analysis, the film's visual and narrative concern is centered on the coming-of-age of a teenage boy, Mitya. Like *Repentance,* the film portrays the confused relationships in a complicated "family." At the film's beginning and end, which show an offbeat character living in the communal apartment that is the focus of the film, we hear an audio-tape reporting the "medical death of Stalin."

Between these two references appear a host of images and words reflecting the psychological implications of that death for Soviet culture and, ultimately, for Mitya as an individual young man. At one point he is told "You are nobody's son," a line that, to use Peter Blos's term, suggests the difficulty Mitya is experiencing in growing to maturity in the midst of such chaos.

Solovyev's film appears as something of a parody of the attempt to find any meaning in (re)considering the Stalinist past. Contemporary scenes are interrupted by a sequence in which "Stalin" has a bowel movement under the supervision of his Jewish physician. Perhaps the most strikingly original shot is the one in which "Stalin" and the doctor examine the leader's stool in the toilet bowl, after which a title card appears on the screen: "Hard Constipation Chased Stalin."

Absurdity is pushed further than ever before on the Soviet screen as Solovyev employs some of the spirit and techniques of the Soviet avant-garde movement known as "parallel cinema" to present a sequence in which "Stalin" visits Mitya's apartment with a full entourage, including the young "Brezhnev." "Stalin" says to the boy, "You have suffered a lot. What do you want?" Mitya replies, "To be a marine." "Stalin" requests that "Brezhnev" help the young man. Mitya is then given a marine's outfit of the period, and Solovyev intercuts shots of the battleship *Aurora*, which played a significant role in the Revolution and which appears throughout the film, with shots of a naked woman, bringing sensuality and revolution together in a manner reminiscent of Dusan Makavejev's playful collage montages of twenty years ago in such films as *W. R.: Mysteries of the Organism* (1971) and *Innocence Unprotected* (1968).

As Svetlana Boym has pointed out in "Kitsch as Satire in Recent Soviet Cinema," Solovyev's film is perhaps best taken as kitsch rather than as a serious (re)presentation of the past and present. But in terms of our consideration of fathers and sons, we can note that "Stalin" confers his blessing on Mitya by coming through death and time and space to Mitya and granting his wish. The blessing, however, leads not to maturity but to further confusion, as we see the battleship blowing up and as the scenes and images become increasingly surreal. As one character comments: "Everything is confused in our country. I am forty, but I feel as though I am in the tenth grade." Under such conditions, no coming-of-age seems possible.

Clearly Soviet audiences in 1990 were tired of such cinematic confusion, even if it did contain Stalin's feces and rock music by popular

Soviet groups. There were lines for *Gone with the Wind* and Arnold Schwarzenegger's films rather than *Black Rose*, which closed its initial Moscow run after two weeks.

GENRE FILMS AND THE GHOST OF STALIN

Soviet cinema did not have to wait for Gorbachev in 1985 before it began to critique Stalinism and socialism, however mildly or indirectly. In the 1950s, probing directors found that genre films could be used to frame criticism. Chapter 5 will detail the development of Soviet genre cinema, but we should mention here that Iosif Kheifits's *Rumyantsev Case* (*Delo Rumyantseva*, 1955), for example, used the detective formula to suggest disgust with bureaucracy. Yuli Raizman, working with screenwriter Yevgeni Gabrilovich, opened up the worn-out "production" and "positive hero" genre films of the Stalinist period with such openly critical works as *The Lesson of Life* (*Urok zhizni*, 1955) and *The Communist* (1957). During Khrushchev's "thaw" even such a controversial film as Andrei Tarkovsky's *Andrei Rublev* (1967), coscripted with Andrei Konchalovsky, presented metaphorical depictions of excesses of violence and persecution under Stalin.

The Polish filmmaker Andrzej Wajda made perhaps the earliest and strongest condemnation of Stalinism in his renowned 1976 production, *Man of Marble*. In Wajda's film, the crimes of Polish Stalinism are brought to light in an investigation similar to that in *Citizen Kane*, as a young student filmmaker investigates the rise and fall of a model bricklayer of the 1950s. In the Soviet Union, the first five years of glasnost did not produce a film equal in stature to Wajda's. But two extremely popular films, Alexander Proshkin's *Cold Summer of '53*, written by Edgar Dubrovsky, and Vladimir Khotinenko's *Mirror for a Hero* (*Zerkalo dlya geroya*, 1988), written by Nadezhda Kozhushannaya, suggest how critiques of Stalinism can be framed by genre films.

The Cold Summer of '53 is a taut tale of violent action set in a northern Russian village shortly after Stalin's death. The film is constructed using codes and formulas mirroring those of the classical American Western, but operating for clearly Soviet ends. Its very simplicity, like that of films such as John Ford's *Searchers*, makes it complex.

This immensely popular film was seen by many millions more than *Repentance*, and outsold all other Soviet films, including *Little Vera*, in foreign sales (twenty-six countries) in 1988. It follows the terror unleashed on a village by a gang of criminals freed after Stalin's death. This depleted village (many of its men had never returned from the war, or had been deported to Stalin's camps), like the towns in so many Hollywood Westerns, is helpless before the destructive demands of the rampaging gang of four. The drama builds as the gang is confronted and ultimately wiped out by two political prisoners exiled to the village for "anti-Stalinist activities." The older man is Digger, played by Anatoly Papanov, a famous comic actor who died soon after shooting was completed. Digger is a former engineer separated from his wife and son since his arrest in 1939 as a British spy. The younger man, Chaff, was in his pre-exile days Sergei Basargin, a former intelligence officer. He is played with Gary Cooper–like control and quiet intensity by Valery Priemykhov, who is also a well-known screenwriter and director.

A major debate in Soviet cinema circles since the 1920s has been how to make a truly popular film that offers a "correct" socialist vision. In 1929, for instance, director Pavel Petrov-Bytov wrote in *Zhizn' iskusstva* that the works of Eisenstein, Pudovkin, and others did not qualify as "Soviet cinema" despite their formalistic virtues because "people do not want to watch these films" (Taylor and Christie, *Film Factory*, 259). That year, critic Adrian Piotrovsky wrote in the same journal that Soviet filmmakers had much to learn from Hollywood, especially in terms of "plot tension, precisely what is lacking more than anything else in our cinema" (ibid., 269). In chapter 5 we follow in more detail the influence of Hollywood and genre on Soviet filmmakers.

The Cold Summer of '53 manages to build a popular Soviet film with plenty of plot tension on influences from Hollywood Westerns such as *High Noon*. Consider the elements that go beyond the simplistic "good guys"–"bad guys" dichotomy. On the primary level, the Western is a genre concerned with the mythical existence of what George M. Fenin and William K. Everson state is an "ideal ground for a liaison and re-elaboration of the Olympian world, a refreshing symbiotic relationship of Hellenic thought and Yankee dynamism" (*Western*, 6). For Americans, the Western is, in even its simplest form, a complex discourse on American frontier history and American dreams of an eternal frontier and manifest destiny. The contradictions set up an endless number of dramas in which the landscape itself becomes a character, and in which the hero is traditionally a loner treading a fine line between violence and civilization, opposed to "evil," but unable to settle down, establish a family, become a joiner. As Will Wright has pointed out in summing up a number of studies of the Western, the romantic myth of the West offers a discourse on law and morality and on the conflict between individualism and the necessity of community (*Six-guns and Society*, 7).

Proshkin and Dubrovsky have adapted these elements to the wide-open spaces of the bleak northern Russian landscape with marked success. Absent from the film are the characteristics of so many of the formula socialist films: the "production" plot, the endless debates and discussions that make such films language-intensive rather than visual, and fancy or formalistic styles of montage and shooting. The cinematography (by Boris Bzhozovsky) is as simple and direct as that of John Ford's cinematographers. And, like John Wayne or Gary Cooper, Valery Priemykhov speaks with his eyes and fists more often than with his tongue.

Within this Western formula, *The Cold Summer of '53* plays out an anti-Stalinist morality tale. Chaff and Digger are good men wronged under Stalin. They are men of principle who have suffered exile for no just reason. Those without morality, the common criminals, are the ones unleashed by order of secret-police chief Beria shortly before his own arrest. Like the ghost of Stalin, they continue to plague Soviet citizens. The citizens themselves, represented by the few villagers seen in the film, are the law-abiding folk, confused by the political battles that are acted out elsewhere but have an effect on them, and unwilling to go too far in supporting any cause.

Proshkin captures this morality drama concisely. In one scene, the local militiaman—an honest man just doing his job, which includes watching over the exiles—returns from a trip to district headquarters, rips Beria's portrait from the wall, and burns it. The official in charge of the landing pier stares in disbelief. The militiaman explains: "Exposed. Removed from his post. Arrested. That's all." How swiftly history can be altered, "air-brushed," in Milan Kundera's words. What we see in the official's eyes is the confusion and uncertainty of how one should act in an ideologically shifting universe.

Chaff negotiates his way through the crisis, relying on his intelligence, cool reserve, and physical strength. There is a tentative romance with a village girl, but she is raped and murdered while trying to help the exiles. Chaff must ultimately bear the responsibility of carrying the burden of his companion's life and death. Before Digger dies, he explains that he wrote his wife after his arrest that, in order to protect herself and her son, she should not try to get in contact with him. For all those years there had been no contact. What has been his one desire? "I'd like to live a normal life and to work," Digger says modestly.

The ending of the film is a variation on a Western theme. Instead of a simple fade-out as our hero leaves town, we cut to Moscow two years later (1955). Chaff visits Digger's wife and scholarly son. He tries to explain to them what happened, how dignified Digger had been, how much he had lived for them. But the wife had wiped her lost husband from her memory years before, and the son has no desire to learn more about the past, about his father. There is nothing more Chaff can do. He leaves and walks through a park alone. An old man asks for a light for his cigarette.

Chaff gives him one and walks on. As in a Western, Chaff moves on, alone and unsettled.

If we return to Blos's paradigm of the maturing son, we find another danger signal in *The Cold Summer of '53*. While *Repentance* treats complicity (Abel as Varlam's son) and defiance (the grandson), Proshkin's movie ends with a willful dismissal of the past. Digger's son simply does not care. Once again, the important adolescent phase of receiving a blessing from the father has been skipped. This time, however, the absence of the father figure has been imposed by the Stalinist times. We cannot totally blame the son for dismissing the father he never knew. But the film's closing is ominous: a rejection of the past will haunt the young man's future and make any sense of maturation difficult at best. Chaff, on the other hand, by circumstance or by choice, has become neither a father nor a husband. With a past such as his, he will have a troubled future.

A Mirror for a Hero offers a father-son reconciliation that, at least on the level of cinematic narrative, provides a means of coming to terms with the Stalinist past. The film is constructed around a father-son conflict that is ultimately resolved. The genre formula employed is that of the American teenage subgenre exemplified by Robert Zemeckis's *Back to the Future* (1985), *Back to the Future II* (1989), and *Back to the Future III* (1990), in which a contemporary teenager resolves his personal problems by confronting his parents before they met in the 1950s. Comedy and pathos cross in this reverse Oedipal time-travel situation, as a lost childhood that never existed (that is, childhood from an adult perspective) is (re)captured.

While the American subgenre is played mostly for laughs, *A Mirror for a Hero* probes deeper, exploring both the Stalinist 1950s and a family's development. The son, Sergei, who resembles a younger Harrison Ford, is hardly a teenager; in his thirties, he is told by his father, Andrei, a retired mining engineer who has become a novelist, "Young people have nothing to believe in. No motherland."

Soon thereafter, while watching the shooting of a film about a robbery set in the past, Sergei collapses and finds himself back in 1949. For a day he observes his father, his mother, and himself as a child. All the scenes that are humorous in the American versions of this formula have a political edge in *A Mirror for a Hero*. When people in the past discover Sergei's strange Soviet currency from the present, they suspect him of being a spy. In another scene, his meeting with a young beauty is interrupted by his modern digital watch with its musical alarm.

Besides the intriguing and complex implications that such a time trip has for Sergei's personal and family relationships, the film captures what seemed at the time like honest enthusiasm for Stalinism. There are gatherings to celebrate Stalin as "the best worker among a nation of workers." Such phrases, said with straightforward gusto, make Sergei feel both the irony of these moments and a kind of nostalgia for a time when Soviet people who were not informed of the atrocities could be naive and trusting.

There is no need to detail the entire convoluted plot. What is important is that Sergei's odyssey becomes the means by which he finally accepts his father. As the film returns to the present, father and son meet and embrace. All gaps are bridged as an old hymn rings out with the words, "You forgive all our sins." The father's dismissal of Soviet youth becomes a form of blessing passed on to his son. No words are spoken: it is an emotional and spiritual exchange that bonds them, uniting the past and the present.

The mirror in the title is much like Alice's looking glass. It is a way into an inverted world, a wonderland, where the son comes to understand the complexity of a way of life he has glibly condemned before. In a sense, we have a model Gorbachevian ending: the film critiques and forgives simultaneously. Gorbachev has trod carefully in condemning Stalin. Like Khrushchev, he has often mentioned Stalin's accomplishments in the same speeches that deplore his antidemocratic practices. *A Mirror for a Hero* likewise creates a sympathetic mood, a Christian sense of refraining from casting the first stone (the hymn adding a spiritual dimension), and an idealistic Frank Capra–like vision of reconciliation between generations, especially between fathers and sons. Depending on how one views such a reconciliation, therefore, the film can be seen either as the most positive of the lot or as the most cautious, cashing in on the popularity of "Stalin bashing" without offending anyone. Critics have taken both positions.

A final observation: Khotinenko succeeds in doing with Stalinism what Louis Malle does with fascism in *Lacombe Lucien* (1973). By following the life of a young peasant who becomes seduced by the glamor, power, and sexuality of nazism, Malle suggests how easy it was for the French to become Nazi collaborators, as many did, during the war. Likewise, Khotinenko takes us through an emotional sequence in which we are made to feel the haunting effect of experiencing the Stalinist past as well as seeing it with the eyes of the critical present. Furthermore, unlike the films previously discussed, *A Mirror for a Hero* is weighted toward the younger generation. It aimed to pull into the theaters—and did—many of the Soviet youth who did not line up to see *Repentance*. Sergei is, at one point near the end, tempted to stay in the past. But his final decision is: "We can't live here. It's like a game. These people are ghosts."

Whatever artistic or ideological complaints might be leveled at the film, it does make us feel how real those ghosts continue to be. The final image, of Sergei standing alone in the doorway of the empty cottage he rented for his father, an image that suggests his father's death, leaves us with a sense of hope. The father and son have at least had the chance to celebrate and fulfill their personal histories despite the obstruction of a national history. Whether one takes the ending as a contemporary socialist "happy ending" or as an honest effort at closing the generation gap and moving forward, Sergei's wise glance in the freeze-frame at the end is less troubling than the blank stare of a hypnotized girl who cannot tell black from white (*Is Stalin with Us?*), or the shattered face of a youth who has committed suicide rather than accept the guilt of his family (*Repentance*), or the unconcerned stare of a son who has simply turned his back on his own and his nation's history (*The Cold Summer of '53*).

Consider another direction, taken by Alexander Pankratov's *Farewell, Street Urchins* (*Proschai, shpana zamoskvoretskaya*, 1988). Set in 1956, this film follows the harsh life of a young street urchin, Robert, whose father is still in a political prison three years after Stalin's death. The story follows Robert's life without a father; his difficult relationship with his mother, who is accused of stealing money from her office; and his first romance and sexual experience, with Milka, a neighborhood girl in their working-class area. The film is a melodramatic look at the harshness of life at that time and ends in Milka's rape and death at the hands of a street gang. The conclusion, as in *A Mirror for a Hero*, is the reunion of a father and son. Robert's father finally returns from prison, saying "Let's embrace, son." The film ends with a fade-out on their embrace and all that it implies. The focus has shifted from the horrors of camp life to the grinding hardships of daily civilian life without a father. While politics is seldom discussed directly, the implication throughout is that it is the "situation" that has shaped this environment and turned these youths into street urchins.

STAGNATION IN MOTION: BREZHNEV ON AND IN FILM

Francine du Plessix Gray makes this telling remark about the Soviet male under glasnost: "*Perestroika* is about waking up the *lichnost*—individualism—in our men—so that they cease feeling superfluous" (*Soviet Women*, 189). It is an interesting aspect of the cinema of glasnost that many filmmakers have begun to explore lichnost not through the present, but under the safer umbrella of the recent past, the Brezhnev years.

The casting of recent narratives within the period of "stagnation" produces a complex and frequently highly ambiguous double image. On one hand, there is an attempt to understand the present as it has evolved from the recent past. On the other, however, the Brezhnev years serve as a convenient way for filmmakers to make strong remarks that are also about the present, without being held accountable for such directly critical discourse.

Sergei Snezhkin's film *The Incident on a Regional Scale* (*ChePe raionnogo masshtaba*, 1988) serves as a clear example. Is the film a wise critique of a crumbling socialist system or a sophisticated endorsement of the "true" socialist spirit? Snezhkin casts his narrative as a confrontation of public (Communist) and private lives, leaving the answer in doubt.

Nikolai is a promising Komsomol (Young Communist) leader on his way up. In the film's opening, he presides over the dishonest initiation of inarticulate, alienated young people into the Komsomol and then, with other leaders, proceeds to enjoy a decadent evening of wine, women, and nude bathing before returning home drunk and exhausted to his wife and child. Nikolai is a model socialist in public, but, as Snezhkin and scriptwriter Yuri Polyakov present him, he is "stagnating" as a person, a husband, and a father.

Everything begins to unravel when his office is broken into and the local Komsomol banner is stolen. The bust of Lenin is also left shattered on the floor. We have no difficulty reading the implications of a shattered Lenin, which the filmmakers drive home with a relentless lack of subtlety as Nikolai later speaks in voice-over to the bust before placing the pieces in a safe for "protection." The narrative never reconstructs the broken bust. The implication is that socialism itself is fragmented and under lock and key. But the film does provide a curiously positive ending that can be read as reinforcing the ultimate power of communism. The turning point comes as Nikolai confesses his dishonesty and inauthenticity in public and in private. At a Communist party meeting he delivers something akin to a homespun Capra-like plea for honesty, ends by telling the members, "Don't be afraid of the bosses, because they are afraid of you," and then storms out, assuming that his career is finished. What occurs, however, is in keeping with the socialist-realist model: the hero's honesty leads to a transformation of the corrupt socialist model, as factory workers rally behind him and the party decides to include "lessons of sincerity" in all future meetings.

The iconography of the film is even more blatant. Lenin's bust is left in pieces, but that of Brezhnev is not. Early in the film, Nikolai walks past a series of posters of Brezhnev and the Politburo. In the final shot, we see Brezhnev again, yet this time Nikolai, somewhat older, is depicted on the wall as a Politburo member.

Pytor Smirnov's warning about the ambiguity of evoking and destroying icons of the past, which nevertheless remain icons, applies here.

That audiences were confused by the film underlines Smirnov's point. Some took it as a stirring revelation of the corruption in the Komsomol and the party under Brezhnev. Others saw it as a veiled condemnation of the Komsomol and the whole socialist system, past and present. Still others found it a conservative, safe film that attempts to consume its glasnost and have it too. There are critical scenes, but the overall effect is to suggest that sincerity within the system will lead to a stronger, healthier communism—which is the essence of Gorbachev's reformist rather than revolutionary ideology.

Lichnost in this case is incorporated once more into the public (socialist) domain. The filmmakers, either purposely or inadvertently, have failed to distinguish between irony (in which case the positive ending would be read against the narrative grain) and straightforward socialist-realist narrative in the classical mode. We are not singling out *The Incident* as the lone example of doublespeak or, at best, ambiguous speech; far from it. Rather, the film is representative of many works produced under glasnost that attempt to be daring and cautious at the same time, as if driving with one foot pressed to the floor on the accelerator and one on the brake.

A less ambivalent portrait of the period is presented in Anatoly Vasilyev's *That's All the Love* (*I vsya liubov'*, 1989). In many ways, this straightforward work is the Soviet version of Wajda's *Man of Marble* told from the worker's point of view. The film belongs to what might be called an "agrigenre" (films set on collective farms), and focuses on how a young woman, Valentina, on a collective farm is turned into a national "worker hero" by the local party bosses. It shows, predictably, how she sells out, as fur coats, champagne, and a life of privilege swiftly replace the worn-out values of her working-class background and as sleeping around subverts love and affection.

The setting is the Brezhnev years, when the increasingly consumer-oriented Soviet culture needed to pretend that it still had working heroes on the farm. In terms of cinematic language, the film builds on the standard socialist-realist model, only to overturn it and expose the means by which such myths are created. Such a work, in contrast with a "director's film" such as *Repentance*, cleverly subverts the cinematic as well as the political clichés from within. Instead of long shots of tractors harvesting bumper crops, we have close-ups of sex as rape, of violent confrontations without tenderness. In place of stirring Soviet music on the sound track, there is a continual drone of clashing noises, voices, drunken songs, and televisions broadcasting Brezhnev's speeches in the background. The model collective is exposed as a personal hell without privacy.

A shot near the end shows the clash between the mythologized image of progress under Brezhnev and the impoverished reality. Valentina's neglected worker-husband stands on a frozen avenue in Moscow watching his famous wife on the world's largest television screen, which is forty feet high. She appears above the freezing crowds quoting Brezhnev and radiating warmth and confidence, while her pathetic husband looks on without hope or comprehension. In the next scene, he finally breaks down, shouting "We have nothing to eat," and accusing his wife of being a whore. "Life is a zigzag," says one of the high-ranking party bosses at a decadent party. In such telling clashes of myth and reality, Vasilyev and his scriptwriters, Sergei Bodrov and Irina Vasicheva, deconstruct the traditional socialist-realist cinema with a newly polyphonic (zigzag) camera.

THE DAY OF THE SOVIET JACKAL: *THE MANSERVANT*

There is no ambiguity about the relationship between the Stalinist and Brezhnevian past and the present in Vadim Abdrashitov's *Manservant* (*Sluga*, 1989). Abdrashitov and scriptwriter Alexander Mindadze, perhaps the most respected filmmaking team in contemporary Soviet cinema, have throughout their career together focused on intense moral dilemmas, using a predominantly psychological form of narrative development. (See our discussion of their film *Plumbum* in chapter 2.) *The Manservant*—which echoes Joseph Losey's taut existential allegory *The Servant* (1963; script by Harold Pinter), but which the filmmakers claim they did not see before completing their film—tackles both a universal and a historically determined issue: at what point does the servant become the master, and vice versa, in a relationship mapped by class and political differences? Specifically, how entangled is the present with the Soviet past from the 1950s through Brezhnev's stagnation period? The answer is forthrightly and grimly stated as a message of exchangeable identities and inextricable intertwinings of past and present.

Abdrashitov and Mindadze have always been able to tell a moral fable with a sense of narrative drive uncommon to many of the poetic directors, especially those under the influence of Andrei Tarkovsky. The plotting of *The Manservant* departs from their more usual straightforward narrative, continually switching from past to present and back again. But unlike the phantasmagoric *Repentance*, *The Manservant* is a relentlessly controlled chamber drama involving two characters: Pavel, who is presently a famous orchestra conductor, and Andrei, now a tramplike outcast but once a high-ranking Communist official who "created" Pavel and even married him off to one of his mistresses.

The austerity and relentlessness of Abdrashitov's style are part of his message. For audiences as well as for the characters, this intense psychopolitical drama offers no escape, no hope. We begin in the present with the former boss, Andrei, outstaring a jackal in a forest, and we end in the past, with Pavel, described throughout the film as a "jackal" by his son, his wife, and others, seeing his "master," Andrei, off at a train station as Andrei heads for Moscow to become a higher official.

Moving within this framework, the film suggests that the present is clearly the servant of the past. Toward the end of the film, in a moment of self-reflection, Pavel talks to a priest in a church: "Perhaps we are guilty, in that we made them [children, others] who they are." The interlocking of present and past is established visually near the beginning: Andrei and Pavel drive into a tunnel in the present and emerge from the dark in a Volga sedan with Pavel as chauffeur (a more accurate representation of what is meant here by "servant") in the 1950s.

The film is textured with layer upon layer of cross-influences and power-oriented relationships between servants and masters. One narrative strand concerns Pavel's son. A student of philosophy, he comes under the influence of Andrei, who teaches him to tap dance, an art diametrically opposed to Pavel's "serious" music. In *The Manservant* the son rejects any blessing from the father. That the son is "blessed" by Andrei offers no encouragement for the future. Such a blessing suggests that the future will simply be a repackaging of the Stalinist-Brezhnevian past.

"I died last year, but they revived me," says Andrei to Pavel about his "clinical death." The bitter irony of the line echoes throughout the film, into the past and present and future. On an Aesopian level, the cynicism of the remark suggests that instead of tossing the corpse to the vultures, as in *Repentance*, many in Soviet society have brought the dangerous ghost of the past back to life—a notion reflected in the news as rightwing youth groups and Stalinist organizations spring up throughout the Soviet Union.

The Manservant unabashedly presents a male universe. In many East European films, sex is often represented onscreen as rape. In *The Manservant*, that convention is followed as Pavel brutally rapes his wife. The next scene suggests how glasnost has begun to challenge cinematic clichés, however. After the rape, she coldly states, "You are a jackal," pushes him aside, and leaves him looking helpless, pathetic, and confused. Women are still more often objects than subjects, but at least Abdrashitov and Mindadze present the possibility of deconstructing the male power structure.

BREZHNEV AS PIGGY BANK AND BEYOND

In Oleg Fialko's film *God's Tramp* (*Bich bozhii*, 1989), a character holds up a piggy bank shaped like Brezhnev, complete with bushy eyebrows. "I paid twenty rubles for it at the Odessa cooperative," quips the owner. It is hard to avoid the Brezhnev period in films set in the perestroika present. Even in such playful moments, the humor comes from the realization of how fast Soviet culture has changed in a short time. That the bank is sold in a cooperative store, a transition toward a private economy, underlines this.

Yet whether references to Brezhnev and the past are used to create a historical setting for the dramatic action (as we shall see is true for *Assa*), or are simply passing remarks made in the present, many films portray a psychological form of repression rather than the more common physical suffering of Stalinism.

Sergei Selyanov and Nikolai Makarov's *Name Day* began as a homemade, "parallel," avant-garde film and emerged in 1988, after years of work, as a feature-length "experimental" work, highly regarded by many young Soviet critics. It makes no effort to specify the period of stagnation. But in this tale told by an idiot, or holy fool, we realize that given the youthful Mafusail's age, he lived much of his life during the Brezhnev era. Like Faulkner's *Sound and the Fury* and Gabriel García Márquez's *One Hundred Years of Solitude*, with a poetic sense of cinema echoing Tarkovsky, *The Name Day* talks to us through Mafusail's unbalanced voice-over and visual perceptions. It focuses on history as a jumble of images, sounds, and words inside the mind of a boy who was born prematurely and who, like Oscar in Gunter Grass's *Tin Drum*, refuses to grow.

While much of this black-and-white film may look a bit too much like European and American avant-garde works of the 1960s, its implications and wry absurdist humor are specifically Russian. Mafusail's refusal to grow is, in effect, a refusal to accept the icons of Soviet society, including Lenin's portrait, and the language surrounding him in his family-oriented existence. This is lichnost with a vengeance. The refusal to grow up is also the denial of being or becoming a man. Mafusail's mother is never mentioned. The absence of a mother, of a woman's touch, seems particularly telling in this young wise fool's free-floating rather than "stagnating" reality. "I liked my life. I don't know why," he says about the liquid mosaic of his existence.

Toward the end, he remarks, "We need to live in a new way. But I don't know how to do this at all." The psychological jumble of the past and of Mafusail's eternal present begins to offer the possibility of a future, a glimmer of hope denied in films such as *The Manservant*. With the playful enthusiasm of youth, some directors appear to suggest that even without a mother and without the blessing of a father, the son may one day begin to change. "This is a search for new possibilities in the language of the cinema" says the press release for the film, and we can agree. Mafusail's contemplation of the future is a hopeful sign. Though he spends his life entirely within the relative safety of his home, he may eventually venture out into the larger, ever-shifting world.

LIKE A ROLLING STONE: THE SOVIET ROAD FILM

In terms of film language, the mixing of past and present is, as *The Manservant* demonstrates, most often handled by crosscutting between past and present. But with glasnost and the exploration of new cinematic subject matter, another movement has appeared: horizontal motion through space and time. Thus we see the beginnings of a broadly based Soviet "road movie" genre. The road film has seemed a particularly American genre. As Mark Williams notes in *Road Movies*, the existential sense of movement in space and time is caught in Jeff Bridges's cry to Clint Eastwood in *Thunderbolt and Lightfoot*, "Wherever we're goin', man, I'm ready!" (6). Wim Wenders has adapted this American formula to his own European themes in films such as *Alice in the Cities* (1974), *Kings of the Road* (1976), and *Paris, Texas* (1984). Now the Soviets under glasnost are free to suggest that the open road may be an internal as well as an external journey.

The Name Day presents a free-floating psychological state in which history and the present mix inextricably. Films such as *God's Tramp*, *Freedom Is Paradise* (*SER*, 1989), and *BOMZH* have added long-distance travel and a sense of the possibility of drifting within a culture.

Ukrainian director Oleg Fialko's *God's Tramp* is framed by the opening and closing scenes of the main character, Leonid, a *bomzh* (drifter), on the street. In the first sequence Fialko's camera does an excellent job of simply following a bum around, including the sly satire of "the new documentary": "What do you think about cooperative toilets?" a documentary filmmaker asks Leonid as he washes up in a public bathroom. Leonid replies, "One must think about one's soul." The line is funny, ironic, and a foreshadowing of the film, for it is his soul that Leonid ultimately cares about. Much of the film becomes a series of flashbacks while Leonid rides a train and meets a woman who is being seduced by a bureaucrat. What the images of the past dredge up is a strong condemnation not simply of the Soviet school system (Leonid is expelled from school), but of an entire system in which the rules of survival are cynically taught. Leonid learns: forget rules; have patience; learn to do what others cannot do; and if someone wrongs you, seek revenge. Leonid's problem is his desire to be honest. It is this trait or flaw that makes him God's fool. The film ends as it began: Leonid is on the street, this time in Moscow, meeting up with another bum after refusing a ride in a fancy official car with the bureaucrat he met on the train. Leonid, whose name ironically evokes Brezhnev's, is offered the official "blessing" of those in power, but rejects this false blessing in favor of the freedom of the street.

Freedom Is Paradise is discussed in the following chapter. But we should close our discussion of the (re)presentation and representation of the past in feature narratives where we began: with the ending of *BOMZH*, as the drifter sits by a campfire with a young teenager who is not his son.

Nikolai Skuibin's film is the first feature about drifters in the Soviet Union. Although there are thousands, the subject was previously taboo. Skuibin shot his film in black and white, with a directness, simplicity, and austerity for which "bleak" is not a strong enough term. Here there are no poetic montages, as in Tarkovsky, no flashbacks to provide at least some conventional Aristotelian motivation and visual relief from the present. Skuibin's style is as grim as the landscape and the main character's life.

Unlike Leonid in *God's Tramp*, Victor, the protagonist drifter (played with moving intensity and humor by Vladimir Steklov), is silent for the first few minutes of the film. He is a tramp, but there is no hint of God. We have no idea who he is, where he has been, or where he is headed. Skuibin and screenwriter Valery Zolotukha imply that all we need to know is on the screen. The past is visible in Victor's grim, unshaven, yet somehow sympathetic face. Gone is any possible "symbolic" or Aesopian approach to the past. The distance between the cinematic language of *Repentance* and *BOMZH* is enormous. In its refusal to name names, be they Stalin, Brezhnev, or others, the film keeps a tight focus on the personal rather than the public world of contemporary Soviet people.

A stirringly original scene occurs after the long introduction, during which Victor takes a Moscow metro to a suburban train and finally reaches a frozen landscape in a small city in the provinces. He stands in the middle of nowhere and talks on a pay telephone. The absolute bleakness of the moment, in every sense, is striking. In the first words we hear from Victor, we learn that he is talking to the wife he abandoned more than thirteen years before. From the one-sided conversation it becomes clear that she has remarried and does not want to see him, and that their son, Vitaly, will not be allowed to see him. We hear her voice on the phone saying, "A father is someone who brings up a son, *not you.*" We are left with the expression on Victor's face as he hangs up, standing alone against the snow and the dreary apartment buildings in the distance. He is judged not to be a father; he does not know his son.

The subsequent tracking down of the youth he believes to be his son, the emerging friendship based on the pretense that "you look like my dead son, Vitaly," becomes the major part of the narrative. At the conclusion, Victor has broken down in complete despair. When the boy asks Victor to call him by his own name, the boy's words are a way out for Victor, a means of resolving his troubled past and his present anguish. As the film ends, they are together, walking away, able to communicate honestly.

We have suggested that the treatment of the Soviet past on the glasnost screen can be fruitfully considered from the perspective of the giving of a blessing from a father to a son. By closing this chapter with *BOMZH*, we are suggesting what the filmmakers represent: that at times the process can be reversed. Perhaps it is possible, given Soviet reality and the past, for the son to bless the father so that both can begin to mature.

On the other hand, a number of films suggest that no blessing at all is being given or received. In the 1991 film *Coming Closer* by Georgian director Alexander Rekhviashvili, we see Gorbachev on a television set in a Georgian home as the male protagonist goes about his work. Neither he nor we hear Gorbachev, since the character has turned off the sound. Nor can we see the leader clearly, for the reception is poor, with static and lines running through the image as it fades in and out. But the character is not worried, for he is not paying attention anyway. Gorbachev has, the filmmaker suggests, become a fading image in the background of daily life.

Fredric Jameson remarks about the dynamics of presenting and (re)presenting history, "The dilemma of any 'historicism' can be dramatized by the peculiar, unavoidable, yet seemingly unresolvable alternation between Identity and Difference" (*Ideologies of Theory*, 2:150). The Soviet dialogue with the past, on and off the screen, is the no less important struggle to establish personal identities as well as national ones, and to know the difference.

"We Are *Your* Children": Soviet Youth, Cinema, and Changing Values

We don't give a damn about anything. We just want to have a good time.
—A YOUNG MAN in *Is It Easy to Be Young?*

COMMUNISM, YOUTH, AND CINEMA

A YOUNG SOLDIER with closely cropped hair faces the camera and says without expression, "There is nothing worth dying for, nothing worth living for." When pressed by the unseen interviewer-filmmaker, he offers only this further thought: "I doubt my generation can bring about any changes." Earlier in the film we have seen the same fellow at a rock concert, moving to the beat, long hair flowing. These words sting; the images burn.

The impact of moment after moment of similar scenes helps explain why Latvian director Juris Podnieks's feature documentary *Is It Easy to Be Young?* (*Legko li byt' molodym?*) became the most popular Soviet film released in 1987. Such a statistic, however, hardly captures the shock the film caused when it opened. Soviet critic Alexander Kiselev writes, "When the picture was finished, it created such furor that it can only be compared to the reaction to a terrorist act in the heart of a Communist capital. Indeed, a bomb placed somewhere near Red Square would not have caused more excitement" ("Wuthering Voids").

Our task is to describe and to begin to evaluate the ways in which such cinematic bombs have been planted, detonated, and received. While each Soviet critic has his or her own personal list of the most important films made since the beginning of glasnost, a compiled listing we have made (*The Russians Are Coming*) points to five of the top ten as being youth-related movies: *Is It Easy to Be Young?*, *Plumbum*, *Assa*, *Little Vera*, and *The Needle*. While *Little Vera* is discussed in the next chapter and *The Needle* in chapter 7, we now turn to a study of the remaining three and others, and their implications. As Nancy Traver details in her study of Soviet youth, *Kife: The Lives and Dreams of Soviet Youth*, the contradictions and agony of the present are even more sharply felt and observed by today's troubled youth. Soviet film scholar Nina Tsyrkun has been even more pointed: while at first glance the various behavior patterns of contemporary Soviet youth may seem negative, it is more accurate to read such actions as "a positive reaction and separation from an adult generation they feel has failed them" ("Youth Cinema"). Troubled youth present a search for new values and thus a challenge to a crumbling socialist tradition.

Eastern European cinema has a long tradition of distinguished hard-hitting documentaries about troubled youth that simultaneously serve to critique elements of socialism. In Hungary, for instance, Pal Schiffer, Jr., has become well known for intense documentaries focused on individuals whom he gets to know, thus achieving a remarkable closeness with them. His *On Probation* (1980) traces ten years in a village boy's life, from the ages of seven to seventeen. We see in this nonfiction feature a young man who is in and out of prison from the age of fifteen because he fits neither into the changing village environment nor into the alienating city landscape as it has emerged under communism. The film gives us no reason to hope that he will find a "normal life."

It can now be said that Soviet filmmakers are surpassing what has been done in Eastern Europe, both in the number of films about troubled youth and the variety of approaches. This phenomenon is all the more startling given the previous vision of youth in Soviet culture.

Soviets have since the Revolution paid special attention to children and young people. They were seen as embodying the future of socialism, the hope for a new world and the betterment of mankind. The history of Soviet cinema is also the history of a fine tradition of children's films and of adult films that use the perspective of a child or adolescent— especially since the 1960s—to portray the horror of war, the crushing injustice of life before socialism, the failure of bourgeois culture. After all, the scene everyone remembers from Eisenstein's *Battleship Potemkin* is of the baby carriage rolling down the steps. The first Soviet sound film, Nikolai Ekk's *Road to Life* (*Putyovka v zhizn'*, 1931), proved to be an extremely popular treatment of the problem of the *besprizorniki* (homeless orphans) after the ravages of World War I and the subsequent Soviet civil war. During World War II, films that portrayed young "positive hero" martyrs to the cause, such as Lev Arnshtam's *Zoya* (1944), were inspirational for millions of war-besieged citizens.

In Mikhail Kalatozov's *Cranes Are Flying* (*Letyat zhuravli*, 1957), made during Khrushchev's thaw (*ottepel'*), the image of youth shifted from positive hero to victim. This dramatic and lyrical hymn against war as it affects the young became world-renowned.

Then, during the 1960s, as the period of stagnation (*zastoi*) began, filmmakers struggled against Stalinist clichés and sentimentality without giving up a certain poetic romanticism. One senses in such films a delayed response to the portrayal of war-afflicted youth in Italian neorealist works such as De Sica's *Bicycle Thief* (1949). Georgi Danelia and Igor Talankin's *Seryozha* (1960) and Marlen Khutsiev's *Two Fyodors* (*Dva Fyodora*, 1958) both use a child protagonist not as a martyr or a hero, but as a child, presenting point-of-view shots of war, grief, and destruction that go beyond what adults experience. *Ivan's Childhood* (*Ivanovo detstvo*, 1962) launched Andrei Tarkovsky's remarkable career as a poetic prophet of the cinema by creating a powerful impressionistic view of a war-torn world robbed of its innocence as seen through a young boy's eyes. The film is one of the rare evocations of childhood by an adult, full of what feels like almost purely intuitive insight into a child's relation to nature, to adults, and to experience.

The 1960s were also known for a popular subgenre of the youth film, the "school film." This movement began with Yuli Raizman's *And What If It Is Love?* (*A esli eto liubov'?*, 1962) and has continued to the present. The subject of the school film is not education, but the moral upbringing of children. The central collision—a conflict between teachers and high-school students—almost always concerns the teachers' recognition of the students' dignity and human maturity. From the first confession of love in the classroom, the scene usually cuts to the teachers' lounge, observing the clash between "good" and "bad" teachers (the professional qualities usually overwhelmed by the moral ones) about their students. The cry of the school films—including Stanislav Rostotsky's 1968 hit *We'll Survive Till Monday* (*Dozhivem do ponedel'nika*), and the debut film *Practical Joke* (*Rozygrysh*, 1977) by Vladimir Men'shov, who then made *Moscow Does Not Believe in Tears*—in contrast to the glasnost youth films, is not "We are your children!" but rather "We are people too!" The school films are also colored by their appreciation of teaching, viewed in these films as the most noble profession on earth.

The 1970s ushered in films that treated troubled youth in contemporary society more directly. Nikolai Gubenko's *Orphans* (*Podranki*, also known as *Angels with Broken Wings*, 1976), for instance, is an update of the World War II orphan genre. Here we have a prince-and-pauper story of brothers separated by war. When the film switches to the present and the reunion of the Soviet "yuppie" brother, a rich architect, with the writer-protagonist of the film, Alyosha, and with the third brother, now in prison, Gubenko (in 1991, the minister of culture in the USSR) manages to question the values of the stagnation period under Brezhnev. The film concludes with the strong suggestion that the traumatic war period, when the protagonist was a homeless orphan pretending to be mute, may have been the happiest time of his life.

A basic contradiction has developed over the years in the Soviet Union. Children and childhood are national preoccupations, yet although the Soviet Union has more than a hundred puppet theaters, roughly seventy circuses, and the largest children's toy store in the world, Moscow's Detsky Mir, studies show how little room for free play and individual expression exists. David K. Shipler comments that in Soviet classrooms, it is rare to find children's art or schoolwork or photos of the students displayed, as they commonly are in many preschool and elementary classrooms in the United States. "Fantasy," Shipler writes, "exists in well-defined formats such as old Russian fairy tales, circuses, and cartoons, but it is often discouraged by adults when children try to practice it in drawing, storytelling, or make believe play" (Russia, 61).

Such regimentation at home and in the classroom accounts in part for the sense of alienation and disorientation felt by many Soviet young people today. But the "we don't give a damn about anything" attitude reflected in the opening quotation from Is It Easy to Be Young? forces the viewer to look beyond the youth problem to Soviet society and the ideology that has formed it. As another young person says in Podnieks's film, "We are your children": ultimate responsibility rests with the older generations.

"I don't live my real life. I only live the life I invent for myself," says rock singer turned actor Bananan in Sergei Solovyev's 1988 hit film Assa. These words capture the spirit of many Soviet fiction films about youth made since 1985.

The ingredients for such fiction films have been simmering for at least a decade. Leningrad director Dinara Asanova, who died an untimely death in 1985, is particularly associated with honest films about youth. In Woodpeckers Don't Get Headaches (Ne bolit golova u diatla, 1974), The Key Not to Be Passed On (Kliuch bez prava peredachi, 1976), and Tough Kids (Patsany, 1983), Asanova portrayed difficult youth in a way that reached young and adult audiences alike. Her influence can be seen in many of the new films, particularly those of her collaborator, Valery Priemykhov. He wrote some of her films, played the lead role in Tough Kids (and The Cold Summer of '53), and now has begun to direct his own films. His 1989 film Pants (Shtany) is a complex perestroika drama of an actor-father who takes a murder rap for his son. In the concluding scene the son is sentenced to three years of prison as an accomplice to the murder; as he leaves, he says "Father, I am your son."

Another significant youth film released just before glasnost was Rolan Bykov's Scarecrow (also known as Chuchelo [Weirdo], 1984). This heavily allegorical tale, cowritten by actor-director Bykov and Vladimir Zheleznikov, stars pop singer Alla Pughacheva's mesmerizing thirteen-year-old daughter Kristina Orbakaite in a melodramatic moral parable about a young girl wrongly persecuted for her beliefs by a group of her peers. As Neya Zorkaya notes, Soviet audiences were moved to tears and to debate about the film "by the ethical problems raised . . . and by its topicality: . . . children's cruelty that can either stay within the limits of practical jokes . . . or turn into an evil doing" (*Illustrated History*, 301). As a psychological study of Lena, the young girl, and her nonconformist, art-loving grandfather, the film can be viewed as a critique of the "herd mentality," of the self-imposed censorship of the Stalinist period projected into the present, with echoes of Dostoevsky's moral debates.

The development of youth films under glasnost follows two striking paths: opening up subject matter within a rather traditional, linear narrative structure, as in Vadim Abdrashitov's *Plumbum, or A Dangerous Game* (*Pliumbum, ili Opasnaya igra*, 1987), and experimenting with form as well as content, as in Solovyev's *Assa* or Nugmanov's *Needle*.

As a point of comparison, we should first note the parallel but differing emphases between the cult of the American teen films of the 1980s and the Soviet youth films. Thomas Doherty's *Teenagers and Teenpics: The Juvenilization of American Movies in the 1950s* provides a thorough review of how American movies "reflect teenage, not mass—and definitely not adult—tastes" (1). This phenomenon first became prevalent in the 1950s, with the release of films in a variety of teen genres, including rock and roll films (*Rock around the Clock*), dangerous-youth films (films starring James Dean, especially *Rebel without a Cause*), teen horror films (*I Was a Teenage Werewolf*), and clean teen films (*Bernardine*, with Pat Boone). This trend has continued into the present, with the box-office triumph of sterile coming-of-age films by John Hughes (*Sixteen Candles, Pretty in Pink, Ferris Bueller's Day Off, The Breakfast Club*), which mix realistic dialogue with an ideology supportive of the status quo. Studies yet to come will presumably follow through on the observation that the increasing domination of the American box office by teenagers in the 1980s coincided with the conservative Reagan years. This double phenomenon accounts for the twin directions taken by American teen movies in the 1980s: the John Hughes films, with their white, suburban, upper-middle-class conservatism (Ferris Bueller takes a day off, but he is no threat to the status quo) on the one hand, and the Steven Spielberg–George Lucas adventure-fantasy features, which avoid all unpleasant contemporary crises in favor of expensive cinematic daydreams, thus reflecting a neoconservative 1980s perspective.

It is possible to view some of the new Soviet youth-oriented films as conservative as well. But many are not. Because a disillusioned Soviet youth represents a failure of the older socialist generation to nourish the future of communism, youth-oriented feature films have become an important part of the discourse between various levels of Soviet society. These films differ from American teen movies in a notable characteristic: the amount of narrative time and energy given to the interrelationship of the youthful protagonists and their parents and elders.

A HARD LOOK AT IS IT EASY TO BE YOUNG?

Is It Easy to Be Young? is an anthology and a pioneering text for documentary and fiction films made under glasnost about young people. The film's importance to the documentary movement and ethnic cinema will be explored below. Here, we examine more closely its significance as a complex discourse on and with contemporary Soviet youth.

The new wave of Soviet documentaries about youth demonstrates how well film can evoke a feeling for the times and a sense of current crises. It is difficult to find many American documentaries that address youth problems with such intensity. Martin Bell's *Streetwise* (1984), however, comes close in its gut-wrenching view of teenage vagrants living and dying on the streets of Seattle.

Is It Easy to Be Young? is a prime example of the new Soviet documentaries about young people. The film resembles Michael Apted's *28 Up* (1985) in that it follows various teenagers over a period of time (less than two years, in this case). While Apted's sociological documentary of the British class system includes interviews with a diverse group of English youth over a twenty-one-year period, from the ages of seven to twenty-eight, Podnieks's work begins with a rock concert in Riga, the capital of Latvia, on 6 June 1985, and pursues its young subjects (not all of whom are present at the concert) for almost two years. The film's power comes from the simple honesty of the young people interviewed no less than from the complex construction, aesthetic form, and rhythm.

The opening rock concert is in itself an important statement about the increasing significance of pop music in Soviet youth culture. By Western standards, both band and audience at this particular concert appear well-mannered, tame, and vaguely reminiscent of a pre-Beatles period. Yet the images are read differently by Soviet youth. Until only a few years ago they were not allowed to hold such concerts openly. To start the film with so many Latvian teenagers "just having fun" at a pop concert, therefore, is significant. Podnieks succeeds in capturing these young people when they feel most "free," and he has recorded a last fling of adolescence before each is forced to choose a direction in life.

The rock concert makes an important statement about the increasing significance of pop music for Soviet youth. Artemy Troitsky, a Soviet rock critic, explains in his history, *Back in the USSR: The True Story of Rock in Russia,* how rock evolved as a counterculture from the 1950s *stilyagi,* the first hipsters, through Beatle-like groups in the 1960s playing in garages and at small, unofficial underground gigs in the major cities, to the wide-based movement today, which involves large officially sanctioned outdoor concerts with groups singing in Russian. (Through the 1960s, most groups simply imitated Western bands and sang in English.) In exploring how Soviet rock culture differs from its Western counterpart, Troitsky makes two major distinctions.

First, he sees the lyrics and "literary level" of Soviet music as far more important than the technical and musical levels, which are usually stressed in the West. Second, he finds a strong Soviet emphasis on social issues in the lyrics as they affect the individual. As he says of one popular group, Time Machine, "there's not a single clear-cut love song, let alone one about sex" in their entire repertoire (41). The final song quoted in the book serves as a good example. In 1986, the year *Is It Easy to Be Young?* was first shown, another popular group, Aquarium, recorded a song satirizing old Russian-Soviet culture as represented by *babushkas* (traditional grandmothers). The lyrics run, in part:

> Why does the game always have only one goalpost?
> And why are there always so many umpires on the field?
> Excuse us, babooshkas, we are very tired of you.
> Go and find somewhere else and a proper job to do.
> And we will quietly sigh and wipe away a tear
> And wave you all bye-bye, waving white handkerchiefs.
>
> . . . .
>
> But whoever told you that you have the right to rule us?
> A flock of babooshkas flies through the night sky.
> Fly, darlings, fly away. (136)

Clearly the Soviet rock singer and composer sees himself or herself taking on a number of roles, including social bard and poet. The music thus highlights the message, and the message is conveyed through language. As Troitsky states, the rock tradition in the Soviet Union has strong ties to the Soviet literary tradition of expressing social injustice and exploring moral values. This does not mean that all disenchanted Soviet young people have embarked on a positive search for a better life. But it does suggest that for many young Soviets, and East Europeans as well, part of the difficulty of being young arises from their moral and ideological differences with the dominant Communist superstructure.

The growing influence of pop-rock music in Soviet culture came to American attention in the summer of 1989 with the mammoth heavy-metal concerts on two days in August, as roughly ninety thousand people gathered each day for about eleven hours of music in Lenin Stadium. As the American performers Ozzy Osbourne, Bon Jovi, and Mötley Crüe jammed with Gorky Park and other Soviet groups, any remaining barriers between the Soviet and Western youth cultures tumbled. Futhermore, the beginning of a "Russian invasion" of the American rock scene is a further sign of normalization of the cultural life of once antagonistic countries. A double album released in the United States in 1987, "The Red Wave," increased the Americans' exposure to this music. The lead singer of Aquarium, Boris Grebenshchikov, is only the most visible of Soviet pop singers who have cut American albums and begun to tour widely in the United States. The late Victor Tsoy and his group, Kino, Gorky Park, Zvuki Mu, Autograph, and others have made Western albums and videos, and have begun to receive airplay on Western radio stations and television.

Is It Easy to Be Young? is non-narrative in any traditional, linear sense. Rather, the audience is drawn in by the time-capsule effect of watching each individual open and reveal himself or herself more fully, for better or worse. One is struck by the diversity. Several young fellows wind up on trial for hooliganism after trashing a passenger car on a train as they are returning from the concert; we are taken into the courtroom for the sentencing. Others become extreme examples of "punks" who view Soviet reality as "upside down" and blame the previous generations for falsifying everything. A sixteen-year-old girl accused of stealing a dress tries to commit suicide by jumping out a window in a police station. A young man becomes an amateur filmmaker making a Kafkaesque avant-garde film (of which we see several scenes), while another youth becomes a follower of the Hare Krishnas. Several other young people say they have turned to drugs since alcohol has become so difficult to obtain (because of the party's strict attack on alcoholism). Another fellow working in a hospital dies, while a teenage girl who appeared in the opening as a child having a good time now has a child of her own and no idea what her future will be.

Then there are those who join the army and are sent to Afghanistan. The film's structure moves us from the opening rock concert to scenes with the wounded and disillusioned Afghan veterans toward the end. Afghanistan is clearly the Soviet Union's Vietnam. But part of what is surprising in this film, especially for American audiences, is the extreme candor of such a documentary made *while the war was still being fought.* We in the United States, for instance, had no documentary of similar strength made about the effects of the war on veterans who returned home before the Vietnam War ended.

Though the film captures the problems of being young and male much more successfully than it does those of being young and female (only the two women mentioned above are covered, and they are only briefly sketched in), the Afghan veteran sequences bring the film to a stirring conclusion. The switch from the carefree youngsters seen at the opening rock concert to the grim-faced survivors of battle is startling. One wounded veteran who will never recover tells us, "Every time I think about it, I get mad." Another veteran is shown as a city fire fighter now that he is no longer fighting Afghan rebels: he claims war taught him to be "humane." Finally, we are shown a group of veterans gathering around a campfire and embracing a wounded fellow veteran with hugs and tears. "You value life more from the experience," one veteran tells us in the voice-over. "*There* everyone had a common destiny."

Throughout the film, we hear and occasionally glimpse the filmmaker, questioning, on the move. We feel how personal a film it is for Podnieks, and the degree to which he pushes himself, his camera, and his subjects, like Vertov before him, to create a contemporary Kino Eye (Vertov's term for Soviet documentary film), one that will be, as Vertov called for in 1923, "the sensory exploration of the world through film" (Michelson, *Kino-Eye*, 14). One can hardly imagine, however, two filmmakers more different in ideological approach (as distinguished from cinematic style and technique) than Vertov, the enthusiastic defender of the Communist cause, and Podnieks, a sharp commentator on the flaws of the system as it relates to young people.

Podnieks's approach might be called expressionistic cinema verité, a style that has become popular with many new documentary filmmakers. The film is both a searing investigation (in its interviews) and an angry personal statement (in its montages, editing, and structure). At times the camera conveys the immediacy of being at an event while it unfolds, as in the courtroom in which the group of youths is on trial. But Podnieks colors his film in an expressionistic manner through his sudden juxtapositions of images, his escalation of interviews (culminating in those with the Afghan veterans), his off-camera questioning, often with a "come on now, tell the truth" approach that clearly oversteps the polite rules of traditional documentary discourse, and through juxtaposing color shots of the past with "present" scenes often captured in black and white or sepia. There is an electronic sound track of disturbing music that puts us on edge, allowing us no chance to feel comfortable or complacent.

In this sense, Podnieks has already answered the title's question for us. (The original title was *It Is Difficult to Be Young*, but Podnieks al-

tered it in order to receive a general release on the "advice" of the censorship committee.) Clearly it is hard to be young in the Soviet Union
today, and it is even more difficult to become an adult. Two closing
images, one of despair, the other of hope. As the synthesizer music plays,
a partially lame veteran walks through the rain on a desolate street to
catch a bus. We fear for his future. Finally we see a group of people standing in a lake shot through a blue filter. It is the final scene in the young
man's film we have witnessed in progress throughout Podnieks's film.
Why blue, asks Podnieks. "Blue is the symbol of hope. The whole world
is hoping." What has gone before undermines any easy sense of hope, yet
the nervous probing of the camera itself is hopeful. The exploration of
problems may lead to understanding and discussion, which can lead to
change. This is the unspoken message of the film language used, since
the film is just as much (and at times possibly too much) a questioning
of how a documentary is made as it is a study of its subject.

The film had an impact on Soviet audiences. Soviet critic Lev Anninski noted that the film forced audiences to consider questions of youth
and freedom, maturity and responsibility: "It would have been easier for
us if the omnipresent 'officials' had suppressed such a film. Then we
would pass our complexes with relief on to the 'officials' and we would
explain it all with the fact that 'they' shut us up. However, the film came
out and we have to answer aloud for our children" ("Is It Easy to Be
Grown-Up?").

But what of those outside the Soviet Union? Each time we have seen
the film projected in the United States, many in the audience have spoken of it as one of the stronger documentaries they have seen. American
audiences speak of the honesty of the film in depicting so widespread a
sense of confusion, disappointment, and antisocial feeling. *Is It Easy to
Be Young?* points toward four growing areas of youth films: films ori-
ented toward rock and pop music, films about youth in the cities,
movies about young people and drugs, and films concerned with Afghan
veterans and the effects of the Soviet version of Vietnam.

ON A ROLL WITH SOVIET POP-ROCK FILMS

In documentaries, rock music itself comes into strong focus in Alexei
Uchitel's *Rock* (*Rok*, 1988), which covers five leaders of Leningrad rock
onstage and at home: Yuri Shevchuk of DDT, Victor Tsoy of Kino, Boris
Grebenshchikov, who was, at the time, with Aquarium, Anton Adasin-
sky of Avia, and Spitball of Auction. Rashid Nugmanov's first film, a
short docudrama, *Yakh-ha!* (1987), includes bands such as Kino and Zoo,
as well as a glimpse of underground ("parallel") life-styles in Leningrad.

While Hollywood fiction films in the 1980s catered to youth as it was sheltering them from many of the real issues facing them in American culture, a surprisingly large number of the Soviet youth films made since 1985 have taken the opposite tack, confronting social issues with unusual candor. The teen horror genre is not likely to become popular in the Soviet Union. Certainly the 1980s films combine elements of rock and roll and danger, like America's youth films of the 1950s, but viewed from a clearly Soviet perspective. For example, Leningrad director Valery Ogorodnikov's pop-rock crime film *The Burglar* (*Vzlomschik*, 1987), starring rock star Konstantin Kinchev, capitalizes on and exploits the theme of Soviet dropouts in a melodramatic yet powerful way that echoes Marlon Brando's 1954 performance as a motorcycle gang leader in *The Wild One*. We should also note that Soviet rock stars are much more prevalent in Soviet films than are American rock stars in Hollywood productions: think of how many American rock luminaries either have never tried cinema (Bruce Springsteen, for instance), or tried and failed miserably (Bob Dylan, James Taylor, Ringo Starr). Although we can point to Elvis, Cher, and Diana Ross as some American exceptions, this point suggests, as we shall discuss, a more direct link between audience and screen, youth culture and cinematic narrative, in the Soviet Union.

Tragedy in Rock (*Tragediya v stile rok*, 1988) by Savva Kulish takes on sex, drugs, and rock and roll as symptoms of a sick society rather than as causes of rebellion. Victor, an idealistic eighteen-year-old who looks like a Soviet yuppie, descends through an inferno of Soviet subculture, becoming a drug addict, a dealer, a lost soul. The title itself announces the combination of opposites in this film as it attempts to wed a classical structure, tragedy, with the contemporary culture of rock. The sound track is drenched in overpowering synthesizer music by Sergei Kuriokhin, and before Victor commits suicide by ramming his car into a wall, we see and hear music by the leading rock groups Brigada S, Pop Mechanics, and Time Machine, we see the dancer Igor Garkusha, and we are offered what appears obligatory in recent Soviet films, at least one Beatles tune: "Michelle"—a reminder that the Beatles have been the single most significant influence on Soviet popular music. Yet the counterweight of "tragedy" announces that the film's language and form are not postmodern; they are Hellenic, traditional, ancient.

If perestroika is a period of transition, it is hard to imagine a film that embodies opposing tendencies more clearly than *Tragedy in Rock*. What we should realize, however, is that since "tragedy" is the narrative conception and form, it dominates the cinematic effect, employing "rock" as content, atmosphere, and rhythm within the genre of tragedy—new wine in a very old bottle.

In terms of story and theme, the abuses of the son are clearly marked in this traditional, linear narrative as the result of the sins of the father. Once more, it is the father-son narrative that embodies the contemporary Soviet crisis. The son idolizes his bureaucratic father, who is sent to prison for compromising a "boss," a Mafia-like figure. This evil, paternal Mafia figure replaces Victor's father and pulls the boy and his girlfriend Lena into a nightmare of twisted sex, hard drugs, and loss of identity. A particularly chilling scene is one in which Victor shaves not only his head but his eyebrows as well, becoming another creature entirely.

We have seen that the transitional phase of glasnost has moved some directors, like Khotinenko in *A Mirror for a Hero*, to find a reconciliation between father and son and thus between the socialist past (with all its dark secrets) and the polyphonic present. But true to its title, *Tragedy in Rock* allows no such illusion. Victor commits suicide when he learns that his father is part of the evil game. After the father attends his son's funeral and discovers a tape Victor had made with such messages as "rock music is a symbol of our times," he leads the Mafia figure and his henchmen into a trap and blows himself and them up in a fiery conclusion. Fire destroys and purifies. The director leaves the audience, however, with a mixed message that is both pessimistic (the main figures are all dead) and moralistic: Victor's tape contains the further reflection that "children brought up on lies cannot be moral." The fireball at the end thus suggests that it is not merely *something* that is rotten in the state of the Soviet Union, but everything. This apocalyptic vision offers no hint of salvation, no blueprint for self-improvement. Furthermore, it appears judgmental about youth culture in that the energy and power of rock music, for instance, are associated with negative images of decay, decadence, and drugs. As a child of the Khrushchevian "thaw," in his fifties today, Kulish, despite the use of surreal montages and psychedelic manipulation of images, remains outside the modern culture he attempts to capture on film. There is also a hint of pretentiousness in linking this contemporary tale with tragedy. Greek tragedy concerned man's battle with his own limitations, fate, and the will of Zeus: Kulish's film points indirectly to the socialist system rather than to Zeus, and to human nature as the virus infecting these figures. After an initial flurry of interest, the relatively low box-office turnout for the film, less than ten million, suggests that Soviet audiences also sensed a mismatch between form and content, concept and execution, in this early glasnost youth narrative.

Much more successful in narrative construction and audience appeal has been the young Belorussian director Valery Rybarev's *My Name Is Arlekino* (*Menya zovut Arlekino*, 1988). Rybarev has a feel for gang life today. "We are outsiders from birth," Arlekino, the fatherless (bastard) protagonist and gang leader, says at one point, and the film helps us understand from the inside how it feels to be part of this world without goals, values, or joy. We feel how trapped the right is in such a youth culture: its adherents reject the corruption of their parents' generation, but do not embrace the decadence of the freewheeling hippie culture. We see them watching American black-market videotapes (dance sequences from *Streets of Fire*), putting Bruce Lee posters on their walls, and attacking a long-haired hippie and shaving him.

The director tries for no special flourishes, no fancy surrealistic montages, none of the expressionistic touches of Francis Ford Coppola's *Rumblefish*. Instead, Rybarev shapes a narrative that brings out the clash between newly formed social classes in contemporary Soviet culture. Arlekino is of the working class, living with his mother in a communal apartment. His girlfriend, Lena, hangs out with the "new rich" class that has emerged, dating one of the "golden boys" whom Americans would label preppies; they have cars, expensive clothing, and money to spend.

The conclusion, however, leaves the audience with a dash of romance and hope. Despite the bleak landscape and the final obligatory gang fight as the golden boys stomp one of Arlekino's friends, Lena returns to Arlekino. Youthful love wins out over corruption, fascism, and consumer materialism. *My Name Is Arlekino* is much more realistic and hard-edged than American teenage romances. But the happy ending no doubt helped explain the high box-office appeal of the film during 1989 despite its mixed critical reception.

POSTMODERN CINEMATIC ROCK NARRATIVE: *ASSA*

The first major attempt to wed rock culture and a nonlinear narrative cinema was Solovyev's *Assa*. Sergei Solovyev had previously explored childhood in his lyrical coming-of-age films *One Hundred Days after Childhood* (*Sto dnei posle detstva*, 1975); *Lifeguard* (*Spasatel'*, 1980); *Heiress Apparent* (*Naslednitsa po pryamoi*, 1982), and *The Wild Pigeon* (*Chuzhaya belaya i Ryaboi*, 1986), which depicts a young boy in 1946 and his complicated relationship with his father, shot in a style the director calls "eccentric realism." *The Wild Pigeon*'s thematic and associative, rather than plot-driven, development prefigures the wildly anti-narrative structure of *Assa*. Clearly *Assa* (which is supposedly the word Noah said upon seeing the world after the flood; it is also a popular Leningrad underground yell) was conceived as "hypereccentric realism." To describe a plot that involves elements of a teenage romance, a rock and roll musical, a gangster film complete with dwarfs, and a historical epic detailing the downfall of Czar Paul in 1801, shot in styles that suggest Godard, Fassbinder, Fellini, and Buñuel wrapped up in one, would be to miss the point.

Instead, one feels the film asks to be viewed as a "happening," a new order of film narrative, a new species of media event. At the center of the film is Sergei Bugayev, a well-known Leningrad showman and rock and roll playboy. He sings songs by the rock group Aquarium such as "Sponge Blues" and "Air Force," which were once banned and circulated samizdat style on illegal tapes. These numbers work well as ironic, irreverent, and humorous send-ups of the status quo; one of the musicians is a Russian black, a surprise for non-Soviet audiences. And Bananan himself, who is like a younger David Byrne, combines a certain hipness with anarchistic characteristics that make him appealing as a screen presence.

Set in a snowy Yalta resort in winter, the film, written by Solovyev and Sergei Livnev, catches audiences by surprise with many inventive touches. Bananan gives his girlfriend Alika (played with zombielike passivity by Tatyana Drubich) a "communication tube" and explains various "positions" for receiving and sending messages. There is a nod to silent comedy, and Chaplin in particular, as Bananan takes Alika to see Chaplin in *Easy Street*; on a serious note, there is a topical handling of how prisoners (Bananan in this case) can be badly beaten by other prisoners at the suggestion of the police in exchange for favors and shorter sentences. With a nod to early Godard, there are title cards interspersed at unexpected moments, including a "slang dictionary" series, which defines words such as "MOTHER: What we address to any female object."

To enhance the perception of *Assa* as part of a happening rather than just a movie, many of the early screenings were preceded by an art exhibit of new-wave art and followed by rock concerts for a total evening lasting more than six hours.

Finally, though the film is set during the stagnation period under Brezhnev (there is a shot of his picture on one wall early on), a strong pitch is made for glasnost and social change at the end. After Bananan has been murdered by a Godfatherlike Soviet Mafia figure for stealing Alika and for discovering the Godfather's dirty deals, the rock musicians try to get jobs in a restaurant. (A title appears on the screen: "This is not the end of the story.") They are asked where they live. "Nowhere" is the reply. "We are musicians." They receive no permit, but they decide to play anyway.

Thus the film ultimately embraces freedom (which is the theme of

The Wild Pigeon as well) and the need to go beyond "the regulations." It ends with a live concert at night with roughly sixty thousand young people swaying in the dark, holding candles and matches as they sing along with the Soviet-Korean rock star Victor Tsoy, bandanna around his head à la Bruce Springsteen, "Our hearts demand change."

The film was popular. But it did not catch on to the degree that the filmmakers would have liked. What failed? According to many Soviet critics, the film, in trying to burst the seams of the previously restrictive Soviet film language, ended up communicating little. Alexander Timofeevsky, for instance, comments, "Sometimes it seems that not the director but the material dominates" ("In the Tenderest Shroud"), as if the director hoped the material would speak for itself. By going in so many directions simultaneously, and by switching moods constantly, the film left audiences more confused than enlightened or entertained. In a word, Solovyev has "overcooked" his raw material: Soviet youth culture today. We sense that the film is trying too hard to impose a studied chaos on the audience while at the same time asking to be taken seriously as a thought-provoking piece on changing regimes (1801 and the present). The main plot line involving the older gangster, Krymov, and his opposition to Bananan for stealing his girlfriend, Alika, becomes a trite melodrama with a dubious ending: Krymov kills Bananan and Alika shoots Krymov (which parallels the assassination of Czar Paul, and simultaneously reflects the stagnation period under Brezhnev during which the film is set). Caught between being a concert or rock performance film and a narrative film too closely imitative of "old" French new-wave techniques, *Assa* sinks into an ambiguous middle ground. It is unable to sustain a mood or theme—or to "stop making sense" completely, in a purely lighthearted anarchistic use of genre, as in the recent Hollywood production *Earth Girls Are Easy.*

Our point is not to castigate one film's shortcomings. To the contrary: *Assa* exemplifies to what degree these first years of glasnost have been a transitional phase. Given the freedom to work much more openly and experimentally, many filmmakers will inevitably go overboard in an effort to find their individual voices. *Assa* is three or four feature films edited into one; it fails to hold together as a postmodern metanarrative. Yet such overreaching ambition should, we suggest, be deemed a healthy reaction to those times when it was difficult to make personal or eclectic films, not to mention anything resembling postmodernism. For this reason, many Soviet filmmakers feel feature films are some three to five years behind the documentary movement. The documentary film has already chalked up a remarkable list of successes and connected with a large and varied national and international audience. The feature film is still in its formative stages.

One final example of such a film would be *The Green Fire of the Goat* (*Zelyonyi ogon' kozy*, 1989), a film about a lost generation, made by members of that generation in their twenties. A first feature by Anatoly Mateshko, written by Arkady Vysotsky, the son of the famous actor and ballad singer Vladimir Vysotsky, *The Green Fire of the Goat* has the feeling of spontaneity, anarchy, and pretentiousness of many of the now-forgotten first films made in the late 1950s in France, along with the memorable works of Godard, Truffaut, Chabrol, and Rohmer. The film drew little critical attention and an even smaller audience. Yet for our purposes, it deserves mention both for its representation of a particular slice of the youth culture and also for its self-indulgence.

Much of the statement of the film is made in the casting itself: "parallel" filmmakers and numerous nonactors who are "personalities" around Moscow have found their way into bit parts, including film critic turned independent producer Andrei Dementyev. But the picaresque narrative, such as it is, follows twenty-five-year-old Nikita (Vladimir Mashkov) through a day and a night in Moscow. He encounters several women, including Tanya, with whom he has had a child, rock groups, whores, gangsters, and, finally, his parents for his birthday party. Though the film fails to bridge the distance between the avant-garde and hipness, it nevertheless has a series of striking images taken from the street and from the bizarre life-styles of many Moscow youth. Musically too, the film presents an eclectic reflection of the times. Along with Soviet rock groups, the sound track features Michael Jackson, the Beatles, and, most important for the protagonist, Tom Waits and his "Rain Dogs" album.

Despite the final aesthetic or cinematic limitations of this first feature, it is of curious interest because Vysotsky and Mateshko have captured something of Tom Waits's boozy, sleazy, nightmare world of fallen ideals, cheap violence, and lost love. The title refers to a childhood memory awkwardly dropped into the film of an innocent time when Nikita received a toy goat.

The unresolved question of fathers and sons is central to Nikita's confusion as well. In the birthday scene to which the film has built, albeit slowly and by indirection, Nikita turns to his father and says, "Father, there are many things I have to tell you." The father replies in a distant voice, "Talk with your brother first." Rejected once more, Nikita wanders the streets of Moscow at dawn, bleeding, as we hear Tom Waits singing about being "inside a broken clock."

The Green Fire of the Goat will not be long remembered in the history of contemporary Soviet film. But because it is made by young filmmakers and actors who are of the generation they treat on the screen, the rhythms and spirit of the youth culture, including an international blend of music and life-style, is striking.

BEYOND THE LOOKING GLASS: URBAN YOUTH
IN CONFLICT

Films about troubled urban youth abound. We began our introduction by mentioning the Estonian documentary by Mark Soosaar, *A Life without* . . . , about teen suicide. This documentary is powerful not simply because it is about one teen who kills himself. Rather, the young boy's death becomes the key with which the filmmaker begins to unlock the personal and social circumstances that cause frustration and needless friction for all those living within "the system."

A Life without . . . is also a film without. It is without fancy camera work, complicated editing, manipulative sound tracks. We are discussing not merely a documentary recording of "reality," but a conjunction of aesthetics, ideology, and documentary. On the surface Soosaar appears simply to be documenting the aftermath of the boy's death, showing us a legal inquest and interviews with family and friends. But we soon realize that there is an unstated agenda. We are also given a glimpse at the system that created the tensions and contradictions that led the young man to the point of desperation.

Furthermore, Soosaar manages to create a delicate but distinct shift in audience sympathy during the film. At first we feel that the mother is the most immediate and direct cause of her son's death: her manner of speech, her hostile attitude toward her son's girlfriend, whom she labels a whore, and her seeming insensitivity toward her son's needs seem clear causes for the boy's distress.

Yet when the film switches from the inquest to "a day in the life of the mother," we come to feel quite differently. We watch a woman who goes to work before dawn by bus to a factorylike dairy miles from her urban apartment. Once she is at work, the cows arrive by conveyer belt and she begins the hours of mechanical drudgery alone. Then comes the telling moment when she shouts angrily at a cow who does not cooperate with her. We suddenly realize that this woman works alone in a highly depersonalized environment that leaves her little space to be a human being.

The final scene, in which she breaks down on camera, thus elicits sympathy from us, even though we previously felt ready to condemn her for apparently being the prime cause of her son's death. The problems of youth become those of the adults living in a dehumanizing environment. No voice-over narrator preaches to us; the camera simply reveals. The effect is devastating. We feel, as we do with many contemporary Soviet documentaries, that we are watching drama in its purest sense, and we are even more deeply touched because we know the subjects in the film are real.

One other documentary in this category stands out. The most popular American teen gang in recent years is seen on television and on film: *Teenage Mutant Ninja Turtles*. But teen gangs in the Soviet Union are not cute cartoon figures. Director V. Kuzmina's *And What about You Guys?* (*A u vas vo dvore?* [*In Our Courtyard*], 1987) treats the problem of ultraconservative teenage male street gangs in the city of Kazan in the autonomous republic of Tataria, where the rate of crime committed by teenagers is the highest in the country. In a brief twenty minutes, this black-and-white film takes us inside the activities and the minds of the Cascade gang, one of forty in the city. As in *Is It Easy to Be Young?* the film proceeds as a voice-over dialogue between the filmmaker and several gang members. These neatly dressed, crew-cut teenagers all express a similar point of view: being a member of the gang means, as one member says, "We're strong, and no one can break us up."

Americans viewing the popular *Little Vera* were puzzled by an early scene at an outdoor dance for teenagers where lines of youths facing each other suddenly pounce on each other and begin what looks like a prearranged brawl. Viewing *And What about You Guys?* makes it clear that this dance–fight sequence is a common event in Soviet urban areas. Here we see lines of youths, some skinheads, others punks, and still others the neat ultraconservatives of the Cascade gang, facing off and moving to the rhythm as a group. "This is not a dance," one gang member tells the filmmaker. "It's a ritual."

Kuzmina's film would be less shocking if it were about punks or skinheads: we expect them to be antisocial. But the film is all the more troubling because these body-building, reactionary kids are a ludicrous parody of communism. They openly declare their goal: to "fight for world communism," and to do so as "good guys" who are "going to fight the bad."

Clearly the gang gives them what the official party cannot: a sense of belonging, of action, of excitement, of something to believe in. There is one classroom scene in which a stiff schoolmarm states that the class should consider how to "mold the new Communist morality." She calls on a bored class to help define the characteristics needed for such a new morality. Only the inarticulate Cascade members attempt an answer. No one seems to have a clear idea of what that morality might be.

The film ends in the violent death of a Cascade member during a courtyard battle. Kuzmina concludes by cutting to the gravestone of an Afghan soldier and contrasting it with a young gang member killed "in peacetime." The narrator notes sadly that there are tragedies happening in real life that do not appear in the papers. The film closes with a dramatic question: "Can they be helped?" No answer is given. Once more, questions raised by filmmakers are left to audiences to answer.

THE NARRATIVE FEATURE YOUTH FILM:
A TROUBLED SLICE OF LIFE

Assa suggests a postmodern approach to narrative films about today's Soviet youth. Other films, however, choose a more traditional format, yet nevertheless situate their discourse on youth within a multilayered narrative, mixing genres and employing a many-charactered framework.

Consider, for instance, the 1989 feature *Assuage My Sorrows*, directed and written by Alexander Alexandrov and Vladimir Prokhorov. This is a slice-of-life *(bytovoy)* film with echoes of Italian neorealism and the British Angry Young Man, kitchen-sink films of the 1950s. But Alexandrov and Prokhorov have mixed family melodrama (three generations of characters) and the youth film genre with an ensemble cast that strains to create an epic of the everyday. The jagged transitions between scenes mirror the jagged edges of the characters' disjointed lives. But such extreme fragmentation means that, as in *Assa*, the film is successful only for individual moments rather than as a whole. We remember the sad-eyed ten-year-old son, Zhora, crying as his hair is shaved in a barbershop; the camera tracking over the old ceramics on the wall of the crowded communal apartment as an old woman, Maria Nikolayevna, explains to Zhora what they represent to her about her past; and the dark farce of Boris, the thirty-five-year-old protagonist, overturning the car belonging to his wife's lover on a dark street in frustration over their confused relationship. But like the 360-degree spinning point-of-view shot in the dance class scene when Boris dances "the dances of the world" to an old Russian Jewish tune, the film itself careens from scene to scene, from life to life, leaving the audience dizzy with underdeveloped possibilities for the picture as a whole.

Such films are difficult to rank aesthetically. They suggest both a pretentiousness of purpose and an unfocused development. But as cultural texts of Soviet society in flux, such works become invaluable windows onto the confusion of the times.

"NOVY REALISM" IN THE FICTION FILM
ABOUT URBAN YOUTH

We note once more that a major feature of glasnost cinema is the breakdown of the traditional boundaries dividing documentary from fiction filmmaking. Those youth films with a documentarylike quality and a straightforward narrative and thematic intent have been much more successful at honestly balancing aesthetics and topicality. We are speaking of films that have aimed for a style and narrative thrust much closer to Italian neorealism, which can be called "novy realism."

Abdrashitov's *Plumbum, or A Dangerous Game* is illustrative. Written by Abdrashitov's permanent partner, Alexander Mindadze (*Fox Hunt* [*Okhota na lis*, 1980], *The Train Stopped* [*Ostanovilsya poezd*, 1982], and, as we have discussed, *The Manservant*, 1989), this linear film tells of a teenager from a middle-class family who becomes a little fascist dedicated to turning in criminals in order to "keep my city clean." Played with frightening intensity by Anton Androsov, Plumbum at first amuses those around him (and us) with his antics. After all, he appears to be an adult trapped in a child's body. But the script cleverly draws the audience in by being entertaining, and then delivers several strong punches that force the audience to consider the magnitude of the issues of justice and personal freedom more seriously.

It is genuinely funny to see this youngster lecture the police after he catches a thief: "I hate evil. I'll give my life in the struggle." The camera scans the faces of the confused policemen; they have no idea what to think about such a seemingly "perfect," zealous youth. We realize this obsession goes beyond that of being a miniature Clark Kent with a dual personality, however, when he forces a young woman he caught along with the mobsters to imitate a chicken loudly in a restaurant in what is clearly an exercise in sadistic power and control.

The final blow comes as he turns in his father for poaching fish. Plumbum then proceeds to conduct the police interrogation. "Maybe it's power you like," his father says in a moment of growing awareness. Abdrashitov and Mindadze thus manage to offer a complex meditation on the corruption of power in the hands of those too immature to use it by using an extremely simple and direct narrative.

For Soviets, Plumbum appears not only to be a seemingly normal child who becomes a fascist: he is also a little Stalinist. Part of what is so effective about the film is that, unlike most films about troubled youth, including *Scarecrow*, this one dares to make the protagonist the villain instead of an innocent corrupted. Plumbum is impenetrable. Soviet critic Lev Anninski puts it well when he observes, "Can you catch the moment when 'evil and good exchange places' in Abdrashitov's films? Perhaps they don't 'exchange.' They somehow exist here in another way. They look at each other" ("Softness of *Plumbum*"). As in *The Lord of the Flies*, William Golding's popular study of youth and evil in the 1950s, *Plumbum* offers no consoling and simple explanation for why this young fellow is the way he is. He simply is.

For audiences conditioned to read allegorically, even such a seemingly nonmetaphorical film suggests more than appears on the screen. In terms of Peter Blos's reading of father-son relationships discussed above,

Plumbum appears to be a child who has bypassed adolescence altogether and jumped into adulthood before resolving his Oedipal situation. The adolescent phase of resolution of son with father will never take place for Plumbum since he is a little old man cheated out of his youth for reasons that are not made clear. But Abdrashitov and Mindadze's darkly realistic morality play implies more. We must remember the youth's cry in *Is It Easy to Be Young?*: "We are your children." Society (and those who shape it), not Plumbum, is guilty from such a perspective. Such an ideological reading of Plumbum's behavior suggests that Plumbum is the perverted ideal of socialist justice carried to ludicrous and terrifying ends. Given a choice between family and the "code" or "law," Plumbum cold-bloodedly and sadistically carries out the letter of the law.

One of the first true examples of perestroika in cinema, *Plumbum* closes with a devastating sequence. Plumbum is chasing another boy across rooftops when Sonia, his sweet and innocent girlfriend, who is nearby, decides to go up on the roof as well. Clearly her attraction to Plumbum is like that mixed fear and curiosity seen in the relationship between Dostoevsky's self-tortured, saintlike women and their troubled male lovers.

In trying to reach Plumbum she slips and, in slow motion, she falls and dies. The film is over. The shock value of the ending deserves comment. As we have suggested earlier, such an ending would be totally out of character in the American neoconservative, upbeat teen films of the 1980s. This contemporary Soviet film even goes beyond the haunting anguish of François Truffaut's debut feature, *The 400 Blows*, as Antoine, Truffaut's autobiographical childhood double, is caught in a close-up freeze-frame that suggests his no-win confusion. *Plumbum* allows us no chance for reconciliation or improvement. Sonia is dead, and nothing suggests that Plumbum will ever change.

While there are numerous examples of youth features made in the past five years, three others will help clarify the dimensions of the youth film under glasnost. Karen Shakhnazarov's *Messenger Boy* (*Kourier*, 1987), made during the first year of glasnost, is a milder, much lighter look at contemporary youth surrounded by contradictions that seem to have no resolution. Shakhnazarov proved earlier with *Jazzmen* (*My iz djaza*, 1983) that he could spin an entertaining tale and make a point without turning either pretentious or overly philosophical. *Jazzmen* details, with plenty of humor and good music, the trials and ultimate victories faced by the first Soviet jazz band. *The Messenger Boy*, based on his own novel, is stronger than John Hughes's brand of American teenage comedy. It more closely represents the kind of Soviet youth film being made that catches the sounds and flavors of life for Soviet teenagers today without exaggerating the problems presented.

Ivan (Fyodor Dunayevsky) is the middle-class son of a divorced couple, living with his mother. His pent-up frustrations (toward his father, for instance) come out in his poor performance at school and his sudden outbursts: at one point he starts a fire in the apartment in front of his mother. Everything changes when he falls in love with a professor's daughter, Katya (Anastasia Nemolyaeva), and is introduced to a world of culture and refinement far beyond the environment in which he has grown up.

Much in the film would seem familiar to any middle-class European or American teenager: skateboarding, karate films, and break dancing abound, and marijuana makes its appearance here as well. (Soviet teen films also include what seems to be an obligatory "robot dance" sequence, with teenagers dancing with mechanical movements to electronic music.)

Unlike *Ferris Bueller's Day Off*, however, to which this could be compared overall, *The Messenger Boy* is a tale about a clearly materialistic child (in the Brezhnevian sense of the cultivation of consumerism and materialism above all else) who grows toward a wider appreciation of life's possibilities. (Both films evidence a concern for the workings of the upper middle class, though *The Messenger Boy* explores class difference, as the protagonist is from the working middle class and his girlfriend is from the aristocratic-artistic upper middle class.) Ferris Bueller, on the other hand, appears to have learned nothing in his day off that will seriously alter his acceptance of white, suburban upper-middle-class Chicago life.

As has often been the case in the Soviet Union since 1985, the characters in this film do not talk so much as conduct interviews centered on self-analysis and self-definition. "What do you want?" asks Katya's father, a professor, early in the film. "A good salary," Ivan answers, in his usual half-mocking tone, "a nice apartment, a dacha in the country." The professor replies without irony, "It's not criminal to want basic material things. But it's not enough."

This questioning continues in the office in which Ivan is a messenger boy. A young man and a secretary exchange their secret dreams; hers is to marry a Japanese man because "they have the most advanced technology." When they turn to Ivan, he says with a straight face but tongue in cheek that his dream is "that communism triumphs over all the world." The young man and the secretary stare at each other, not sure how to take such a ridiculous answer—which is, nevertheless, what everyone had grown up being told to believe. (This ironic response on Ivan's part is a line repeated several years later by Vera on the beach with her lover in *Little Vera*.)

The Messenger Boy is much less ambitious than the darker film *Assuage My Sorrows*. But it succeeds because, since it is a smaller film, Shakhnazarov has space and time to explore each character in more detail. While adults often make almost no appearances in American teen films, or do so in caricature form, here we are given a sense of Ivan's closeness to his mother and his loneliness as he thinks about his father on assignment in Africa.

Caught between the highbrow art world of Katya's family and the hard realities of Ivan's divorced parents, Ivan and Katya invent an imaginary marriage and pregnancy with which they shock their parents. The wrath that follows leads to the breakup of the romance and Ivan's retreat. In the final sequence, set in a freezing, drab winter landscape, Ivan asks his unkempt sidekick friend, Bisone, what he wants. While Ivan is being as philosophical as he was at the beginning, Bisone turns practical. "An overcoat. Winter is coming." Ivan takes off his expensive coat and puts it around Bisone. Like a holy fool, Ivan is learning to share, to give to others, to think past his own material needs.

Though this film, like so many popular contemporary Soviet films, presents life from a clearly middle-class perspective, it goes beyond many of the so-called stagnation pop films of the Brezhnev era, which offered comedy and drama in a noncritical, consumer-driven context. *The Messenger Boy* leaves the audience doing what perestroika has encouraged: questioning. *Ferris Bueller's Day Off* has a happy ending: suburban life will go on as usual. *The Messenger Boy* suggests that there must be, as Katya's father suggests, "something more."

TOUGH-MINDED REALITY LONGING FOR PARADISE

Novy realism is most clearly present, however, in Sergei Bodrov's 1989 film *Freedom Is Paradise*. This film is an extremely simple, direct, uncluttered narrative about a thirteen-year-old, Sasha (Volodya Kozyrev), in a reform school, who escapes for a brief taste of freedom. The title, like the film, is deceptively simple: beyond a sense of freedom, Sasha is actually seeking commitment and family. His mother is dead and his father, whom he has never met, is serving time in a Siberian prison camp. Even less sentimental than Truffaut's *400 Blows* and more in line with Buñuel's *Los Olvidados*, *Freedom Is Paradise* takes us beyond the comforts of middle-class life to view the life of youth on the edge.

The film is uncluttered partly because it does not deal with those issues that everyone mentions when discussing young people: sex, drugs, rock and roll, alienation. Sasha is not turned off; he is simply not connected. He has no roots, and yet the yearnings are there. In paring down his narrative to such simplicity, Bodrov avoids the dangers of the poetic and prophetic auteurs in "overdetermining" their films. Here the image is allowed to speak for itself, and the audience is also free to experience the intensity of this simple, documentarylike tale. Sasha escapes, hopping a train, meets a variety of people, and winds up spending one night with his father in prison before the guards take him back to school.

This son-father film gains in resonance because of the attention to mise-en-scène as opposed to montage. The film builds up to the evening spent in prison. What Bodrov, who also wrote the film, allows for that is refreshing for Soviet cinema is the quiet moment, the privileged instant, when we are allowed to watch a father and son together without dialogue or camera work or music or special effects. The faces, the gestures tell all, and when the dialogue arrives, it is extremely brief and telling.

The beauty of the scene is that Bodrov reverses our expectations. After a stony silence in which neither father nor son can find the words to begin to reach the other, the father breaks down and begins to cry. He says that in his life he has "never had anything." Sasha comforts him, pointing out that he only has another eight years to serve. After that, Sasha says, they can live together. "Maybe we can buy a bicycle or something. Find an apartment."

To return to our father-son paradigm: the scene is effective not only because of the exposure of the bleakness of their lives or the pathos of a son who takes on a fatherly role toward his own father; it is also because the moment generates in the audience a degree of hope. Maturity in a male, as Peter Blos suggests, depends on the adolescent receiving the blessing of the father. This, we feel, has taken place. The final freeze-frame of the film, therefore, which holds on Sasha's confused and angry face as he tries to break free from the guards who are to take him back to school, is not actually as desperate as that of Truffaut's young man, who truly feels he has no one to go to and nowhere to go at the end of *The 400 Blows*. As Bodrov's film ends, freedom has been experienced, a father has been found, and Sasha has begun to be connected to life.

It is telling that this film was chosen Best Film at the 1989 Montreal Film Festival. Not only was such a decision a vote for an unknown film and director's quality and power; it was, whether consciously or not, a nod toward an unadorned, direct language of filmmaking as opposed to the other Soviet film in competition, Alexander Sokurov's *Save and Protect* (*Spasi i sohrani*, 1989), which, in its approach and style, clearly was influenced by the Tarkovsky mode of poetic-prophetic Soviet filmmaking. As important a film as *Save and Protect* is, clearly the jury felt it had seen this kind of Soviet filmmaking perhaps once too often. *Freedom Is Paradise* is thus not only another film about troubled youth; it is a film that has found a voice, a use of cinematic language that helps challenge more traditional Soviet filmmaking.

TOWARD A "MIDDLE" REALISM: *BLACKMAILER*

Another film suggests a middle ground between the harshness of *Plumbum* and the much milder vision of *The Messenger Boy*. Valeri Kurykin's *Blackmailer* (*Shantazhist*, 1988) presents a harder look at much the same territory covered in *The Messenger Boy*. Once again, a young man, Misha (Mikhail Efremov), is the product of a broken home and an absent father. Misha lives with his mother, but is almost totally alienated from others. When he takes photos, which is his hobby, they never include human beings.

The narrative traces Misha's gradual movement from the hardened philosophy "it's no good being kind in our times" to a more vulnerable position because of his love for a young girl, Alionka (Marina Starych), and his friendship for and antagonism with a classmate, Genka (Andrei Tikhomirov). Contemporary youth plot elements include a joyride sequence in Alionka's father's "borrowed" car, robot dancing, and the theft of a school video camera to pay for car repairs after an accident. The blackmailing comes as Genka's father insults Misha's mother at a school parents' meeting. Misha blackmails the man to defend his mother's honor. But once again we feel the weight of psychological complexity behind this action. Misha is striking out against the double standard of the adult world, and, we feel, against a life without a father.

The result is that Genka must come to his father's defense. He does so with a shotgun. He empties the gun into Misha, and in a close-up, we watch the pain, the tears, the real emotion he has been denying for so long suddenly well up as he dies. To end here would be to leave us with the shock impression of *Plumbum*. Kurykin takes us one step farther, however. We see a montage of photos Misha took of children in a park after he began to open up to Alionka. Suddenly we see that an internal change had been going on in Misha. Unlike the coldly abstract and depersonalized photos he took before, we see playful and moving shots that capture children as children in all their moods, shots taken with a sensitivity to childhood. That the old ways of thinking (blackmail, distrust, revenge) dominated the lives of these youths, alas, remains the sobering message of the filmmakers.

DRUGGED YOUTH:
THE MAKING OF A DRAMATIC DOCUMENTARY

The drug problem is one without easy solutions and one toward which, under perestroika, filmmakers have turned their documentary lenses. One of the most widely seen and hotly debated films on the subject has been Georgi Gavrilov's *Confession: Chronicle of Alienation* (*Ispoved': Hronika otchuzhdeniya*, 1988), which is described as a journalistic feature film. The film details the downfall of a drug addict named Lyosha, his girlfriend, Sveta, who dies of an overdose (Lyosha: "For an hour and a half I tried to make you breathe"), and their blank-eyed baby, Vera. Gavrilov, who wrote the film with Yuri Kotlyar, has created an unusual and sometimes disturbing blend of fact and fiction based on the lives of those depicted. The genre is not docudrama (the reenacting of events at a different time with a different cast). Here we have the "original cast" filmed documentary-style, but with some scenes staged or re-created after the fact.

That the film is a depressing glance at drug addiction is an understatement. "There is no place for me in this world," says the spaced-out protagonist, who looks like Charles Manson and speaks in a monotone. The film is a chronicle of turned-off and tuned-out human beings of all generations. We see the pregnant girlfriend on drugs and later the child (literally another "little Vera") unable to recognize or respond to her parents, and we listen with shock as Lyosha's mother emerges as a matriarchal Stalinist, claiming that "children should fear their father," while the grandmother, who has a portrait of Stalin in her home, threatens to turn the youths in to the KGB.

With *Confession*, we move away from the strong personal documentary style of the films discussed above and enter a zone in which we must ultimately hold the filmmaker even more responsible. The new Soviet documentarists strive for moral and ethical and ideological discourse through a combined expressionist-impressionist and realist approach; Gavrilov has blurred the edges of life and fiction to present a narrative shaped as a chronicle. The controversy over the film in the Soviet press hinges on this in-between approach. Certainly both camps have their reasons: yes, film is such a powerful medium that in having the original participants play themselves we are tricked into thinking we are watching a pure chronicle or documentary, and yet we are aware that in literature, for instance, the constructed "documentary," be it *Don Quixote* or *Robinson Crusoe* or *Pamela* or *The Persian Letters*, is a time-honored tradition.

Whichever side the viewer takes, however, audiences do realize that

Gavrilov is, like so many of his filmmaking peers, using a particular story to discuss a general theme. The story—drugs and young people—is presented in a wider political and ideological framework. This is made apparent by the opening and closing montages. The series of images that opens the film ties together Brezhnev, babies, soldiers, children with guns, American troops, a burning man, children's eyes, rock music, drug needles, sad youths, and a quote from Dostoevsky: "There is no such notion as a future." Near the end of the film another montage presents a Soviet train wreck, the Chernobyl nuclear accident, bodies floating in the sea, dolphins dying, and images of the destruction of the planet. The "no future" theme is reflected on a small scale in Lyosha's poisoned life, but it is also applicable to the world in our time.

The quotation from Dostoevsky is helpful. It signals to us the approach Gavrilov takes to his subject. Gavrilov has gone beyond documentary and has carried on the Russian tradition of the artist as apocalyptic visionary, part prophet, part philosopher. The dangers of taking on such all-encompassing roles, however, are evident. When the film works best, it effectively conveys the painful suffering of young drug addicts. When it is least successful—in the use of staged documentary and the simplistic montages described above—it appears proselytizing. In other words, one dogmatic approach (socialist realism, for instance) is being replaced by another.

A film such as *Confession* leaves us aware above all else that Soviet filmmakers are still in transition, searching for a voice and a cinematic language as free as possible from the clichés and dangers of the confining languages they wish to escape.

AFGHANISTAN AND SOVIET YOUTH

The appearance of the Afghan War veteran in Kuzmina's and Podnieks's films suggests how prevalent the "Afghan question" has become for Soviets.

One of the first strong films about the veterans has been young filmmaker Tatyana Chubakova's hard-hitting, seventeen-minute black-and-white film, *Homecoming* (*Vozvrascheniye*, 1987; scripted by Sergei Bobrov). A desperate male voice-over whispers "Hear me, Motherland" as eerie music clangs harshly on the sound track and we see cinema verité shots of the mountains of Afghanistan and the abandoned wreckage of Soviet military vehicles by the roadside. The plea is heard not by an abstract "Motherland" but by the audience. The cry for help can only be answered by those who see the film. This cry is a call for awareness, anger, understanding, and healing on behalf of the physically and mentally crippled, disturbed, wounded veterans whom Chubakova interviews in the film.

According to one veteran, the war was "bad for the soul." Against grim shots of young soldiers being returned to the Soviet Union in coffins, another veteran states flatly, "Nobody wants us." Another disturbs the viewer with his apparent moral numbness to the whole experience: "I was told to kill and I killed. It was exciting. Like hunting a hare."

The trajectory of the film leads to a mother's grief. We see her at her son's tomb and then in his room, which looks like any youth's room anywhere today, complete with a poster for a cheap Italian film, *Johnny Chicano*. She reads passages from her son's letters. With the line "Too bad boys are trained to kill against their will" from yet another returnee, the restless camera returns to a carnival of Soviet wreckage in Afghanistan and more of the grating electronic music.

The toughness and the personal nature of the new school of documentary films must be seen in part as a reaction against the many years of predictable, "factual," state-produced documentaries in the Stalinist mode. *Homecoming* is clearly as far from the traditional Soviet documentary as possible. Its empathy for the disenchanted and its manipulation of sound and image to stir the audience's emotions leave little room for "objectivity." (There is one sequence suggesting a "positive" direction for grief, as we see a veteran dedicating himself to constructing a home for the deaf.) Such extremes of filmmaking have raised critical eyebrows as well as praise for charting new directions under perestroika. Some have suggested that such films run the risk of exploiting explosive subjects without "digesting"them fully. Others feel that this is not the time for digesting but that the filmmakers on the front line need to find their voices by exercising them in whatever way suits them.

A more thorough and less manipulative look at the moral and psychic cost of the war for youth and the nation as a whole is Sergei Lukyanchikov's feature-length *Pain (Bol'*, 1988). With narration provided by the writer Ales' Adamovich and the priest Viktor Radomyslensky, the Belorussian production provides an intricate compilation of interviews with mothers and young widows of soldiers lost in Afghanistan, as well as with friends, military experts, and other relatives. What emerges is both a personal history of the war, complete with documentation of the suffering caused by loss, and the beginning of an open dialogue on a more objective, less emotional level in an attempt to understand and prevent a repetition of the mistakes of the past.

We do not need to detail the familiar litany of pain expressed, but we do wish to comment on the opening and closing frames of the film. The filmmaker has chosen to introduce a religious dimension; the film begins and ends at a Russian Orthodox church service. The takes are long and the religious chants soothing. The pain, therefore, is embraced, enveloped by a thousand-year-old tradition dedicated to easing personal and worldly burdens. While *Homecoming*, with its jarring, rough music, is geared to upset us, *Pain* hints strongly at the possibility of healing and relief. That a priest has been involved in the making of the film simply underlines this notion. No direct appeal to prayer or to Orthodox liturgy is made. But the evocation of such an important part of the Russian past is a test of the new plurality of spirit in the Soviet Union, and thus a challenge to the monopoly of communism on offering guidance and solutions to the people's pain.

Finally, we learn that the Orthodox service is a baptism. The closing image is a close-up of a child's face with eyes full of wonder at the flickering candles and the rich chanting filling the church. Pain has been transcended, though the memory of Afghanistan lingers.

PARALLEL AND ZIGZAG ALTERNATIVE CINEMA

All the films discussed above were made by adults, most of whom are already over thirty. The complicated system of becoming a filmmaker in the Soviet Union has, in the past, almost guaranteed that young people have not been able to produce images.

That is beginning to change, because of perestroika and also because technology is changing. The advent of video has been a boon to young would-be filmmakers, and has helped foster the beginnings of an independent and, at times, underground avant-garde.

The most active group of young people producing films and videos is composed of the avant-garde filmmakers in Leningrad and Moscow known as Parallel Cinema. Sergei Dobrotvorsky comments that such a "free cinema" has sprung up on super-8, 16 mm, 35 mm, and video; complete with "its own authorities and connoisseurs, it has festivals and even a special magazine, *Cine-phantom*." (See his "Most Avant-Garde.") The movement, which he terms "aesthetic terrorism," is alive and growing, he notes, in Riga, Lvov, Minsk, and other cities.

What are its characteristics? Those who practice and comment on these works agree: parallel cinema is naive cinema, it is an ironic and humorous medium, and it is energetic in its denial of any influences. Also, subgroups or movements within the movement have appeared. In Leningrad, for instance, a group ironically named Che-payev (after Chapayev, the hero of the most popular film of the Stalinist period, and Che Guevara) produces films that work against such previously cherished socialist myths. Films such as Yevgeni Yufit's *Suicide Wild Boars* (*Vepri suitsida*, 1988), Yevgeni Kondratiev's *Daydreams* (*Grezy*, 1987), and the Che-payev collective series *Parallel Movement* (*Parallel'noye dvizheniye*, 1988) and *The Struggle for a Fleet* (*Bitva za flot*, 1989) play with image, sound, and meaning in anarchistic ways in keeping with the filmmakers' mission as cinematic terrorists.

One of the most striking examples is *Tractors* (1987), a half-hour, black-and-white tongue-in-cheek pseudodocumentary about . . . tractors, made by the Moscow-based Aleinikov brothers. Blending old newsreels with their own black-and-white footage, they have assembled a hilarious parody of Stalinist educational films, centering on that most sacred of production icons, the tractor. "Tractors can be used in different ways," says the female narrator, who later notes, "People love the tractor and call it a steel horse." Suddenly, however, the traditional documentary language and imagery break down as the camera begins to swirl and focus inappropriately on details, and as the narrator begins to speak in a frenzied, passionate, and then hysterical voice. "You feel death all around you," she says as the camera tilts, bobs, weaves, goes out of focus, and then suddenly swish-pans the barren horizon. "Your blood screams, your head is numb," she adds. She then begins crying, screaming as the image fades to white. "There is only me and the tractor" she intones as a sarcastically patriotic Communist song comes on the sound track and the final image of a statue of Lenin appears.

Such a movement clearly heralds the possibility for youth to have its own voice, to conduct its own experiments free from the pressures— ideological, financial, and bureaucratic—of the Soviet studio system of Goskino. A space has opened for films as divergent as the mysterious Che-payev Group's *Struggle for a Fleet*, which presents images of "industrial civilizations" rather than a story, or Yevgeni Yufit's "necrorealism" movement, which asserts that "totalitarian ideology always causes violence" as he uses film tricks such as fast motion and pixilation to bring corpses to life. "Necrorealism is neorealism," stated another avant-garde filmmaker, Boris Yukhananov, at a press conference at the Moscow Festival in July 1989, in the deliberate, ironic, playful voice characteristic of such films.

That youth are beginning to find the means to say what they wish to say, in the manner in which they feel most comfortable expressing themselves, to audiences they wish to reach, is a positive sign. This road will not be an easy one. Alexander Kiselev notes, "Many parallel filmmakers would have no truck with official filmdom, but are ready to deal with any film industry that has hard currency" ("From Euclides to Lobachevsky"). But such movements, and the restructuring of the studios and unions to encourage younger talent, suggest that under perestroika young people may become subjects as well as objects in an ongoing process of social and cultural change.

That the Aleinikov brothers and Yevgeni Yufit have begun to work within the studio system is a harbinger of change and a sign of the beginning of the end of the original avant-garde movement. The Aleinikovs' 1989 short feature (or long short), *Somebody Was Here* (*Zdes' kto-to byl*), was financed and supported as a very low-budget experimental film by the largest of all studios, Mosfilm. Shot in color with high production values, this wry existential tale looks neither like true parallel cinema nor like traditional film. Again, we are speaking of a transitional phase.

If there are mixed feelings about the Aleinikov brothers turning commercial, there has been almost universal recognition of the importance of the so-called Kazakh New Wave cinema, headed by Rashid Nugmanov, especially as demonstrated in his first feature film, *The Needle* (*Igla*, 1988). Nugmanov represents not a parallel movement but what could perhaps best be described as "zigzag cinema": an offbeat approach to working within the evolving studio system.

The Needle is a film about youth made by young filmmakers and actors who grew up inside pop culture. "I was born the same year as rock and roll," Nugmanov, who is in his mid-thirties, commented (Horton, interview, New Orleans, April 1989). "It was a great influence on me. I believe that rock, like film itself, is international. So you could say that I'm representative not of Soviet culture, but of a Soviet subculture, which until recently had always been underground."

Unlike *Assa*, *The Needle* speaks to us with the voice of someone comfortable with the culture he films, and who thus uses cinema as a natural extension of a world he is familiar with—as opposed to a subculture being investigated from the outside (as in *Assa*). That the film sold millions of tickets in 1989 alone and has been acclaimed by critics as one of the top ten Soviet films of the glasnost period, and by some as the major film of the period, is testimony to its importance.

With *The Needle*, youth and filmmaking find a hopeful, playful, progressive, postmodern language in which to speak to a mass audience on a cinematic and cultural level simultaneously. *The Needle* is a landmark film; it suggests directions for many young Soviet filmmakers to explore. And certainly part of its importance is that it is a Kazakh and not a Russian film. Soviet critic Avdotya Smirnova remarks, "*The Needle* looks at a vice [drugs] with an oriental wisdom. The film speaks not about a vice, but a fate" ("The Discreet Charm of One Film"). Critic Marina Drozdova observes that this tale of "postpunk playfulness" starring rock star Victor Tsoy avoids melodrama and indicates a new direction for Soviet cinema by demonstrating how to make "the emotions, the living feelings, run run run, like the White Rabbit in *Alice in Wonderland*" ("A Dandy of the Postpunk Period, or Goodbye, America,

Oh! . . . "). And Olga Reizen notes that *The Needle* succeeded in reaching a broad audience of all ages, not just a teenage crowd. In watching the film at several public screenings, she observed that "people seem to feel a sense of mystery and surprise that they seldom see in Soviet films. Older people liked the hero and the young crowd enjoyed the music" (Horton, interview, Moscow, October 1989).

"Wherever Will I Begin?" Soviet Women in Cinema and on Film

It's the happiest time of my life, but I want to cry all the time.
—VERA to her girlfriend in *Little Vera*

THE CHANGING ROLE OF SOVIET WOMEN

IN EXTREME CLOSEUP, a woman in her thirties with troubled eyes looks at herself in a mirror and sings to herself in a harsh voice:

> It's evening
> And Masha is sad.
> Wherever will I begin?
> What, oh what, shall I start with?

She then turns and faces us and pauses. In that silence and through those sad eyes, we are in direct contact with a woman attempting to define herself, to speak to herself. The film is the 1989 production *The Husband and Daughter of Tamara Alexandrovna (Muzh i doch' Tamary Alexandrovny)*, well received at the 1989 Venice Festival and other festivals. It was directed by Olga Narutskaya and scripted by Nadezhda Kozhushanaya, who also wrote *A Mirror for a Hero*.

The woman seen in the opening, Tamara Alexandrovna, soon disappears from the film, taken to the hospital. She never returns. We then follow the two people who mean the most to her and who must cope with life without a wife and mother. The female filmmakers make it clear by the end of the film that coping is indeed difficult. The daughter, Katya, is poised on the edge of sexuality and aware of the abuse she is receiving from men around her, while the husband, Valeri, badly beaten by a gang of men and hospitalized at the end, sings in a harsh voice similar to Tamara's at the opening of the film.

But Tamara's question remains a pressing one for Soviet women today: "Wherever will I begin? What, oh what, shall I start with?" Social scientist Elvira Novikova, who has studied the position of Soviet women for many years, notes "that all upswings in public life in this country were accompanied by upswings in the women's movement" (Kraminova, "Politics Not for Women?" 14). Indeed, glasnost and perestroika have intensified the need for Soviet women to question and to reformulate their roles in Soviet society and thus to redefine their own identities. That change is strongly reflected in cinema, in terms of the women who have entered filmmaking and of the representation of women on the screen.

One of the most striking facets of the issue of Soviet women and cinema to the Western observer is the absence of a clearly delineated contemporary feminist movement. While feminist movements have played a role in the Russian "women's question" at least since the late nineteenth century, the 1980s and early 1990s still have seen no significant feminist presence. A common phrase heard in the past few years from women filmmakers and women critics and scholars in the USSR is "I'm not a feminist, but as a *woman* I feel . . . ," an attitude well documented by many, notably Francine du Plessix Gray in her study, *Soviet Women: Walking the Tightrope.*

If we are to look at recent films as examples of possible new directions in Soviet cinema for the depiction of women (especially by women), we cannot expect to find committed women's films like those existing in Germany, Italy, and other Western countries. Donna Seifer has shown that almost no Soviet women filmmakers are willing to speak of the existence of a "women's cinema" in the Soviet Union. Director Nana Djordjadze appears typical of many questioned: "It seems to me that there is good cinema and bad cinema, your style, not your style. But 'women's' or 'men's' cinema? No" (Seifer, "What Is Women's Cinema?" 8).

This chapter treats the complex issue of women and cinema in the Soviet Union today. Dzhordzhadze's remark is a striking example: is it a reactionary dismissal of gender differences, or simply a different language for speaking about male and female? Even the awarenesss of difference appears to fall into prefeminist stereotyping. While the presence of women in filmmaking and the representations of "woman" onscreen vary widely, perhaps the emerging view held by many women filmmakers is best expressed by director Lana Gogoberidze, the first president of a worldwide association of women filmmakers, KIWI: "Women by their very nature are invested with gentleness and the capacity for self-sacrifice and another quality, which I think is the most important: the ability to understand a stranger's point of view" (ibid., 9). American feminists might bristle at such language. Coming as they do from a "progressive" contemporary woman artist, these words could be seen as stereotypical descriptions of woman's nature within a patriarchal structure. Nevertheless, Gogoberidze represents a movement toward a new perspective that acknowledges difference in gender terms and in all that such terms imply.

Once again, such changes in perception owe much of their impetus to glasnost. As Soviet feminist Nina Belyaeva notes, "The absence of the independent, organized, active role of women in our politics is the last bulwark of the totalitarian iceberg that has inhibited a normal, natural life in civil society" ("Unmarked Road," 12). Perestroika has helped make the gap between such deep-rooted "matriarchal qualities" and the surface influence of male power more obvious.

Teresa de Lauretis has written, "Although the meanings vary with each culture, a sex-gender system is always intimately interconnected with political and economic factors in each society" (*Technologies of Gender*, 5). This was known in Russia long before the Soviets came to power. Richard Stites has documented the rise of the women's liberation movement as a three-pronged phenomenon from 1860 to 1930: feminism, nihilism, and Soviet communism-socialism, in *The Women's Liberation Movement in Russia*.

The development of Marxism-Leninism, however, while vaguely espousing gender equality, actually supported the patriarchal family structure and puritan sexual values, and thus never delivered true economic, social, personal, or psychological freedom for women in the Soviet Union.

Since every aspect of Soviet culture has been influenced directly or indirectly by Communist ideology—an ideology shaped almost exclusively by men—we must first look at the changing role of women in light of Communist theory and practice. Lenin is often quoted as having noted the difficult role of most Soviet women during pre-Revolutionary days and having stated, "It is only with the help of the woman, her thoughtfulness and social awareness, that the new society could be consolidated" (Kraminova, "Politics Not for Women?" 14). Due to the Revolution and the depletion in the number of men in World War II, 92 percent of Soviet women have jobs outside the home. The bind, however, is that they still have to manage the domestic sphere as well as their outside employment, a bind that leaves them little room for personal satisfaction or self-esteem.

Kerry McCuaig cites one Soviet statistic: a mother with young children has an average of seven hours and thirty-six minutes a day to herself, including time for sleep ("Effects," 11). She documents that there has been no real economic improvement for women during the first five years of glasnost, though she notes that *"perestroika* means giving the most oppressed group of women—mothers with young children—more time" (12) through new legislation, which extends maternity leave from one to two years, with job security for three.

Politically, though women make up more than half the population, they have accounted for only roughly 30 percent of the members of the Communist party, and only 6 percent of the female party members have held elected offices. With the introduction of limited democracy in 1989 through the People's Congress, women's political power has been ironically further threatened, notes Elvira Novikova. In the election for the People's Congress, only 198 of the candidates out of 880 contending for 750 seats were women. At 22.5 percent, this means that the proportion of representation has actually declined under "democracy." Alexandra Biriukova was perhaps the most important female political figure in 1991, as she had held the position of secretary of the Central Committee and an alternate to the Politburo.

Change is in the air. But many people agree that women are still second-class citizens. Even though they hold 51 percent of the jobs, and represent 75 percent of all teachers, 69 percent of all physicians, and a surprising 87 percent of all economists (Smolowe, "Heroines of Soviet Labor," 29), only one woman appears on the most powerful governing body of the country, the thirteen-person Politburo. Divorce has reached a million cases a year, with roughly 25 percent of marrying women pregnant at the time of marriage (ibid., 37). This adds up to half the marriages ending in divorce, and hundreds of thousands of children being raised by single-parent families, which in the Soviet Union almost always means by working mothers (Mann, "Vox Populi Sovietskaya," B3).

Particularly for those outside the Soviet Union, Raisa Gorbachev appears to embody the Soviet ideal of the good mother and wife and career woman. Many Soviet women, however, are resentful of this highly visible woman with a doctorate in social philosophy, the mother of a daughter, the wife of the president of the Soviet Union, and the daughter of a railroad engineer. Many accuse her of having risen not so much because of her talents as because she is Gorbachev's wife. Other Soviet women seem disturbed that she wears expensive clothing that is denied other women in the Soviet Union, and that she is too "pushy" about appearing in the limelight to a degree inappropriate for a Soviet leader's wife (Chua-Eoan, "My Wife," 43). Yet one senses that Raisa, as she is known around the world, is more a victim of conflicting attitudes existing in Soviet culture toward women and among women ("Wherever shall I begin?") than she is guilty of crimes committed as an individual.

We will examine more closely the conflict surrounding the nature and role of women today in the Soviet Union with three topics in mind: the changing state of women working in the film industry, the nature of the films made by women, and the representation of women in films made by men. Such a broad perspective should help guarantee, as Lucy Fischer suggests in *Shot/Countershot: Film Tradition and Women's Cinema*, that we see "women's art" not as an isolated genre within an overriding patriarchal system, but as "an ongoing *intertexual debate*" in the dominant culture and between women themselves (12).

WOMEN IN FILM

A number of Soviet film dictionaries and encyclopedias published before 1980 list not a single female filmmaker. Though few, they did exist, and they played a greater role than has been acknowledged. The successful efforts of the San Francisco Women Make Movies Festival each year to bring Soviet women filmmakers and their films have made it evident that even in the silent era, women played a role in shaping Soviet cinema. Soviet film scholar Frijeta Goukassian has documented the work of nearly sixty Soviet women filmmakers and has put together much of this research in an anthology she has edited for KIWI, *Women in World Cinema*.

The classical Soviet silent-film canon, of course, is that of Eisenstein, Vertov, Pudovkin, and Dovzhenko. But one can begin a reassessment of the canon by noting the important roles played by the wives of many of these filmmakers, especially Yulia Solntseva, who was Dovzhenko's wife and coworker. Beginning as the talented star of *Earth*, Solntseva became Dovzhenko's lifelong assistant on projects and then, after his death, not only the one to complete many of his unrealized projects, but, as Vance Kepley, Jr., notes, "an accomplished artist in her own right" (*In the Service of the State*, 179).

Other women associated with the origins of Soviet cinema include Lili Brik (especially for her playful avant-garde work *The Glass Eye* [*Steklyannyi glaz*, 1928]), Olga Preobrazhenskaya (consider her lyrical study of the possibilities of a "new peasant woman" in *The Peasant Women of Ryazan* [*Baby Ryazanskiye*, 1927]), and Esther Shub, whose *Fall of the House of Romanov* (*Padeniye dinastii Romanovykh*, 1927) has been hailed as a triumph of the use of actual newsreel footage in a variety of styles to create a montage of great power. Jay Leyda states, "By the juxtaposition of . . . 'bits of reality,' she was able to achieve effects of irony, absurdity, pathos, and grandeur that few of the bits had intrinsically" (*Kino*, 224).

Few women, however, have risen to prominence in Soviet film circles. Of those in more recent years, three names have stood out: Larissa Shepitko, Dinara Asanova, and Kira Muratova. Director Larissa Shepitko, who died in a car accident before glasnost began, has in recent years received well-deserved attention for her brief but important contribution to Soviet cinema in *The Homeland of Electricity* (*Rodina electrichestva*, 1957, released in 1988), from a short story by Andrei Platonov, *Wings* (*Krylya*, 1966), *You and I* (*Ty i ya*, 1971), and *The Ascent* (*Voskhozhdeniye*, 1977). Her accomplishments have inspired younger women filmmakers, though many have noted her "manly" drive and courage in succeeding in such a male-dominated industry. Still, as Barbara Quart has written, "the more you admire her work, the greater the sense of loss" ("Between Materialism and Mysticism," 5).

While there is not space to do justice to all women filmmakers, Dinara Asanova, who died in 1985 as perestroika began, should be mentioned. As Anna Lawton has noted, Asanova in her eight films showed a flair for capturing and entering "the world of adolescents, with all the uncertainty and uneasiness of a time of transition, and their troubled relations to adults" ("Toward a New Openness," 14). Once again, however, the focus is not on women's issues per se but on those of being young.

Glasnost, in contrast, coincides with the rising awareness among Soviet working women of the need to organize themselves better in order to get what they want and need. At the initiative of the Soviets, for instance, an international press club for women journalists was established in 1988 with its headquarters in Moscow. In film, a similar international organization, KIWI, was established at a conference in Tbilisi in 1988 with Georgian director Lana Gogobezidze as the first president. It is significant that the initial call for such an organization came from Soviet women filmmakers. At its inception, it numbered about a hundred women. KIWI has continued to meet each year as membership has grown to several hundred women from at least ten nations. As Natalia Pozharskaya, a consultant working in the Leningrad division of the Soviet Filmmakers' Union and a member of KIWI, has said, "As an organization, we must help women in professional ways and in a purely human sense" (Brashinsky, interview, Leningrad, August 1989).

KIWI planned a series of international meetings focused on specific areas of filmmaking in order to help women in those areas. There were plans, for instance, for a conference of makeup artists and another for assistant directors, both roles traditionally dominated by women in Soviet cinema.

Furthermore, the Soviet Women Filmmakers' Union was set up in 1988. The membership is small, however, and few specific programs have been formulated. A number of women filmmakers we interviewed stated that they did not belong and had no plans to join. In Leningrad, for instance, women directors make up only 10 percent of all feature directors (five out of about fifty), but they constitute 50 percent of the documentary filmmakers. Many women, on the other hand, work in film administration. At present, some twenty women in Leningrad belong to the Soviet Women Filmmakers' Union—about half of the women involved in the industry there. As Pozharskaya suggests, this is at least a hopeful beginning. The major problem at the moment, members contend, is a lack of funding to carry out their programs. Glasnost has not ushered in a wholesale shift of career possibilities for women in the film industry. But changes, however slowly, are taking place.

KIRA MURATOVA

I talk like I feel.
—NATASHA in *The Weakness Syndrome*

Kira Muratova is the most highly regarded Soviet woman filmmaker. Her reputation was made some twenty years ago, but she has had a "second life" since 1985. Her early works, *Brief Encounters* (*Korotkiye vstrechi*, 1968) and *The Long Farewell* (*Dolgiye provody*, 1971), were intensely personal, honest, and original studies of men and women coming to terms with relationships. In fact, these films were considered dangerous, and were some of the many works shelved for years until 1987.

The rediscovery of Muratova's unique cinematic voice coincided with the release of her first film in four years, *The Twist of Fate* (*Peremena uchasti*), which is loosely based on a Somerset Maugham story. A militant feminist might have used this rather traditional tale of a married woman caught in a triangle that leads her to murder her lover to deconstruct patriarchal systems of control over the wife, Maria. Certainly one would expect a woman director to build sympathy for the female hero-murderer.

But Muratova's first film under glasnost unfolds in no such simplistic manner. In her hands, the camera remains for the most part in the middle distance, denying us the close-ups that would automatically win us over. Instead, the long takes and multiple flashbacks distance us so that we view Maria almost clinically; at the same time, they trap us in a spiral of confusion as we work to make narrative sense of the complex web of passion in which Maria becomes entangled. Muratova therefore neither judges nor pities her female protagonist. Her steady camera allows us the opportunity to study a woman in conflict in much more detail than traditional (male-directed) narrative films.

Her next film, *The Weakness Syndrome*, caught even those who admired her previous work off guard. Quite simply, it emerged as one of the most remarkable films made during the first five years of perestroika. Whether or not one is prepared to agree with critic Andrei Dementyev that the film "is the only masterpiece of glasnost cinema" (Horton, interview, New Orleans, 22 April 1990), it is clear that with *The Weakness Syndrome* Muratova is striving for her own language, voice, and tone, beyond her earlier experiments and certainly beyond the scope of traditional Soviet cinema. *Variety*, for instance, noted that *The Weakness Syndrome* makes *Little Vera* look like "a vicarage tea party" (Strat, "*Weakness Syndrome*," 26).

The Weakness Syndrome defies simple description. Its strengths and weaknesses arise from the same cause: it is all things at once. Documentary, melodrama, allegory, farce and black comedy, "a woman's film" and a troubled man's drama mix, collide, separate, come together, and, finally, coexist. Yet if we approach this complex collage from the perspective of gender, we find we have a strongly emotional tale of a female doctor not only on the verge of a nervous breakdown, but actually in the midst of a complete spiritual breakdown caused initially by the death of her husband (who, in looks, resembles Joseph Stalin). The core of her concern in the film, Muratova explains, is this: "I don't like the way we mistreat one another and torture animals" ("I Make Films," 19).

The strongly emotional world of Natasha is contrasted with the "sleeping" universe of Nikolai, the male protagonist, who manages to outdo that emblematic embodiment of the Russian male character, Oblomov, in lethargy, by simply falling asleep anywhere he happens to find himself: at home, at work, at school, in meetings, and ultimately in the metro. The film that begins chaotically with three women shouting at us such lines as, "In childhood, all it took to be good would be to read Tolstoy," ends with Nikolai asleep in an empty metro car, stretched out in a crucified position as an old, sappy swing song in English plays on the sound track: "Chiquita, Come Back, My Darling, Chiquita."

In terms of "the woman question," the first half of Muratova's film is especially telling. As in many Soviet films today—but to a greater extent here—boundaries of fiction and documentary break down. Narrative moments in any Aristotelian cause-effect relationship are brief and fleeting. What Muratova provides instead is a rich polyphony of colliding events and shots and scenes that, in a postmodern sense, the audience must handle by itself. The opening shots seem to have no relation to each other: three women shouting at us (the camera), a boy blowing bubbles, two men talking about eating. We then switch to a funeral, which we come to learn is that of Natasha's husband. But it is significant that Muratova keeps us off balance from the beginning.

The viewer is clearly being signaled: "Stay awake and watch out. Surprise and dislocation are the organizing principles here." The narrative disruptions, blended with documentarylike shots, are reflections of the protagonists' fragmented grasp on reality in the present situation. At the funeral, for instance, silence mixes with music in a stop/start rhythm in tune with the widow's grief (much like Jean-Luc Godard's asynchronous use of music in many of his films). Then when Natasha shouts out to those at the grave site, "Go to hell, everybody," we suddenly have a haunting silent montage of the faces of those present.

This lonely woman is not searching for a life companion, however. Muratova does not take us beyond the state of her "syndrome," her moment of crisis, to let us see if she evolves into a new woman or a more independent self without her husband. What Muratova does stunningly capture is the pain and confusion of Natasha's crisis. She confronts men in the metro with a string of profanity (this and the male nudity caused censorship problems for the film); she knocks men down in the street; she drags a drunk off the street and orders him to strip in her apartment before becoming hysterical and tossing him out. She is a medical doctor, but she turns down sick neighbors who need help. As a doctor and as a woman, in fact, she seems unable to get hold of her own life. Without doubt, however, Muratova has captured in the portrayal of Natasha a searing image of the complete Soviet woman—wife and career woman—coming undone.

Despite such a seriousness of purpose, Muratova is not without a dry sense of humor. Halfway through the narrative, we learn that the film of Natasha is actually a black-and-white film being projected in a theater. As the audience in the film streams out of the theater, a cultural official tries to lead a group discussion about the film, claiming "it is a rare opportunity to talk about film seriously. You know, about Kira Muratova and Alexei Gherman and others." No one appears to hear or care. They are gone.

The masses leaving the theater become the masses in the metro who discover Nikolai asleep on the subway, and the second narrative strand, filmed in color, begins. What ultimately joins these two major divisions of the film is neither Natasha nor Nikolai, but the "collective hero." The film appears balanced between moments featuring our protagonists, on the one hand, and those favoring "the group" or individuals scattered throughout the film, on the other. In a strangely appropriate way, perhaps Muratova has taken us back to Eisenstein's effort to create a "mass" protagonist. *Strike* (*Stachka*, 1924) features the Soviet masses rising up in protest against a corrupt bureaucracy and government. *The Weakness Syndrome* finally goes beyond questions of male and female to the level of us against them. It is the masses, confused, angry, and . . . sleeping, against the system.

One can argue that, like many glasnost efforts, this director's film is overdone. A drawn-out scene of dogs waiting to be exterminated, for instance, feels self-indulgent, and a schoolroom scene in which a teacher asks students how to spell the word *future* may go on too long. But un-like the self-reflexive humor of the audience storming out of the art film within the film, Muratova's film does invite discussion, pondering, questioning. For while we have here a clear portrait of the crisis of con-temporary Soviet women, Muratova wants us finally, through her explo-ration of film language, to realize about the present that, as one character says, "Nobody likes to look at it, to think about it."

BEYOND A WEAKNESS SYNDROME: *COMA*

Muratova has been deepening her established art in recent years. We now turn to a young woman beginning her career under perestroika. Nijole Adomenaite, born in Lithuania in 1958, completed her theater production degree at the Leningrad State Institute for Theater, Music, and Cinema in 1987. Her first feature is *Coma (Koma,* 1989), which she researched and coscripted with Yuri Makusinsky (in collaboration with Mikhail Konovalchuk), and codirected with her husband, Boris Gorlov.

The particular sixty-two-minute film grew from Adomenaite's memories of her father's imprisonment in 1952 for a twenty-five-year term, of which he served four years (Horton, interviews, Moscow, July 1989, and New Or-leans, October 1989). Adomenaite comments that knowing that a parent served in a camp "definitely makes me feel different from others." In-stead of focusing on her father's experience, however, Adomenaite chose a subject never before covered in Soviet cinema: women's prison camps. Researching thousands of women's cases and interviewing hundreds of survivors, Adomenaite fashioned a lean script that follows the fate of one woman in 1950, Maria.

The particular accomplishment of Adomenaite and Gorlov is to cap-ture the camp experience from a female perspective, managing to avoid the expected melodrama of the prison camp genre. Certainly the harsh realities of camp life call for an emotional response; Adomenaite has gone further and included the first lesbian love scene in Soviet cinema and the first scene of a woman performing oral sex on a man (the camp commander). Neither event, however, is exploited for its sensational-ism. The lesbian scene is presented as a playful romp in the women's barracks as other women sing, sew, and carry on everyday activities. The lovemaking is viewed as nothing out of the ordinary.

The same may be said for Adomenaite's presentation of oral sex. The act takes place outside, in the snow, at night, in a long shot, as the fully clothed officer has his back to the camera and as we hear the sounds of men shouting in the distance and of a women's folk chorus on a radio. What Adomenaite and Gorlov suggest is the absolute lack of passion in such acts of violence forced on the female prisoners.

By making a film about women's camps, Adomenaite begins to fill in yet another blank page in Soviet (film) history, thus adding more women's history to the general Soviet cultural dialogue. Here the attraction of the film is our desire to know how similar and yet how different women's experiences were (and are) in camps. Many of the women, for instance, were serving time not for anything they themselves did, but simply because they happened to be married to men who were condemned. Certainly the level of sexual harassment aimed at the women differed from men's experiences in camps run by men.

The protagonist is sensitively pictured. She is caught in a no-win situation. At the beginning of the film we learn that she and a prison guard have been living almost as man and wife. She has given birth to a baby as a result of this liaison. In one painful scene, we see her reduced to tears as she tries in vain to breast-feed her child in the brief minutes allowed by the prison hospital before handing the child back through the nursery window. But she must also spend time in the women's barracks, where she is hated for her special treatment. Furthermore, she becomes the object of the commanding officer's desire, and thus is forced to participate in the arrest of her lover and guard. Caught among these conflicting forces, she is finally thrown out of the barracks one night by the other women and left, we assume, to freeze to death in the winter of the northern Russian tundra.

The complexity of this portrait alone makes Coma one of the most important recent Soviet films made by women. But Adomenaite's form of presentation goes even further. Instead of offering the usual personal melodrama of the heroine, the filmmakers opt to present the camp and its workings and environment as a whole for more than ten minutes right at the beginning. Only then, when we have begun to be disoriented, numbed, bored, or overstimulated (the overdetermined sound track assures us that camp life allows for no restful stretches of silence), do we enter Maria's world. Even more than in Muratova's Twist of Fate, we are allowed no easy access to Maria's life. (She is portrayed by an interesting but not beautiful actress, Natalia Nikulenko, which helps us experience the narrative in ways beyond the accepted star system.) We sense how much the camp environment is the overriding influence in her life. Her "death" scene (we assume she dies but do not see her actual death), for instance, is filmed in long shot in almost complete darkness, so we are not given the immediate emotional impact of a close-up. She is alone in the cold night, crying. Such a distance leaves us free to identify more broadly with her condition than with her personality.

As in other Soviet films made by women, the thrust of the narrative in Coma emerges not as feminist but as humanist, seen through a woman's eyes. Like Irina Ratushinskaya's prison autobiography, Grey Is the Color of Hope, Adomainate's film is of immediate interest because of the subject matter itself. But what remains especially significant in *Coma* is the manner of narration. Although it is not consciously feminist, it nevertheless derails the norms of Soviet (male) narrative, which, like classical Hollywood narrative, has tended to focus on the Aristotelian concepts of character and plot. For many of the reasons detailed here, *Coma* received favorable attention at a variety of international festivals in 1989 and 1990, including those at Venice and Berlin, the Los Angles Women in Film Festival, the New Orleans Film Festival, and the Montreal Festival of New Cinema.

WOMEN AND THE NEW DOCUMENTARY

Women have begun to make a larger contribution to the documentary field. Marina Goldovskaya stands out as the most prominent woman documentary filmmaker. The creator of the much-praised and widely viewed *Solovki Regime*, a chilling documentary about Stalin's first concentration camps for political prisoners, Goldovskaya has entered the ranks of those filmmakers who have promoted a national dialogue on the past through the medium of documentary. A 1963 graduate of the National State Institute of Cinema (VGIK), her first film focused on a woman, *Raisa Nemtchinskaya, Actress of the Circus (Raisa Nemtchinskaya, actrisa tsirka,* 1970), followed by a work on the first woman astronaut, Valentina Tereshkova. Her wide range of interests is also reflected in her 1987 film about a Soviet Jewish Musical Chamber Theater tour of the United States, *Let There Be Theater! (Tumbalalaika)*. Besides making films, Goldovskaya is also a film scholar of note at the Film Art Institute in Moscow. None of these previous works, however, suggests the scope, depth, and power that *Solovki Regime* was to have. Goldovskaya's film has become one of the most highly regarded documentaries of the glasnost period.

THROUGH A GLASNOST DARKLY: IMAGES OF
WOMEN IN SOVIET FILMS

We live in constant bullshit. We think one thing and we do another.
—TANYA in *Intergirl*

How have women been represented on the Soviet screen under perestroika? Judith Mayne remarks in her study *Kino and the Woman Question: Feminism and Soviet Silent Film*, "A representation of woman is not the same thing as a position for women" (5). Her study of "woman" in Soviet silent films comes up with a largely negative view of how the Revolution and the young (male) filmmakers such as Eisenstein and Vertov presented "woman" on the screen. "Too often ambiguity and play rely on the position of woman defined in a decidedly unradical way," Mayne notes (188).

Women as represented in sound film, a period that began with Stalin's rise, fared little better. It is difficult to find a film, even among those made under Khrushchev's "thaw," that portrays women in more than traditional roles. Think, for instance, of Grigori Chukhrai's *Ballad of a Soldier* (*Ballada o soldate*, 1959). The young soldier's brief odyssey is a homecoming from the front to his mother before returning to battle, where we discover he will die. The final scene is a poignant one—a reunion of mother and son. But the mother is given no personality, no function beyond that of being "Mama." (Mayne, in her examination of Pudovkin's *Mother*, demonstrates that this "revolutionary" film only portrays the mother's evolution away from her husband to an embracing of her son's cause, a "substitution of one traditional gender role for another" [189]). Even the young woman the soldier meets and falls in love with on the train is traditional. In fact, in the initial scene when the soldier approaches her, she raises her hand in fear and utters "Mama." While the film beautifully captures the transitory sense of young love during wartime, there is nothing in the depiction of the young woman or the romance that is beyond the scope of traditional depictions of screen courtship, whether Soviet or Hollywood.

BETWEEN JOY AND SUICIDE:
FATHERS, DAUGHTERS, AND *LITTLE VERA*

Glasnost has, however, begun to change the representation of women on the screen, as we have begun to explore in the films of Muratova and Adomenaite. Certainly Vasily Pichul's *Little Vera* is an important contribution to this small but growing list.

Little Vera (1988) had fifty million Soviet viewers during its first year and an enthusiastic following abroad wherever it was shown. In the United States, it was the most successful Soviet film since *Moscow Does Not Believe in Tears*. On the most immediate level, the film can be seen as a clear example of glasnost. But it is much more: one of the most popular films of the first five years of perestroika is about a young provincial Soviet *woman*.

While not a feminist film per se, this work, set in a drab Ukrainian industrial town, was written by a woman, Pichul's wife, Maria Khmelik, and centers on Vera (Natalia Negoda), an eighteen-year-old Russian woman whose disjointed emotional life suggests significant questions of gender as well as of glasnost. The raw edges of *Little Vera*'s narrative are those of an Oedipal and patriarchal system (political, economic, cultural) of signification and representation that are showing serious signs of disruption and change.

Three early shots set the tone and direction for the rest of the film. The establishing shot is of a bleak industrial town on the banks of a large body of water before dawn. The second is a morning scene on the balcony of a cheaply built apartment house, as Vera is told in a brusque and unsympathetic manner by her mother, "Make something of your life . . . as your brother has done." Shortly thereafter, again on the balcony, Vera's working-class father quietly tells her, in a comforting voice, "Cherish your youth" (a paraphrase of a famous line by Pushkin).

Little Vera is striking, in part, for its many firsts. As a low-budget Soviet feature, it is a debut film by a young husband-and-wife team, the first Soviet film with a sense of sexual candor (the actress Natalia Negoda gained instant celebrity status in the United States for her May 1989 cover appearance in *Playboy*), the first mention of AIDS in a Soviet feature film (a passing joke about government warning pamphlets), and the first direct suggestion of nonwhite children as the offspring of white mothers.

Our focus here, however, is on the strength of the film as a refreshingly straightforward portrait of a contemporary provincial young woman and her relationships. In particular, it is her close ties to her father that hold a special interest. But it is also important to view the film in relation to the changes being wrought under glasnost since filmmakers began to replace bureaucrats in the hierarchy of the Soviet film industry in 1985. From this perspective, Pichul's film is notable on at least four counts: it is made by a director who came from the working-class provincial background he treats on the screen (he is of Russian origin from Zhdanov, a Ukrainian industrial town on the Sea of Azov); it dares to show rough edges in terms of cinematic style—a direct alternative to the long tradition of "well-made" Soviet films, including even the auteuristic and lyrical works of Tarkovsky, the folk-mythic surrealism of Paradjanov, the sense of robust humor of Georgian comedies and satire (Otar Ioseliani's *Falling Leaves* [*Listopad*, 1967] and Irakli Kvirikadze's *Swimmer* [*Plovets*, 1982]), or the imaginative mixed-media films (drama and documentary) of someone like the president of the Filmmakers' Union from 1986 to 1988, Elem Klimov; and it is an important contribution to a growing number of films that honestly capture the "no-win" mood of many Soviet youth today, as opposed to the forced optimism of so many socialist-realist films of the past.

Maria Khmelik's script found no sympathetic producer for four years, or in other words until glasnost had come into being. She wrote it in

1983 after visiting her husband's native town and family, and it captures Vera's marginal, "on-edge" existence. The film chronicles a few brief weeks in Vera's life. The driving force of the narrative is her romance with an engineering student, Sergei—a Dionysian free spirit. We observe their engagement, separation, and eventual reunion, tentative though it may be, on the evening that Vera verges on suicide.

Khmelik depicts a life without spiritual or even passionate materialistic values, a life in a vacuum, affected by the vestiges of stagnation and decay. Vera is at the same time empty and cramped. She is cramped by the drabness of her town and her job (she is a switchboard operator), by the lack of physical and psychological space in her family's apartment, and by her general absence of alternatives to the roles that appear laid out for her. And she appears to have no clue as to how to break out of her environment. Her name, of course, is emblematic. "Vera" means "faith"; thus "little Vera" reflects her age and position and her lack of hope or, conversely, the glimmer of hope that may exist. Both readings make sense given Pichul and Khmelik's diegesis.

Vera is on the edge of perceiving how her life is predominantly defined by the men who surround her. There is her successful doctor brother, Victor, who has managed to move to Moscow. Andrei is the ineffectual young man, "calm and polite," who pursues her like a puppy dog and who thus offers her a traditional romance, marriage, and social status, which she rejects. More important, however, Vera exists between the sympathetic acceptance of her quietly desperate alcoholic father and the antisocial freedom represented by Sergei and their tempestuous affair. Neither wholly modern (despite her streaked hair and mod clothes) nor traditional (despite time spent helping her mother cook and clean), Vera is caught squarely in the middle with little hope of escape, an accurate portrait, according to many Soviets, of a young woman from a blue-collar family today.

Little Vera does, however, chart this young Soviet woman's movement away from her father and toward her fiancé. While much of feminist theory details the importance of the mother-daughter relationship in its reevaluation of Freudian psychology (the Demeter-Persephone pattern, as Carol Gilligan and others note), little work has updated Freud's brief exploration of the Electra complex (a daughter's adoration of her father). While there is much in literature and film about daughters under the spell and shadow of domineering or impressive "successful" fathers, there has been relatively scant attention given to the possibility of nurturing relationships between an "unsuccessful" and basically nondomineering father figure and daughter. *Little Vera* explores this terrain. (While there are a few scenes in which mother and daughter share their troubles, the mother is portrayed as more distant and hostile than the father and thus as less of an influence on Vera.)

From the beginning, Vera's life is overdetermined: there is literally and psychologically no space or time she can call her own. Because of the distance between her mother and her father, Vera chooses to play wife and mother to her father. Thus while the father realizes Vera should "cherish her youth," Vera is, in fact, the one who takes his complaints about his heart trouble seriously and who then undresses him and tucks him in bed in a clearly mixed mother/wife/daughter role early in the film.

The developing conflict of values within Vera comes to a crisis once Sergei is officially her fiancé. At a birthday party for her father, confusion reaches a climax. Pichul and Khmelik effectively structure Vera's dilemma. Almost every scene starts on a seemingly congenial note and then proceeds to break down; the birthday party is no exception. Vera is caught in the middle once more as the two main people in her life suddenly quarrel and come to blows. Sergei, who operates on spontaneous passion with no apparent respect for anyone, beats up Vera's father and tosses him into the bathroom, locking him in. The scene ends as the father frees himself and stabs Sergei, sending him to the hospital in critical condition.

Afterward, as Vera attempts to cope with her divided feelings, the family plans a picnic by the sea. That moment dissolves into bitter antagonism as her mother shouts at Vera, "I never wanted to have you anyway." She goes on to say that she only kept Vera in order to get a larger apartment. Denied maternal friendship and support, Vera retreats to the edge of the sea in a rainstorm, only to be followed by her father. He holds her gently and quietly says, "My little daughter." Pichul holds the moment long enough for us to feel their mutual understanding and shared loneliness. He manages to do so without pushing the scene into traditional melodramatic forms (the absence of underscoring music alone is one example).

Vera is unable to negotiate her emotional and psychological life between her father and Sergei. If her father had been a traditional Russian patriarch, the separation would have been easier. But though Vera herself never verbalizes her anxieties, we sense she glimpses the limiting realities of life with either man and, as presented in the film, has not yet reached a level of consciousness in which she would consider life alone. Consider how such a dilemma contrasts with the strong ending of Abram Room's *Bed and Sofa* (*Tret'ya Meshchanskaya*, 1927, coscripted by theoretician Viktor Shklovsky), in which the young heroine, caught between life with her husband and with her lover, walks out on both, claiming "Neither of you is worthy to be the father of my child."

Unlike Room's heroine, Vera finally cannot face the tough decisions she must make and so tries to kill herself. In a terrifying depression involving booze and pills, she clasps a childhood photograph of herself to her chest. Her brother and Sergei (who has escaped from the hospital) reach Vera before she loses consciousness, and soon thereafter she and Sergei are shown together again in Vera's bed, exhausted, frightened, quiet. "Do you love me?" she asks Sergei, as she has throughout their relationship. "I was afraid," he replies. They are not yet married, and they have no apartment to go to, no careers unrolling before them. Vera still has little faith in her own identity. However, they are together . . . alone.

A little hope.

But the film closes with two final images: the father keeling over in the kitchen, followed by another long shot of the small city similar to the opening image. The mother has no role in this resolution. Whether her father is dead or having another heart attack, it is clear that Vera has already begun the difficult task of growing up and leaving her childhood behind. As comforting as her father's affection has been, it was not enough, could never be enough. Pichul ends as he began, with another dawn shot. Hope or life repeating itself? We, the spectators who have lived vicariously through her experiences, and Vera are free to decide.

In the spaces created by such "unfinalizedness" (to use Bakhtin's term), the Sphinx has a chance to set an alternative agenda in the Oedipus tale without the need for suicide and self-sacrifice.

The British phase of neorealism in cinema in the late fifties and early sixties was characterized as "kitchen-sink" realism; *Little Vera* would have to be dubbed "kitchen-table" cinema, a "novy realism." Pichul's unflinching camera grounds Vera in a literally cramped familial environment (the apartment), centered further on the kitchen table and the different functions it serves for the family—work, meals, and conversation. Even the finely etched scene between Vera and her girlfriend at her apartment is set around the kitchen table as Lena, her friend and the mother of the half-black child, announces she is content to settle for a relationship with a boring but well-meaning middle-aged man because he is "calm and polite." In the same scene, shortly before what is to be Vera's wedding, Vera, who has been on edge throughout the film, suddenly breaks into tears: "It's the happiest time of my life, but I want to cry all the time."

We sense here not only the general confusion of the times in the Soviet Union, but that of women in particular. Vera's line sends us back to Tamara Alexandrovna's cry in Olga Narutskaya's film, "Wherever will I begin?" But the cries are coming from two different ends of the female spectrum. Vera's cry is from a young woman on the brink of living her life for herself. The middle-aged woman in *The Husband and Daughter of Tamara Alexandrovna* cries out, having tasted the pleasure and pain of motherhood and married life and found herself unable to cope (her first words to anyone else are to scream at her daughter, "Don't shout!").

Seen as companion pieces, the stories of these two women present a troubled view of Soviet women indeed. As noted, Tamara Alexandrovna simply disappears from the text, offscreen, hospitalized and thus institutionalized where she will not have to cope with her conflicting roles. Furthermore, consider how different is the lot of women portrayed in contemporary Soviet film from the images of women dominating the American screens of the same period. *Little Vera* offers none of the upbeat, feisty range of possibilities suggested, for instance, by Melanie Griffith's performances in *Something Wild* or *Working Girl*, both of which, despite contemporary touches, uphold the classical American film emphasis on happy (optimistic) endings. Such American films—and one can add those made by American women directors, such as Susan Seidelman's *Desperately Seeking Susan* (1984, written by a woman, Leora Barish)—place a premium on winning. This is not to say, however, that most American women do in fact win, but simply that the representation of women onscreen belongs to the American tradition of the protagonist Coming Out on Top. Ironically, a Soviet film that won an Oscar, Vladimir Men'shov's *Moscow Does Not Believe in Tears*, in following the spunky rise of the provincial young woman Katya to fame and fortune (thus presenting a positive heroine) was meant to be imitative of American models, according to the scriptwriter Valentin Chernykh (Horton, interview, Moscow, October 1989).

There is one positive note, however, in the extended scene with Vera's girlfriend. Maria Khmelik has written an honest scene about the importance of girlfriends, of women trusting and supporting each other. The scene exists as something of a female oasis in a male world. In what becomes one of the genuinely comic and touching moments of the film, Vera learns from Lena one way to express her frustration: a kind of Zen primal scream that involves rising on one's toes, shouting, and collapsing to the floor. We laugh when Lena demonstrates. We are moved when Vera, drunk on vodka (and thus indirectly communicating with her father by sharing his sickness), rises unsteadily to her toes, screams, and falls. Nothing has been solved, but, as written by Khmelik, much has been shared between women. The scene reaches a level of honesty beyond the new American subgenre, the "female buddy film," as practiced, for instance, by Bette Midler (*Outrageous Fortune, Big Business, Beaches*).

Such a scene—and the film is chock full of revealing "everyday" moments—suggests how far contemporary Soviet cinema has shifted from the false enthusiasms and wooden idealism of socialist realism in its most rigid forms. There is an engaging offhandedness about many of the sequences that suggests a blend of improvisation and keen writing paired at a conceptual level. Such a disjointed approach to narrative reflects Vera's youth and her perspective as a woman who is unhappy with her lot, but not yet articulate enough to determine her own destiny.

Some of the images, lines, and contexts may be striking but not completely intelligible to a non-Soviet audience. In a beach scene, for instance, restless youths tattoo large images of St. Basil's Cathedral on their backs. A sign of protest, or of religious belief, or of some kind of joke? Perhaps a blend of all three. On the beach, Sergei asks Vera, "What is our common goal?" and she replies "Communism" in a voice tinged with irony, with parody, but also, we sense, with the leftover response of years of conditioning that has lost all meaning. "The challenge today," Pichul explained during his first visit with his wife out of the Soviet Union, "is to find some spiritual values in this life."

Pichul is more modest than some Soviet critics, who have already dubbed *Little Vera* "the first honest Soviet film." To the then-twenty-eight-year-old director, "What's great is that we actually made it," he explained in Montreal where the film was awarded Best First Feature (Horton, interview, Montreal, August 1988). It also received Best Film at the 1988 Chicago Festival. Thus his answer to those who felt the overall impression of the film was one of a crushing hopelessness was revealing: "The film is an attempt to come close to the abyss of our life today. Actually our real life is even darker, and yet I remain an optimist. Making a film is an exercise in hope"—a fitting remark for a film about a woman named Little Faith.

Pichul's sense of hope has most immediately been transferred into the establishment of his own independent film production company (a cooperative), Podarok (Gift), one of the first examples of independent filmmaking in the Soviet Union. It is through this company that he managed to coproduce his second feature, *Dark Nights in Sochi*, once again written by his wife and starring Natalia Negoda. While such possibilities for individual production are encouraging, *Dark Nights in Sochi* nevertheless emerged as a disappointing second feature in almost every aspect.

A complex contemporary ensemble film that traces the fate of a variety of characters in the seaside resort of Sochi (Stalin's favorite retreat), this film creates a role for Natalia Negoda as a young free spirit that does little to reveal an image of women beyond that of being the not-so-secret objects of sexual desire. The icy reception of the film at its Soviet premiere in Moscow in early November 1989 at Dom Kino was further testimony that the creators of the vital and original *Little Vera* had lost their focus and drive in this second feature, which clearly aimed to be more commercial.

A final note should be devoted to Natalia Negoda. Her performance made her the "best actress of the year," according to a readers' survey vote in the USSR's leading film magazine, *Sovetskii ekran* (*Soviet Screen*), and at a festival of debuts in Brussels. Clearly the image that twenty-five-year-old Negoda projects has connected and met the approval of millions of Soviets. Her blend of troubled youth, native intelligence, sensitivity, vulnerability, strength, and lack of fear in expressing her sexual desire clearly signals a new image of young Soviet women.

But not everyone in the Soviet audience felt comfortable with the film. Cinema critic Nina Agisheva warns about a new sense of intolerance emerging under glasnost that may become a poison to social and political reform. In the search for scapegoats for social ills, she notes, some have even gone so far as to "blame *Little Vera* for a 10th grader's unwanted pregnancy" ("Intolerance Again?" 3). Natalia Negoda has commented that she has received a lot of hate mail from men and women, including one letter from an irate man who claimed he hated the film so much he had seen it eight times (Barringer, "Glasnost in Wide Screen"; see also Span, "Bare Facts about Glasnost").

HARD CURRENCY, SOFT PORN, MAMA, AND *INTERGIRL*

Little Vera suggests an accurate representation of a young Soviet woman caught up in the confusion of the times. Another box-office hit made a year later, *Intergirl* (*Interdevochka*, 1989), is indicative of a much more confused approach to representing images of Soviet women today.

A Swedish-Soviet coproduction written by Vladimir Kunin and directed by Pyotr Todorovsky, who also directed *The Wartime Romance* (*Voenno-polevoi roman*, 1984), *Intergirl* embraces a number of timely issues for Soviets: hard-currency prostitution, marriage with foreigners, and the good life in Western Europe. Instead of a hard-hitting portrait of a contemporary prostitute, however, as seen in Alan Pakula's *Klute*, *Intergirl* is of interest because of its narrative confusion in general and its contradictory representation of Soviet women in particular.

In fact, one can separate out at least five films or narratives within this one work about a Leningrad prostitute who marries a Swede and moves to Sweden, only to discover she is bored by materialism and misses her mother and her home, Mother Russia. The opening sequence suggests a light sex farce in the Italian or French tradition, yet the comedy soon breaks down. Other scenes suggest that the film is working hard to be the first Soviet soft-porn film, but, whether due to self-censorship or studio control, the filmmakers never present any real nudity or images of lovemaking beyond shots of the prostitute's troubled face. There is also the possibility of romantic comedy in the Hollywood mode, as Tanya and Eddie, her bald, stocky husband, appear as a mismatched couple that might make a true relationship through wit and love. Yet here again, there is no real romance (clearly Tanya is using Eddie to escape the USSR) and no wit. Next, we have many of the elements of a family melodrama centered on a poor, struggling mother whose daughter becomes a prostitute and leaves; the young girl next door is later in danger of repeating this pattern. But this direction is not followed through with any detail that would add up to something like a Soviet *Terms of Endearment*. A fifth possibility is for a picaresque road movie involving Tanya's movement from Leningrad to Sweden and her brief relationship with a handsome, good Soviet truck driver, followed by her death in a car crash at the end. But we do not have enough of the road to follow through in this genre either.

It would be easy to dismiss this film as a cheap attempt to cash in on some scandalous contemporary themes. During the 1989 IREX conference in Moscow, the Soviet critics and scholars wished, at first, to do just that. Yet the film is important, we believe, as an example of what happens when perestroika leads to commercial cinema for filmmakers used to making "directors' films." Furthermore, the confused or even schizophrenic depiction of women necessarily follows from the confused narrative strategies presented.

Tanya (Yelena Yakovleva) is an updated version of the whore with a heart of gold. If an individual character is the sum of the discourses with which he or she comes in contact, as Bakhtin suggests, then Tanya is a polyphony of contradictions with no center. She is the good-bad girl who works as a nurse (good) by day and a whore (bad) by night. She is attracted to life in the fast lane, which includes pop fashion and material goods, and yet she is repelled by it as well. She wants to leave the confusion of Soviet life today, and yet is unhappy abroad, away from her roots. Her death (implied, not stated; we see a freeze-frame of her agonized face as we hear the sound of a crash) is the inevitable conclusion to such inconclusive "voices." Teresa de Lauretis has built on Laura Mulvey's remark that "sadism demands a story" to explore how often the death of a woman is demanded as the price for desire in Western narrative (*Alice Doesn't*, chapter 5).

It is possible to rewrite such traditional narratives by having the woman take charge of her own existence, sort out the various contradictions in her life, accept them, and reorient them toward a higher self-awareness and ability to act in society, as seen in a film such as *Desperately Seeking Susan*. *Intergirl* hesitates between seeing woman as object (of desire) and subject (of her own desire), and thus ends by presenting woman as victim in a way *Little Vera* avoids; Vera's attempted suicide leads to the need for her to come to grips with life as it is and live her own life. Certainly Tanya's line "We live in constant bullshit. We think one thing and we do another" is central to an understanding of the film and of Kunin's and Todorovsky's representation of Tanya. But, the male filmmakers suggest, no resolution of this contradiction appears possible except through Tanya's convenient death.

If we read the film against the grain of the surface narrative structures, *Intergirl* does, however, reveal some extremely important images of Soviet women as represented during this turbulent period. A deeper contradiction in the film is between the contemporary surface and gloss of the film and the underlying conservatism of much Soviet behavior. As an object of desire, Tanya is never presented fully nude, or in provocative poses, nor is she allowed to show true passion in any of her couplings during the film. In fact, the only time anything approaching tenderness and affection is represented is in a scene involving Tanya and her hooker friends. Tanya has become so drunk at one point that several of her prostitute comrades come to her assistance. Her limp, pale body is treated with compassion by the other women, who are concerned about her state. This rare moment among women in the film opens a space in the otherwise heterosexual emotional wasteland presented.

In familial terms, a complicated drama is carried out as Tanya's father turns out to be a black-market con man who blackmails his own daughter. In order to marry her Swedish friend, we learn, Tanya is forced back into prostitution to pay off her father. A deeply ambivalent view of men comes out in other scenes too. During a drunken party in Sweden, one of her husband's friends attempts to rape Tanya in her bedroom. Much to our surprise, she clubs the fellow, pushes him down the staircase, and holds a shotgun on him, on the verge of killing him. She does not pull the trigger. But this moment, coupled with the tenderness of the scene with the other women, definitely points to the beginnings of a new awareness of male-female relationships and power alignments.

The traditional ideology of the film, however, leads Tanya back toward Russia and her mother. Her final drive is accompanied by a highly nostalgic Russian folk ballad heard earlier when she was departing the Soviet Union:

> By Lake Baikal a vagabond is traveling
> With his knapsack on his back.
> He sings this sad song.
> The vagabond crosses the lake
> And sees his dear mother.

Tanya's death comes as she tries to leave all that is modern and contemporary and materialistic and democratic in Western Europe and return to her roots, her mother, and her mother's sufferings within her traditional world, which are exacerbated by the confusion of modern life. Is the film an exploitation of the current muddle of values or an accurate representation of the times? Perhaps both. If so, between *Little Vera* and *Intergirl*, Soviet filmmakers do not offer much hope for the young Soviet woman during this period of social and political flux, when patriarchy is perhaps crumbling but still in power, and the power of women is untried and unsure.

SEXUALITY AND SOVIET CINEMA: FROM OBJECT
TO SUBJECT OF DESIRE

Filmmaker Alexander Sokurov deliberately avoids a contemporary narrative in order to examine sensuality and women. In *Save and Protect*, he recasts Flaubert's *Madame Bovary* with a French-Greek actress, Cecile Zervoudaki, in a landscape that is purposely meant to be "non-European" (Horton, interview, Montreal, September 1989).

If *Little Vera* supposedly contains the first Soviet sex on film and *Intergirl* the first full treatment of prostitution on the feature screen, Sokurov's *Save and Protect*, completed less than two years after *Little Vera*, suggests how far Soviet cinema has come under perestroika in permitting an exploration of sensuality and sexuality in women in narrative film.

There are clear signs that such a permissive atmosphere means that sex scenes will become increasingly obligatory and gratuitous in many Soviet films; *The King of Crime* is one example of this pop Soviet trend. But Sokurov's film is unusual in its complex portrayal of a woman's conflict between sensuality and responsibility. Flaubert's accomplishment was to allow us access to Bovary's mind as she thought about her experiences, desires, and conflicts. Sokurov's talent is for the extended visual experience of observing, and coming to feel on a quite tactile level, Bovary's passions; one senses the heat, humidity, and physicality of many scenes, especially through the carefully constructed sound track, with its constant buzzing of flies.

The limited visual vocabulary in world cinema for representing sexuality has often been noted. Much of the filming of sex has more closely resembled rape than the physical coupling of two human beings attracted to each other. (It is an alarming trend in Soviet youth films that almost every one includes a rape scene.) Sokurov's film broadens the lexicon on this subject, both because he focuses on passion from a woman's perspective and because he downplays "plot," as he does in all his films, in order to explore the moment. In *Save and Protect*, Sokurov's camera captures not only the heat of passionate sex, but also the quiet moments before and after sex, the tender physicality that does not necessarily lead to sex, and the sensuousness of the body that is not always associated with male-female coupling. There is, for instance, a simple, joyful moment when Cecile Zervoudaki walks nude, holding her young daughter, who is also naked. The sensuous pleasure of the mother-daughter moment carries no trace of sexuality. But it speaks pages about yet another dimension of a woman's experience with and through her body.

As in Muratova's *Twist of Fate* and Adomenaite's *Coma*, Sokurov's casting of Zervoudaki as Bovary is a choice that cuts against the expectations of popular cinema. Rather than selecting a starlet with a pinup's body, Sokurov has opted for the far more intriguing and realistic exploration of a woman who is not a beauty but whose attractiveness is one of character as much as it is of the flesh. *Save and Protect* seems, therefore, a hopeful example of how male Soviet filmmakers can portray a broader range of women's experiences without exploiting them as mere objects of male fantasy. (Leida Laius's *Games for Schoolchildren* [*Igry dlya detei shkol'nogo vozrasta*, 1985] is another example of a sensitive portrayal of women.) But Sokurov's film is available only on video; it has yet to find a Soviet theatrical release. With *Save and Protect* we sense that Soviet women are being represented as subjects of desire rather than as victims or objects.

ALMOST LIBERATED:
A LONELY WOMAN LOOKS FOR A LIFE COMPANION

Soviet women, on film and in cinema, have come a long way in recent years, especially under glasnost. Yet by their own admission and according to the cultural and political statistics we have presented, they are increasingly aware of the distance they must still travel if they are to be accepted and perceived as true equals of men. It is not a hopeful sign that so many contemporary films, including *Coma*, *Little Vera*, and *Save and Protect*, end in the female protagonist's death or attempted suicide.

Sokurov's *Save and Protect*, for instance, ends with a roughly twenty-minute sequence devoted to Bovary's funeral. On one level, of course, he is, as he has explained in interviews, exploring the tension between the material and the spiritual realm. The absence of physicality and sensuality after so many scenes of it before highlights the past and at the same time provides a calming distance from passion. Also, the richness of the Orthodox chanting and music as we watch, in a long shot (after so many medium close-ups), the procession to the cemetery, leads us to contemplate eternity. Though Sokurov is not in any sense didactic, the film evokes a fuller range of responses beyond this simple dialectic. We clearly sense how incompatible Bovary's desires are with the practices of the society into which she has been born. Will this always be the fate of women? Is it only a nineteenth-century vision? Does it apply to Soviet contemporary women as well? Sokurov leaves it for us to determine.

Perhaps one of the most fitting titles for a film representing an image of Soviet women today is the early glasnost film *A Lonely Woman Looks for a Life Companion* (*Odinokaya zhenschina zhelaet paznakomitsya*, 1987). Vyacheslav Krishtofovich's film stars Irina Koupchenko as a beautiful, bright, single designer with a stylish apartment in Kiev (which is also the location where the film was shot, and Krishtofovich's home). Of all the films discussed so far, this one comes closest to representing a contemporary middle-aged Soviet woman in the emerging Soviet middle class. Without resorting to the extremes of melodrama or genre, Krishtofovich's patient camera and pacing allow us to observe a woman under the influence of loneliness in a culture that appears to award women who have careers with an empty success.

In many ways the film would remind Western audiences of Paul Mazursky's *Unmarried Woman*. The structure of the film resembles the American screwball-comedy tradition pushed to a contemporary level of uneasiness. Certainly the setup allows for much gentle as well as dark humor: a lovely woman out to get a companion by tacking up personal ads around town. Such a "screwball" is obviously setting herself up for trouble. Krishtofovich has fun presenting several losers who show up as suitors.

The screwball formula is further suggested by the male lead, who begins to take center stage even though he is the most unlikely candidate of all. As in the American tradition in which lovers of divergent socioeconomic backgrounds team up, the protagonist of *A Lonely Woman* settles for an amiable alcoholic dropout as her companion—a man who plays the holy fool to our heroine's screwball.

Part of what is refreshing and encouraging about this subtly realized production is that instead of pushing the representation of woman to the clichéd ending of death (*Intergirl*) or the desperate conclusion of attempted suicide (*Little Vera*), *A Lonely Woman* remains within the confines of loneliness rather than desperation, despair, or nonbeing. The protagonist is in control of her life; she makes choices. She has a career and enough money to be what to most Soviets would be almost an impossible dream: a woman alone with money and an apartment.

Such materialism is not enough, however. She does want to share her life, but she is not so desperate that she will compromise or destroy what she has made of herself. The ending resembles *An Unmarried Woman* in presenting the protagonist alone on the street, wiser from her affair, but, like Chaplin at the end of his films, continuing by herself. She spends much of her time with the alcoholic dropout feeling how mismatched they are as a couple. Yet she finds herself accepting him as well, and even falling into traditional domestic roles as she tries to darn his jacket (only to give up and toss it out).

When he disappears at last, she goes in search of him. In the final scene she sees a bum being led along by two policemen and, thinking it is her "companion," she calls out that he is her husband. When she sees the man up close, we realize it is merely another bum. She is alone in the dusk of another urban twilight.

The sophistication of the film is also reflected in its avoidance of an easy romantic comic ending, as in *Working Girl*, in which the woman wins all: career and her corporate mate in a Manhattan paradise of glass and steel. By resisting such narrative conveniences and by allowing many of the scenes to be played out quietly, often with only the protagonist alone in the frame with no music, and even sometimes with an empty frame to suggest her state by her absence, *A Lonely Woman* suggests an important middle ground for Soviet filmmakers in focusing on contemporary women during the glasnost period.

"Go to hell, everyone!" shouts Kira Muratova's troubled hero at her husband's funeral in *The Weakness Syndrome*. Natasha, however, is the one experiencing hell. Her cry is partially that of honest grief for a lost life companion. But it is also a cry of uncertainty, as Natasha realizes she must begin to redefine herself as subject (a woman responsible for her own life) rather than as traditional object (wife)—something the film demonstrates as sharply as any film made in the Soviet Union in the first five years of glasnost. A large part of what makes Muratova's film so important to the cinema of glasnost, especially to a cinema made by Soviet women, is its refusal to subscribe to a sense of closure. Such a state of "unfinalizedness" is hopeful for future Soviet films by and about women. Whether they admit to it or not, Soviet filmmakers are beginning to share a feminist viewpoint. As Laura Mulvey comments, "A feminist perspective should insist on the possibility of change without closure" (*Visual and Other Pleasures*, 175).

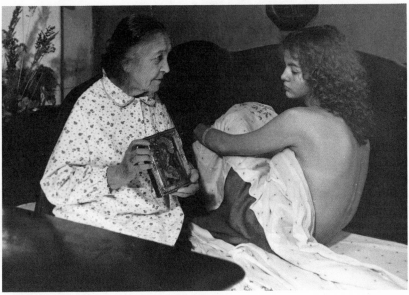

1. *Commissar* (*Komissar*, 1967). Mother or Commissar? Nonna Mordyukova (left) stars in Alexander Askoldov's rediscovered classic.

2. *Assuage My Sorrows* (*Utoli moya pechali*, 1989). The only thing con-
necting generations in this film is an old icon. Directed by Alexander Alexandrov and Vladimir Prokhorov.

3. *BOMZH* (1988). Vladimir Steklov is the father tracking his son. Directed by Nikolai Skuibin.

4. *The Name Day* (*Den' angela* [*Day of Angel*], 1988). Sergei Selyanov and Nikolai Makarov in their debut film, in which they experiment with the time and space of film as well as of the Soviet Union.

5. *A Mirror for a Hero* (*Zerkalo dlya geroya*, 1988). Waltzing around the gates to nowhere in Vladimir Khotinenko's fable in the *Back to the Future* vein.

6. *Assa* (1988). Rock star Victor Tsoy closes out Sergei Solovyev's "film-happening" with a rousing concert performance.

7. *Is It Easy to Be Young?* (*Legko li byt' molodym?* 1987). Afghan vets
smile through their pain in Juris Podnieks's ground-breaking popular documentary about troubled youth.

8. *Assa* (1988). Soviet postpunks fight crime using rock and roll as a weapon in Sergei Solovyev's postmodern film.

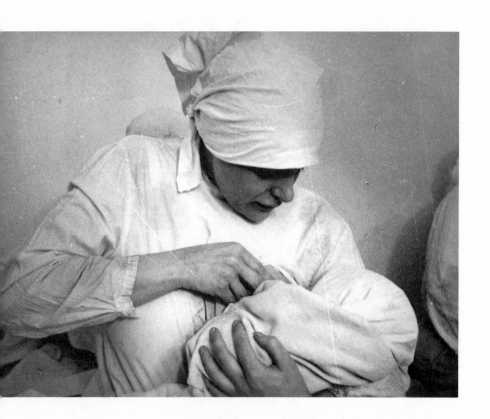

9. *Coma* (*Koma*, 1989). Motherhood in a Stalinist prison camp for women in the late 1940s. A debut film by Nijole Adomenaite and Boris Gorlov.

10. *Little Vera* (*Malen'kaya Vera*, 1988). On the beach with Little Vera as her boyfriend Sergei asks, "What do you belive in?" Vera answers, "Communism, of course." A typical ironic exchange in Vasily Pichul's hit debut film.

11. *Intergirl* (*Interdevochka*, 1989). Looking for a hard-currency customer: Elena Yakovleva stars as a hip hooker in Pyotr Todorovsky's film.

12. *Is Stalin with Us?* (*Stalin s nami?* 1989). Tofik Shakhverdiev's disturbing feature documentary about the still-popular Stalinist cult in the Soviet Union, here depicting some of the old newsreel footage used.

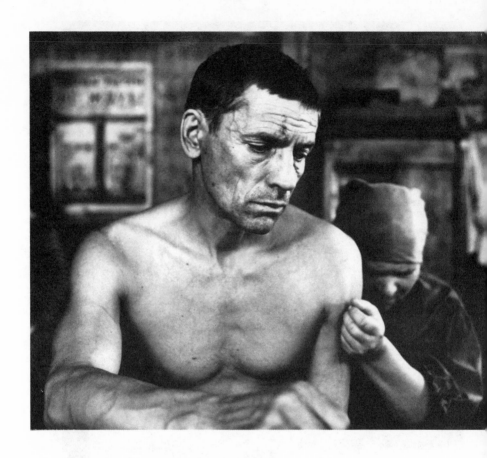

13. *The Cold Summer of '53* (*Holodnoye leto '53-go*, 1987). Valery Prie-mykhov in Alexander Proshkin's anti-Stalinist Western more closely re-sembles Henry Fonda in *My Darling Clementine* than a Soviet officer in forced exile.

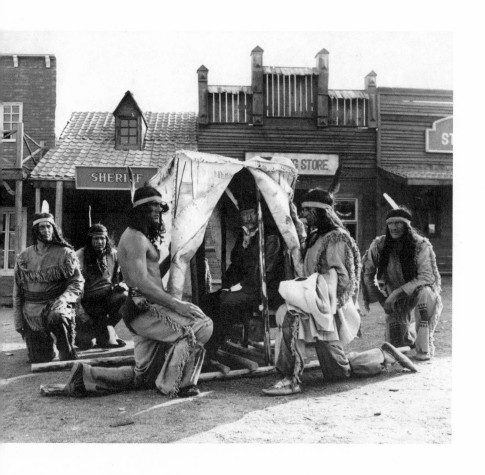

14. *The Man from Capuchins Boulevard* (*Chelovek s bul'vara Kaputsi-nov*, 1987). Glasnost, American Indian style. The late Soviet comic idol Andrei Mironov (center) stars in a Western-parody slapstick farce directed by Alla Surikova.

15. *Zerograd* (*Gorod zero*, 1989). Leonid Filatov (left) receives a birthday cake shaped like his own head in the absurd world of Karen Shakhnazarov's realistic fantasy.

16. *The Fountain* (*Fontan*, 1988). Communist slogans on faded signs are used to hold up a collapsing roof in a Leningrad apartment building in Yuri Mamin's biting satire.

17. *The Photo with a Woman and a Wild Boar* (*Fotografiya s zhenshchinoi i dikim kabanom*, 1987). A Latvian femme fatale seduces an Afghan vet in Arvids Krievs's drama.

18. *Repentance* (*Pokayaniye*, 1984). Georgian director Tengiz Abuladze depicts the victims of the film's composite tyrant as buried alive in one character's dream sequence.

19. *Taxi Blues* (1990). Piotr Mamonov as Lyosha, the alcoholic Jewish jazz musician, having a rough night on the town in Pavel Loungine's film.

▼ P A R T   T W O ▼

GLASNOST:
DOWN
WITH
STUTTERING

CHAPTER

Is It Easy to Be Honest? Glasnost in the Documentary Film

If we do not find anything pleasant, at least we shall find something new.
—VOLTAIRE

A SEEMINGLY ENDLESS LIST of names pops on and off the black screen. These are names of Lithuanian boys who have committed suicide in the service of the Soviet army, in the dedicatory epilogue of the 1988 Lithuanian documentary *The Brick Flag* (*Kirpichnyi flag*).

Serving in the special Internal Troops (one of the duties of which is to guard convicts on their way from court to an out-of-town prison), Arturas Sakalauskas, an eighteen-year-old Lithuanian recruit and the hero of *The Brick Flag*, was tortured and raped by his fellow soldiers of different nationalities in the train's sleeping compartment. In desperate response, he killed eight of his attackers with his machine gun, then escaped, turned himself in, and, during the investigation, went insane.

This twenty-minute film by a young Lithuanian director, Saulius Berzhinis, is thoughtful and unsentimental. The film investigates Sakalauskas's case, which became a symbol of the destructive dominance of the Communist system, represented by the Soviet military machine, over human nature. Through interviews with Sakalauskas's parents and psychiatrists, relatives of the murdered torturers, army officials, and even the criminals who were guarded by Sakalauskas's unit, the makers of *The Brick Flag* try to understand who is the victim and who is the real perpetrator in this appalling case. The film exposes different truths, not pretending to possess the ultimate one. It shows and listens; it does not interpret. The actual zeal of it is clear, however: both the murdered and the murderer were victimized by the inhuman and powerful system.

In the Baltic states, the release of *The Brick Flag* caused pickets demanding reforms in the army. The documentary undoubtedly played a role in Lithuania's decision to struggle for independence. Meanwhile, the fate of Arturas Sakalauskas was still in question.

Another question, also direct and urgent, was raised after the screening of *The Brick Flag* at the First International Festival of Nonfiction Film in Leningrad in January 1989. The question was put in the form of a piece of paper attached to a small restaurant table splashed with champagne, in the spacious hall of Dom Kino in Leningrad. The paper said: "The Collection of Signatures in Defense of Arturas Sakalauskas." The address: "Mikhail S. Gorbachev, Kremlin."

This question, which left all theoretical disputes about the documentary film far behind, was: Is it possible for art to intervene in reality and change it? The previous day, Errol Morris's *Thin Blue Line* had been shown to the Leningrad festival audience, though no one knew then that the release of the picture in the United States aided the release of its imprisoned protagonist. So the universal question could have been addressed even more specifically: Can glasnost in art revolutionize reality? Can a film and the voice of its viewers save an endangered human life?

That a documentary inspired a campaign, no matter how small, in defense of its protagonist suggests a positive answer, or the hope of one. In hundreds of other cases of Soviet documentaries since perestroika began, the question of actual participation in daily reality, as opposed to its documentation, has been raised and left open. But in spite of this uncertainty, the question itself testifies to the radical changes in Soviet culture and in the art of documentary as one of the most progressive parts of that culture.

The issue of the vanguard role of the documentary leads us back to the nature of changes in the Soviet Union under Gorbachev. Perestroika does not equal glasnost. Glasnost (openness) is an ideological, or rather cultural, category, while perestroika (restructuring) is practical: economic, political, social. Glasnost can produce truth, which was banned under the Communist regime for years; perestroika must produce butter and cheese for people, some of whom had gotten used to the idea that these are not necessities.

From the beginning of the reformation period, glasnost took over and left perestroika behind. Today one can speak openly in the Soviet Union, and that is what people do as they stand in line for meat or toilet paper. Furthermore, while glasnost gives people the right to criticize society, it is the duty of perestroika to provide guarantees of this right, which is, after all, the first indispensable condition of a democracy. Today, the Soviet people still have no guarantees that totalitarianism will not reoccur tomorrow, as the turbulent events of August 1991 showed.

Culture (glasnost) found itself ahead of life (perestroika) in Gorbachev's Soviet Union. This is not only because in Russia, traditionally, to speak was always more convenient than to do, but also because, when the curtains blew apart, the amount of information exceeded all expectations. No wonder that the documentary, the only art dealing directly with reality, emerged as one of the most active expressions of glasnost. The cinematic qualities of the documentary naturally stepped back; subject matter came into the limelight. Today the documentary competes not with the fiction film, but with the press and television. It is widely accepted in the Soviet Union that fiction filmmakers have a long way to go to catch up with the powerful documentaries of the last five years. At the same time, as the poet Andrei Voznesensky, in reviewing a book on Chekhov for the *New York Times*, commented:

Unfortunately, readers in the Soviet Union now have not the time nor the ear to catch Chekhov's subtleties. The newspapers drip with the blood of Stalin's victims, the diamonds Leonid Brezhnev is said to have stolen dazzle their eyes; there are demonstrations in the streets and vehicles rumble past loaded down with the latest Soviet rockets. Who has time for "The Cherry Orchard" when the orchards near Chernobyl are turning black? ("Prophecies," 3)

The documentary is placed between cinema and the mass media. Being more influential than the fiction film, but less mobile than television or the press (due to its production facilities and the routine of the film industry), the documentary has to find new ways to stay tuned to the times. The competition is certainly helpful to the development of the documentary, although the documentary might lose the first rounds. The qualities the documentary has gained by competing with the glasnost media, interacting with them, and using them are:

1. *An instant responsiveness.* The documentaries on ethnic clashes, for example, made with dispatch, sometimes on video, were shown right away, even before the party's opinion was formed.

2. *An investigative spirit and social activism.* Actuality is approached in most of the new documentaries as a field for critical social and moral analysis and as something that can be changed.

3. Finally, and most important, *an openness of discourse.* No recipes or prescriptions are being given to the viewer anymore; on the contrary, the filmmakers share with the audience their questions and demand the viewer's participation in the search for answers.

All this became possible only after rejecting the past tradition shared by the documentary and the mass media under Stalin and Brezhnev—the tradition of public lies. To those who question how a document, something taken from reality and fixed on paper or on film, can lie, the recent documentary *Chronicle of a Parade* (*Hronika demonstratsii*, 1989) gives a spectacular reply.

Young filmmakers from Leningrad, led by director Dmitry Zhelkovsky, took newsreels of the Communist parades on Revolution Day from Brezhnev's era and reedited them into a new film, adding nothing, not even a new voice-over. No change of meaning was attempted. The result is a scary joke. All the old Communist lies appear onscreen in their nakedness. All the faked party slogans, all the notorious Soviet myths are there, unmasked. Elderly Communist leaders, like windup toys, automatically wave to the crowds, and "happy" crowds "enjoy" rain and freezing temperatures merely for the chance to scream "Long live the party!" All this, which was filmed not long ago as "documented truth," is now turned into parody. The film looks almost like an absurdist comedy and today causes nervous laughter in the rows of Soviet viewers who might have recognized themselves on film.

Soviet documentaries in the past followed, with rare exceptions, the tradition of the Nazi documentary championed by Leni Riefenstahl: they created myths that showed how the rulers wanted the times to appear. There had been a "triumph of the will" in the Soviet documentary ever since Stalin turned even the most challenging filmmakers, such as Dziga Vertov, into obedient though enthusiastic chroniclers of a nonexistent reality. The documentary became and stayed the major tool of Communist propaganda in art.

Under glasnost, a switch as crucial as the change from lies to a search for truth has been made: from a documentary statement to a documentary question. As opposed to a propagandistic exclamation mark, the Soviet documentary of the anxious era of perestroika might be symbolized by a huge question mark. The range of puzzles to be solved is immense; it starts with eternal questions Shakespeare posed in *Hamlet* and comes to a point when it is neccessary to find out how a country that occupies one-sixth of the world reached the verge of total collapse.

DOCUMENTING THE SHAME: REMEMBERING THINGS PAST

The popular Kirghiz author Chingiz Aitmatov, in his novel *The Day Lasts More than a Hundred Years*, creates an Asian myth in which one conquering tribe enslaves another by turning its members into *mankurts*. Their heads covered with a stretched piece of raw camel skin, the victims would lose all memory as the skin contracted and camel hairs continued to grow, penetrating the captives' heads. They were driven to the brink of insanity as they became wordless animals without history who suffered a sort of ancient lobotomy. According to Aitmatov, "The *mankurt* did not know who he had been, whence and from what tribe he had come, did not know his name, could not remember his childhood, father or mother—in short, he could not recognize himself as a human being" (126).

For obvious associational reasons, *mankurt* has entered everyday speech in the Soviet Union as an appropriate metaphor for the effects that the repression and misrepresentation of the past have had on the Soviet people. This exploration of the past, in newspapers and magazines, on television and in documentaries, has become a major area of concern under glasnost.

Soviets do not want to be mankurts anymore; glasnost helped them realize that without a past there is a miserable present and no future at all. In an existential way, the revived Russian tradition suggests that which had been almost completely lost in Soviet culture under Stalin and Brezhnev and in American culture since Faulkner and the Southern School: the past is something a person must always bear in his or her heart. Aitmatov's attitude illustrates the typical approach: no past means no human being. In a practical sense, the investigation is urgent: most present Soviet troubles are rooted in previous historical periods, and to extirpate the weed one has to find its roots.

The material the past provides to glasnost is boundless. Soviet (and sometimes Russian) history for seekers of truth is like a child's puzzle: it must be reconstructed from tiny pieces of desultory knowledge, and it is hard to leave it incomplete. The difference is that in the Soviet case there is no box with the completed picture to follow. Glasnost sees the previous study of history either as totally faked (it has been admitted that all the history textbooks were falsified, and because of this history exams in Russian schools were temporarily canceled in 1989), or as a gap to be filled anew. Perestroika-oriented historians today are no less popular in the Soviet Union than are Johnny Carson or David Letterman in the United States. They are not scholars anymore, but public spokespeople and television (or documentary) stars.

From admitting "certain mistakes of the past," Soviet society in the course of perestroika has moved closer to understanding the past as one enormous mistake. This mistake, however, is rarely seen as a fatal one, which colors the documentary reconstruction of the most gloomy pages of Soviet history with degrees of faith and hope. One of the first steps of glasnost was the reevaluation of Stalin and his role in Soviet (and world) history. The avalanche of facts, names, and numbers started from the top of this major peak in the Soviet past covered with a snow-white veil of taboo and ignorance. Documentary, which rushed after the avalanche, found itself in a beneficial position: a large amount of priceless documentary footage of the Stalinist times was found shelved in the national film archives. The struggle for its unshelving has begun.

As usual, television reached the finish line first with epic documentary surveys such as *More Light* (*Bol'she sveta*, 1988), *Risk* (1988), and *The Trial* (*Protsess*, 1987). Sequels followed: *Risk II* and *The Trial II*. None of these hour-long or feature television documentaries, full of sensational footage, seriously analyzed the issues of the past. But they were marked with excitement at the ability to show everything without prohibition. They were tasting freedom, not living fully in it.

Risk, a Soviet equivalent of *Atomic Cafe*, directed by Dmitry Borshchevsky, zooms in on the nuclear researches of the 1930s to the 1950s and switches from the superpowers' secret games to timidly anti-Stalinist narration on the troublesome destinies of the major Soviet physicists. The boundary of courage, over which the filmmakers did not step as they compiled *Risk* from archival footage, is marked by analogies of Stalinist Russia with Nazi Germany.

The Russian title for Igor Belyayev's *Trial*, *Protsess*, could also be read as *The Process*. As such, it fits with our understanding of glasnost as a process of liberation in Soviet culture. This two-part documentary study of the Stalinist trials of the 1930s went further than *Risk* in the de-Stalinization of Soviet society, and met more resistance in its broadcast. The second part, focusing on the witch-hunt inside the party, had been suppressed for months and was finally shown on national television only in May 1988, before the Reagan-Gorbachev summit in Moscow. For the first time, Soviet audiences were seeing footage of how Stalin methodically set up and eliminated many of those who had been close to Lenin, including Bukharin, Kamenev, and Zinovyev. While the press had previously carried rough estimates of the number of Stalin's victims, this film came out with a more accurate number of the "enemies of the people" murdered: twenty million.

The message carried by *The Trial* strongly affected Soviet public opinion. The evening the film was broadcast the traffic in major Soviet cities was much lighter than usual, a phenomenon that would not have occurred five years earlier. No documentary filmmaker could have dreamed of competing with a Soviet detective series or a Western soap opera. Obviously that night people were home watching *The Trial*. During the next week, this film was discussed more often than President Reagan's upcoming visit. However, many Soviet viewers evaluated *The Trial* as "not going far enough." Partly, this was because the film was a tyro, entering the unknown field of freedom. Partly, though, it was the result of the neverending competition under glasnost between television and cinema.

The bottom line in this competition is that television, in contrast to the film industry, has never tried to separate itself from the state and the party. Therefore, television has always been under much more powerful control and censorship by the government than has cinema. Being relatively open in its talk shows, Soviet national television turns conservative when it comes to documentaries. The broadcast of documentaries is extremely complicated. A documentary movie meets a whole hierarchy of obstacles before it reaches the air. Several television chief executives have been forced to resign during perestroika for letting "too much" information be broadcast. Such a situation has not happened in the film industry since the new minister of film took office in 1986. The general distrust of television can be spectacularly illustrated: before the First Congress of People's Deputies began in 1989, Gorbachev himself had to reassure people officially that all meetings of the Congress would be shown on national television and that nothing would be cut out.

That is why documentary films, although they may not be shown to a television audience of many millions, have the opportunity to be more honest and less censored than television documentaries. The documentary makers in film did not wait long before they analyzed the issue of the past, with a broader and deeper perspective than that on television.

The first major success in this field was *Solovki Regime*, a feature documentary made by Marina Goldovskaya at the Mosfilm studio (not the documentary studio) in 1988. Originally, this renowned director had planned to make a "cultural documentary" about an ancient Russian Orthodox monastery called Solovki, "an imposing red-brick citadel on an island in the White Sea off the northern coast of Russia," as characterized by David D'Arcy in an article appropriately entitled "Finally, a Documented Documentary" (14). In the course of preproduction research, however, Goldovskaya and her scriptwriters Victor Listov and Dmitry Chukovsky learned that from 1923 to 1939, that remote monastery was transformed into a prison camp where, along with common criminals, Stalin's first political prisoners were locked up. They included priests, writers, anarchists, old Communists, and common citizens such as students and peasants who, bearing no subversive potential for Stalin, simply filled in the gaps in the required percentage of "political opponents." One of them, for instance, was arrested as "an American spy" coming back from the United States where he, a young engineer, had been sent to study modern technological methods. "This Solovki Camp was the first cancer cell which gave birth to the whole gulag system," said Goldovskaya. "The methods were being experimented with there, and then they expanded throughout all the country" (ibid., 14).

Solovki Regime is a mosaic: it combines old newsreels with the beautiful landscape of the site today, letters from prisoners to their families in voice-over, prison songs, and a historical survey of the place from the founding of the monastery. But the most striking combination of different textures and meanings is found in the contrast between the live interviews with aging survivors and the footage of a 1928 public-relations documentary about Solovki Camp.

This 1928 documentary, accidentally discovered by Goldovskaya, was made on the special order of the GPU (the KGB under Stalin) to promote successful "reeducation programs" in Solovki and to counteract rumors about the brutality of Soviet prisons. In the late 1930s, when the Stalinist regime had tightened its nets over the country, this propaganda became useless. The film was banned and, fortunately for the future documentarians, ended up on the shelves of one of the archives.

Today, the old footage seems almost comic. The prisoners are shown eating healthy meals on lace tablecloths, working out, and reading newspapers. The reality of the camp, of course, was nothing like this fancy resort; the former prisoners make this clear in the interviews crosscut with the sequences of the sixty-year-old "documentary." Some of them are interviewed in front of a screen on which the Stalinist film is projected, which makes the contrast between lies and truth, propaganda and reality, the past and the present, even more dramatic. Interviewees, among whom are the academician Dmitri Likhachev, the writer Oleg Volkov, workers, and intellectuals, tell breathtaking stories about their lives and sufferings in the camp. Here we find a controversial feature of the new form of Soviet documentary: its "talking heads" are no less and sometimes more exciting artistically and informationally than any newsreels. This feature is controversial because, objectively, "talking heads" pull the art of documentary away from formal experiments. Many Soviet filmmakers underestimate the power of "talking heads" in their search for "artistic qualities." But in Russia, the authorities have been silencing the most interesting individuals in the country for so long that nothing is more helpful today than to listen to them.

Marina Goldovskaya, however, who began her career twenty years ago as one of the first female cinematographers in the Soviet Union, found in *Solovki Regime* a masterly balance between interviews and other documentary techniques. Consider one of the stories verbalized on the screen with almost no visual accompaniment: a prisoner, a former Red Army commander serving as a supervisor for a prisoners' unit in Solovki, withdrew his subordinates to the *taiga* (an impenetrable northern forest) for work and wound up like Marlon Brando's character in *Apocalypse Now*: he declared himself Emperor of Russia. The continuation of the story is beyond imagination. The camp authorities used this case as a pretense for a mass political execution. From the sixteenth century to the beginning of the twentieth century, 316 people were put in Solovki monastery prison. In stark contrast, during the night of 28 October 1929, 300 innocent "politicals" were shot without trial, accused of creating a local coup d'état.

Those who tell this and other stories on the screen, giving terrifying details and numbers, overcoming sixty years of silence, are mainly sad and thoughtful. They observe their past as an unwritten book of sufferings and humiliation, but it is still the past, not forgotten but lived through. In rare instances, however, hidden emotions emerge, and the director does not edit out these moments. One of the interviewees suddenly bursts out crying and asks the filming to stop. The rest of his monologue goes on over the black screen, and the impression it makes is stronger than any possible visual image. The film, restrained and severe in the beginning, gains emotional depth and ends up as a requiem to the victims of Stalinism.

The significance of *Solovki Regime* is not only in its emotional vigor, but in its analytical energy. The film provides a historical concept of Stalinism and the seventeen years of the Solovki Camp, which was established during Lenin's decline and closed in the most ruthless Stalinist prewar years. Goldovskaya shows how the former torturers had been tortured themselves; more than twenty thousand KGB executives were repressed and replaced under Stalin, says the film. The major goal of *Solovki Regime* appears to be an analysis of the regime itself and of the mechanics of its machinery, and the main conclusion a viewer may reach is that Stalinism aimed to establish small, isolated state regimes within a huge all-embracing regime. Those smaller regimes, like that of Solovki, had to have their own hierarchy—"tops" and "bottoms," gods, heroes, and convicts; but the law for all of them was the same: fear and violence.

It could be considered lucky for the Soviet documentary that the first seriously analytical film about the Stalinist past, *Solovki Regime*, was devoted to the roots of Stalinist totalitarianism, and to the first years of Stalin's dictatorship. Nevertheless, the glasnost documentary has not chosen a chronological method of investigating the past, and neither will we. A whole variety of aspects coexist in new Soviet documentaries, reminding us once again of a puzzle rather than a harmonious history textbook. For instance, a group of biographical films has emerged, unveiling the lives and times of eminent figures of the Soviet past.

One subdivision of this group has marched along under the banner of the theme "an artist and his epoch." Among these films are *African*

Hunt (*Afrikanskaya ohota*, 1988) by Igor Alimpiev, a strongly metaphorical and darkly poetic evocation of the life of poet Nikolai Gumilev (1886–1921), who was shot as a "counterrevolutionary"; *Dmitry Shostakovich: Sonata for Viola* (*Dmitri Shostakovich: Al'tovaya sonata*, 1987) by Semen Aranovich and Alexander Sokurov; and *Maxim Gorky: The Last Years* (*Maxim Gorky: Posledniye gody*, 1987) by Semen Aranovich. The latter two are devoted to the most "official" Soviet composer and author who, as the films discover, lived and worked in a state of continual, risky confrontation with the regime. All these films try to combine broad historical contexts with biographical motifs and a documentary symbolism appropriate to the discussion of an artist's creative world.

Another biographical subdivision speaks of prominent army leaders from the 1920s to the 1940s who were either banned or misrepresented in official Soviet histories. In accordance with Gorbachev's concepts that Stalin distorted Lenin's line of Communist development and that the purpose of perestroika is to come back to Leninist principles, it was finally admitted in Soviet public opinion that Stalin annihilated the top members of the Leninist party and army in an attempt to rewrite the history of the Revolution and the Soviet civil war and put himself first. But even those of the new Stalinist generation who played leading roles in World War II, the film biographies show, have been balancing on the blade of Stalin's mania for power and paranoid fears.

Marshal Blucher: A Portrait against the Background of the Epoch (*Marshal Blucher: Portret na fone epohi*, 1988), by Vladimir Eisner, is dedicated to one of the Red Army commanders who was declared an "enemy of the people" and perished in Stalin's prisons in 1938. *Marshal Rokossovsky: Life and Times* (*Marshal Rokossovsky: Zhizn' i vremya*, 1988) by Boris Golovnya and *A Story of Marshal Konev* (*Povest' o Marshale Koneve*, 1988) by Lev Danilov are both concerned with the key figures of World War II. All these documentaries use the same biographical-narrative model to unlock the riddles of the Stalinist past.

Revolution Square (*Ploschad' Revolyutsii*, 1989) belongs to the same category of documentary biographies of "important people." What makes it stand out is the archival footage it includes. The film, like many of its kind, restores the good name of a Civil War cavalry commander, Filipp Mironov, who was one of the first to be slandered and shot by the Communists in the first postrevolution years. The gimmick is that scriptwriter Lev Roshal and director Alexander Ivankin used the sequences from the revealing film *The Trial of Mironov* (*Protsess Mironova*), made by the pioneer of Soviet cinema, Dziga Vertov, in 1919. Undoubtedly, Vertov was sincere in his revolutionary enthusiasm, but what in 1919 was supposed to accuse and ruin a "traitor" in 1988 was turned to defend and rehabilitate a "hero."

More challenging and innovative than this traditional trend in Soviet documentary is one that aims at the same target—unlocking historical riddles—from the opposite direction. It looks at history from the point of view of ordinary people, and it discovers history in the lives of ordinary people, not immortals or heroes.

The documentary camera may be placed on both sides of the "barricade" dividing victims and butchers. Thus, a 1989 feature documentary, *I Was on Service in the Guard of Stalin* (*Ya sluzhil v okhrane Stalina*), directed by Semen Aranovich, a film and television director from Leningrad, and coscripted by Yuri Klepikov (*Asya's Happiness*), focuses on one of Stalin's aging bodyguards, a simple man named Rybin. He worked for the leader for thirty years, day in and day out, often around the clock. By interspersing Rybin's direct commentary on his own life with newsreels of the times, the viewer comes to have both an intimate and an objectified view of the epoch and of why someone would devote his life to a tyrant.

The monologue of Stalin's bodyguard in *I Was on Service in the Guard of Stalin*, like the monologues of surviving prisoners in *Solovki Regime*, leads paradoxically to a dialogue and polyphony of voices, as opposed to the entirely monologic structure of the Brezhnev-era documentary. While history has been approached exclusively as Communist party history in the previous decades and written according to the party's guidelines, the historical documentary has followed a simple rule: nothing live is allowed on the screen, only newsreels. The rule was rather clever: nothing unpredictable or undesirable could be expected from a newsreel; on the contrary, history could be easily falsified by simply reediting old footage. Even the best documentaries of the past decades, such as Mikhail Romm's *Ordinary Fascism* (*Obyknovennyi fashism*, 1966), or the twenty-part Soviet-American series *The Unknown War* (*Velikaya Otechestvennaya*, 1978), directed by Roman Karmen and others and narrated by Burt Lancaster, did not make use of witnesses when compiling their historical truths at the editor's table.

What the late Communist leaders were afraid of most—ordinary people recalling their extraordinary past—has swept over the glasnost documentary screen at last. In the new documentaries we see people who do not want to be manipulated any longer, people who want to speak. The influence of television is obvious in this breakthrough, as a Soviet expert on documentary, Victor Listov, points out in "History on the Screen." Television influences documentary all over the world, but the specific glasnost competition of television and documentary in openness and sincerity makes any live appearance on film even more significant. Consider this example.

In 1937, a group of children from "the middle of nowhere" in the far north wrote an idealistic book called *We Are from Igarka*. The scriptwriters Vyacheslav Romanov and Olga Bulgakova and the director Sergei Miroshnichenko planned to film a touching reunion of the "kids of Igarka" fifty years later. But another childhood was revealed during the preproduction period, quite different from the one described in the book. Thus a feature documentary *And the Past Seems But a Dream* (*A proshloye kazhetsya snom*, 1987) was born, a controversial compound of sweet memories of childhood and nightmarish pains of the worst Stalinist years.

The striking effect of the film is that what from the filmmakers' objective point of view, supported by the passionate live narration by the writer Victor Astafyev, a native of that land, looks horrifying and inhuman, from the subjective standpoint of the witnesses seems nostalgic and warm. Even huge prisonlike barracks where children, the sons and daughters of exiles, lived and where clothes froze to the plank beds during the long polar nights could smell like home if they happened to be one's childhood home.

"I don't have people any closer and more dear to me than those whom I was brought up with," says an aging woman from the screen, a former "Igarka kid," describing the little pleasures of the miserable past. Put in the broad context of the Stalinist terror of the late 1930s, the private lives of ordinary people who finally can speak for themselves create in *And the Past Seems But a Dream* a multidimensional, truly historical picture.

Common voices, stunning revelations; breathtaking details and unique destinies. What unites these documentaries and makes them essential works of glasnost, aside from the subject matter of the painful past, is the openness of their attitude (another dimension of glasnost). The past is not being observed in them as something hermetical and segregated, as something finished. On the contrary, in the new documentary an almost surgical operation of revealing the country's true past is performed in the present and for the future. We are back to Aitmatov's concept: no past means no human being.

IS STALIN WITH THEM?

The strands that tie the past and the present in the uncuttable Gordian knot are versatile and endless. Generally, purely historical analysis is hardly acceptable for glasnost. *Solovki Regime*, for instance, may seem to present this type of analysis, but in fact the film's bottom line—the idea of numerous "states" inside the state, each of which serves as a support for oppression—is of high priority in today's Soviet Union, where old Stalinist social and political structures still survive and resist perestroika.

While films such as *Solovki Regime* are seeking the present in the past, another group of films emerges to unmask the past in the present. Although they are highly topical, they do not necessarily present an openly political discourse. Take, for instance, a short film, *Subway* (*Metro*), made by the students of VGIK, the national film school, in 1986. On the surface, it is nothing but a "watercolor study" of one day in a Moscow metro, lacking any serious message. In essence, it is a dramatic poem that speaks with grief and a sarcastic energy of how a Stalinist culture exists today and keeps repressing people in the most unexpected ways.

A "silent" film with music by Dmitri Shostakovich, *Subway* opens with a series of still shots of the interiors of the metro built under Stalinism from the 1930s to the 1950s. Astonishing witnesses to the baroque gigantomania of Stalinist aesthetics, these interiors present monumental frescoes from farm life. The peasant women's breasts seem more likely to feed the whole country than do the cows, and the phallic ears of wheat construct a dome over people's heads. Enormous ironworkers smile from their pedestals, raising threateningly their enormous hammers, and the stone soldiers look into the distance with a firm resolve not to miss an enemy.

To understand this brilliantly absurd Orwellian design, we have to consider that Stalinist fine arts and architecture had the same goal as the Gothic religious style: to overwhelm and crush one's personality, to make one feel tiny and negligible in the face of the grandeur of the state, just as a cathedral in the Middle Ages made people feel insignificant before the church. Today, people never look at their underground environment, but it still influences them subconsciously, turning them into a horde of ants. *Subway* shows this by switching angles from medium shots of the interiors to long shots of disorderly crowds and close-ups of faces void of any expression.

Under glasnost, however, openly political discourse is preferred. That is why *Subway*, made in the childhood of perestroika, passed almost unnoticed in limited distribution. The most successful of the films revealing the past in the present was a 1989 feature documentary by Tofik Shakhverdiev, *Is Stalin with Us?*

In its opening shot, a handsome teenage boy who looks like a Soviet version of the young American star River Phoenix appears in close-up, confessing to the camera: "I admit that I was a spy and committed acts of sabotage. I handed over much information about our country to alien states. . . . I am tired of leading a double life. . . . I no longer consider myself a human being." The monologue goes on as we try to reconcile these guilty words with the image of this innocent young face. Somehow the two seem totally incongruous.

At that point we hear laughter and applause. Then another male voice, off-camera, explains that the young man will "wake and come out of this stupor." As the camera pulls back, we realize that the young man is onstage before an appreciative audience and that the second voice belongs to that of a master hypnotist. The bewildered youth has not committed any of these crimes; he has simply repeated what was offered to him under the power of suggestion.

This is an ironic and metaphorical opening for a film about how Stalin's image has not been erased. In fact, Shakhverdiev offers shattering proof that Stalinism is alive and well throughout the Soviet Union. What occurs in the seventy minutes that follow is a complex interweaving of interviews, documentary footage of the Stalinist period, and cinema verité shots of group discussions about Stalin. There is no off-camera "voice of God" narrator to the twenty-seven sequences that make up this inquiry into the title's question. Instead, as in so many Soviet documentaries in recent years, it is the viewer who is challenged.

The material for this is abundant, since the concept of the film, cowritten by Shakhverdiev with the noted glasnost political writer Anatoly Strelyany in consultation with the popular socioeconomist and author Nikolai Shmelev, is to create "an encyclopedia of Stalinism," as another glasnost celebrity, sociologist Len Karpinsky, pointed out in his review of the film. "People whose mentality shows the results of Stalinism [in *Is Stalin with Us?*] give evidence concerning people who caused these results," writes Karpinsky ("Is Stalin in Us?" 4).

In an early sequence, a sweet little old lady talks to her parakeet and explains that she chose not to have a husband or family, but rather became a school principal. "My family is only one person," she says confidentially. "And it is for his sake that I live." But it takes her another minute or two to get to the punch line: "I love Stalin. I adore him. . . . I love him so much!"

If we are surprised by the hypnotized youth, we are shocked by the Stalinist "granny," and even more so the more she speaks. Her voice-over continues as she strolls through a park and brushes leaves away from a bizarre statue of Stalin, which is simply a six-foot image of his face sticking out of the ground—a trace of Khrushchev's de-Stalinization, when all statues of Stalin were ruined. The millions who were condemned to camps and died, propagates this educator of the younger generation, "went on believing in socialism, in the correct line followed by our country. And glasnost always was there: they were being sentenced openly and executed openly."

This moment is followed by and juxtaposed with a newsreel of Stalin's seventieth anniversary in 1949, and a teenage girl (the schoolmarm might once have been like this girl) singing a song: "Our thanks to Him who brings us joy." Then, right away, a newsreel of the trial of "Trotskyists-Bukharinists" adds a new, controversial tone to the polemic documentary discourse.

But this is only the beginning of the polyphonic dispute of *Is Stalin with Us?* which revolves around personalities of aging (and sometimes middle-aged) Stalinists. One of them, a man named Alexeyev, discusses his past and present adoration of the dictator in his kitchen. The point is not so much Alexeyev's lavish praise of Stalin, but the context of his presence and interaction with those seated in his home around him. First of all, we note the patriarchal structure of the scene. Alexeyev speaks in a monologue, as one used to speaking as much as he wishes for as long as he chooses (and with an eye often on the camera). A young woman listens quietly, often with her head bowed, and when she does try to contradict him, her contradictions come in the form of questions. They must in fact come as interruptions, since the Stalinist's monologue allows no natural entry, no way of participating in a dialogue.

But a much older man confronts Alexeyev directly. Their talk becomes a shouting match, a jockeying for verbal power that leads finally to the old man saying, "Please! I insist that you and your kind still cannot break with the enchanting image of the faultless leader. But I'm glad that such things can be freely expressed! We are locked in combat. Our ideas are wholly antipodal, and you're suffering from the Stalin syndrome. I would like to take you across the country, letting you say all you wish, so as to make people see what madness leads to!"

At that point the young woman joins in again, and Alexeyev, feeling under seige, barks out, "I want to get through! I want to say something. Where have you brought me, to what circus? Is this a dispute? Do you call this a talk?!" The Stalinist's discomfort with open discussion is clear. But what the film actually suggests is that Stalinism is a blind and aggressive faith knowing no pity or doubt.

Shakhverdiev's documentary itself strongly reflects glasnost by allowing people to speak for themselves according to Voltaire's formula, assumed by glasnost: "I disapprove of what you say, but I will defend to the death your right to say it." The film also observes glasnost in practice, not in the Kremlin or in party meetings but where Gorbachev's policies most affect an average citizen: in the home, in the emerging need for people to reevaluate their roles in relation to others.

That the film itself invites, and in fact demands, audience participation and thus a dialogue, is finally seen in the fragmented interweaving of scenes and sequences within the documentary. The mixture of contemporary interviews with newsreels and propagandistic pro-Stalinist footage builds to a carefully orchestrated crescendo. From the Stalinist schoolmarm to the raging, "deaf" Alexeyev to an old Georgian peasant who says "We need faith, and only Stalin had given it to us" to a truck driver convinced that "Stalin is alive and will be alive forever," the film moves to a concluding segment. This involves a middle-aged Stalinist Cossack, an army journalist who interviews prisoners. One of them is a nameless "hooligan," a witty anti-Stalinist with Stalin's portrait tattooed on his chest. He is a brilliant and paradoxical alter ego of the film's director, who not only criticizes Gorbachev from the sarcastically interpreted Stalinist perspective, but who also views prison as the perfect "minimodel of accomplished socialism, the Stalin way." As he notes, with a subtle and organic irony, in prison people "need no passport, no worrying about a job. As for the amenities, cultural life . . . we march in line. We lead a modest life, yet a merry one."

Is Stalin with Us? develops the concept of *Solovki Regime* in presenting prison as a leading motif, a model of the state structure, a state within the state. Shakhverdiev's film also gives a stunning turn to Aleksandr Solzhenitsyn's *One Day in the Life of Ivan Denisovich* (1962). From Solzhenitsyn's withering depiction of life in a Stalinist prison to the film's sardonic "acceptance" of Stalinist socialism as parallel to prison existence is indeed a great shift. Both are condemnations of Stalinism. Yet the distance between 1962 and 1989 is between a simple yet powerful direct rendering of Stalinist reality and, as in *Is Stalin with Us?*, a complex, multilayered presentation that condemns through irony as much as through emotional appeal.

In the coda, Shakhverdiev returns to the opening sequence. After a cheery march tune accompanying the prisoners' shuffle around the drab jail yard, and after footage of mass hysteria in different totalitarian societies—Stalin's, Mao Ze-dong's, Hitler's—a teenage girl is shown onstage, hypnotized by the same master we saw in the opening. He holds up a white paper and asks her what color it is. "Black," she responds. And she answers "white" when a black sheet is presented. Then the credits begin to roll.

The effect is chilling; the message is clear—so clear that Georgia Brown of the *Village Voice*, who wrote that Shakverdiev's point "is that amnesia is a universal affliction; to some extent we're all secret Stalinists," unintentionally called the film by its initial title, which was changed by the censors—*Stalin Is with Us*, without a question mark (Brown, "Bird Watching").

What can the stunned viewer of recent historical documentaries expect after the total and detailed denunciation of Stalinism? What can be added to this résumé of a Soviet film published in a Soviet magazine:

"Stalinism is a natural historical phenomenon having its organic roots in adaptational instincts of weakly developed people in the underdeveloped country" (Karpinsky, "Is Stalin in Us?" 5)?

Can there be any further surprises? Yes—and the new Soviet documentary begins to realize this. A young Soviet critic writes:

> Everything [in the historical documentary] is a documented truth. . . . But why is this truth so exhaustingly monotonous? Haven't we gotten some kind of new aesthetic stereotype? . . . Almost every director, today, feels obliged to show, in slow motion, an explosion of a cathedral, or plunder of churches. . . . It seems to us that we fight against Stalinism, but, in fact, aren't we fighting against an image of Stalinism? (Shumakov, "Are the Russians Coming?" 11)

What the critic suggests is that Stalinism, like any historical occurrence, has its origins not only within itself but "outside," in the previous periods. As one Soviet historian put it, "A tyrant does not beget totalitarianism; totalitarianism begets a tyrant" ("Film of the Totalitarian Epoch," 116).

SIGHT, SOUND, AND FURY: CHRONICLES OF THE PRESENT

Is It Easy to Be Young?, discussed in detail in chapter 2, was the first Soviet glasnost documentary to attract national attention, to cause a storm of controversy and ecstasy, to become an event of social, not only artistic, importance in the Soviet Union. People standing in grocery lines, for instance, might discuss the rumor that "Himself," meaning Gorbachev, had seen the film and what he said afterward.

Today *Is It Easy to Be Young?* would scarcely be seen as such a courageous and ultimately truthful film, since the criteria of fearlessness and openness have advanced so much during glasnost. But Podnieks's film deserves a place of priority in our discussion of new Soviet documentaries about the present.

It is not a coincidence that the first documentary success under glasnost was a film about the problems of young people. Here it was, a new Soviet documentary, addressing two major sources of pain: the shameful past and troublesome youth. *Is It Easy to Be Young?* opened the theme both to the art of documentary and to broad public discussion. The Latvian documentary, structured mosaically according to different aspects of the problem (or rather, problems), offered a compendium of questions that included the seeds of all the documentaries to follow. In its enumeration of the possible exits for youth from the room of discontent and indifference, *Is It Easy to Be Young?* mentioned juvenile crime, teenage suicide, and drugs. As later documentaries such as *And*

What about You Guys, This Is How We Live, A Life without . . ., and *Confession: Chronicle of Alienation* demonstrated, these topics are of vital importance to the whole Soviet Union, and not only its young population.

As in *Is Stalin with Us?* there is a question mark at the end of the film's title, there are no ready answers, and, correspondingly, there is no "voice of God" off-camera narration to suggest ideas and solutions to the viewer. Instead, there are many voice-over interviews covering almost every moment of the picture, as if the filmmakers were afraid to lose a word of what has been said by their heroes.

Before we turn to the conclusion of Podnieks's documentary, which discusses one of the sharpest sources of pain for the Soviets' aroused consciences, the Afghan War, we must mention two other subjects that *Is It Easy to Be Young?*, this encyclopedia of Soviet youth, leaves out: prostitution and AIDS. These issues are out of the closet, but they have not yet found a powerful realization, either in documentary or in fiction film.

Prostitution has been exploited rather than examined in several almost identical documentaries: *Dignity, or the Mystery of a Smile* (*Dostoinstvo, ili Taina ulybki*, 1987) by Sh. Mahmudov, *At the Bottom of Life: How Much Is Love* . . . (*Na dne: Skol'ko stoit liubov'* . . ., 1988) by Yevgeny Katz, and *How Do You Do* (1988) by Sergei Baranov. The filmmakers move from prosecution through pity to a near-admiration of the attractive and fearless "priestesses of love," and even if they go so far as to decode "STD" as "socially transmitted disease," they do not explain these diseases seriously enough.

The AIDS issue, one of the newest revelations of glasnost, was in an even more ambiguous position. While the disease is "officially admitted" in the Soviet press, the subjects related to it are still held back; moreover, there is still a special article against homosexuality in Soviet law. To be sentenced is to be imprisoned. However, the only film discussing AIDS in the Soviet Union, an hour-long video documentary called *Risk Group* (*Gruppa riska*, 1988) by Andrei Nikishin, focuses on carriers of the virus and identifies them. Between dry and frightening statistics and revelations of blind public rage (the voice-over in the beginning reads a letter from a large group of medical students who demand a stop to all medical help to drug addicts, prostitutes, and gays, so that when they die society will be cleaned up), the interviews with members of the "risk group" show the causes of the disease. The major merit of the film is that it deals with the issue tactfully and unsentimentally. Its problem, despite the quality of the film itself, is that it stands alone in a vast field of willful and unwitting ignorance about AIDS, and it is not strong enough to overcome that ignorance.

Clearly, the films discussed answer the question posed by *Is It Easy to Be Young?* It is hard to be young. From youth lost in crime, suicide, and drugs, the Latvian documentary turns, for the first time on a Soviet screen, to Afghanistan, which adds to the picture of total alienation new political and moral dimensions. The Afghan sequences in *Is It Easy to Be Young?*, complemented by two later documentaries—a Moscow-made short called *Homecoming*, by Tatyana Chubakova, and a Belorussian feature, *Pain*, by Sergei Lukyanchikov—provide a shockingly realistic picture of the war as well as of a new class in Soviet society: the war veterans who are called "the Afghans." These films also present a sudden switch in Soviet ideology, from the glorification of the "liberating mission" of "Soviet soldiers and internationalists" to disillusionment and denunciation of the meaningless and unfair slaughter.

The words spoken on the screen by the veterans are stunningly reiterative. "Why have we been there? I don't know" (*Is It Easy to Be Young?*). "Nobody asked my generation whether we should have this war or not" (*Homecoming*). "I have no idea why I've been there" (*Pain*). "No one wants to know the truth about this war" (*Is It Easy to Be Young?*). And ultimately: "No one needs us. . . . I've never seen them show the truth about us" (*Homecoming*).

The pain of the homecoming, as well as the urge for it (with "home" understood as normal conditions of human existence and elementary moral values), is, to a large extent, a major concern of all Soviet documentaries dealing with the problems of youth. They try to understand the generation that grew up in the cynicism of the stagnant 1970s and early 1980s, and excitement of the "anything goes" perestroika years. They try to reclaim this generation, which had appeared to be lost to itself and to society. But in order to do it, they know, society must be changed first, since no one wants to return to an old, rotten building. "We have forgotten how to live in peace with ourselves," says an Afghan War veteran in *Is It Easy to Be Young?* Anyone in the Soviet Union today might have said this.

One 1991 feature documentary takes this point even further. Instead of focusing on veterans, *Demobilized* (*Dembil'*), directed by Alexey Khaniatin, follows a group of young men through their army experience. Beginning with the moment they kiss loved ones—mostly mothers and girlfriends—goodbye and climb into an army bus, Khaniatin captures, step by step, the systematic breaking down of individuality that the Soviet army practices on its recruits. Ironically, instead of watching demobilization—the return from army service—we, the viewers, are locked into the army system for almost two hours. Scenes of lonely silence mix with ones of noisy humiliation, ranging from the shearing of hair to the scene in which recruits are forced to go through an absurd ritual of jumping in and out of bed in the middle of the night, standing at attention, and returning to bed. There are vast panoramas of an empty landscape near the Chinese border where recruits from the main cities feel totally isolated from life as they knew it. Sepia coloring alternates with black and white, with only occasional use of color, all reinforcing a feeling of abnormality, boredom, and danger.

More than an hour into the film, we are told that we are now entering the second year of service. We begin to see the same routines and rituals repeated, only this time with some of the recruits we followed through the first year administering the hazing and the humiliating tasks.

Then comes the finale: a freeze-frame on the face of one man, with the information superimposed on his face that in 1990 he hanged himself. In a brisk montage we quickly see many of the key scenes captured before: the young man kissing his mother goodbye, the ripping off of his shirt by his mates, the haircut. For this young man only death itself, and a suicide at that, is a form of demobilization.

The film was completed during the same week in January 1991 that troops fired on and killed young men in Lithuania because they were not reporting for army service. The heavy irony was clear to all Soviets: young men were being shot for not joining, and were committing suicide once they were inside the system. Such powerful works not only document reality, but stand, metaphorically, for the illness that Soviet culture is enduring.

COUNTERCLAIM: DOCUMENTARY AS A
VOICE OF PERESTROIKA

Introducing the Glasnost Film Festival that traveled around the United States in 1989, an Oscar-winning documentary filmmaker, Vivienne Verdon-Roe, wrote: "For the first time, Soviet documentary filmmakers can show Soviet life through their own eyes, without the restrictions of the past. The door to a forbidden room has finally been opened. And what we find is somehow disturbingly familiar" (Verdon-Roe, "Introduction," 2).

Industry's disregard for public health and the environment; squalid housing and depersonalized working conditions; alienated youth; disenchanted elderly people; the disillusionment of war—all those problems that Vivienne Verdon-Roe calls "disturbingly familiar"—drive Soviet and American realities so close to each other that some neglected citizens of Flint, Michigan, if allowed to watch new Soviet documentaries, might have become confused for a minute about which country they live in. Such confusion, however, might have never occurred to a Soviet viewer of Michael Moore's *Roger and Me*. This is not only because Soviet economic and social troubles are incomparably worse than American ones. It is also because to Soviets, *Roger and Me*, in contrast to the social turmoil of perestroika and the public and private wars in Soviet society and on Soviet screens, would not seem sharp enough.

In this section, we shall discuss the branch of glasnost documentary that an expert on nonfiction film, Erik Barnouw, would call the "cinema of advocacy": films of civil activism, revolutionized documentaries that turn a filmmaker-advocate into a "bugler" in a time "when film makers, surrounded by the rumble of explosions, would not be asked to probe issues, but to sound the call to action" (*Documentary*, 139).

The war situation that Barnouw describes as giving birth to the filmmaker-"bugler" is fully applicable to perestroika. Perestroika as a clash occurred side by side with perestroika as change. But what in the first years of Gorbachev's rule was a regular confrontation of the old and the new, conservative and progressive, stagnant and reformist, has in the course of glasnost become an immense range of conflicts in which everyone is fighting against everyone. The clash in the government, the conflict in the Communist party, the struggle between the parties, the combat between Westernizers and Russophiles, nationalists and cosmopolitans, left-wing radicals and left-wing liberals, right-wing liberals and right-wing radicals, the republics and Moscow, Gorbachev and Yeltsin— all these have brought the Soviet Union to the verge of civil war and created the unique atmosphere of a neverending, multifaceted fight. Even the definition of democracy in the changing Soviet Union is "the culture of fighting." Having no experience with democracy, the Soviet people are engaged in a philistine fight. But there is no way for any citizen, from the president to a peasant, to stay out of it.

The initial conflict between the old and the new, with the old being the state bureaucratic machine, is reflected in the documentaries *Theater in the Times of Perestroika and Glasnost* (*Teatr vremen perestroiki i glasnosti*, 1987) and *Counterclaim* (*Vstrechnyi isk*, 1988) by the Belorussian director Arkady Ruderman. Ruderman touched the forbidden zones in the body politic in the former film, which ironically finds the "enemy of perestroika" in what is commonly called in the Soviet Union "the state and party apparatus," which usually stays anonymous but here was named outright. Demonstrating that the fate of glasnost in the provinces is more questionable than it is in the "center" (in Moscow and Leningrad), the Belorussian party officials banned the film, and Ruderman had to emigrate from his republic. His next film was made in Leningrad.

Counterclaim, which Ruderman codirected with Yuri Haschevatsky, is based on the trial of Ales' Adamovich, one of the leaders of the movement for glasnost, who was brought to court by an aging Stalinist on a charge of "contumely of Stalin's dignity" in the press. Adamovich turned the trial into a "counterclaim" of glasnost against conservative forces. The directors use footage from the trial (also used in *Is Stalin with Us?*), combined with shots of Adamovich's social activities provocatively described by offscreen voices of imaginary KGB agents who follow Adamovich everywhere, as a symbol of the general fight for democracy in the Soviet Union.

A more complex image of wartime chaos under glasnost is provided by another documentary, *Modern Times* (*Novyie vremena*), made by Georgi Negashev in 1988. In a light, fake cinema verité tone that anticipates *Roger and Me*, this "documentary farce" runs through everyday life in the Soviet Union and ends up in a labyrinth of ideological confusion. This seemingly chaotic film is held together by the protagonist, a funny, simpleminded plumber with a bicycle, who even physically reminds us of Michael Moore, and who, "hired" by the film crew, penetrates the "perestroika opposition camp" by pretending to be a Stalinist. There is not much informational novelty in the hero's bicycle tour around the circles of disorder; neither are *Theater in the Times of Perestroika and Glasnost* and *Counterclaim* full of news and facts (the information deficit distinguishes these glasnost documentaries from those that investigate the past). The plumber encounters Nina Andreeva (an antiperestroika celebrity who was the first to raise her voice against Gorbachev's policies and who advocates "socialism Stalin's way") and Lazar Kaganovich (Stalin's right-hand man, who died in Moscow in 1991), who, like a resigned Soviet "Roger," does not allow the interviewer to talk to him. These encounters are brief and almost meaningless. But the feeling a viewer captures from them is like Hamlet's: "The time is out of joint."

With the feeling of upheaval suggested by the skeptical filmmaker-politicians who have thus far stated the multitude of indirections, rather than by indirections finding directions out, we leave the screening room and this group of films to turn to other aspects of documentary social activity.

AGAINST THE CURRENT: DOCUMENTS OF ENVIRONMENTALISM

The new wave of Soviet documentary was not heralded by documentary statements about sociopolitical disorder. Positive criticism, so long awaited, was the stream that burst through the dam of stagnant social "benevolence." "The first wave of today's advocacy cinema dealt with ecological disasters, or, more precisely, ecological crimes," wrote Soviet film critic and author Sergei Muratov in an essay prepared for the Glasnost Film Festival in the United States ("Restored Vision," 1).

Ecological crimes are part of what made Vivienne Verdon-Roe call the documented Soviet reality "somehow disturbingly familiar" to Americans. Polluted waters and cities, dying seas and soon-to-be-extinct birds—the catastrophe shared by every civilization, has, however, different social and economic roots in the West and in the East. Under Soviet communism, it is the legacy of what is called in the Soviet Union the "command style of economy," as one of the first of the numerous "environmentalist documentaries," *Computer Games (Kompyuternye igry)*, pointed out in 1988.

The "command style" means the blind management of the economy from above or from the center, which is concerned only with the plan and not with the beseiged environment. While the major economic goal of perestroika was to eliminate this system by giving more power to local authorities and local management, documentaries began to attack the command style from different perspectives. The enemy provided many conspicuous targets.

There is a large synthetic-protein plant in the small town of Kirishi, in Dmitri Delov's *Against the Current (Protiv techeniya, 1988)*. "We couldn't breathe," a young woman shouts at a rally. "We coughed, we itched, we buried our children!"

We see other rallies in the states of Latvia and Belorussia against the erection of a dam across the Daugava River, in Latvian Romuald Pipars's *Hour of Democracy (Chas demokratii, 1988)*. While the dam threatens to upset the natural balance in the region, people go into the streets to protest.

In the polluted, suffocating Ukrainian city of Zaporozhye in *Exhausted Towns (Ustalye goroda)*, doomed children play on the doomed land. Burning and abandoned houses in the area of an artificial flood of a major Sayano-Shushenskaya hydroelectric power plant appear in Boris Shun'kov's *Flooding Zone (Zona zatopleniya, 1989)*. The plant became useless, but the makers of the film are more concerned with the residents of the area.

A new Soviet bourgeoisie—the fruit of stagnant thinking—messing up the environment of the Caspian Sea is the subject of the vitriolic documentary satire *Weekend on the Caspian Sea (Weekend na Kaspii, 1989)* by Valery Grunin. A tragic coda to all these images of human neglect is an Uzbek documentary, *Cosmogony (Kosmogoniya, 1988)* by N. Mahmudov, which predicts total destruction of the planet. "Remember! Remember! Remember!" runs a neon ad over a sleeping city. "Coming soon," the ad continues, and what is advertised here is universal collapse.

Some pictures, such as *Against the Current* and *An Hour of Democracy*, portray glasnost protests against social ignorance and indifference. "We can't put up with it anymore," shouts a young woman at a rally in *Against the Current*. It is certainly glasnost that has given her and millions of others the opportunity to confront the decisions made at the top. But doubts would occur to a regular Soviet viewer watching these rallies, emerging from the traditional Russian conflict between words and deeds. People protest, but nothing changes, a skeptic would note. Glasnost versus perestroika: revolution in words versus stagnation in deeds.

An image of a quiet, nonverbose, "personal perestroika" can be found in the short documentary *The Wood Goblin* (*Leshii*), shot in 1987 by director Boris Kustov. It concerns a weird old man who lives alone in the woods with a cat and two dogs, in a hut he built himself. During World War II, he commanded a tank company; after the war he became a local Communist party chief. Fired from his position after a smear campaign, he went away to live in the woods and defend them against resourceful poachers and woodcutters. "I joined another party," he comments. "The party of the green world."

An almost idyllic victory of "ordinary perestroika" over Communist doctrine, as in *The Wood Goblin*, is not typical of the new documentary. On the contrary, an apocalyptic mentality, such as that of *Cosmogony*, became a trademark of glasnost for environmentalists. The Chernobyl disaster played the key role in shaping this mentality.

Consider the first feature documentary on the issue, *Chernobyl: Chronicle of Difficult Weeks* (*Chernobyl: Hronika trudnykh nedel'*, 1986), called by a commentator on the CNN network "another radical departure from the past Soviet policy, documenting the nuclear disaster with candor and honesty." The fate of the film was no less dramatic than the events described onscreen. The film crew, led by the late Ukrainian director Vladimir Shevchenko, was the first into the disaster zone, but it took weeks for them to win the right to film there. When permission was finally given, the crew shot continuously for more than three months. What appears on film looks like the set of a science fiction horror movie: a lifeless town, empty villages, a dead forest. Some shots are exposed with white blotches from radiation leakage.

Neither the heroism of the filmmakers nor the urge to publicize all aspects of the disaster, however, meant automatic permission for the film to be distributed. *Chernobyl* was banned, despite glasnost. Then the director died of radiation poisoning in 1988. Only after his death, a year after the actual events took place, was the film unshelved. *Chernobyl* shows the disaster itself; later documentaries expose and analyze the consequences. What is captured in them is even more horrible as the filmmakers show close-ups of the destinies of common people, victims of the catastrophe.

The short Ukrainian film *Zone* (*Zona*, 1987) by Murat Mamedov presents the absurdly dramatic celebration of Victory Day (9 May, which is considered the anniversary of the end of World War II in the Soviet Union) in a village within twenty miles of the "first-degree danger" around Chernobyl.

In another post-Chernobyl documentary, *Microphone* (*Mikrofon*, 1989), also Ukrainian and also banned in the Ukraine, director Georgi Shklyarevsky edits shots of the zone with scenes of public protests against the hushing up of information about Chernobyl's consequences. After we see the mutant plants and animals held by women who say they are prohibited by local authorities from getting pregnant, the camera switches to Kiev's central square, where the speaker accuses party officials of misinformation. When his speech comes to a crucial point of desperate criticism, the microphone in his hands goes dead and the crowd of thousands cannot hear a word he is saying. It is not a coincidence, but a planned party provocation, as the film makes clear.

Glasnost on the screen, and a lack of glasnost in reality; new questions, old answers. But today, this dilemma cannot stop the filmmaker-"buglers," as it would have five years ago. Watching their films, one might wonder if anything could stop them at all.

TOWARD AN "ECOLOGY OF SPIRIT": BETWEEN *HIGHER JUDGMENT* AND *FINAL VERDICT*

A rather poetic term, "ecology of spirit," appeared under glasnost when it became clear that the whole nation and every citizen in it requires protection just as much as the environment does. While the old Stalinist slogan "Nature is not a temple but a workshop" concealed the ravages of the environment, the false Brezhnevian motto "All for the good of a human being" masked the state's neglect of the conditions of human existence in the country.

The first task of the new documentary has been to reveal how people live, and what has appeared on the screen has been a desperate cry for help. With indifferent and mechanical movements, female workers stuff live chickens into metal containers in Sergei Bukovsky's *Tomorrow Is a Holiday* (*Zavtra prazdnik*, 1987). There is not much difference between the executioners and the victims. The working women keep singing songs "to avoid," as they put it, "crying or swearing." Murat Mamedov's *Early on Sunday* (*V voskresenye rano*, 1987) presents another season and other faces, but the same reality. On Sunday mornings in winter, old village women go to the forest to gather wood. Doing hard work, chopping down sturdy pine trees and carrying logs, they sing and banter about life, hiding their pain and despair from us and themselves.

Armenian director A. Khachatrian in *Kond* (1987) brings us into another setting, suburban this time. We see everyday life in one of the neighborhoods of Yerevan, the Armenian capital, which resembles Brazilian slums or the South Bronx. The images of weddings and funerals, births and fires in Kond, combined with interviews with Kond's inhabitants, suggest a hopeless conclusion: there is no way out of here.

Perhaps people in Moscow, "the center," live better. Director Yevgeny Golovnya, in his feature-length documentary *Limita, or The Fourth Dream* (*Limita, ili Chetvertyi son*, 1988), discredits this provincial dream. *Limita* is a new Soviet slang word for people who come to the capital for a better life and find themselves a segregated minority. They possess "limited rights" and encounter hostility from native Muscovites, who approach them as intruders.

Hard and ill-paid labor, poverty, and hatred are the actual protagonists of *Limita*. Its intention, however, goes further than a pure statement of an unbearable situation. Disillusionment is what the makers of *Limita* and many other "SOS documentaries" mean to present to the viewer. Some of them provide nothing more than "first aid." Others analyze and deconstruct the Communist mythology of the past decades.

The crew of Leningrad director Alexander Sokurov made a short documentary on an exemplary collective farmer about ten years ago. At that time the film seemed too pessimistic to the film authorities, and it was banned. When the crew went back to the same village ten years later, it turned out that the woman had committed suicide. The conflict between the outdated footage and the woman's actual fate became the subject of a two-part documentary, *Maria* (1988). No explanations are given, but what the grey atmosphere of the film suggests is that the Communist myth, along with personal failures, killed ordinary, simple, kind Maria.

Another angle on the same subject, treated earlier in fiction film in Andrzej Wajda's *Man of Marble*, is taken by the Leningrad documentary *Our Mother Is a Hero* (*Nasha mama, geroi*, 1989) by Nikolai Obuhovich, which was also banned for several years. In the limelight once again is an ordinary woman who becomes a symbol of an exemplary worker. She starts shopping in special stores and visiting top meetings, but actually stops working. Behind the scenes is her family: desolate children, an enervated husband who becomes a housemaid, and a television screen on which, along with falsified Brezhnevian propaganda, we see her, a "hero" of that, not this, reality.

These films explore Communist myths and the distorted worlds of the people who lived under and inside those myths. One of the "crazy Communist way" men, the hero of the documentary satire *The One with a Song* (*Tot kto s pesnei*, 1989) by V. Tarik, has found a "golden vein": he wrote a song glorifying a factory and now sells it to different factories, simply replacing the name of the business in the lyrics. Another character from Nikolai Obuhovich's *Fourth Dream of Anna Andreevna* (*Chetvertyi son Anny Andreevny*, 1989), an aging woman from the countryside, wrote a "theoretical treatise" that substantiates a new model of a "Communist paradise" in openly religious terms. Now she writes letters to Gorbachev to apply her theories to life.

The heroes of both documentaries, as well as the protagonist of *Our Mother Is a Hero*, might a few years ago have become characters in regular propaganda films: a progressive worker, a self-made composer, an ideological genius "from the heart of the people." Only the new perspective made it possible for these alienated, Brechtian documentaries to become indictments in defense of people's spiritual health.

If the "grand illusion" inherited from the past enters the picture in the documentaries discussed above, the actual disillusionment of the present colors Vladislav Mirzoian's *Tailor* (*Portnoi*, 1988). At first glance, this fifty-minute documentary seems to be the private story of a divorce, told intimately and tactfully. No old newsreel, no Brezhnev, no Gorbachev appears on the screen, just a crisscross conversation among the director, a man, and his former wife. But the deeper the story goes, the clearer its actual theme becomes to the viewer. "It is a picture about the lost generation of forty-year-olds, who started out in life with faith," as critic Sergei Muratov put it (Muratov and Topaz, "Screen").

Marc was a successful television director when his troubles began. Once, during a public lecture, he gave a eulogy for rock and roll. Ruthless persecution followed, with secret denunciations and slander. Marc was expelled from the Union of Journalists for "susceptibility to foreign influences"; his dismissal "for political immaturity" was yet to come. It happened in 1985. Marc became a private tailor; then his wife left him. Today, these people are hollow; they look bored, and they sound faithless.

In the Soviet documentary, wrote Vivienne Verdon-Roe, "we see a society that is taking a moral inventory of itself" ("Introduction," 2). But this society presents itself onscreen as hollow. Director Alexander Sokurov pictures a Victory Day demonstration in Leningrad in *The Evening Sacrifice* (*Zhertva vechernyaya*, 1987) as a senseless herd of people. What can save them? What can save Marc, this crowd, and this country? The answer is in the new Soviet documentaries: an old Orthodox prayer is heard on the sound track of *The Evening Sacrifice*, juxtaposed to a picture of the "heartless" crowd.

"Back to the spirit" is a credo for the "ecology of spirit" ideology. Some filmmakers, such as Sokurov and Vladimir Dyakonov, director of the feature-length documentary *The Temple* (*Hram*, 1988), devoted to the anniversary of the arrival of Christianity in Russia, interpret these words as meaning "back to religion." Others—young director Algis Arlauskas, for instance—would say "back to charity." Arlauskas's short film *A Touch* (*Prikosnoveniye*, 1987) uses a small provincial school for blind and deaf children as a symbol of charities the whole society should help. A third group, containing the makers of *The Wood Goblin* and the Latvian Ivar Seletskis, director of the award-winning *Poperechnaya Street* (*Ulitsa Poperechnaya* [*Transverse Street*], 1988), sees the alternative to the voids of Soviet communism in a return to the organic spirituality of ordinary people who live on the margins of society.

The most impressive and controversial argument on moral issues comes from a Latvian feature-length documentary by Hertz Frank, *Higher Judgment* (*Vysshii sud*, 1987). Included in the program of the Glasnost Film Festival in the United States, the title of the film was translated as *Final Verdict*. The gap between the original title and its translation demonstrates the whole message of Frank's documentary.

There is no final verdict in the film. It does, however, show a convict sentenced to death. His story does not at first engage us: a spoiled child, a troubled teenager, and a black-marketeer in his twenties, the hero ends up in prison for double homicide, propelled by a thirst for easy money. We have neither sympathy nor pity for this banal case at the beginning of *Higher Judgment*. What is unusual, however, is that the murderer is not presented as evil. Looking like an ordinary student, he just sits in front of the camera and speaks. His autobiography sounds like regular Russian "kitchen talk" at first. The switch occurs when he finds out his sentence. The interview turns into a confession scarcely imaginable on the screen (or anywhere else). The fascinating courage of the filmmakers (the cinematographer's hair turned grey in the course of the filming) is that they bring us face-to-face with death, a process that develops like photographic film in the eyes of the hero. From the motivation behind the tragedy, the film goes much further, beyond the boundaries accepted in art, to the higher judgment of the highest moral imperative, which the hero imposes on himself: the killer must become a saint. The confession goes so far that at some point we come close to accusing it of profanity. But the film does not allow us to, as we know that tomorrow this man will die. Hertz Frank's camera follows him everywhere: to the prison barbershop, where his hair is cut for the last time, to the prison cloakroom, where he is dressed in the shroud; it stops only when the guards lead the hero away down an interminable corridor that, as we know, ends in the execution ward. Then we see an empty one-man cell, and this is the end, of a human life and of the film.

With its social message, *Higher Judgment* strongly argues that the death sentence does not remove the guilt of the murderer: it imposes it on society, as the film itself imposes it on us. By its ethical appeal, Hertz Frank's documentary calls for the realization of the price of a human personality, and does it through death, with Dostoevskian "ruthless spirituality," with the ultimate glasnost.

INSTEAD OF AN EPILOGUE

What the reader might have concluded, in following us on this journey through glasnost documentaries, is that the road is smooth. There are, however, other opinions. Consider an interview with Vladilen Kuzin, a chief executive of the most prominent Soviet documentary studio in Leningrad. Kuzin writes:

> Documentary today faces the threat of an extremely serious crisis. For one thing, there is confusion about the new times. There is a creative and psychological crisis in all of Soviet cinema, and probably also in the whole social consciousness. On the other hand, there is a crisis in administration and management that threatens our documentary with extinction. ("Documentary," 9)

By "a crisis in administration and management," Kuzin means the new model of film production, which switches the film industry from state subsidies to self-financing.

Kuzin explains the "creative and psychological crisis" thus: first, a "direct orientation toward sociology, and the obvious domination of political enthusiasm over art. Besides, this enthusiasm . . . often turns into a declaration of new banalities." Second, a "superficial, often ignorant analysis of history. . . . One semitruth is being replaced by another, new semitruth." Third, the "rejection of all moral norms, of elementary ethics in approach to the characters for the sake of 'drama' and 'expressiveness'" (ibid., 11).

Considering *Solovki Regime*, *Is Stalin with Us?*, *Is It Easy to Be Young?*, *Higher Judgment*, and other discoveries made by the new Soviet documentarists, we disagree with the Leningrad chief executive. In these films the balance between political enthusiasm and art is superb; they are far from being superficial and ignorant in their analyses of the past and the present; and they do not reject moral norms in their approach to people as the most priceless "material." The makers of these films are honest, even when it is not easy to be so.

What is apparent, however, is that the turmoil of hope, uncertainty, and frustration on the screen reflects the turmoil behind the screen, which drives Soviet filmmakers to document life in the volcano. Nonetheless, the major novelty is that instead of disguising the volcano as a peaceful valley, or even merely listening to its hollow voices, Soviet documentary, like all glasnost cinema, talks to the volcano. The dialogue with the controversial, frighteningly unknown, and exciting reality is underway.

CHAPTER

Down with Stuttering: Soviet Popular Genres and the New Film Language

Which genre do we make the picture in? In the genre of decay.
—SERGEI SOLOVYEV

BACK AND DOWN TO THE ROOTS

AN INNOCENT provincial girl goes to the big city in search of fortune and true love. Eventually she meets a successful man who turns out to be a bad guy when he gets her pregnant and then disappears. Years pass and the girl becomes an attractive, prosperous woman in charge of a big business, with a grown-up daughter sharing her fancy apartment. She has gotten a lot out of life, except happiness and love. But it is never too late: on a night suburban train she finds both in the person of an ordinary, middle-aged man, a common worker. After a couple of misunderstandings caused by their social inequality, the couple happily settles down; class conventions are surmounted by these two lonely hearts longing for warmth.

It would be useless to look for this story in the credits of Karel Reisz (*Sweet Dreams*) or Bob Rafelson (*The Postman Always Rings Twice*, 1981), as useless as to employ a more sophisticated vocabulary in the description of the plot. It is also not *Working Girl II*. This typical Hollywood melodrama, *Moscow Does Not Believe in Tears*, was made in the Soviet Union, and received an Academy Award for the Best Foreign Film of 1980, beating out Kurosawa's *Kagemusha* and Truffaut's *Last Metro*, also nominated. The previous year, a good harvest of Oscars was reaped by Robert Benton's *Kramer vs. Kramer*, starring Dustin Hoffman and featuring the same melodramatic kind of "my-pop-and-mom-kissed-watching-this-movie" production, only with a male protagonist.

Why did Hollywood, for the first time in thirty years, honor the Soviet picture? Why, if not because it recognized itself on the screen, even though it was dressed in exotic Russian fabrics and set in scenic Russian landscapes? The late 1970s, when *Moscow Does Not Believe in Tears* was made, were the climactic years of Brezhnev's stagnation period. The whole country paused at the edge of the abyss, in calm and obedient inertia. What could have been a better time for genres to spread, clouding reality with temptingly sweet dreams? Yet *Moscow Does Not Believe in Tears*, well packaged and performed, was not a typical stagnation movie. Except for rare cases, which will be discussed below, Soviet genres jelled during the universal stagnation. The favorites of the time were war films, essential for Russian culture ever since World War II, and the ugly Communist creation, "industrial films," in which the only conflict was "will the party plan for the plant be fulfilled or not?"

"The structural similarity of 'war' and 'industrial movies' in our cinema is spectacular," writes Soviet critic Mikhail Yampolsky.

This similarity is not occasional. As a matter of fact it is based on the flourishing, in the economy of this country, of a "command" style of management, which was transferred to our industry directly from the army troops. However, this explanation is not sufficient. A normal plant is not a good base for intense dramatic collisions. To make "industrial movies" somehow attractive, they are being dramatized according to the "war model," the universal dramatic model for Soviet art. ("Cinema without Cinema")

This explanation of the phenomenon of the "genre of invalidity," however, is still incomplete. Yampolsky goes further in pursuing his target of "cinema without cinema." Accusing contemporary Soviet films of "supplanting visual and audio elements with a verbal one," Yampolsky asserts that "verbosity kills our cinema."

If, in this opposition of verbal and visual or word and image, the former part belongs to Soviet film, the latter one definitely belongs to genre. Industrial films, filled with verbose fights between bosses and workers and loquacious expositions of five-year plans, are a good illustration of the anticinematic monopoly of "the word" on the Soviet screen. These films also expose the eternal desire of the Soviet state to keep at any price the tyranny of a single language, as opposed to the democracy of many languages.

A major goal of the totalitarian regime was to force people to believe that the unified language thrust by the rulers on the people under the solemn (though meaningless) rubric of "socialist realism" was the only possible one. The projection of this aim on film resulted in film's total domination by speech and the neglect of visual imagery. No wonder the popular genres, as the breeding grounds for various art languages, fell into disgrace.

Besides, genres in the modern sense have never been a Russian inheritance. One of the reasons, perhaps, is that the Russian instinct is to avoid formulas. Pretending to be free behind bars for centuries, Russians increased their creativity by distrusting any deliberate cages, including art as a canon. Dostoevsky picked up the plot of *Crime and Punishment* from a police report in a newspaper, but stepped as far away from the detective story as he could without slipping into shapelessness. Tolstoy has been celebrated for his epic genius as well as for his disorderly style. Style in general was usually considered something opposed to the spirit, and spirit was always preferred.

Modern culture inherited popular genres from the "mass" or "lower" cultural layers, conceived on Parisian boulevards, not in fashionable salons or artistic garrets. The Russian classical tradition, with its spiritual obsessions, always disregarded these layers as cheap and antispiritual.

Surprisingly, this attitude outlived many other Russian prejudices. "Soviet cinema," writes Yampolsky, "has an abundance of top-notch films but entertaining popular cinema is extremely weak as it is cultivated mainly by the second-rate professionals. This situation is easily explained by the whole native tradition in which the contempt for 'lower culture' is stronger than anywhere else" (ibid.).

Genres came to Russia from the West, owing to another controversial national feature: a readiness to be influenced. Genres hit Russian culture in the first quarter of the nineteenth century, along with a general passion for everything French. Classic tragedy in theater was replaced by vaudeville shows and melodramas. Adventure novels took over bestseller lists. But silly husbands, suffering Camilles, and invincible dandies still looked like foreigners on tour on the Russian cultural stage.

Early pre-Communist Russian film followed the European tradition submissively. But when recognition of film as an art began, catalyzed by the Communist Revolution in 1917, Americans got their turn to be the model for Soviet screen inspiration. One of the first revolutionary Soviet movies (and perhaps the best early Soviet eccentric comedy), *The Extraordinary Adventures of Mr. West in the Land of the Bolsheviks* (*Neobychainye priklyucheniya mistera Vesta v strane bol'shevikov*, 1924), preceding Eisenstein's *Battleship Potemkin* (1925), Pudovkin's *Mother* (1926), and other classics, was made as a vitriolic parody of and a polemical challenge to Hollywood productions.

The film exposes a sanctimonious and puerile American, Mr. West, hunting the "big buck" in the young Communist Russia, led by his childishness into trouble and rescued by intrepid Soviet workers. But while the ideological discourse of the film is openly antibourgeois, its form is deeply rooted in the bourgeois American tradition of slapstick comedy.

Lev Kuleshov, the director of *Mr. West*, who had been attacked for "imitation of capitalist patterns," wrote in his defensive article "Our Life and Americanism" (1924), "Today, the majority of filmmakers is theoretically keen on Americanism. . . . Psychological and typically Russian motion pictures are being shaped in the American fashion. . . . Thus they try to link Russian psychology to American dynamics. It's an incredibly absurd and amateurish effort" (*Essays and Materials*, 126–27). But in spite of this ideology, *Mr. West* displayed its cinematic novelty by playing with "Americanism," which was not an imitation but a close encounter indeed. What was being approached in this "Americanism" was nothing other than genre.

By the 1920s, Hollywood had already become the biggest "genre corporation" in the world. If the Russians needed a skilled instructor, they had to turn to the United States, not to the closer examples of Europe. And they did need to learn, since the new Soviet film had been urged to unite aesthetics with propaganda. This meant that it had to be the most democratic of all the arts not only in terms of distribution but in terms of its artistic language as well—and there is nothing more democratic in the language of culture than genre.

The problem, however, is that genre in modern culture is nonrealistic at heart while being realistic on the surface. Genre is the biggest cultural lie: it is a distorting, though pleasing, mirror of life. Confronting the argument between fiction (as a formula, a canon, a tradition) and reality, genre always takes the side of fiction. The harder the life, the greater the chance for genre to obtain a dominant place in a culture. Soviet society in the 1920s did not really need genre understood in this way; that culture was truly optimistic and healthy enough to manage without any consolations. The time of genre's Pyrrhic victory came in the 1930s with Stalin's "iron hand."

It is well known that the Soviet Union at that time had been turned into a labor camp with millions of victims executed or missing, with thousands of informers, and with only a handful of fearless people. Take artistry and style out of Orwell's *1984* and that is what you have: Stalinist Russia. What is not so well realized, though, even by Orwell, is that such a country needs a cheery, jubilant, effervescent art. Totally idealist Stalinist culture turned the bleeding country into a wonderland inhabited by cheerful lads and lasses who were generously endowed with flesh but not with substance, a singing people devoid of memory, just as happiness is devoid of memory, and free of complexes, just as health is free of them. Those people used to make love through song, without undressing, but friendships were valued more: the friendship of swineherds and shepherds, the friendship of nations, the friendship of the hammer and the sickle. That wonderland was a realm of film, which became more important than it had ever been. That cinema was an empire of genre, in which the Communist state fulfilled its dreams and desires.

Never were the film cultures of America and the USSR closer to each other in intent and design than in the 1930s. It is not that the genres were similar. While Hollywood was ruled by the magnificent three, the Western, film noir, and comedy, Stalin's favorites were musical comedy and the heroic epic. Soviet comedies, such as Grigori Alexandrov's *Happy Guys* (*Veselye rebyata*, 1934) and *Volga, Volga* (1938) or Ivan Pyryev's *Tractor Drivers* (*Traktoristy*, 1939) and *The Swineherd and the Shepherd* (*Svinarka i pastukh*, 1941), mostly concerning farmers' lives, had only one goal: to suggest and animate Stalin's notorious statement that "life has become better; life has become more fun." The epics, such as the Vasilyev brothers' *Chapayev* (1934) and Dovzhenko's *Schors* (1939), were mostly dedicated to the recent history of the Revolution and the civil war in Russia and destined to become a cornerstone of Stalin's rewriting of Soviet history. The similarity was that both "factories," American and Russian, were manufacturing dreams and myths, and used genres to accomplish this feat. Moreover, Hollywood was officially set up as the model for Soviet directors to emulate. Thus, the Soviet cinema finally discovered the mythological potential of genre.

In answer to the question "why did America provide the model?" it would not be enough to say that Hollywood has kept its world championship in genres as well as in film in general. Paradoxically, there are many more similarities between America and the USSR than are apparent from both shores—and many more than between Russia and Europe. In fact, the USSR, which is geographically divided into Europe and Asia by the ridge of the Ural Mountains, has something of each, but is neither. Russia is undefinable and unpredictable, although its ingenuous, childlike openness and vast spaces bring it close to America, despite all the social and political contrasts. According to Milos Forman, who emerged as a European director and then found a new homeland in the United States, nowhere in the world was the reaction to his *One Flew Over the Cuckoo's Nest* as American-like as in Moscow, where the film was screened at the central stadium with fifteen thousand spectators. Forman gives an original explanation for this phenomenon. "The Soviets and Americans," he says, "began with the same: they created a lot of official institutions intended to serve people, but in the course of time those institutions seized power and made people serve them" (Brashinsky, "To Tell an Interesting Story," 111).

LOOK WHO'S TALKING: FREEDOM IS SPEECH

One would imagine that the liberated Soviet film of the perestroika epoch would clutch at genres as if to lifesaving straws. Films today have to make money, and the financial state of Soviet cinema is miserable. To realize, however, why nothing of the sort has happened, imagine a mute being miraculously granted the gift of speech. The first thing he buys is a microphone to show everyone that he can talk. The first thing he does is verbalize that which has been building up inside him for years. The first thing he forgets is the style of his speech. Nothing is of such great import at that moment as what is being said. He rushes, he chokes with words, he mumbles and screams, and he will not stop until he is empty. This model precisely fits the Soviet situation as glasnost began, also because *what* has been ever more significant for the Russians than *how*.

Soviet cinema, like all Soviet culture, was unable to speak normally for such a long period of time that what "normality" meant had almost slipped its collective mind. This cinema used Aesopian language for so long that it had forgotten the subjects hidden behind the symbols. While being forced to speak, the honest branch of Soviet culture had been leaning over backward to save its dignity. For too long it had trained its subconscious to be conscious. When the lock was finally broken, it had to kill the censor in itself.

Meanwhile, the range of subjects, banned or forbidden under Stalin, Brezhnev, and even Khrushchev, grew enormous, in direct relation to the range of social ills undermining the country's health. Corruption and prostitution, drug abuse and the decay of the family, Stalinism and national poverty, anti-Semitism and failure of the ethnic policy, the Afghan War, homelessness, unemployment, a lack of necessities and of ideals—everything since glasnost had to be named. Certainly the first interpretation of glasnost was "freedom of speech." As no one knows how long it would take to tell the whole truth, this concept still dominates Soviet public opinion. But while admitting that such naming is desperately needed, we have to realize the danger of this concept for a culture.

The danger is that glasnost, understood this way, has nothing to do with art itself. It requires *what* and not *how*, words and not style. An avalanche of films investigating the crimes and misdemeanors of the state and the party, past and present, fell on Soviet audiences. *Plumbum* and *The Messenger Boy*, *Games for Schoolchildren* and *Dear Elena Sergeevna* (*Dorogaya Elena Sergeevna*), *The Burglar* and *The Arsonists* (*Podzhigateli*)—these are only some of the notable films that deal with the pains of Soviet youth, lost in the jungle of Communist morals and ideology. The films may be better or worse, more or less truthful. They are certainly very unlike one another; the only strong resemblance they bear is that their creators are apparently trapped by reality, and sacrifice the language of art to the problems and facts. The informational novelty in these films is fully apparent, but if the Soviet cinema consisted only of such films it would still be twenty years behind the rest of the world.

Glasnost begat a new set of clichés and stereotypes. Rarely did Soviet films of the late 1980s manage without either Stalin (if the director looked back at the past), or the madhouse (if he or she focused on the present), or both. In terms of the viewer's perception, this leads from the boredom of the closet, where these images were locked up, straight to the boredom of contemporary platitudes. In terms of artistic language, the new symbol stereotypes add little to the grammar of film.

One glasnost neologism, however, is worth mentioning in this discussion of speech as opposed to language. This is *chernukha*, a Soviet slang idiom meaning something like "pitch darkness"—the new semigenre, or even antigenre, zooming in on all the dark, nasty, clumsy, ugly, barbaric, immoral . . . (the list may be continued by the reader) sides of contemporary Soviet life, and private life, in particular. The word *genre* appears in the definition because this phenomenon, in spite of being brand-new, already has a tradition, a certain atmosphere, and an inevitable set of characters. In other words, it is a canon.

It is not a valuable genre, however, since its artistic language is still neglected. What we see in chernukha films is the common language of the Soviet cinema of the past two decades, and what we hear is contemporary slang and "dirty" language, much less censored now than in the recent past. The generic formula is wholly based on the subject matter, which is "life itself," "life in general," the favorite Russian expression meaning formlessness (what can be more harmful to any genre?) and symbolizing, according to the young Soviet critic Marina Drozdova, "the sweetest uncertainty" (Drozdova, "Midseasonal Anarchists").

The chernukha formula is at once simple and intricate. Its necessary ingredients are:

1. The family, agonizing or already collapsed.

2. Average Soviet citizens unmasking their animalistic natures, ultimate immorality, and unmotivated cruelty, which perfectly illustrates the popular Russian proverb "who keeps company with the wolf will learn to howl."

3. The death of all former ideals, leaving no hope for the future after the closing credits.

4. Packed everyday conditions in "communal apartments" where

several families live sharing all utilities, with the cockroaches being thrown in the neighbor's soup, naked light bulbs and torn wallpaper in the hallways, dirty graffiti on the staircases, with the attendant "communal" psychology and forms of communication.

5. Senseless hysterics and fights arising from nowhere and dying down in the middle of a scream.

6. Usually, a few "adult" scenes.

In general, this formula could be described as "the unbearable blankness of Soviet being." *Little Vera*, by Vasily Pichul, so welcomed in the United States and cited by Vincent Canby of the New York Times as one of the ten best movies of 1989, is one of the lightest examples of the chernukha film. *The Husband and Daughter of Tamara Alexandrovna* and *Assuage My Sorrows*, unknown in America, are the most dramatic ones.

Tamara Alexandrovna, who gave her name to the film, appears on-screen only in the prologue, singing an insanely mournful folk song. The rest of this two-hour film is shot with a ruthlessly sharp camera, which switches suddenly from long shots to close-ups and back, with nothing in between. We are drawn to the picture of the complete moral and physical decay of Tamara Alexandrovna's husband (played by Alexander Galibin), who lives in the same apartment building, though he does not live with her. All relationships in the film are turned upside down. One of the first scenes, where the husband goes to his daughter's school to talk to her gymnastics instructor about the girl's misconduct, gives a good start to this inverted reality. The young instructor turns out to be the man's ex-lover, and the normal teacher-parent scene explodes into an ugly fight comparable to American professional wrestling.

The closing shots perfectly accomplish the picture's goal—to leave the audience nauseated. The daughter, who also suffers from the lack of a sense of direction, wants to lose her virginity but at the last moment gets scared and changes her mind. Her deceived partner (who is also her classmate), accompanied by his grown-up drunk friends, follows her father through the busy Moscow streets and beats him almost to death. The only help the hero gets from fellow citizens is when he, bleeding and weakened, screams not "Help me!" but "Help a 'Spartacus' fan!" ("Spartacus" being the most popular Soviet soccer team)—which is typical of social and human relations today in a society that has always preferred a collective "we" to an individualistic "I."

Assuage My Sorrows deals with the same type of hero and situation. The main character (Sergei Koltakov), enervated by constant fighting with his ex-wife (Yelena Safonova), with whom he is forced to share the apartment (the eternal Soviet real estate problem!), tries to rent a room. Making new acquaintances (his landlady, the neighbors, the young woman who lays claim to the same room and eventually becomes his lover) and trying to come to grips with his wife and son, the protagonist shows only total groundlessness and futility. He deserts his past, he lounges in the void of the present, and he faces no future.

If one happened to wonder just how much darker a chernukha film could become, even by the dark Soviet standards set forth here, 1990 offered one of the bleakest ever in Leonid Menaker's *Dog's Feast* (*Sobachii pir*). The productive Soviet screenwriter Victor Merezhko has shaped a minimalist tale of an ugly train-station cleaning woman, Jeanna (played by Natalia Goundareva), who drags home an alcoholic, Arkady (played by Sergei Shakourov). He pays her less than no attention, though it is clear he cannot function on his own. These two outcasts at the bottom of the Soviet social ladder are two against each other and against the world.

The relentless grittiness of Jeanna's apartment, the shabbiness of their personal lives (Arkady tries to have an affair with the next-door neighbor), and the hopelessness of their situation (both are alcoholics), leads to a suicide-murder conclusion. Jeanna turns on the gas while Arkady is asleep and climbs in bed with him, as the soon-to-be-dead but unsuspecting Arkady calls out, "You're a real human being, Jeanna."

Dog's Feast has flashes of humor and touches of pathos. There are also jabs at perestroika, which provoke audience laughter (Jeanna calls out, when everyone is shouting at her while she is trying to work, "I ask you, is this a true pluralism of opinion?"). But the overall impression left with the viewer is one of suffocation and utter depression.

Whether the genre of chernukha, represented by these and other films of the glasnost years, has a future in the Soviet cinema is rather questionable. As a temporary stage in the process of liberation, this semigenre may produce inventive movies struggling for freedom of speech. What it certainly cannot give us is a model of filmic language that could provoke a search for and that might be identified with genre in the classical, though not antiquated, sense. That Soviet audiences are starved for real, pure genre is evident. *The Bondmaid Isaura*, the Brazilian miniseries melodrama broadcast on national television in 1989, became for Soviet viewers even more powerful than David Lynch's *Twin Peaks* did for American viewers: streets throughout the country were desolate during prime time, and who knows how many gallons of tears were shed over the unhappy fate of the pretty Brazilian maid? Apparently, the genre baggage with which Soviet cinema arrived in glasnostland was not sufficient.

THE CHERNUKHA BUDDY FILM: *TAXI BLUES*

Nineteen-ninety did bring one interesting twist in the chernukha formula, as well as a Cannes Film Festival Best Director award for a Soviet filmmaker. We are speaking of Moscow-born screenwriter Pavel Loungine's debut film from his own script, *Taxi Blues*. This gritty tale of Shlykov (played by Piotr Zaitchenko), a redneck Moscow taxi driver, and Lyosha (played by Piotr Mamanov, a rock star and composer of the group Zvuki Mu, with an unusual face that looks as if it were etched by Modigliani), a down-and-out alcoholic Jewish saxophone player, blends heavy doses of Russian chernukha atmosphere with a genre framework that suggests American buddy films and urban crime flicks. A joint Soviet-French effort (Lenfilm and ASK-Europe with the French-based MK2 Productions), Loungine's down-and-dirty film exists somewhere between Martin Scorsese (*Taxi Driver*) and Dostoevsky. The attempt, therefore, is to search for a new language using Russian speech and American cinematic grammar.

The American influence is found in the film's speed, shape, and sharp edge. Just as *Taxi Driver* is a realistic 1970s update of film noir, shot in harsh, dark colors with clearly contemporary implications (Robert De Niro's Vietnam veteran protagonist's angst), so *Taxi Blues* uses the city at night as the backdrop for a race at breakneck speed through the dark night of the glasnost soul. Many Soviet films seem slow to Western audiences, but *Taxi Blues* moves at the speed of a racing taxi. Part of Loungine's accomplishment is this sense of constant, uneasy motion. There is simply no place, no space in Shlykov's life for peace, stillness, or contemplation; all is frenzy, noise, movement.

Like the new American cinema represented by *Taxi Driver*, the location shots in *Taxi Blues* introduce us, in a way that a Mosfilm studio film never could, to the underbelly of Moscow (and Leningrad, since the film is actually a composite city), with subcultures ranging from marginal people living in abandoned train cars and bums in trash-filled alleys to teen gangs and harshly lit police stations.

Furthermore, the tight focus of the narrative on two males suggests that durable American formula, the buddy film. But Loungine alters this American grammar for Russian purposes. Whereas the American buddy film, from *Butch Cassidy and the Sundance Kid* to *We're No Angels*, depicts opposites who come to appreciate each other and work together with a deepened appreciation for each other, *Taxi Blues* offers no such easy sense of growth, maturity, or acceptance.

Enter chernukha's speech. True to chernukha's basic negative aesthetic, *Taxi Blues* highlights the unbridgeable gap between the two men.

Shlykov is a marginal worker (taxi driver), while Lyosha is an artist (saxophone player); Shlykov is a Russian nationalist, while Lyosha is a Jew who, during the film, calls himself a Buddhist at one point and is told he plays the sax "like a Negro" at another.

The Russian version of the American subgenre means the film carries an "overdetermined" weight that plays against the existentialist-realist feel of the American version. Loungine has explained the liberating effect of being able to write such a script, one in which, "for the first time, I didn't have to hide my personality" (Sipe, "In Competition," 32). He added that in *Taxi Blues*, "I described my reactions to my country, which I love and hate at the same time."

For all its American speed and surface, *Taxi Blues* explores many of the themes and obsessions that are important to glasnost cinema. A closer look at the "buddy" structure, for instance, reveals that we are once again looking at the failure of communication between fathers and sons. The film actually creates a triangle in which the fun-loving, free-living female protagonist (played by Natalia Koliakanova) is not so important as the old man (played by Vladimir Kashpour) who shares Shlykov's dingy communal apartment. In this sense, the lack of communication between the old man as the father and Shlykov as the son suggests that there is no possibility of a "blessing." "You would sell me for seven rubles" is Shlykov's response to one of the old man's anti-Semitic tirades about the corruption of Russia.

But Shlykov is no better. He plays the overcontrolling father figure to Lyosha's "bad son" as he constantly strives to "make a man" out of the artist. That the intense love-hate relationship between these two represents an Aesopian look at contemporary Soviet culture cannot be denied. No solution is possible to such a stridently male-oriented standoff; this is made clear not only by the final smoking images of wrecked cars but also by the tacked-on epilogue, in which we learn that Lyosha becomes a jazz star in New York, cutting his second album, while Shlykov buys his own car and forms a co-op, a personal attempt to survive under perestroika.

Loungine directs with enough high-voltage energy, however, to keep the rather obvious metaphorical readings of his dark tale from completely overdetermining his narrative. His success is visible, for instance, in an extended scene involving Shlykov, Lyosha, and Ira, the woman in Shlykov's cramped apartment. She dances to Lyosha's sax playing by herself and then does a jitterbug with Shlykov. Next she pours champagne over both men, saying "the music makes us *feel* something," as Lyosha upsets an increasingly jealous Shlykov by saying "women call my instrument a *sex*ophone." Ira then begins to dance with Lyosha while he continues to play. Shlykov cannot tolerate this, and he leaves. Lyosha begins "kissing" Ira using his saxophone. Attracted to each other, they dance happily on the bed until Shlykov returns to smash the sax. Lyosha then trashes the whole apartment, much as Kane destroys Susan Alexander's room at the end of *Citizen Kane,* and Shlykov responds by strangling him, only to be attacked by Ira. Lyosha leaves, shouting "I'm sick and tired of you all," while Shlykov ends the sequence with a brutal form of sex with Ira in the kitchen, a physical act expressing violence rather than tenderness, force rather than shared joy.

True to chernukha films, such a scene is "too much," even when measured against the charged bleakness of a film such as *Taxi Driver.* But Loungine explains that this is life as he sees it today, full of "patriots and crooks" ("Releases," 17). The driving power of this mixed-genre film, therefore, is its hard-hitting depiction of a no-win reality. The reason the film has won international audiences and an American release is perhaps that no easy solutions are offered to those suffering from taxi blues—or, more correctly, perestroika blues.

Taxi Blues suggests yet again the crisis of male identity under glasnost. Mark Gerzon has suggested that, in contrast, a new face of American manhood has been emerging. According to Gerzon, the "emerging masculinities," as he calls them (*Choice of Heroes,* 235), are characterized by a variety of roles that include healer, companion, mediator, colleague, and, finally, a role more traditionally associated with motherhood: nurturer. "A Nurturer inspires men to empower others," comments Gerzon (258). *Taxi Blues* is a window looking onto a dark view in which none of these roles is appropriate or possible. Chernukha, even when crossed with American film genres, has no lasting space for such growth and satisfying maturity. Such bleakness, despite the international awards and worldwide attention, may have finally become too much even for Soviet audiences. The Soviet release of *Taxi Blues* attracted only mild attention and a limited audience during a short initial run. Such a reaction definitely suggests that the chernukha film, in any form, has only a limited future.

LOVE, CRIME, AND PUNISHMENT: MELODRAMA AND
THE DETECTIVE FILM

Of the traditional film genres, the Soviet favorites for a long time were melodrama and the detective film. The explanation—at least the most apparent one—for this preference is that of all the genres, these two are, as the Soviet cultural authorities would put it, the most realistic. They are rooted in life more deeply than others; they are more dependent on subject matter. It is hard to imagine a regular detective story in which the mystery lies in the mode of storytelling rather than in the plot, although many thrillers are thrilling because of their language and despite disappointingly poor narratives.

Neither melodramas nor detective stories provoke the darker sides of ourselves. They do not appeal to the audience's suppressed desires and subconscious instincts (as popular culture usually does); they employ the "innocent" centers of a human organism: lachrymal glands in the case of melodrama, and the sections of the brain that control curiosity for the detective story. Neither genre requires a big budget nor suffers from a lack of special effects, which helps when the technical base of a film industry is as miserable as the Soviet one. Finally, two points the Communist state could always admit more or less painlessly: in a society of "developed socialism," men still abandon women (which is the ground for melodrama), and crime continues to occur.

Melodrama and the detective film survived the years of stagnation, giving rare but sure signs of life, but they met an uncertain fate with perestroika. Perhaps the best melodrama of the early 1970s was *Romance of the Lovers* (*Romans o vliublennykh*, 1974) by Andrei Konchalovsky, who in the early 1980s moved to the West and made *Runaway Train*, *Shy People*, *Tango and Cash*, and other movies in Hollywood.

In *Romance of the Lovers*, Konchalovsky tried a risky experiment: to exploit the formula of melodrama, to make a pure genre film with extreme situations and open emotions, with all its sentimentality and even silliness. Surprisingly, this required the establishment of an exclusively conditional reality. All the characters speak in verse. The first, "happy" part of the film, where the lovers are delighting in their romance, is shot in color. At the end of this part, the hero leaves for his army service and is reported killed during maneuvers. Soon after that his fiancée marries another man and settles down to a normal, prosaic existence. During the rest of the film, shot in black and white and spoken in prose, the hero, returning alive, tries to get a grip on himself and outlive the death of his love.

The result of Konchalovsky's experiment was rather positive. But the film, as well as the response to it, proved that pure melodrama is as alien to Russian culture as skyscrapers or hamburgers. While *Romance of the Lovers* was taken for tasteless kitsch abroad, at home it was received as something alien. Never since the Stalinist genre exploded in the 1930s had Soviet melodrama laid claim to such genre purity. Usually melodrama is mixed with either a comic or a heavy dramatic element, reflecting the traditional Russian passion for psychology and the investigation of grim social problems.

Even the brightest examples affirm this rule. In *Moscow Does Not Believe in Tears* (1979), a genuine melodrama is immersed in a circumstantial picture about two decades of Soviet life, and it looks rather like an epic. In *The Wartime Romance*, the best preperestroika melodrama of the 1980s, the classic genre triangle of a man torn between two women is drawn by director Pyotr Todorovsky toward psychological drama with a Chekhovian slant. In the end, when the hero leaves his love's wedding party (she left him for a serious, normal, wealthy official) and is being arrested by a police officer on a Moscow street, at dawn, his wife finds and rescues him. They stay on the lonely street, two suffering hearts, and the coda of their screen life could be borrowed from Chekhov's *Uncle Vanya*: "What's to be done, we must go on living! We shall go on living."

Perestroika, which brought novelty into life and art, added almost nothing to the genre of melodrama. Benevolent critics, praising Eldar Ryazanov's *Forgotten Tune for the Flute* (*Zabytaya melodiya dlya fleity*, 1987) as the first satiric comedy of the perestroika era, have forgotten to mention that it is also the first melodrama of the glasnost era. But if the comedy in the film is colored by perestroika (the target of satire is the Soviet bureaucratic machine), the melodrama is as old as the world, or at least as the genre itself.

A high-ranking married functionary, a Communist yuppie named Filimonov (played by Leonid Filatov), falls in love with a nurse. In addition to being torn, as is usual, between two women, he gets a split personality: the comic bureaucrat from satire in him fights with the passionate, almost childlike, heroic lover from melodrama. The only alteration Ryazanov brought to this collision is the solution of the problem, unsolvable within the boundaries of one genre, of the hero's generic duplicity. In the finale Filimonov dies of a heart attack during one of his official meetings. He goes straight to purgatory, where he meets his parents along with Afghan War victims and other interesting candidates for heaven. Meanwhile, his lover feels that something is wrong; she rushes to Filimonov's office, and while the paramedics helplessly report that he is dead, she magically brings him back to life with a kiss.

The originality here is a mixture of cheap mysticism adopted, as Soviet critic Alexander Timofeevsky noticed, from an American book called *Life after Death* (which, although never published in Russia, was a best-seller by word of mouth) and an archetypal fairy tale, "Snow White." The resolution of the conflict, which was forced by the "melo-satire" genre's duality, showed that social sharpness (within the genre of satire) itself can neither save the hero nor improve the genre of melodrama.

What Ryazanov also did by mixing the genres exemplifies a strong tradition in Russian art. The genre, usually called tragicomedy, is apparently derived from Chekhov's drama; it could also be defined as "comedy with a dramatic ending." After going through various stages of development, it was transformed eventually into a trend that was particularly popular in the Soviet cinema of the 1970s and 1980s. The trend, called sad comedy, in fact gave birth to comic melodrama. Its leaders at that time were Georgi Danelia, who made his best film, *Autumn Marathon* (*Osennii marafon*, 1979), on the dividing line between melodrama and comedy, and Ryazanov himself, who provided Soviet screens with a kind of Russian *It's a Wonderful Life* when he made *The Irony of Fate, or Hope You Enjoyed Your Steambath* (*Ironiya sud'by, ili S legkim parom*, 1975). The film has little in common with Frank Capra's 1947 classic, except that it, too, is shown every Christmas on national television.

The hero, quite an ordinary man, gets awfully drunk at the ritual bathing with his friends on New Year's Eve and ends up going from Moscow to Leningrad. There he goes "home," having no idea that he is in another city, and since Soviet architecture and town planning are so homogenized, there happen to be a similar street, house, and apartment in Leningrad. Even the lock on the door is the same. Thus the hero enters someone else's apartment—and there finds love and happiness.

In spite of the apparent weakness of *A Forgotten Tune for the Flute* in comparison with *The Irony of Fate*, one marginal detail makes the former film significant and the comparison meaningful. In both Ryazanov films, as well as in Pyotr Todorovsky's *Wartime Romance* and others, the love triangles are centered on a man who is presented as a melodramatic hero, which certainly contradicts the traditional melodrama scheme (manifested by early silent melodramas or by the characters played by Greta Garbo and Marlene Dietrich in the 1930s) with a woman as hero and victim. This phenomenon could have been explained by the lack of a feminist movement and feminist consciousness in the Soviet Union. But women in Russian melodrama are stronger than men—which in a way reflects Russian reality. It is not accidental that many female protagonists of Soviet melodramas, as in *The Old Walls* (*Starye steny*, 1974), or the notorious *Moscow Does Not Believe in Tears*, are businesspeople in charge of big businesses; this signifies the sublimation of a "matriarchal complex" in Soviet culture. After perestroika this trend is still dominant. The rare outbursts in the opposite direction do not yet herald a radical change.

Ryazanov himself made an effort to break the trend in his 1984 film *The Ruthless Romance* (*Zhestokii romans*). But this "romance" was an adaptation of a classic Russian play of the nineteenth century, *The Dowerless* by Alexander Ostrovsky, set correspondingly in the past. One of the few entirely modern examples of an alternative approach to melodrama in the glasnost period is *The Frozen Cherry* (*Zimnyaya vishnya*,

1987) by Leningrad-based director Igor Maslennikov. It presents a typical emancipated working woman in her thirties, familiar to Americans from soap operas. But the Russians have no soap operas, which also strongly encourages melodramas. The heroine of *The Frozen Cherry*, Olga (played by Yelena Safonova, the future star of *Assuage My Sorrows* and *Dark Eyes*), is dissatisfied with her life as well as with her men. She is not really involved in her routine job; she also is not a good mother to her five-year-old son by a former marriage. All her energy is aimed at the settlement of her private life. Her credo is "Family is like a homeland: everyone must have it." She rushes from one man to another in search of stability, but cannot find it. Men here represent a materialistic, practical, prosaic entity, conflicting with an idealistic though not unworldly feminine spirit. The sympathies of the male director are on Olga's side, but despite the director's benevolence, the sexist attitude of the film, hidden even in the title (she herself is a "frozen cherry"), is evidenced by the heroine's fake independence; what she depends on most of all is men.

Similarly, a secretly conservative and confused morality can be found in another glasnost melodrama from Leningrad, *Forgive* (*Prosti*, 1988) by Ernest Yasan. To unlock this one-dimensional story, the publicity synopsis, written in the plain style of an administrative report, is more than enough:

> Young and beautiful Masha Antonova seems to be content with everything in life: she has a considerate and loving husband, Cyrill, a ten-year-old daughter, and many friends. *However, the office where she works consists of women, and differences of opinion often result in conflicts.* Such a case happens today. Masha clashes with a female colleague because of a phone call *from an unknown woman informing Masha of Cyrill's faithlessness.* [Italics added to emphasize the *Fatal Attraction*–like, male chauvinist concept of the "she-devil" in this "feminist" movie.] Something is breaking to pieces in her well-balanced life, though at first Masha does not realize it. She goes to a friend's party; she accepts an invitation from a stranger. Suddenly an idea flashes in her mind: it is late and her daughter is alone at home. She starts home but is attacked by a group of ruffians. . . . Having experienced suffering, humiliation, and shock, she reaches home where she is awaited by her daughter and Cyrill rejoining the family. He has realized that responsibility for his wife and daughter is much stronger than a brief flame.

Forgive was the first film in Soviet cinema to present a rape scene (euphemistically called "attack of a group of ruffians" in the synopsis). All the rest of *Forgive*, though, is stagnant both historically and cinematically.

Another minor but growing trend in contemporary Soviet melodrama is worth mentioning here. This is the "genre-for-export," evidenced in Pyotr Todorovsky's 1989 Soviet-Swedish coproduction *Intergirl*, and most spectacularly in Nikita Mikhalkov's *Dark Eyes*.

One of the leading Soviet directors of the middle-aged generation, Mikhalkov moved to the West after a stormy though brief romance with contemporary Russian reality in his last Soviet films, *Kinfolk* (*Rodnya*, 1982) and *Without Witnesses* (*Bez svidetelei*, 1983). This Italian movie (*Dark Eyes* is not even a coproduction; it was made with Italian money and an Italian crew), a free adaptation of the classic Chekhov short story "The Lady with the Pet Dog," is a spicy, though rather tasteless, cocktail of Western and Eastern sensibilities. Not sure which star was more striking—the aging Marcello Mastroianni as a jaded traveler who falls in love with an attractively mysterious Russian lady, or the young glasnost—Mikhalkov let them costar: a sappy love story stands side by side with openly critical but beaming pictures of good old "Mother Russia": immense, impenetrable, and incredibly backward in her bureaucratic hypocrisy.

The melodrama in *Dark Eyes* (which is also the title of a famous Russian-Gypsy love song) is executed perfectly, although it is not the film's main attraction. What the West might buy, Mikhalkov calculated, was a "Russian toy." The result was a shameful sellout for the director: what he presents as the essence of the "Russian spirit" is in fact kitsch (*kliukva*, as it is called in Russian—cranberry). Interestingly, genre refused to help Mikhalkov in his effort: melodrama in *Dark Eyes* (as well as in *Intergirl*) is separate from the Russian texture. Both directors executed melodramas simply as universal trademarks that guarantee the audience's appreciation.

The detective film, unlike melodrama, has been a symbol of mass culture in the Soviet Union since the 1960s. Not accidentally, the person who publicly accused Soviet film culture of a snobbish neglect of the box office as well as of an elitist neglect of democratic tastes and needs was director Stanislav Govorukhin, who specialized in the detective genre. But what was portrayed as an "elitist plot" in Govorukhin's article published in a leading newspaper, *Sovetskaya kul'tura* ("Soviet Culture"), in 1988, was, in fact, a hereditary Russian inability to execute genre fearlessly and skillfully.

The detective genre, after all, has never been neglected in Russia;

Govorukhin, for instance, magnetized the entire country in the late 1970s with his five-part television series *The Meeting Place Cannot Be Changed* (*Mesto vstrechi izmenit' nel'zya*, 1979), starring the Soviet dissident singer-actor, the legendary Vladimir Vysotsky, as a cop fighting a gang in post–World War II Moscow. The series was well done and stylish; all the period-piece rules as well as the genre rules were carefully observed. The plot, for instance, focused on a classic pair of cops—the lead, and a rookie (Vladimir Konkin) who discovers the secrets of life and his profession through the mistakes he makes in the investigation. The same scheme can be found in recent Hollywood productions, such as Ridley Scott's *Black Rain*, Clint Eastwood's *Rookie*, and John Badham's *Hard Way*.

This series was at least the third major success of Soviet television in the detective genre. The first one, *His Excellency's Aide* (*Adyutant ego prevoskhoditel'stva*, directed by Yevgeny Tashkov), was made in 1970 and released as a movie in 1972. The narrative was set in the 1920s in the headquarters of the czarist White Guard, which was fighting the Communists, and the protagonist, a Communist spy, for many hours of national prime-time television stole enemy secrets and helped the Soviets win the battle and establish the new regime.

The second and more successful picture, *Seventeen Moments of Spring* (*Semnadzat' mgnovenii vesny*, 1973), was also a spy movie rather than a pure detective one, and also set in the past. Director Tatyana Lioznova put the Soviet intelligence officer in Hitler's headquarters in Berlin. The rest is history: all the characters, including real Nazi figures (only the Führer never appeared onscreen) and the protagonist, Schtirlitz, became national cult heroes, and the series gave rise to numerous jokes. The script was pulled apart bit by bit into aphorisms and maxims still familiar to any Russian teenager. The lead, Vyacheslav Tikhonov, became the number one star; the film has been rerun at least a dozen times, and captured the National State Award. The only unsolved puzzle was why a series called *Seventeen Moments of Spring* had only twelve parts. The significance of all three of these films transcends their individual qualities; they are examples of a specific approach, both to a genre and to the past, widespread among Soviet filmmakers in the stagnant 1970s.

Since social life under Brezhnev was so boringly predictable, so comatose, so idle, so all-embracingly mendacious, all art that was not serving the party turned to various modes of escapism. Genre and the past happened to be the most accessible of them. Both were stylish, as opposed to the styleless, grey Soviet reality; moreover, both allowed nonconformist directors to avoid Communist ideology without embarking on a confrontation with the regime. Uniting them killed two birds with one stone.

What the Kremlin ideologists had not forgotten, however, was Lenin's notorious tribute to film as "the most important art," which could promote Communist ideals in the most simplistically "democratic" form. That is how the subgenre of the "political detective film" was born. The favorite settings for these films were small Latin American or Asian countries—"developing countries," as they were called in the Soviet propaganda lexicon. The favorite collision was the struggle of Russian Communists against Western capitalists for influence in this "disoriented" part of the world. The narrative scheme was multiplied in dozens of similar movies in the 1970s, and perestroika, surprisingly, brought nothing new. The description of such a movie can simply be reprinted from the advertisement, since its cinematic imagination went no further than to invent a new name for the "imaginary" country. Here is the plot of a political detective film, *Hunting the Dragon (Ohota na drakona*, 1988) (typical of many, including *Bringing to Bay, The Mystery of Villa "Greta," The Ransom*, and *The Werewolf's Tracks*), taken from the Sovexportfilm catalogue of 1987–1988:

> A small Latin American country, Guadiana, is regularly attacked by devastating waterspouts in the form of a dragon coming from the ocean. During a hurricane a Soviet scientist, Gribov, disappears. Studying climatic abnormalities in this region, Gribov suspects that the calamities are of an artificial origin. Gribov's diaries have also disappeared. Many dramatic and mysterious events take place before we learn that the hurricanes have been caused by meteorological rockets launched from a secret base on the territory of the neighboring state. Operation "Dragon" was carried out under the command of CIA.

"Operation Dragon" would seem too dull even for Rambo. The attraction of this kind of movie for the filmmakers, though, was that it gave them the opportunity to go overseas to the most realistic locations (almost all of them were Communist bloc coproductions; *Hunting the Dragon*, for example, is a coproduction with Nicaragua). Today, probably, the stream will become shallow: crossing the national border in Russia is much easier than it used to be.

This is not the only likely change perestroika will bring to the genre, if we consider the nonpolitical, standard detective film and its escapist attitude. It took only a little while for escapism to lose favor under glasnost. Everyone began to promote social and political activity because under perestroika it is no longer shameful to do so. Furthermore, there is not much room for escapism: the Soviet past has become one of the vital questions of the present. Perhaps genre films are the last opportunity for escapism, but no one seems to need it anymore.

Stanislav Govorukhin can once again serve as a model figure. He started his glasnost period with a purely commercial adaptation of Agatha Christie's *Ten Little Indians* (*Desyat' negrityat*, 1987), intended to be a blockbuster. However, neither the openly expressed attitude that it was no longer shameful to make money nor the first-rate cast could save the meaningless film.

What might ten years before have been seen as a well-costumed British society puzzle caused embarrassed bewilderment in light of glasnost: why such a film now? What is such a masquerade for? Can this multiple murder set in an alien world, shot in a fancy Russian resort, compete with the most mysterious and horrible detective story of all time—the investigation of Stalin's homicide of millions—broadcast daily on national television? But even if we look at the discourse of the movie rather than its political context, we will see that it is done inertly, without spirit and inspiration; the director obeyed the story and apparently never asked himself the question he might have been asked afterward: why all this elegant reshuffling?

Perspectives change, however. After *Ten Little Indians*, Govorukhin produced the controversial documentary feature *We Cannot Live This Way* about the horrors of daily life in the USSR. The switch of focus is significant for all Soviet films. Perestroika detectives, or detective films set in the present, dedicated to current domestic problems and lit by the light of glasnost, are still in short supply. Perhaps the genre is too irrelevant for contemporary Russia—or is it too mild and intellectual? Do gangster films or thrillers fit better with perestroika? As the "Book-of-the-Month Club News" put it when promoting "a first-rate post-glasnost thriller," *Soviet Sources* by Robert Cullen, "The good news is that glasnost and perestroika haven't meant the end of the political thriller."

The danger, of course, is that even this tried-and-true formula may self-destruct with overindulgent glasnost filmmaking. *Fools Die on Friday* is the catchy title of a 1991 Soviet-Bulgarian coproduction directed by Rudolf Frountov that in January 1991 was the only Soviet film in Moscow theaters. The film tries to be all things to all audiences: an intellectual European thriller (a detective who finds out that the murderer is his longtime detective colleague); a soft porn movie (the gangster in the film has a dacha that seems to house a nonstop orgy); and an American-style action police film, as cars chase, smash, and crash into each other throughout the film. Such an "in-between" production is all the more flat because it misses the one element that helps define the genre in Europe and Hollywood: a sense of humor.

HOLLYWOOD ON THE MOSCOW RIVER: AMERICAN GENRES
AND SOVIET CINEMA

The Gangster Film

The southern Russian Godfather is more sophisticated than Mr. Brando,
and no less powerful. The high life of the low-level Red Mafia; sex under
the broiling sun of Soviet Georgia; a burning-hot iron on the belly as a
weapon of the mob; the sawing-off of human arms to the music of Bizet's
Carmen—kitsch is all the rage in the first Soviet thriller under glasnost.
The *King of Crime* (1988) is as smooth as a Ping-Pong ball and re-
bounds off everything in a similar style. In this typical gangster film
with a sociohistorical subtext, as in Mikhalkov's "Russian melodrama,"
Dark Eyes, the temptation to follow a genre competes with the appeal of
perestroika. The film opens as pure genre entertainment, slightly funny
because of the parodic flavor and because recognizable Soviet citizens
are being endowed with the exaggeratedly tasteless passions of a classic
melodrama-thriller. A "good guy," a local gangster, and his *Blue Angel*–
like sexy lover—the paradigmatic love triangle—find themselves involved in the turmoil of a gangwar with all the attendant consequences.
There are shoot-outs on the streets, bloody signs of revenge, terrific car
chases, and deaths, deaths, deaths.

The major thrill of this film comes from its treatment of subjects
formerly considered taboo in Russia: prostitution, the Mafia, and corruption in the KGB, whose agents collaborate with the gangsters. But,
apparently fearful of being misunderstood, the director, Yuri Kara,
who debuted in 1987 with the melodrama *The War Was Tomorrow*
(*Zavtra byla voina*), set in the time of Stalin's witch-hunts, soon un-
masks his true intentions. It turns out that the film, for all its social zeal,
is actually about the stagnant past and not about the sunny glasnost
present: the walls of the film are hung with portraits of Brezhnev, not
Gorbachev.

One can certainly commend the director's uncanny ability to follow
the party line of "permitted criticism." But the execution of the genre is
both timid and pretentious. In their search for the origins of the gangster
film, the filmmakers went no further than Francis Ford Coppola's *Godfather* or Sergio Leone's *Once upon a Time in America*. But even in re-
considering these thrillers, they use gimmicks, symbols of the genre,
instead of learning the rules. While the lack of education and tradition in
genre culture is an obstacle to, rather than a fault of, the makers of *The
King of Crime*, their amateurish irresponsibility to the genre does not
bode well for the future.

The following years brought less controversy but more focus to the genre of the Soviet thriller. Such films as Mikhail Tumanishvili's *"Wreck,"* the *Cop's Daughter (Avaria, doch menta*, 1989), Alexander Muratov's *Criminal Quartet (Kriminal'nyi qvartet*, 1989), and Sergei Bodrov's and Alexander Bourovsky's *Card Player (Katala*, 1990) show that the first lessons well learned by Soviets about the thriller were durability and balance of style. In *Criminal Quartet*, for instance, four Soviet "musketeers," a prosecutor, a journalist, and two cops, played by four first-rate stars, Nikolai Karachentsov, Vladimir Steklov, Boris Scherbakov, and Vladimir Eremin, fight for a prosecutor's son, kidnapped by Mafia thugs, and they do it with the finesse of the best examples of the genre. The useful novelty of the film for the Soviet screen is that the heroes—the official guardians of justice, who are definitely "good guys"—do not even bother to involve the state police in their operation and often violate the law themselves. Call it "thrillerstroika" in action.

The thriller seems more than likely to continue in the cinema of perestroika. Like the Great Depression era that gave birth to the genre, Soviet reality today, with all manner of violence engendered by freedom, reminds one of a thriller movie: chaotic and unpredictable.

The Western

Paradoxically, one of the first glasnost-born films and a hit at the box office was the Western *The Cold Summer of '53*. However, if the frankness of tone of the narrative dedicated to the Stalinist years fascinated Soviet audiences, the use of American genre codes was not a striking novelty.

The first Soviet Western was made in the dawn of the stagnation era, in 1970. Vladimir Motyl's *White Sun of the Desert (Beloye solntse pustyni)* tales place during the Soviet civil war in one of the Soviet Asiatic states, where the lonely Red Russian soldier Fedor Sukhov (Anatoly Kuznetsov) fights a gang of local bandits, *basmatchi*, who are trying to restore feudal order to Soviet Asia.

The story has many comic elements that add a peculiar attractiveness to the genre: the duty Fedor Sukhov is discharging is to escort the khan's harem, liberated by the Bolsheviks, to a safe place across the desert. A somewhat strange simpleton from a traditional Russian fairy tale, writing bombastic letters daily to his bride in Russia, Fedor Sukhov keeps finding himself in odd situations amidst a horde of silent women whose faces are always veiled, according to the Muslim tradition. Also humorous is Sukhov's companion and guide, a kind of local Sancho Panza, filled with Asian wisdom and unshakable inner peace. The essentially dramatic situation, however, is presented by director Motyl seriously and with a deep respect for the Western genre. The laconic romanticism of the hero and of the desert location recall John Ford's classics. Tense action, dynamic fight sequences, and generic morality—all these attributes of the Western make *White Sun of the Desert* one of the rare Soviet classics of genre.

The film begat a slew of similar movies that, partly ironically, were called "Easterns." The trademarks usually were the same—the Soviet civil war, set in an Asian locale and with an Asian flavor, horses, and army caps (replacing cowboy hats)—but the quality of these clones never reached that of *White Sun of the Desert.*

The next step forward (and back to the origins of the genre) was taken four years later, in 1974, by Nikita Mikhalkov (*Dark Eyes*) in his debut film, *At Home among Strangers, a Stranger at Home (Svoi sredi chuzhikh, chuzhoi sredi svoikh)*, a thrillingly expressive mystery tale, set, once again, in the 1920s, full of surrealistic symbolism and giddy narrative twists. While the artistic mode of the movie is even closer to the classic Western (the counterrevolutionaries wearing cowboy hats rob the train in search of the Bolshevik's gold), the innovative style of the film completely overwhelms the subject matter and moves it even further away from the Soviet reality and ideology, providing a nearly ideal formula for the genre escapism of the 1970s.

The Cold Summer of '53 can be considered the first Soviet Western, or "Eastern," if not the first Soviet genre film, that has no escapist goals. This is not an unconditional merit of the movie, but rather the source of its dual nature. The film has some penetrating scenes where the bullet, flying along the trajectory of the Western, hits the mark. But overall, the director, Alexander Proshkin, evidently foreseeing that the Soviet audience was not ready to accept the painful subject matter of the past interpreted as a genre-game, stopped halfway and produced a "film centaur" in which incomplete historical truth is expressed within an inferior genre, overloaded with psychology and lacking strict Western features. Nevertheless, the director and his creation received credit and applause for being first.

Other Genres

Why do Soviets have no real horror or suspense films? The answer is at hand, and it is as banal as it is truthful: because audiences cannot even imagine that a Soviet clerk dressed in a cheap suit may turn out to be a perverted scoundrel, that an ordinary Soviet husband may try to kill his wife with an axe, that Satan may move into a Soviet child. Even in Soviet melodrama there is a lack of natural villains, though they are required by the canon. Old, pseudomoral ideological stereotypes are still deeply set in the Soviet subconscious; it is not even a matter of censorship or lack of freedom today. Besides, the Russians, with rare exceptions such as Mikhail Bulgakov's novel *The Master and Margarita*, have always had problems with the supernatural in art, and if they deal with it, they prefer an officially approved hypnotist-exorcist, who relieves the tension of perestroika while appearing regularly on national television, to the real *Exorcist* (which, as it happens, was never released in the Soviet Union).

"Our film industry is indeed not ready to produce trilogies about 'star wars' or Indiana Jones's adventures," writes Vladimir Dmitriev, a Soviet expert on American film.

> But could not we make our own *E.T.*? Its story line is rather simple; any lesser scriptwriter could have written it. Its special effects are ordinary and would have been all right for our supervisors. There are almost no complex sets. What else? Well, the Extra Terrestrial itself, a moving toy, Carlo Rambaldi's amazing creation. It is hard to construct it, but not impossible. So we *could* have made something like that even before Spielberg, and achieved incredible success in the world market. What impeded it? Two things, I suggest. First, the lack of imagination, the mental laziness, the habit of following familiar routes. Second, the fear of breaking the tradition. ("Waiting for the Oscar," 17–18)

The fate of the other indigenous Hollywood genres, despite the desire of Soviet filmmakers to catch up with their genre predecessors, has always been shaky. The Soviet musical, for example, so favored by Stalin in the 1930s, never recovered from the "cult of personality," perhaps because of the audience's guilt about being happy and lively while millions were being killed. The disaster film sent forth some promising shoots at the beginning of the 1980s, particularly in Alexander Mitta's 1980 hit *The Crew*, a Soviet variation on *Airport* and *Airport 75*, but soon the disaster genre died out, apparently because it was too expensive for the Soviet film industry.

Under glasnost, however, those filmmakers who chose to search for a new film language had to establish new rules, familiar to any American teenager but completely unknown to the best Soviet film professionals. These efforts, so far, are rather timid and unskillful, though no one would discount the directors' courage or their progressiveness.

Oleg Teptsov, a young director from Leningrad, debuted with *Mr. Designer*, in a genre that could be classified mystery-suspense at a video store. This typical "tale from the dark side" tells the story of a young designer who fashions a female mannequin for a fancy store; she comes to life and he falls victim to her predatory powers. The decadent Russian Art Nouveau atmosphere and the talent of the male lead, Victor Avilov, a theater actor with the face of a young Donald Sutherland trying to portray Dennis Hopper, made *Mr. Designer* a favorite among alternative-film buffs. However, the attempt to combine the classic Hollywood genre with the traditional Russian mode of an "intellectual" film—

slow, lacking in narrative strength, and "hypersignificant"—turned out to be rather pretentious and only partly rewarding. The major problem is the weakness of the script, written by the avant-garde poet and screenwriter Yuri Arabov. The script, which scores points for weirdness but has no chance against the genre competition, reveals one of the major problems of the Soviet genre cinema in general: the lack of screenwriting skills. Sulambek Mamilov's *Day of Wrath* (*Den' gneva*, 1987), a werewolf-suspense variation on a political theme, suffers from a pale script and the lack of skill of the director, which results in inconsistency. More and more "film-centaurs" are torn between old fears and new temptations.

One final example. The 1991 film *Death in Film* (*Smert' v kino*) takes film centaurism to new and frightening heights. It is hard to imagine a more talented crew and cast than the ones assembled for this Soviet-American coproduction. The script is by the veteran writers Eduard Volodarsky and Valentin Chernykh, and the film is directed by Valery Frid and Konstantin Khudyakov and stars Ivan Bortnik. But here the talent ends and the process described in the self-fulfilling title begins. This tortured existentialist tale of a pseudomurder (as it turns out) on a film set, staged by the director to bring out the best in his overstressed actors, ends in the predictable death of the cinematographer. The pretentious final shot (in both senses) of the bullet shattering the screen (the camera lens) is followed by a shot of the bloody hole where the camera operator's eye was. This pays homage to Eisenstein's bloody socket in *Battleship Potemkin* and gives a nod, one assumes, even to Vertov's *Man with a Movie Camera* (*Chelovek s bul'vara kinoapparatom*, 1929) in its self-reflexiveness. The Western viewer is also reminded of the finale of Wim Wenders's *State of Things* (1982), which is unknown in the Soviet Union and therefore an easy film from which to borrow. The intense drama and obligatory brutal sexual sequences suggest an unsatisfying mix of the works of Buñuel, Bergman, Fellini, Coppola, Bogdanovich, and a host of other Hollywood drama-on-the-movie-set films. What is finally so puzzling about *Death in Film* is not just the level of cinematic confusion, but the basic question, "who did the filmmakers feel would actually pay to see such a work?"

The studios' listings of works in progress pledge an increase in Hollywood-oriented genre movies dedicated to urgent perestroika problems. Apparently the favorite of Soviet filmmakers has become the science-fiction thriller à la *Blade Runner*. It may be relatively inexpensive, socially sharp, and potentially successful—these are the three major concerns of the "new thinking" film generation. The artistic significance of these coming films is an open question, though one can still be optimistic.

OLD WORDS, NEW SPELLINGS: POSTMODERN FILMS

Perestroika, despite all its problems and faults, did at least one indispensable job: it blew the doors and the curtains open. Russians found the taste of variety essential to any culture palatable, and the processes vital for contemporary arts found a home in Russia.

Postmodernism, the cultural perspective that unites these processes and to a large degree determines artistic progress today, had been unknown and undreamed-of in Russia. Postmodernism is a "glass bead game," and in previous years, the interpretation of art as a game might have been considered criminal. Art, it was suggested, is a spiritual work, not a game. Therefore, it would be relevant to expect the Russians to view postmodernism as something unspiritual and even immoral. Furthermore, postmodernism is an art language based on the mixture of different art languages. How could it develop in a culture that was totally monolingual?

Meanwhile, postmodernism reflects the changes in human perspective that have occurred in the second half of the twentieth century. To recognize life behind the glass wall culture placed between a man and reality has become almost impossible. We do not compare art with reality anymore; we associate life with art. To say of a painting, "It looks as if it is real," would be a questionable compliment today, though we can say of a landscape seen through a car window, "It looks like a Van Gogh," or of a face, "It's so Felliniesque." *Stagecoach* and *Citizen Kane*, *Scarface* and *Psycho* do exist, and they have influenced human consciousness more than any striking scientific discoveries. Instead of pretending that they have not, which would be merely childish, postmodernism uses them, and anything else that happens to be on hand, to create a new language of old expressions.

In the postmodern cinema, from Wim Wenders to Jean-Luc Godard, from Monty Python to the Coen brothers, from Steven Spielberg to Wes Craven, the classic formulas are always available as a useful framework. Postmodern film, indeed, has different devices to create its "old and new" language. It can take a simple story, approaching it as an "empty space," and fill it out with various quotations from the film tradition, compiling an extravagantly eclectic cocktail of apparently incompatible ingredients, as Terry Gilliam did in *Brazil* (1985). He took the plot and its mood from Orwell, the set from Fritz Lang's *Metropolis*, a shot from Eisenstein's *Potemkin*—and managed to make a surprisingly original picture.

Genre is much more resourceful than mere verisimilitude in providing the rules of the game as well as its contents and spirit. Genre gives a stereotyped language-mask that can cover any face—and that is what postmodernism loves and needs. Wim Wenders's *Hammett* (1982) addresses the correlation of imagination and reality, and that of an author and his creation, although it is wrapped in the cover of a classic gangster film; this illustrates a typically postmodern approach to genre as well as to the film form in general.

Soviet film, at least the part of it that understood glasnost as freedom of expression, not merely freedom of speech, jumped over tradition (or the lack of it) and joined the mainstream with the readiness and the cheek of an infant prodigy. The first attack on postmodernist bulwarks was launched in 1986 in *Assa* by Sergei Solovyev. We need to reexamine this film here in light of postmodernism.

Solovyev, the renowned moralist of the Soviet screen in the 1970s and 1980s, switched channels elegantly: from the autumn mood of his previous teen pictures, which spoke generally of the threshold of spiritual maturity—to the wintry southern town of Yalta, where it never snows but where snow now lies like a heavy cloak, where postpunk youths try to sell their Jethro Tull–like rock music to restaurant customers, and where bizarre adventures wait around the corner.

Bananan, the new Solovyev hero (the name, nonexistent in any language, is apparently derived from "banana"), does not look like the director's former characters or any other characters in Soviet cinema. Bananan is being arrested by a police officer for wearing an earring (or for singing subversively funny songs with serious implications). He falls in love with a girl who is visiting the southern resort with her prosperous older lover, and this lover (played by director Stanislav Govorukhin) not only intervenes in their relationship, which prosperous lovers usually do, but happens to be a mafioso, which they normally are not.

Thus melodrama, eventually descending to the sappiness of *Love Story*, intersects with the thriller, complete with a chase through lonely streets and a final bloodbath. The mafioso, when he sees that blackmailing will not move this half-teenager, half-freak, Bananan, takes him out of town, stabs him with a knife, leaves him to die on a country road, and comes back to meet his own death. Alika, the third point of the triangle, kills him in a bathtub full of red roses whose redness merges with blood. (Film theory suffers from the lack of research on the role of the bathroom in suspense films, from *Les diaboliques*, *Psycho*, and *The Tingler* to *The Shining* and *Fatal Attraction*.)

The thriller theme is the most provocative part of *Assa*. The director's intentions are realized here in full. It is not so thrilling as it is kitschy and bizarre, which is not a fault but a choice. The mafioso is an intellectual. He is, in fact, the smartest character in the movie. Instead of inventing plots, this villain reads a book on the murder of Czar Paul I in the eighteenth century, parts of which, as noted earlier, come to life on the screen. A dwarf couple is involved in the criminal intrigue. They work in a dwarf cabaret and have a normal-size son visiting them on army leave. Being blackmailed by the villain, one of them commits suicide on the deck of a yacht after a theatrically pathetic farewell monologue. The air force officer turns out to be an alcoholic crackpot in costume, and the silly counterpart of the mafioso happens to be a KGB agent. The case for a double bass is employed as a tool for a crime. This weirdness complements the general outlandishness of the set (palm trees under snow), and also suggests that the thriller genre is being used by the director as a game, as a sign, as a language, but not as an essence.

It is harder to say this about *Assa*'s melodrama, which grows weaker as it grows more serious and real. The reason for the director's failure at this point is simple: he loved his heroes too much to treat them as dice in the game. He loved the rock-underground milieu he had entered while making the film, and seriously believed that the future belonged to it. He became pathetic and lost his sense of humor—and the rules of the game along with it.

The initial subject matter of the movie, hidden behind all kinds of aesthetic masks, was supposed to be "the perversity of the stagnation period," the late 1960s to the early 1980s, in which Russia collapsed under Brezhnev. That is why the whole world of *Assa* was turned upside down, including the unusual weather conditions. But the multilayered structure that set out to cover this secret theme (besides the layer of genre, the movie contains those of youth, the rock and roll underground, and history) proved uneven, since some of the layers were treated not as the masks but as the faces. What was offered as language turned into subject matter, defeating the playful postmodern multitude of meanings.

The diagnosis is apparent: the director, Sergei Solovyev, like many of his colleagues, lacking the nerve to dump tradition, old Russian psychology, and linear narrative, stopped in the middle of the road. Nor did he trust postmodern aesthetics, which in this case demanded a whimsical and eclectic mix of popular genres, classical clichés, and improbable hints. What he did have was a taste for the game; what he lacked was the skill and culture of the game. The inherited ignorance in "film linguistics" struck back. However, this first attempt had been made, and it was undoubtedly worth pursuing.

The next attempt was not long in coming. In 1988, a young Kazakh director, Rashid Nugmanov, a student of Solovyev's at VGIK, the national film school, released his first feature, *The Needle*, which pushed his teacher's pioneer attitude further. We also need here to go beyond the remarks about the film made above.

The subject matter of *The Needle*, like that of *Assa*, is social and belongs to a formerly shelved issue: drug abuse. But instead of hiding the subject matter, as Solovyev did, Nugmanov put it into the narrative and allowed it to become overstressed, at which point his interest in it died.

A youngster named Moro (played by the late rock legend from the Leningrad group Kino, Victor Tsoy) secretly arrives in his Asiatic hometown to collect an old debt. In looking for a place to stay, he runs into an ex-girlfriend, Dina (Marina Smirnova), who is using heroin heavily. Moro tries to save her by taking her out of town to the Aral Sea, which turns out to be dried up, and taking up the gauntlet of Dina's abuser (played by Pyotr Mamonov, another rock idol and the future star of *Taxi Blues*) and his gang. In the very unhappy ending, Dina stays on drugs and Moro gets stabbed in an alley at night. The message is simple and clear: do not mess with drugs, and if you do, stay clear of the drug dealers. The only bad news for a potential censor is that the "good guy" finally loses, which is no longer enough reason to ban the movie.

Meanwhile, the real message of *The Needle* is as far from "Caution: drugs!" as the meaning of a television commercial is far from the real product. This message emerges from the director's keen-eyed manipulation of various cultural stereotypes. The film, for example, is dedicated to Soviet television, yet there is not a hint of what is meant by this dedication. Interpretations vary from the director's obsession with reproducing media (besides all kinds of television screens in the film, in the epilogue following the dedication, we see all the critical moments of the movie in instant replay), to the sarcastic equivocation about Communist censorship (the epilogue is simply a compilation of the censored shots), to nothing but a childlike romp.

On another level of convention, every twist of the narrative is foreshadowed by a syrupy radio voice-over in the manner of a children's program. The sound track is full of different languages—Kazakh, Russian, Italian, German, and English—which may have a realistic basis, since all Soviet republics are populated with mixed ethnic groups, but which more likely creates the image of the world as a Tower of Babel.

Yet *The Needle* scores highest in the game based on the public image of its protagonist. Victor Tsoy was known in Soviet rock music as "the last romantic," and that is how he is cast in *The Needle*. This romanticism and Tsoy's performance have much less to do with reality and realism than with the Charles Bronson–Clint Eastwood form of romantic hero: taciturn, morose, and concentrated, an invincible superman with a vague past and, most probably, not a bright future, an introvert who keeps a grain of childhood in his heart and may be charmingly, tenderly in love.

The genre cliché the filmmakers play with in *The Needle* is the action film with a touch of the melodramatic. The rules of the game are not so diverse as they are easygoing and light. Gaps are left, for instance, in place of all the action climaxes into which any Charles Bronson production would plunge. The esoteric location—the dead sea of Aral—makes the hero's image almost sickly sweet. Nugmanov and Tsoy, however, do not let the mocking mask cover the existential problem, which is the real theme of the film—the problem of the lost generation, lost both by society and in the jungle of life. To reach it, a viewer has to try all the colored glasses provided by the game, but the postmodernist secret of vision is that one can stop, satisfied, at any level of the multilayered structure, or just enjoy the motley surface. No one loses in this game.

The Needle is not perfect; what is lacking is the richness of culture, or—and we are back to the initial question of the Russian postmodern project—the knowledge of languages, which still makes it easy to distinguish Rashid Nugmanov from Fassbinder. But it would be ruthless, if not senseless, to demand that a baby taking his or her first steps run a marathon. At the end of *The Needle* the stabbed hero lights a cigarette and walks away into the snowy night, despite the logical death and the rules of socialist realism. The promise of this coda, not necessarily optimistic in the narrative, is certainly optimistic in the context of the new Soviet cinema. It goes far beyond *The Needle II*. The motif of final departure, repeated in such other genre films as *The Cold Summer of '53*, makes it clear: the land of the unknown still lies ahead.

CHAPTER

From Accusatory to Joyful Laughter: Restructuring the Soviet Comic-Satiric Muse

There's nothing to laugh at here, you sons of bitches!
—THE GENERAL in V. Voinovich's *Life and Extraordinary Adventures of Private Ivan Chonkin*

"LAUGHING WHILE THE LASH SWISHES": SOVIET FILM COMEDY AND SATIRE

AT A PLANNING MEETING of the administration of the Central Bureau for Leisure Time, matters appear routine, except the time is 1987 and Gorbachev's perestroika is two years old. The aging, fumbling old department chief asks for reports from his staff, saying, "Let's have it straight, in keeping with the times." At this point a lean, dapper man in his early forties who is the assistant director rises and tells his boss that he is an old reactionary do-nothing and that all the programs they run are useless and ridiculous. The chief and the staff go into shock.

So did the enthusiastic Soviet audiences that embraced veteran comic-satiric filmmaker Eldar Ryazanov's *Forgotten Tune for the Flute*, mentioned in the previous chapter. But the shock of the scene is made suddenly ironic as the scene is repeated with the opposite "script," thus suggesting what really happened as opposed to the playful daydream of the protagonist, Leonid Filimonov. Asked to speak "straight," our antihero talks as we suspect bureaucrats have always spoken: as they feel their bosses want them to speak. Filimonov (played by Leonid Filatov) states that under glasnost there is "too much freedom, and so we need to draw up some guidelines for this freedom."

Between the daydream and everyday reality, the film satirically, dramatically, and comically suggests, Soviet citizens today struggle, half-liberated, half-confused, to find their way under glasnost. The goal of this chapter is to explore how and to what degree Soviet reality has been represented and treated through the twin perspectives of comedy and satire.

The satiric-comic films emerging from the Soviet Union under glasnost call attention to a long and distinguished tradition of Russian laughter in literature. Much of that tradition has been influenced by Western models (Horace, commedia del l'arte, Shakespeare, Molière, Addison), especially in the spirit of the eighteenth century and the Enlightenment's feeling that "the most effective means of correcting faults and vices in society, and of instigating virtue was satire" (Welsh, *Russian Comedy*, 18). More specifically, Russian writers of the past learned the techniques of satire of individuals (from Plautus and Terence) and of a more universal kind, *comédie de caracterè* as practiced by Ben Jonson, Molière, and others, in which it is the "humor" or vice itself, rather than the person, that is mocked. Thus from Gogol to A. N. Ostrovsky to Chekhov, satire and humor have generally been aimed at a serious purpose. Eisenstein, as we shall see, also followed this path, stating, "I adhere to the tradition of laughing while the lash swishes. Mine is the laughter of destruction" (*Notes of a Film Director*, 108).

There is one other element in Soviet culture that may seem foreign to Western audiences but that seems important if we are to grasp the nature of many Soviet film comedies and satires, and that is the function of the holy fool, *yurodivy*, in Russian Orthodox culture. Red Square in Moscow is dominated by the presence of two structures. One is the flat, dark, slablike building housing Lenin's tomb (though given the events of 1991, Lenin may soon be moved). The other is St. Basil's Cathedral, with its wildly diverse, multicolored onion domes rising above the skyline, dedicated to one of the most respected Russian holy fools. Touched by God but outside the normal channels of society, the holy fool traditionally would be that figure who seemed half-crazy and half-admirable (nothing and no one can exercise authority or control over someone whose power apparently evolves from the spirit itself). To speak of the concept of the holy fool, that character existing between the spiritual and the material worlds, is to speak of the influence of the Orthodox faith in general. Clearly the Orthodox tradition, derived from the Greek Byzantine Orthodox tradition centered in Constantinople, had much to do with the shaping of the Russian spirit. With an orientation toward the spiritual and the mystical expressed through the elaborate ritual of the Orthodox ceremony and the rich splendor of Orthodox churches, monasteries, and cathedrals, the Orthodox tradition has existed for a thousand years, most recently in direct tension with the materialist ideology of communism. But there is a further irony. The holy fool, while celebrated by the church, lived outside the influence of the church as well, and thus he or she was truly a simple person, part insane (by modern criteria), part inspired, part human, part saint.

Returning to comedy and satire, we should note that the holy fool transcends traditional Western genres as well. Neither wholly comic nor tragic, the fool truly bridges the emotional and the rational, tears and laughter, at times evoking both. A noteworthy tragicomedy or romantic melodrama—it has elements of each of these—on the eve of glasnost is Pyotr Todorovsky's 1984 film, *The Wartime Romance*, touched on in the previous chapter. To the Western viewer, the film appears to be a bittersweet, straightforward romance with a sentimental touch. An innocent young soldier, Alexander, in World War II, is totally captivated by the mistress of a major who is later killed in action. Alexander's attraction to Liuba is closer to Dante's fascination with Beatrice than to that of a would-be lover. In fact, he tells Liuba when he meets her at last on the battlefield that he hopes she and the major will be happy because just knowing she exists makes him happy.

The narrative then moves forward some ten years. Alexander, a married man and a film projectionist studying to be a history teacher, meets Liuba on a winter street selling hot biscuits; she is a worn-out vendor with a daughter at her side. Alexander's fascination becomes an obsession as he begins to do everything in his power to help her, to make her happy, including becoming a fool himself, selling her biscuits for her as his boss passes him by.

On one level Alexander is simply a fool for love. But the nature of his love—its nonphysical dimension—leads him to risk everything in the eyes of his wife, his boss, friends, and society, and places him in the tragicomic realm of the holy fool. In one scene, he is projecting a Chaplin film in the cinema. He, Liuba, and her daughter are in the projection booth watching the film. Then, after redoing her hair and makeup, Alexander dances with his love as Chaplin romps below in the theater. The scene evokes a smile rather than laughter. Todorovsky's scene does not even approach the level of romantic comedy that is so much a part of American screwball comedy and its contemporary Hollywood variations. Rather, there is a feeling of gentle and even sad amusement and nostalgia as Chaplin's silent image plays against Alexander's silent dance, each commenting on the other, both male figures "gentlemen" out of sync with the society around them. To recognize the Chaplin parallel is enough to enjoy the scene. But in the context of the holy fool tradition, the scene gains in resonance. This is not to say that Alexander is "religious" in the literal sense of the term. But he is clearly a simple person who sees in Liuba a purity, a sense of beauty that the world has otherwise denied him. "You do not know your own worth, do you?" he asks her in the "present" (ten years after the war), and, indeed, the main thrust of the film is that she does not know. That it is this fool who points out a "better way" to her once again suggests the moral and ethical power of this gentle humor, this sentimental comedy.

SOVIET SOCIAL SATIRE VERSUS HOLLYWOOD'S CYNICAL COMEDY

The contemporary Soviet approach to comedy and satire can further be clarified if we take into consideration the Soviet comic film tradition and its contrast with Hollywood comedy in the 1980s and 1990s.

A review of Soviet cinema suggests how important comic and satirical strategies have been since the beginning of the Soviet state. Boris Shumyatsky, writing in his book *A Cinema for the Millions (Kinematografiya millionov)* in 1935, just before the worst Stalinist years, defended the importance of laughter-provoking films under communism with these words:

> Tsarist and capitalist Russia were not acquainted with happy joyful laughter in their best works. The laughter in Gogol, Shchedrin and Chekhov is accusing laughter, laughter derived from bitterness and hatred. . . . We believe that, if Gogol, Shchedrin and Chekhov were alive today, their actual laughter would in the Soviet Union acquire *joie de vivre*, optimism and cheerfulness. (Taylor and Christie, *Film Factory*, 368)

Shumyatsky was defending Grigori Alexandrov's *Happy Guys* (1934) from attacks that said it was the "apotheosis of vulgarity." His emphasis is on the sense of good clean fun that such films offered a Soviet society with a promising future under communism.

Viewed from today's perspective, however, as seen in a film such as *A Forgotten Tune for the Flute*, the Soviet realm of comedy and satire has tilted back to the "accusing laughter" of the Enlightenment in Europe and in Russian drama and literature. Glasnost has provided the opportunity to use a light (farcical) and heavy (black humor) touch to point out the shortcomings, contradictions, and failures of more than seventy years of Soviet socialism.

Irony and accusing laughter are, in fact, a potent form of survival, an alternative worldview as well as an offensive tactic. Irina Ratushinskaya, in her searing account of the years she spent in a political prison for women for human-rights activities under Brezhnev, *Grey Is the Color of Hope*, frequently suggests how often the darkest events—such as the planting of a KGB stooge in their area—brought on deep laughter rather than pure anger. "It was all we could do not to collapse on the grass in helpless fits of laughter. On the whole, though, the situation might be far from funny" (88), she writes, suggesting how intimately laughter becomes, under oppression, a way of distancing oneself from the oppressors and of celebrating one's own sense of self, values, and dignity.

We have touched on the satirical power of many recent Soviet films in earlier chapters. In particular we have looked at Abuladze's allegorical satire of Stalinism in *Repentance*, the multidirectional barbs aimed at contemporary Soviet realities in Pichul's *Little Vera*, and the pop, surrealistic, youth-oriented satire in Solovyev's *Assa*. Now we wish further to examine the implications of comedy and satire for perestroika.

First, however, we need to suggest an international context for our subject. The leading form of comedy in the world is, of course, the Hollywood comedy, a genre that year after year dominates the box office in terms of popularity. In 1988, for instance, six of the top ten money-making films were comedies, led by *Who Framed Roger Rabbit?*

But in the period 1985–1990, there was an important shift in the ideology of much American film comedy that is significant as a stark contrast to the purposeful, critical laughter of so much Soviet film satire. The most popular comedy of all time to date has been Ivan Reitman's *Ghostbusters*, released in 1984 (shortly before glasnost), and followed in the summer of 1989 with *Ghostbusters II*, which topped the original in tickets sold. What emerges as a strong characteristic of Reitman's films and many others such as *Ferris Bueller's Day Off* is how they fit a pattern of what William Paul sees as "Reaganite Comedy" ("Bill Murray," 4). These recent films stand in strong contrast to the earlier tradition of American silent films and the screwball comedies of Capra and Hawkes. The earlier films championed the "little guy," or at least introduced the romantic myth of the possibility of fusing the lower middle class with the American aristocracy by presenting couples from differing social classes. *Ghostbusters* and *Ghostbusters II*, despite their apparent anarchy, are deeply in favor of capitalism and big business, antienvironment, pronuclear, and supportive of an ethical stance in which "conning" rather than truth is what matters. (When Bill Murray tells Sigourney Weaver that he is a scientist, she more accurately evaluates him as looking like "a talk-show host," which, as the film's opening makes clear, he is.) J. Hoberman notes in his review of *Ghostbusters II* how the film can be seen to sum up the Reagan era, especially since the original film came out just before Reagan won the election for his second term. The film is, he states, "the perfect embodiment of Reaganism" since it is "celebrating the creation and exploitation of a false need" ("Suddenly, Last Summer," 65: both films strongly suggest that the Ghostbusters themselves have created the ghosts they claim to attack). And William Paul, observing how Bill Murray and former President Reagan were each given to mockery as a public persona, states that "the mockery seems a necessary defense against a nihilism so deep that neither can afford to confront it directly" ("Bill Murray," 11).

A definite contrast in style and direction arises, therefore, between the predominant Soviet and American comedies of the late 1980s. American comedy has been steadily losing the democratic or populist flavor that characterized it in the past in favor of a "Reaganite," cynical neoconservatism that ignores many contemporary issues such as racial strife, drugs, women's rights, and AIDS. Such comedy ultimately endorses the status quo rather than offering any true critique of it. (It should also be pointed out that much of this comedy is xenophobic: in *Ghostbusters II* the evil threat to New York comes from "Carpathia" in Eastern Europe, and is spearheaded by one Janosz Pha, looking suspiciously like Sergei Eisenstein himself as interpreted by Peter MacNicol.)

In contrast, recent Soviet satire in literature, film, and music has become an important voice in the critical reevaluation of Soviet values. In this sense, even though much Soviet comedy has changed from the toothless laughter of the past to laughter with an accusatory tone, that tone can be read as more optimistic than the smug cynicism of many recent American comedies, for in criticism there is the hope of awareness and thus of change.

Dostoevsky claimed that Gogol's short story "The Overcoat" is the starting point of all Russian literature. But Gogol was following in the satiric Russian tradition of reforming mankind through laughter: "laughter through tears," as he defined his purpose in writing *The Inspector General*. To understand how Gogol's center of levity is anchored in a blend of realism and the supernatural (fantasy and the grotesque) alongside a Christian sense of compassion for the insignificant and downtrodden, and to recognize how much this spirit runs throughout Russian and Soviet literature and cinema, is to see how radically different such satire is from the recent "Reaganite comedy" of self-absorption and conservatism.

DIALECTIC VERSUS DIALOGIC COMEDY

The dialectics of humor under communism present yet another series of issues for our appreciation of joyful and accusatory laughter. But first these too must be seen in the larger context of the nature of comedy itself.

The complexity and ambiguity of comedy and satire have come under close critical scrutiny in recent years. Jerry Palmer, for instance, aptly notes that, "regardless of the specifics of the joke in question, humor is both subversive and conservative, offensive and inoffensive, serious and ridiculous" (*Logic of the Absurd*, 182). As with Irina Ratushinskaya's prison laughter, we are aware that such a comic-ironic response to a clear, present, and yet absurd danger cuts several ways.

In his studies of medieval carnival and Rabelais, Mikhail Bakhtin identifies the importance of "carnival laughter," the laughter of the street and the common person, uncontrolled by the normal social, political, and religious hierarchies of power. Bakhtin, writing much of his work on laughter in the repressive atmosphere of the Stalinist period, saw this laughter of the people in all its constructive and deconstructive forms, its ambiguous and often grotesque expressions, its scatological, sexual, and satirical dimensions, as, ultimately, a means to "consecrate inventive freedom, to permit the combination of a variety of different elements and their rapprochement, to liberate from *the prevailing point of view of the world,* from conventions and established truths, from clichés, from all that is humdrum and universally accepted" (*Rabelais*, 34, emphasis added). Such freedom celebrates the "dialogic" or polyphonic—a multiplicity of expression.

Two observations concerning Bakhtin's emphasis on such a dialogic tradition appear appropriate. First, one would expect that Communist socialism, as a movement of the people and for the people, would, in theory, champion such freewheeling expressions of the common folk. This did not happen. Rather, as we know, the satiric muse during the Stalinist 1930s and 1940s was almost completely silent while comedies took the form of the wildly optimistic musical comedies of Grigori Alexandrov, who had begun his career with Eisenstein. Such films as *Circus* (*Tsirk*, 1936) and *Volga, Volga* (1938) were some of the most popular Soviet films ever. Instead of being examples of "carnivalesque" comedy of the people, however, they offered a vision of a mythologized socialist utopia in which workers were happy, tables were loaded with food and drink, shops were bustling, and progress was everywhere visible. Enthusiastic film audiences of the day had little food themselves and lived lives of fear and drudgery. This effect was, of course, similar to the effect of musical comedy in the United States at about the same time; American audiences attended escapist films about happiness, romance, and wealth while emerging from the Depression. Such "comic" Soviet works purposely shaped cinematic comic realities that contrasted strongly with the actual world in which audiences lived. Dr. Maya Turkovskaya, for instance, has documented the magnitude of this gap for *Volga, Volga,* noting in particular the number of filmmakers connected with the making of the film who were imprisoned or executed before the film was completed ("Behind the Scenes"). As several Soviet critics have noted, comedy in such forms served the purposes of the state by providing an escape valve for pent-up frustrations and a mythological model of what communism hoped to be. What these films clearly were not, on the other hand, were expressions of the people that "consecrated inventive freedom."

Even on a theoretical political level, we see that in Communist ideology, when "the people" and "freedom" are discussed, it is through the limiting funnel of dialectics—carefully identified opposites. In comedy as in all other modes of sociopolitical discourse, the dialogic (polyphonic) became simplistic ("monologic") under Soviet Marxism-Leninism.

The second point in relation to Bakhtin's remarks is to note that a more truly dialogic tradition existed in Soviet film before 1935 and also in the past twenty years. In the 1920s, for instance, farce, satire, vaudeville, commedia del l'arte, and American silent comedies—especially those of Chaplin, Keaton, and Harold Lloyd—made a strong impression on pioneering Soviet filmmakers. One of Leo Kuleshov's earliest and most interesting films is the lighthearted spoof *The Extraordinary Adventures of Mr. West in the Land of the Bolsheviks.* The satire of capitalism is definitely light and the humor joyful and thus in the spirit of, and a tribute to, the "anything goes" flavor of American silent comedy. Vlada Petric has noted that the "film's subtext addresses the viewer's intimate world, touching upon ideas and judgments antithetical to the Bolshevik view of history and society" ("Subtextual Reading"). Dziga Vertov's *Man with a Movie Camera* owes much of its energy and high spirits to the large number of gags and visual jokes employing a playful use of film language, both subtle and obvious, throughout the film, many of them with underlying suggestions of a healthy sense of sexuality. Again, the emphasis is much more on joyful and playful laughter than on satire and biting dark humor, in the spirit of Shumyatsky's description of *The Happy Guys.* Finally, Alexander Medvedkin is the early Soviet director who comes closest to embodying a sense of Bakhtin's description of "carnival laughter." His *Happiness (Schastye,* 1935) is a surrealistic comic-satirical romp that spoofs farm life in both czarist and Soviet times. His innovative use of camera tricks, outrageous absurdity, and slapstick (a soldier rubbing a horse's rear end, a man sitting on a throne in an outhouse, a father and son hitting each other with spoons) still evoke uproarious laughter, as evidenced by a special 1988 tribute to Medvedkin held in front of a full house at Dom Kino, at which the eighty-eight-year-old master of Soviet satire appeared in person.

Eisenstein writes in his autobiography, *Immoral Memories* (1946), that the figure he admires most is the clown. In his essay "A Few Thoughts about Soviet Comedy," he goes further in his description of socialist laughter. American laughter is for the pure pleasure of laughter, he notes, and even Chaplin wins us over as a "grownup behaving like a child" (*Notes*, 110). For the Soviet Union, however, comedy must be satirical: "The time has not yet come for us to indulge in carefree laughter: socialism has not yet been built. So there is no call for light heartedness. Laughter is a new kind of weapon" (ibid., 111).

None of his films is a comedy or pure satire per se except for the short piece he shot as an insert for the well-known stage production of *Even a Wise Man Stumbles*. But traces of both are found in his first feature, *The Strike*, which shows Meyerhold's strong comic and improvisational influence in the surrealistic, circuslike construction, cartoonlike caricaturizing, especially of the fat, ugly capitalists (what he called *typage*), and heavily ironic use of montage in the film. Yet in Eisenstein's hands, the satire is more pointed, more accusing, more dialectic than can be seen in the films previously mentioned. For all its comic touches, Eisenstein's climax is literally deadly serious: in the now-famous cut, he juxtaposes the shooting of workers on strike with the slaughter of a cow, ending with the message: REMEMBER, PROLETARIANS! With such a didactic Marxist message, Eisenstein goes far beyond the confines of the more general and good-natured social satire of the popular playwright Alexander Ostrovsky (1823–1886) in his *Even a Wise Man Stumbles* and other popular works.

Between these twin poles of laughter—Eisenstein's highly accusatory style and Medvedkin's irreverent satirical pleasure—the comic muse under glasnost is developing and finding its own contemporary voice.

RYAZANOV AND THE SHAPING OF GLASNOST'S BARBED LAUGHTER

"Society obviously becomes stronger," writes Soviet critic Boris Berman, "when social criticism comes in the form of open satire, rather than in whispers in the privacy of homes" ("Satire Fed by Candour," 12). What the critic leaves unsaid, however, is that today's barbed satire points, directly and indirectly, at the party itself. Unlike Eisenstein's antibourgeois, dialectical satire, much of the present cinematic accusatory laughter is aimed specifically at the System and thus at socialism itself, as well as generally at human nature.

Cinematic comedy must be viewed in the context of literature. Certainly one of the major accomplishments of modern Soviet prose has been Mikhail Bulgakov's realistic and surrealistic, tragic-absurd satire, *The Master and Margarita*, written during the depths of the Stalinist

1930s but suppressed until its sensational publication in 1966–1967 in the journal *Moscow*. In the early pages of this influential and much-loved work, Satan, visiting Moscow, asks a question of the protagonist that might well serve as a banner for much of the comic satire being produced today: "Allow me to ask you, then, how man can govern if he cannot plan for even so ridiculously short a span as a thousand years or so, if, in fact, he cannot guarantee his own next day?" (*Master and Margarita*, 11). Bulgakov is bitterly critical of communism. But the Devil's words cut deeper to illuminate human nature: ultimately the author who spent so much of his life suppressed by the Soviet regime suggests that the System is simply a multiplication of the shortcomings of each individual. Another sign of glasnost in practice is that the former chief of the filmmakers' Union, Elem Klimov, began working on the film version of Bulgakov's novel in 1989.

In recent years Vladimir Voinovich has carried the literary satirical torch with such imaginative, bitingly comic works as *The Ivankiad* (about the epic attempts to acquire a larger apartment in Moscow) and *The Life and Extraordinary Adventures of Private Ivan Chonkin*, which is very much a Soviet version of *The Good Soldier Svejk* and, though once banned, was recently set for production by none other than Eldar Ryazanov, until complications with the London-based producers led to the cancellation of the project. Bulgakov and Voinovich, with their mixture of general and specific satire, are useful touchstones for us as we return to 1987 and *A Forgotten Tune for the Flute*.

Ryazanov, who studied under Eisenstein and Grigori Kozintsev and who has cowritten almost all his projects with screenwriter Emil Braginsky, has made more than fifteen comedies, ranging from farce to musical comedy, tragicomedy, and satire. For over thirty years he has been one of the most inventive of Soviet satirists, especially in his spoofs on socialist bureaucracy. Beginning during Krushchev's thaw with *Carnival Night* (*Karnaval'naya noch*, 1956), he has produced some of the most popular Soviet comedies, mixing realism, romance, satire, farce, and fantasy. *The Girl without an Address* (*Devushka bez adresa*, 1957), *Man from Nowhere* (*Chelovek niotkuda*, 1961), *Beware, Automobile!* (*Beregis' avtomobilya*, 1966), and *Zigzag of Fortune* (*Zigzag udachi*, 1969) established his reputation for mixing joyful and accusatory laughter. His goal in all his works, however, according to his autobiography, is "I would like people to see in my comedies life as it is."

A Forgotten Tune for the Flute is anticipated to varying degrees by three other works. *The Irony of Fate* (1975) builds on a fantasy of "what if" centering on a man who returns home drunk one night only to discover that he is in the wrong apartment in the wrong city with the wrong woman. The other two prototypes concern the Soviet bureaucracy. With eighteen million bureaucrats, compared to the four million American federal employees (Whitney, "Revolution"), the Soviets have keenly appreciated satire aimed at bureaucracy itself, a central concern for Ryazanov. His use of "miracles" in the midst of a common or even grim reality can be seen in *An Office Romance* (*Sluzhebnyi roman*, 1978), but in *Garage* (*Garazh*, 1980), strong satire begins to emerge and to go beyond the more easygoing humor of his earlier films. Here is a tale of another bureaucracy, this time an environmental institute dedicated to endangered species. The institute and its members themselves become endangered and, in a plot reminiscent in tone and scope of Buñuel's *Exterminating Angel*, the protagonists are unable to leave their building, not because of some mysterious force as in Buñuel, but simply because they do not wish to lose their chance to obtain a private garage. Thus they are forced to come to terms with each other's problems. This dark satire ends ambiguously; the audience is free to decide whether this shared experience will actually change their lives enough for a happy ending or simply allow them to resume their previous banal existences.

A Forgotten Tune for the Flute is both a natural progression from Ryazanov's past career and a rethinking of how satire and comedy can develop under glasnost. Ironically enough, the film is based on the popular Ryazanov and Braginsky play of the 1970s, written during the stagnation period. As an example of an early glasnost work, therefore, it clearly is simply an expansion and updating of the kind of satire already being practiced ten years before.

The dictum "less is more" is certainly not the philosophy of this film, which reflects both the best and the weakest elements of the new Soviet cinema. To separate which element is which is extremely difficult, for the weaknesses (excesses) are also largely the strengths.

Ryazanov and Braginsky have served up the familiar, mundane story of a harried bureaucrat who has an affair with an artistic and beautiful younger woman, in this instance a nurse (played by Tatyana Dogileva) who is also an amateur actor. As is typical for such a bourgeois plot, the main question is whether Leonid will leave his secure position and well-connected wife (it was through her father's pull that Leonid moved from being a mediocre flutist to a leading administrator) for his working-class lover. The decision is even harder here than in Todorovsky's *Wartime Romance*, for while Alexander is from the beginning seen as a fool (different, offbeat, odd), Leonid is painted as a status- and security-seeking Communist bureaucrat.

Were this the entire scope of Ryazanov's film, it would merely be another of the many "safe" pop films made during the Brezhnev era to please large audiences. But the filmmakers have pulled out every possible comic, satiric, and melodramatic stop in order to construct a film that does not clearly fit any one genre. It appears illuminated by all film, stage, and literary comedy, romance, and melodrama. In this respect, *A Forgotten Tune* is, in Bakhtin's sense, quite "carnivalesque," bursting beyond any conventional limits of narrative form and power.

One feels that the film is a mosaic or collage of Russian, Soviet, and Western cultural forms. It would be tedious to trace all allusions; suffice it to say that one senses that Ryazanov began his glasnost phase by building on Gogol, Chekhov, Capra, American screwball comedies, Fellini, Lina Wertmuller, Bulgakov, French bedroom farces, the "Czech Touch" comedies of such directors as Milos Forman and Jiri Menzel, earlier Soviet absurdist-realist serious comedies such as *Autumn Marathon*, and Strindberg's shattering existential symbolist dramas. With such ambitions, the film emerges as experimental and courageous, and at times pretentious and unfocused.

The narrative works on multiple levels. It is a topical satire of a stagnating and corrupt Communist bureaucracy, and thus in line with Ryazanov's previous attacks on crippling bureaucracy. It is also a bedroom farce (a typical comedy of errors as the wife returns home too early and catches her husband and his lover together, for instance), a melodramatic romance, and an absurdist comedy (a funny recurring motif has to do with a chorus of shapely women who were sent by Leonid's office on tour with no specific destination, who got lost, and who now provocatively sing folk songs as they wear traditional costumes and perform on decks of aircraft carriers, at seaside spas, and at Central Asian mountain meadows to aroused and appreciative males). It is also a semifeminist tract. Much of the sexual comedy comes from Lida's contemporary responses to Leonid's male behavior; he tries to be "modern" by asking her if she wants to go to bed with him, and she quips as she eats his caviar and mushrooms (a status symbol), "Nobody ever asked me before they did it!"

Finally, it is also a surrealistic allegory, as Leonid's dream sequences become ever more elaborate and threatening. What begins as a slice-of-life film (opening shot: Leonid leaving his apartment and driving to work) ends as an expressionist tale with religious connotations as he dies. Leonid "sees" a ghostly sequence in which representatives of Soviet culture (workers, soldiers, young lovers, old women, scientists, musicians, and many others, in a sequence that echoes the dumb show at the conclusion of Gogol's *Inspector General*) silently and continually switch seats in an endless procession through several dark rooms, suggesting the flow of Soviet culture. At the same time his deceased parents speak to him. In a heavy-handed manner, Leonid's mother explains to her son that "it's the Last Judgment," and proceeds to chastise him for not visiting their graves.

What immediately draws attention to Ryazanov's film as a glasnost satire is his mockery of bureaucracy and of perestroika itself. Carnival, Bakhtin reminds us, allows for the expression of all voices since, by definition, within the realm of the "carnivalesque," no one is an observer; all are participants. There is, first of all, the theme song, sung as a ballad by a man and a woman, which puts us in a satirical frame of mind; it comments on the Soviet situation today while we are treated to a montage of images of various people, including fat bureaucrats, on their way to work. Leonid himself, as a high-ranking bureaucrat, explains to angry actors when their production of Gogol's *Inspector General* is shut down that under glasnost "we never ban anything. We only make suggestions." The implications are clear, however: bureaucracy speaks its own language, one that can adapt to any situation, with the results being the same. Whether censored or only subject to "suggestions," the play is cancelled. Leonid's cynical wife, Lena, comments halfway through, "This perestroika is only talk anyway."

Many other moments also speak to Soviet audiences about contemporary events. A showdown between wife and mistress is played out against a winter arts auction in a park, reminiscent of the first such open show held under Brezhnev, which ended with bulldozers destroying the artwork as police cracked down on what had at first been allowed. When the old boss suggests that it is time to get the bulldozers out again, a nervous Leonid states, "The time for bulldozers has passed."

Beyond such topicality, the film is finally a comic drama or dramatic comedy of character, much in the tradition of what Harold B. Segel has described as the 1920s absurd and grotesque New Economic Policy (NEP) satires. Segel describes Bulgakov's play *Zoya's Apartment* (*Zoykina kvartira*, 1926) as typical of this strong brand of satire aimed at the failures and contradictions of the party's policies mixed with heavy doses of melodrama and dark absurdity. His description of Bulgakov's play as mixing "absurd, grotesque, satirical, farcical, and melodramatic elements" (*Twentieth-Century Russian Drama*, 198), together with a feel for vaudeville, could just as easily be applied to *A Forgotten Tune*. Ryazanov thus builds his early glasnost effort on a strong tradition of barbed laughter.

Leonid may not be holy, yet he is seen as a fool in every Russian and Soviet sense. He is a man divided. A blatant careerist and an underdeveloped artist (thus the forgotten tune for his shelved flute, which has myriad Freudian implications as well), a hard-nosed administrator and a sensitive and sentimental man ("Don't finish me off," he says, for instance, at one point when his wife is zooming in for the kill), neither he nor the film can ever decide which way to jump, which love to pursue, which life to lead.

As a Soviet Walter Mitty, he is a romantic fool living an alternative and satisfying personal life with his love (he is seen scrubbing the floor of Lida's poor apartment when a coworker arrives to ask a favor). But as a "responsible" husband and Communist bureaucrat, he is as conforming and conniving as is humanly possible.

Ryazanov's film ends without resolving Leonid's dilemma. He has taken over as the new boss of the Bureau of Leisure Time and is conducting his first staff meeting when he sees Lida walk by in the street outside. The fairy-tale ending is that he walks out of the meeting and joins her (she has quit her job as well), and we see them poor but happy and very much in love. Then we are given the realistic version, as he completes his speech about the need to control the arts under glasnost. This conventional speech is interrupted by another heart attack (he has had several by this point). His colleagues call for an ambulance. Lida senses something has happened. He dies as he has the apocalyptic vision described earlier and Lida arrives. Then, depending on how one reads the ending, either he remains dead or her attempts to breathe life back into him succeed. Either way, his resurrection (physical, spiritual, or both) has been accomplished through Lida's love. In short, the film echoes a plot common in Russian fairy tales: the lover saved by a kiss.

As *A Forgotten Tune* suggests, the satirical barbs that were once used by Eisenstein and others against bourgeois and privileged power structures are now leveled at the party's crumbling bureaucracy and, ultimately, at the System itself.

THE GEORGIAN SATIRICAL MUSE

Georgian filmmakers have long exhibited a special flair for comedy and satire, and it comes as no surprise that perestroika has given birth to new dimensions in their use of laughter at the System itself. A film that points the way for many of the satirical films about inept bureaucracy is Georgian filmmaker Eldar Shengelaya's 1984 film, *Blue Mountains, or Improbable Story (Golubye gory, ili Neobyknovennaya istoriya)*. Revaz Giorgobiani plays a young writer who spends the whole film trying to get a publishing house to read his manuscript, "Blue Mountains." Shengelaya choreographs a wry assortment of characters within the world of a publishing house, each obsessed with his or her own project, none of whom manages to carry out the role of the business: publishing. Much to Shengelaya's credit, the central theme—that nobody works—is never belabored. His camera lingers on absurd moments that, like a mosaic, combine to form an overall image, one of helplessness. Yet at the same time, there is sympathy for these characters, none of whom is evil, yet all of whom are to blame for putting up with the System. There are German-speaking secretaries with jealous husbands lurking in the background, bosses who are always on the run and who never actually read anything while they grow plants in the basement, editorial committees that cannot make decisions, and repairmen who turn out to be readers. Shengelaya skillfully builds in the changes of seasons to suggest how eternal is the stagnation in the firm; only nature alters. He makes use of the repetition of lines and scenes to emphasize the hopelessness of it all. Meanwhile the film builds toward the climax as the building is collapsing around those inside. To the tune of a sweet Georgian folk song, the whole edifice crumbles as the boss yells to the young man, while the boss is carried away in an ambulance, that he really will read the young man's manuscript. Fade out.

Those familiar with Fellini's *Orchestra Rehearsal* will see parallels and influences in *Blue Mountains*. Yet what is close to funny tragedy in Fellini's hands becomes satire in Shengelaya's work, a difference that reflects the times.

THE CARNIVALESQUE AESTHETICS OF THE UGLY: YURI MAMIN'S REMEMBERED TUNE FOR SATIRE

"The whole of our country is developing according to a scenario," comments Leningrad director Yuri Mamin. "But let's hope it's a good scenario" ("39 Degrees C," 15). A student of Ryazanov, Mamin emerged as one of the brightest satirical lights on the Soviet horizon of the late 1980s and early 1990s. Clearly he has learned much from Ryazanov and from the Soviet and Russian tradition of satire in general. In describing his award-winning production *The Fountain* (*Fontan*, 1988), he classified the genre as a combination of all genres, "so that one flows into another: it begins as a comedy of situations and ends as grotesque" (ibid., 16). But this younger director who graduated from the Higher Course for Screenwriters and Directors in 1982 has emerged with his own comic-satiric vision and voice. His early glasnost short film, *The Neptune Feast* (*Prazdnik Neptuna*, 1986), is a near-perfect, warmhearted satire of bureaucracy and village mentality today.

The action focuses on a frozen northern Russian village that tries to stage a spectacular outdoor winter show, "Neptune's Feast," to impress a delegation of visiting Swedes. The problem, however, is that no one in the village is actually a "walrus," that legendary breed of tough Russians who plunge into winter waters wearing only bathing suits. Mamin's film refers to the whole "Potemkin villages" deception.

The Neptune Feast seems definitely to have been influenced by Milos Forman's Firemen's Ball; it is also an upbeat version of Gogol's Inspector General. The Neptune Feast manages to engage its audience with its array of foolish villagers incompetently struggling to impress the foreigners while simultaneously distancing us with the absurdity of the situation caused by the System, which is, ultimately, the source of the incompetence and confusion. In this sixty-minute romp, Mamin avoids Ryazanov's trap in A Forgotten Tune of trying to overload the film with too many agendas. Mamin never loses an almost giddy, lighthearted sense of comedy and satire perfectly blended, as in Forman's early work.

In the village of Little Heels (Malye Pyatki), we are treated to a District Party Office where no one is allowed to drink vodka (the reference is to Andropov's post-Brezhnev antialcohol campaign and Gorbachev's more strenuous yet unsuccessful campaign), and where no one wishes to take on the responsibility of mounting the Neptune show. The planned festivity is itself absurd, for they decide to carry out the whole show outdoors when the temperature is thirty degrees below zero, and to do so as a "water show" with the one hundred "actors" swimming in icy water to show the Swedes that the Russians are still tough, superhuman "walruses."

No one, of course, wants to strip down and swim in such frigid waters. Thus another level of absurdity is added: the party members decide to run hoses of warm water into the stage area to heat the water, an absurd gesture doomed to failure.

Mamin, working with coscreenwriter Vladimir Vardunas, casts the film with a wonderful group of peasant faces that the camera captures in comic detail. Mamin orchestrates and paces this minor masterpiece with a sure sense of timing. Detail after detail delights us and feeds the buildup for this bizarre presentation. A farmer is chosen as Neptune and, protesting that "we do everything for foreigners and nothing for ourselves," attempts to commit suicide. Preparations are finally more or less complete, including a hothouse nearby in which participants will keep warm before plunging into the freezing water. The climax of the film, the arrival of the Swedes and the show itself, is set to the score Prokofiev wrote for Eisenstein's "Battle of the Ice" scene in Alexander Nevsky, another level of playfulness that was not lost on Soviet audiences.

At film's end the Swedes have left before the show reaches its climax, but nobody seems to care. The scene is much like the dance sequence in Frank Capra's It's a Wonderful Life in which everyone at the dance who sees Jimmy Stewart and his date fall into the swimming pool under the dance floor decides to jump in as well. Similarly, Mamin's initially reluctant villagers finally charge into the water for the hell of it, having the time of their lives. "Stop!" shouts an official. "The Swedes have left." It does not matter; they are enjoying themselves. Once again, what is pure farce in Capra's film becomes gentle satire in its Soviet variation: Mamin laughs at both the party officials and the notorious Russian "bottomless spirit" which, when provoked, never stops.

There is no question but that Mamin deserves the awards this film has won, including the Grand Prix at the Comedy Film Festival in Gabrovo, Bulgaria in 1987. The triumphant "what-the-hell" celebration by the villagers who finally have fun for themselves rather than for the party or the foreigners makes *The Neptune Feast* perhaps the single most "carnivalesque" satirical comedy yet made under glasnost.

As Bakhtin suggests, in such a "feast of becoming," the people triumph over all obstacles for that moment, that instant of pure carnival. Yet even under early glasnost this seemingly generalized satire had great difficulty passing the watchful eye of cinema officials and only had a limited theatrical release, a form of censorship familiar to Hollywood.

The Fountain, Mamin's first feature, builds on the talents seen in *The Neptune Feast* to create a finely controlled extended satire that was completely in tune with the times when shot in 1988. Working again with scriptwriter Vladimir Vardunas, Mamin grounded his narrative in the closely observed reality of life in an apartment building in Leningrad. But this reality becomes a center from which absurdity multiplies and surrealism develops.

A "story in seven parts," as an early title announces, *The Fountain* is framed in metaphor. The opening shot is of a figure we will come to know as the Composer: he stands atop the apartment building in a Leonardo Da Vinci–like "winged man" outfit, playing a violin. We then cut from this image of Soviet man poised to fly against a grim background while playing classical music, to a desert, as a title card announces the first segment of the film, "The Source." We view a fountain in the rocks that is just a trickle of water. An old Kazakh herdsman patiently holds a small container to the trickle. Suddenly a Russian military truck drives up and soldiers jump out to fill up large water canteens. Discouraged with the slowness of the fountain, they run dynamite to the fountain and push the plunger. The rocks explode and water gushes up into the air, only to die out completely as a soldier attempts without success to fill his canteen. When the soldiers see that there is now no water where once there had been a fountain, they jump into the truck and drive off. The old Kazakh herdsman looks at the dry rocks, and in what becomes the credit sequence, we watch him gather up his family and animals and head into the distance, in search of another source of water. Like much of Chaplin's work, the scene evokes laughter tinged with emotion. As the herdsman, again like Chaplin in the closing shots of his films, walks off into the distance, having failed at what he wanted to accomplish, we are left with a knowing sadness beyond the satire that has gone before.

The rest of the film takes place in the Leningrad apartment building that is the center of the narrative. But this metaphorical opening forces the audience to see in Aesopian style that in the dialectic of tradition and change, custom and "progress," both are often the losers.

The old herdsman, we swiftly learn, is the grandfather of Maya, the wife of the protagonist, Peter. The old Kazakh becomes something of a super-plumber for the apartment building when he arrives to stay with the family. The "frame" of the film is completed in the end when the elevator in the building suddenly goes haywire and ejects the grandfather through the roof, out over the city, into space, and, yes, ultimately back home to his beloved steppe where he and we began. As in *The Neptune Feast*, such an ending places the simple character back in his environment, transcending the System. In *The Fountain* there is also a "carnivalesque" celebration and triumph. After all the disasters that have happened to the apartment house, the inhabitants carry out their own "carnival" of dancing and drinking. There is finally a ceremony in which the building's frozen pipes are warmed with candles. Again we sense a group spirit that bonds diverse individuals together in a common cause beyond the realm of the party and bureaucracy, which have failed the people. Yet the joy of *The Neptune Feast*'s conclusion is not echoed in *The Fountain*, where we are left with a wry awareness that we are back where we began, in a place where the "source" has been destroyed.

Mamin's film, *A Forgotten Tune*, does evoke a number of genres. But Mamin succeeds with far more clarity of purpose in focusing his film and painting a canvas with an array of characters who are, as in his early work, well orchestrated to create a group protagonist. In this sense, Mamin follows the approach of *Blue Mountains* in making all the inhabitants of the building in question the protagonist. But in Mamin's hands, the satire and comedy are pushed to further extremes than in the pre-glasnost Georgian film.

One couple have turned their apartment into an illegal greenhouse where they play music to soothe the flowers and where they prepare their daughter's costume to be a "snow maiden" in a local pageant. A World War II veteran, the father of the greenhouse operator, has no interest in the present other than to plan a reunion of veterans. In another apartment, the elderly widow of a poet listens to ethnographic records of tribal chants, while the composer seen in the opening shot lives in the attic apartment surrounded by various instruments, his handmade wings, and his synthesizer-piano: from time to time we see him "fly" off the top of the building on a wire, across the winter landscape, crashing to the ground each time.

At the center is the family of Peter, a Russian in charge of maintenance, and his Kazakh wife, Maya, whom the grandfather from the steppes visits. Within this household many of the scenes deal with cultural confusion and the clash of traditions as the grandfather insists on facing east to pray to Mecca before eating, while the couple's son feels the old man is praying to the refrigerator. The old man is upset with much he sees, including aerobics shown on television, and, in part as a reaction against such intrusions ("women should not be dressed in such scanty clothing"), he pulls out his old one-stringed instrument and begins to chant tribal songs.

Against this backdrop, the story involves the collapse of the building. (Again, we sense echoes of influence from *Blue Mountains*.) Using Gerald Mast's comic-plot classifications, we could label such a plot reductio ad absurdum, as the whole point is simply to watch everything escalate to one huge disaster (*Comic Mind*, 6), while, in this case, satirizing the system that has made such incompetence possible. The residents of the building cannot stop the building from collapsing around them. All their efforts to get bureaucratic support, party support, official help, fail. In one scene, as the roof is caving in, for instance, men agree to hold the roof on their own shoulders propped up in part by old Communist signs bearing party slogans; yet another satiric visual metaphor. (Their payoff is to be "fed" vodka each hour for their efforts.)

Nothing works, however. With the excellent pacing of this orchestrated chaos, as in *The Neptune Feast*, Mamin drives his situational comedy toward the absurd and ultimately, as he stated, the grotesque. Mamin has, like the Czech directors, an eye for the small details of absurdity that make up life under socialism: people sorting onions, and thus crying, while singing a Communist song called "Our Native Land"; a plaque to a dead poet being dedicated, only to fall off later; television news crews trying to capture the dedication and suddenly becoming a medium for theatrics as one of the women in the building who wishes to be an actor breaks into tears, causing others to do likewise. At no point, however, does this final absurdist-grotesque satire fall into the confusing pretentiousness of the ending of *A Forgotten Tune*. Mamin's world is the world of everyday life simply pushed and nudged further until it becomes what the Yugoslav director Srdjan Karanovic calls a "documentary fairy tale."

Mamin says about his brand of satire, "Some people might be shocked by the raw mixture of images. A lot of people still think that a truly aesthetic picture is one that has leisurely and elegant landscapes. But why should it always be so? After all, there is such a thing as the aesthetics of the ugly. Life is not all about beauty. Vulgarity, chaos, and paradox are all part of our social life, and they prompt the visual solution" ("39 Degrees C," 17).

But Mamin only partially describes the focus and effect of his films by discussing "the aesthetics of the ugly." There is the "carnivalesque" perspective also. Furthermore, we clearly see the seriousness of purpose behind the satire, which, once again, matches Eisenstein's call for comedy to be a weapon in the hands of the revolutionaries. In this sense, *The Fountain*, like many films today, is a tool in the hands of those who see the aesthetics of the ugly caused by the party and the Revolution that did not deliver. The framing sequences in the steppes alone force the audience to participate in the game of reading the narrative as a parable without a verbally stated punchline (though the visuals are obvious), an Aesopian fable about the party. As Kevin Moss pointed out in his study of the popular preglasnost satirical television film *The Very Same Münchhausen* (*Tot samyi Myunhgauzen*, 1983), such Soviet allegories that are missing moral lessons "make the reader name, at least to himself, the Soviet reality to which the text does not overtly refer" ("Russian Münchhausen," 3). The pleasure, therefore, for Soviet audiences is to fill in the blanks, read between the lines, and enjoy the boldness with which contemporary "ugliness" is depicted. *Münchhausen* is an example of such a work, especially because it appeared during the stagnation period.

The Fountain, coming under glasnost, is much more open and thus requires less reading between the lines, which is not necessarily completely positive for audiences used to enjoying the subversive pleasure of figuring out allusions and cleverly worked out references. But Mamin is not totally direct. He describes his work as presenting the everyday situation, rather than a frontal attack on the System. But in a nation where the population is finely attuned to subtle nuances and to getting the point that could not, in the past, be stated directly, most understand that the System has created the situation.

Be that as it may, *The Fountain*, for all its awards, including the 1988 Grand Prize at the first Festival of Genre Films held in Odessa, failed to find a large popular audience. With four million viewers in its first year, Mamin's work must thus be seen as on par with Woody Allen's comic art: much admired by the critics and by a devoted educated audience, but ignored by the general public when compared to the huge audiences found for other comedies and satires such as *Ghostbusters II* and *Batman*. Soviet people interviewed about Mamin's film suggested to us that perhaps the film is too close to real life, that Mamin has succeeded too well in capturing the hardships of daily life. His "aesthetics of the ugly" is something they receive enough of daily in the papers, in conversation, in the effort to get through each day. For audiences used to Aesopian satire, Mamin's new work may appear far too real.

Furthermore, the gigantic box-office success of a film such as *The Man from Capuchins Boulevard* (*Chelovek s bul'vara Kapvtsinov*, 1987) would indicate that the Soviet general public, like its American counterpart, is more interested in seeking entertainment than in gaining Aesopian enlightenment from its comic satires. This observation became all the more apparent with Mamin's *Whiskers* (*Bakenbardy*, 1990), his dark satire of right-wing nationalism and its rabid followers who, in the film, treat Pushkin as their idol and adopt his dress and whiskers. Although completed during the summer of 1990, by January 1991 it had received neither a screening nor a release in the Soviet Union. While admitting that "perhaps this film is too angry to be a true satire" (Remarks), Mamin felt that under perestroika, a new form of censorship emerged. Mamin's film was purchased by an independent distributor who, as it turned out, had no intention of releasing the film. Quite the opposite: the company wished to bury the film so it would not reach the public and further fuel rising tensions among various constituencies in the Soviet Union.

RAZOR-SHARP LAUGHTER FROM AZERBAIJAN

Another complicated reception awaited the excellent 1989 satire from Azerbaijani director Vaghif Mustafayev, *The Villain* (*Merzavets*). Starring the engaging Georgian actor Mamuka Kikaleishvili as Khattam, a simple, good man who becomes corrupted by the times, *The Villain* is a finely worked out comic social satire that clearly blames the System for the transformation of our good man into a villain. Through humor, gentle at times and razor-sharp at others, Mustafayev's film holds up the fun-house mirror of satire to the theme of Mafias and underground economies that have sprung up around the nation in recent years. Even more so than *The Fountain*, *The Villain* is a satire whose mere existence was possible only under perestroika. Before the development of Gorbachev's glasnost, the very admission that Mafias exist would have been rare if not impossible. But the times allow for such an open examination of reality. As director Mustafayev notes, "It's not difficult to become a villain. It's enough to make only one step" (*Sovexportfilm* 1989 catalogue, 101).

Khattam works in a lemonade factory testing the quality of the product, a job that is humorously made to appear totally superfluous. Yet Khattam loses his job and finally turns to crime when he is set up by others to test the limits of perestroika. When he substitutes urine for lemonade, the usually mundane tests run suddenly indicate "danger." As Khattam alerts his boss that the plant must shut down and investigate, thus causing great expense and loss of time, the boss is forced to say publicly to Khattam that he is something of a hero "of the times" for so openly (glasnost) expressing the need for change (perestroika). But in a sharply etched moment, we see the boss's true adaptation to the times. As soon as Khattam leaves the office feeling proud of himself, the boss calls the local party office to have Khattam fired behind his back.

A minor character who underlines the major theme of this film from Azerbaijan is an old-timer who is a kind of aged Chapayev, a grandfather wandering around in his Civil War uniform asking "Where is your revolutionary spirit?" He is both absurd and touching. What would a Chapayev do in Gorbachev's dissolving Soviet (dis)Union?

It is the times that are absurd from his perspective. Nevertheless, the times are the people's reality, and such an "aesthetics of the ugly" is what Khattam must negotiate as a naive good soul or Soviet Candide. Mustafayev has packed the film with telling details, sharper and harder than the more universal satire of Mamin's films. We see a factory foreman who steals equipment from his own factory by night. Why? He has nine children and must feed them. In a marketplace where a fight breaks out between police and others, someone suddenly reaches over and puts a hat over the camera lens: censorship under glasnost. The lemonade boss finally shouts, "I swear, I'm fed up with this democracy!" Apartment houses remain unfinished and grim, children deal in black-market Marlboros, and the Mafia boss bears a clearly intentional resemblance to Gorbachev.

Before Khattam becomes a Mafia boss himself, he encounters the old Civil War veteran once more. The aged man asks again, "Where is your revolutionary spirit?" Khattam pauses. "I have no revolutionary spirit," he responds. It is an electrifying moment. Khattam is in effect not only a good soul but a wise fool. His honest admission of his condition brings into the open the secret admission of millions. In Mustafayev's hands, satire becomes open, with no need for the Aesopian tradition of secrecy and the cat-and-mouse expectations of its viewers. The satire, as in Hollywood's *Being There*, for instance, is direct.

From the moment Khattam descends into villainy, however, the film veers toward the grotesque and the surreal, as dreams are interspersed with reality and ultimately transformed into a Kafkaesque trial and nightmare. Once again, Mustafayev's razor-sharp laughter cuts much deeper than Mamin's Swiftian pinpricks. Humor itself finally breaks down as we witness the complete degradation of the protagonist, and as his love for Natasha, the woman of his dreams, turns into an ugly rape. As he attempts to hang himself, disgusted with the party and the Mafia boss he has become, he suddenly sees himself on television speaking about perestroika. His words ring hollow and unconvincing, and so he hangs. What follows is a dream trial, as the grandfather figure, playing judge, accuses him of crimes against the Revolution.

We learn, however, that his hanging is unsuccessful. A neighbor bursts into his apartment stating, "Voice of America announced you hanged yourself!" In the final shot we see Khattam on the subway, apparently sleeping; it then becomes clear he is dead of a heart attack.

We will now turn our attention to those films that begin in satire and humor and branch into the allegorical grotesque. But it is worth observing that *The Villain* had almost no theatrical audience. The significance of this is still inconclusive, however. On one hand, there is control at the national level of how many prints of a film are struck and which films will be promoted for foreign festivals. This power alone accounts for much of the success or failure of a film, even under perestroika, at the box office. On the other hand, many people we interviewed were honest about stating that the film was doomed to limited distribution despite the quality of the film because it is shot in the Azerbaijan language, not Russian, and therefore would have less appeal than, for instance, Rashid Nugmanov's Kazakh film *The Needle*, which is shot in Russian. Finally, some we interviewed went so far as to say that for Russians in particular, "there would be no interest in seeing a film from Azerbaijan, no matter how fine it was." We run into another paradox of perestroika: there is now freedom to speak openly on film, but it is hindered by the mechanisms of prejudice that work against the distribution and popularity of such a work.

THE ALLEGORICAL GROTESQUE: BELOW ZERO
IN *ZEROGRAD*

The ending of *The Villain* pushes satire into a much darker realm where tragedy and the grotesque meet. Such a mixture of genres is, as we have shown, prefigured in *A Forgotten Tune*. But it is a sign of the times that an increasing number of "directors' films," as opposed to more purely genre movies such as *The King of Crime* and *Intergirl*, have opted for satire that turns serious, allegorical, and ominous.

In films such as Karen Shakhnazarov's *Zerograd* (*Gorod zero*, 1989), Sergei Ovcharov's *It*, and Valery Ogorodnikov's *Prishvin's Paper Eyes*, the alleged bright hope of glasnost is seen as an open Pandora's box of death, destruction, confusion, betrayal, failure, and futility. We have already discussed the nature of the symbolic and grotesque surrealism of history in *It* and *Prishvin's Paper Eyes*. In conclusion, we should take note of Shakhnazarov's uses of dark satire in *Zerograd*, especially since the film stars Leonid Filatov, the protagonist of *A Forgotten Tune*.

Shakhnazarov proved in his earlier efforts, such as *Jazzmen* (1983) and *The Messenger Boy* (1987), that he could tell a simple tale directly, economically, and with dry as well as broad humor. In contrast, *Zerograd*, once again coscripted with Alexander Borodyansky, belongs with the absurd-grotesque-satirical-melodramatic works of Bulgakov and Ryazanov's *Forgotten Tune*. In fact, one senses the jarring conjunction in Shakhnazarov's glasnost film of Buñuel, Kafka, Gogol, and Elvis.

Zerograd picks up where *A Forgotten Tune* leaves off. If Ryazanov's film follows a bureaucrat through bizarre events in a familiar Moscow, Shakhnazarov sends Varakin (Leonid Filatov again) into a provincial town that appears simultaneously ordinary and grotesquely surrealistic. Varakin is a middle-management bureaucrat on an assignment to check on a factory in an undesignated town. All seems normal and mundane until he realizes that the factory manager's secretary is completely naked, yet otherwise a typical secretary, seemingly unaware of the inappropriateness of her appearance.

Varakin falls into a wonderland that, in exaggerated form, mirrors the contradictions of Soviet life in the 1980s, though no specific time is identified (we assume it is in the Brezhnev period). Plot is not the point in this inventive, dark allegory without a punchline. It is enough to know that Varakin is both the hero and the victim of various narrative strands as he is served, in one scene, a cake shaped like his own head, and, in the major scene of the film, he is led through a bizarre museum of living "waxworks" that depicts all of Soviet history, up to and including Brezhnev's period of stagnation.

What matters most is Varakin's situation: like Kafka's K., he is guilty of crimes he does not understand and feels he did not commit. In a reversal of Gogol's *Inspector General*, *Zerograd* suggests that the Inspector Captain becomes a victim of the provincial system's caprices.

Films such as *The Fountain*, *The Villain*, and *Zerograd* attempt to expand the language of Soviet satire by building on previous models. Yet the price for such honest experimentation has been failure or limited success at the box office. *Zerograd* is a significant contribution to the evolving glasnost canon. But it proved too demanding, or perhaps too realistic, in its dark-humored, nightmarish form for Soviet audiences.

As a milestone in the development of a new Soviet film language, however, it merits closer attention. We begin with Leonid Filatov's performance. In *A Forgotten Tune* he was in perpetual motion; if not in control of each situation, at least he reacted swiftly to given disasters. In *Zerograd*, no action seems appropriate. Varakin's body language signals stasis; his expression is one of silent, confused contemplation. Shakhnazarov's film, in fact, is something of a dark hymn to the reaction shot. Perhaps more screen time is dedicated in this film to focusing on the face of the protagonist, in search of a reaction, than in any other film we have seen. Typically, the camera is in medium close-up as Filatov's marvelously expressive face expresses . . . nothing, except mild bewilderment.

This is the main joke, the butt of the film. We as audience members identify with Varakin, for we too are outsiders to this bizarre corruption of life as we know it. The structure and the rhythm of the film, therefore, are carefully orchestrated as a dialectical discourse between these drawn-out reaction shots and the discordant events around Varakin.

The film, shot in a different style with a faster pace, could easily be labeled "comic." But in Shakhnazarov's hands even genre, like the culture portrayed, has broken down. What we have instead are long takes, dim lighting, a generally silent sound track, and a de-emphasis of narrative. All these elements work against the conventions of comedy and even many of those of satire. Instead we are asked to voyage through this dark mirror and to contemplate seemingly disconnected, misconnected events, motives, and results as if we were Varakin. In this sense, the movement of the film is from the mild satire and humor of the naked secretary to the much darker portrayal of Soviet history (as distortion) in the "museum," and finally to the plot that is Varakin's personal history. The protagonist is accused of being the son of the chef who in the past introduced rock and roll to the town, a crime that led to his expulsion from society, and who is murdered or who commits suicide in the restaurant where Varakin is served his pastry "head" on a platter.

The grotesque and absurd in *Zerograd* are clearly shown to be an outgrowth of "history." This brings us back to the elaborately constructed museum scene. Varakin is simply trying to get out of town; instead, he winds up twenty-eight meters below ground in an Ethnographic Museum, which happens to be located in an abandoned mine. The museum guide speaks of all the exhibits as if they were actually part of Soviet history, even when many of them could not possibly have been so. Varakin is told that Priam's grandson is buried there, as well as much Roman material. When Varakin tries to object to this twisting of history, the guide quotes experts "proving" that Trojans reached the area and that a lost Roman legion landed there too. The guide even claims that they identified Attila the Hun by some of his sperm found nearby.

It is at this point that Varakin begins simply to react silently rather than to verbalize his doubts. Why speak when everyone has "answers," "expert advice," false statistics?

Chronology has little to do with the arrangement of the museum, for the exhibit after Attila is that of the first rock and roll dance which, of course, is the event related to Varakin's past. Bill Haley's "Rock around the Clock" plays loudly, much like this film, which also plays with the "clock" of history for its own ends.

The point is that there is no point to the museum, no order to the order presented. We have the head of the Fake Czar, the statue of the first prostitute (but, as with most of the exhibits, we see she is actually alive), the apartment of the railway worker where Stalin spent a night in 1914, the stepson of Maxim Gorky, a plane crash, and even the first citizen arrested for having a relationship with a foreigner. Finally, in splendid parody of Stalinist museum exhibits, we end with two rotating tiered "cakes," with typical socialist workers on one, and, on the other, a frieze of pop culture complete with punks, tourists, bureaucrats, soccer fans, and Afghan War soldiers.

Shakhnazarov allows us no playful laughter in the postmodern vein of Italo Calvino or Borges. This hodgepodge of history elicits no smile on Varakin's face and only faint laughter from us. From such history, Varakin naturally cannot escape or make sense of his own life. He is told soon after visiting the museum, by a psychic young boy: "You will never leave our town. You will die in 2015 and be buried here."

It is very possible that the lad is correct. As the film becomes increasingly bizarre—a prosecutor, for instance, speaks of his passion to commit senseless crimes—Varakin finally appears to accept his fate of being the person (the chef's son) he knows he is not. The film ends after a nightclub scene in which Varakin's "father" is now celebrated at a rock and roll dance. We see Elvis, not Lenin, hanging over the stage, and "Jailhouse Rock" (another suggestive title, given the film's allegorical context) playing on the sound track.

The final sequence is a crosscutting series of scenes. We see the museum guard turning out the lights in the museum; we also see Varakin escaping through the woods, past an ancient oak tree (clearly an emblem of Russia itself as seen in folklore), trying to get away. It is dawn. Varakin climbs into a small fishing boat and drifts out onto the calm, beautiful, misty waters. He is alone, without oars, without direction. No sound. Zero is a number. Zerograd as a place, as a state of being, we are led to feel, is definitely below zero: somewhere beyond our mathematical, spiritual, and psychological understanding.

THE ENJOYABLE LIGHTNESS OF LAUGHTER

The lightest has been saved until last. Beyond allegory, the grotesque, and surrealism, we suggest, is laughter in a joyous, pure state.

Some filmmakers just want to have fun. Such a stance is in itself revolutionary given the general thrust of Soviet laughter summed up by Eisenstein, who saw the comic muse as a weapon rather than a means to pleasure. But what is called "eccentric comedy" existed before glasnost. Nobody, for instance, has had a more appreciated career making eccentric comedies loved by millions for their inventive nuttiness than Leonid Gaidai. Even in person he is described by Soviet critics as having the shape of a "question mark" (Dolmatovskaya and Shilova, Who's Who, 84). Studying with the previous master of Soviet comedy, especially musical comedy, Grigori Alexandrov, Gaidai adapted his zany satirical flair to creating some of the most successful comedies of the 1960s, including The Bootleggers (Samogonschiki , 1961) and especially The Diamond Hand (Brilliantovaya ruka, 1969). The 1970s brought him in contact with some of the great literary satires as he brought Ilf and Petrov's Twelve Chairs (Dvenadsat' stulyev, 1971) to the screen. The film was subsequently remade with less success in the United States by an admiring Mel Brooks in 1974. Gaidai filmed Bulgakov's comedy Ivan Vasilievich in his 1973 movie Ivan Vasilievich Changes His Profession (Ivan Vasilievich menyayet professiyu).

The liberating lunacy of The Twelve Chairs is worthy of attention. Gaidai shot this film in bright, bold colors, with high-spirited, circuslike caricature acting by his cast, who play swindlers chasing after a legacy of diamonds hidden in one of twelve chairs left by an old lady. The film is full of comic cinematic self-reflection as well. Gaidai makes liberal use of silent-comedy techniques, such as having the actors wink at the camera, using pixilation and animation, and providing a conclusion that takes us out of a contemporary Moscow movie theater where the film is playing. As in A Forgotten Tune, there is a nod to Gogol as an influence as the main characters wind up attending a performance of The Inspector General.

Under glasnost, an important director who has taken the form of eccentric comedy to even purer heights is Alla Surikova, whose Man from Capuchins Boulevard was a box-office hit in 1988. It is a hilarious, lighthearted Eastern, complete with barroom brawls with balsa-wood furniture, good guys, bad guys, and Soviet Indians to boot. With an unflinching comic touch, Surikova, who won first prize at the Los Angeles Women in Cinema Festival, is a sterling example of how glasnost has opened possibilities for entertainment that is light without being silly, and enjoyable and clever at the same time. One senses, furthermore, that Surikova has built on the popular prototype of the Soviet Eastern, Vladimir Motyl's *White Sun of the Desert*, set in a Central Asian landscape at the end of the Civil War. Motyl, in contrast, however, used all the structural codes of a Hollywood Western in the context of a Soviet tale. Surikova's contribution has been to deliver the American West in a Soviet landscape.

Half the fun, of course, is watching a Soviet parody of a Western. The actors and set designers have entered this project in the spirit of rip-roaring farce, as every Western cliché is exaggerated here. No American Western bar fight, for instance, broke more furniture and property than this wild comedy, and no John Wayne movie ever piled up more broken bodies than this cartoonlike exercise in comic violence.

Yet while much of the value of Surikova's work is that she proves a good film can be made for fun without sinking under the weight of ideological baggage, there is a self-reflexive level to this tale that lightly leaves the audience a message to consider. The plot, such as it is, centers on a certain Mr. Fest who introduces cinema to a Western town, hoping to civilize these typical cowboy ruffians. There are some very funny sequences as the brawling bar boys quickly become models of decorum and milk-consuming propriety while they are watching polite educational films. The climax concerns the barman Harry's attempt to revive his failing business—selling booze—by introducing his own films of fights, violence, and action, an act that immediately brings the cowboys back to their former chaotic behavior. The conclusion suggests a standoff between culture (Mr. Fest) and the wild West (individualism and capitalism), as Mr. Fest leaves town with the woman he loves.

Georgi Danelia is usually considered a director of more abstract humorous satires about contemporary Soviet life. His *Autumn Marathon* is a well-balanced, sympathetic preglasnost satire of a Leningrad professor of English in the autumn of his life, trying to juggle his career, his marriage, and his mistress. The central metaphor for the film is the effective image of this middle-aged man jogging, jogging, jogging: he is never able to rest, to enjoy, to feel free of the problems he has, to a large extent, brought on himself.

But such a comedy of sentiment does not prepare us for Danelia's truly nutty comedy *Kin Dza Dza* (1987). This science-fiction fairy tale starts in the most realistic, humdrum way. A typical family man in

Moscow goes to the bakery for bread. Running into a young man on the street, he suddenly winds up on another planet. As in any such exaggerated extraterrestrial satire (Speilberg's *E.T.* included, of which Danelia's film is the reverse: humans in space as opposed to the extraterrestrial in our society), the comedy cuts both ways: fun is made of the space beings, but even more of Russians in space.

Slapstick, farce, and a comedy of manners are combined in Danelia's skilled hands. The fun is magnified even further by using the famous Soviet comedian Yevgeny Leonov as one of the leading space beings. Gags abound as the two Soviet men try bribery in space and as they try to adapt to a culture without violence or weapons. A dictionary of the space language is shared with the audience. A host of funny gadgets is employed, including a high-tech spittoon. The ending is circular; we close with the same shot with which we began. Vladimir passes the young man playing the violin. He does not at first recognize Vladimir until both hear the familiar key space word, "koo," uttered by someone else; we are playfully left to ponder which of us in the audience who looks so normal might actually have been transported to another planet and back. Here there is none of Gogol's heavy irony or Chekov's biting social observation: the center is constructed around laughter itself.

The importance of such films, with their joyful sense of play, is that they offer, under glasnost, one bright direction for Soviet cinema. Such freewheeling comedy suggests realms of expression that have long been part of Western cinema but have been underrated and often discouraged under what Solzhenitsyn simply calls Soviet "ideology." In this sense, Jacques Derrida's emphasis on the importance of free play as a counterbalance to any form of authoritarianism or totalitarian power is apt: "To risk meaning nothing is to start to play, and first to enter into the play of *differance* which prevents any word, any concept, any major enunciation from coming to summarize and to govern from the theological presence of a center the movement and textual spacing of differences" (*Positions*, 14). "Comedy is serious business," Woody Allen has said. But in the hands of such directors as Danelia and Surikova, that "seriousness" is allowed to be entertaining, liberating, and fun.

Even this encouraging light approach appears to be turning darker. Danelia's 1991 comic satire, *Passport* (*Pasport*), a Soviet-French-Israeli coproduction, contains many lighthearted moments, especially in the first half, as a young Georgian Jew accidently winds up on a plane to Israel that his brother and family should have been on. The seriousness of the topic—immigration, especially of Soviet Jews to Israel—naturally adds a much darker dimension to the film. Danelia certainly tilts away from carefree laughter and toward a drama of commitment in the end as our good-hearted but weary protagonist is helped to the Turkish border on his roundabout (passportless) road home, only to see a helpful Siberian truck driver who has befriended him die when he steps on a border land mine. That Yakov finally reaches Soviet Georgia, on foot, still without a passport, does not clear away our memory of the Siberian's death. Once more, the continuing darkening of the times appears to be extinguishing those few comic voices that would like to take audiences into less troubled world of the liberated imagination.

PART THREE

THE ISLANDS
OF
THE
CONTINENT

The Islands of the Continent: A Revised Map for Ethnic Cinemas

The unbreakable union of free republics
United forever Russia the great.
—Opening of the state hymn of the USSR

AT A CROWDED high-society party hosted by a police colonel, the host's sixteen-year-old son tears his brand-new red passport to pieces. He hates the notorious "fifth paragraph" in the paper, which certifies his nationality: "Tadzhik." He believes in his country. He wants to read in his passport, "Nationality: Citizen of the USSR." No one offers honor to the young citizen. Instead, he sees ethnic hatred and intolerance. Unable to comprehend or accept his situation, the boy commits suicide.

Whether this really happened in the Soviet Union during glasnost, it certainly happened in the Tadzhik feature film *The Look* (*Vzglyad*),[1] directed by Valery Ahadov in 1988. The problem of Soviet nationalities today is a complex one. Anyone reviewing the ethnic situation in 1990, the fifth year of perestroika, must feel like a survivor of an earthquake, jumping over a crack onto a seemingly safe spot without knowing from where the next danger will come. Since the initial ethnic unrest in Alma-Ata, Kazakhstan, in December 1986, unrest that was ruthlessly suppressed by Soviet authorities, the whole country has appeared ready to explode.

On the surface, each ethnic riot and outbreak of unrest could be classified differently: some are movements for national independence (the Baltics, Moldavia, Ukraine); others are interethnic clashes that seemingly have nothing to do with anti-Soviet or anti-Russian protests and

[1]Original titles of films in this chapter are given in Russian transcription, not in the language of the initial version (Georgian, Lithuanian, etc.).

follow purely nationalistic goals (Azerbaijanis versus Armenians, Kirghizs versus Tadzhiks). But in essence all these conflicts have the same root: inconsiderate, imperialistic nationality policies that for decades were buried under misinformation and false slogans, such as the notorious Stalinist myth about "the harmonious family of Soviet nations."

Today, under glasnost, truth is available. The problem, however, is that the truth changes too swiftly. News from the "nationality front" instantly becomes outdated. This situation provides work for newspaper reporters, but obstructs the writing of a general survey. Between the formation of the Lithuanian democratic movement Sajudis in 1987 and the victory of Lithuanian independence in 1991 there is a political abyss, but a historically trifling period of time: four years.

In this state of political turmoil, film may not seem a pressing issue. Captivated by the enthusiasm of the struggle for independence, ethnic artists transform themselves into politicians. Vitautas Landsbergis, the president of Lithuania, a musicologist by profession, has no time for chamber-music studies. Film, like all the arts, is put aside during wartime.

However, the new policies of perestroika and glasnost have affected every area of culture in the Soviet Union. They have influenced ethnic arts and film cultures as well as ethnic consciousness. Such internationally acclaimed films as *Repentance* and *Is It Easy to Be Young?* demonstrate this brilliantly. The question remains how to approach these films: as Soviet (which is the way they have been approached in the West) or as ethnic, for example, Georgian (*Repentance*) and Latvian (*Is It Easy to Be Young?*).

In this chapter, we try to answer this question, highlighting the ethnic schools of filmmaking, Georgian, Baltic, and Kazakh in particular, as they existed before perestroika and as they have been transformed under the new order. For this purpose, a brief look at the history of the issue may serve as a frame of reference.

"THE UNBREAKABLE UNION": A SURVEY

The Union of Soviet Socialist Republics was established in 1922, five years after the 1917 Bolshevik revolution, right after the Civil War, under Lenin, who died thirteen months later. But the shape of the USSR as glasnost began is primarily a result of Stalin's, not Lenin's, policies. The structure of the Soviet Union was finally formed in 1940 after the Soviet-German peace treaty preceding the German invasion.

"The Soviet Union as it is today," wrote Michael Rywkin in 1989, "encompasses almost as much non-Russian population as its predecessor, the Russian empire. But the differences between the two entities are substantial" (*Soviet Society Today*, 57). Until 1991, the Soviet Union consisted of fifteen union republics, each named after its main nationality. Some of these major units were also divided into smaller parts corresponding to the ethnic groups inhabiting them. Thus, there were twenty autonomous republics (more than two-thirds of which were located in the Russian republic), eight autonomous regions, and several autonomous districts. This account, however, which gives a favorable picture of a fair ethnic system, says nothing about the real state of things. One has to analyze the relationship between the parts of the whole rather than the parts by themselves.

"Both union and autonomous republics can, to some extent, be compared to the states of the United States," wrote Rywkin (ibid.). But while comparing certain specific features, Rywkin did not indicate the general differences that make the comparison highly problematic. First, the American states are not distinguished by ethnicity. This derives from the major contrast between the origins of the USSR and the United States: the Soviet Union was composed from different countries (some of which had lost their sovereignty under the Russian monarchy). The range of dissimilarities between these different countries that made up the USSR is vast: from languages belonging to diverse linguistic groups to divergent sociopolitical and economic structures in the pre-Soviet period, from feudalism in the Asian lands to highly developed democratic regimes in the Baltics.

The second contrast between the Soviet Union and the United States, even more significant for our survey, is that in almost seventy years (counting from 1922), the first Communist state did not achieve what the United States had secured from the very beginning: common nationality based on common sociopolitical, not ethnic, grounds.

The absence of a common nationality that would equal citizenship (as in the United States), and the importance of the "fifth paragraph" in Soviet passports for people's employment, careers, and life in general, both manifest the ambiguous, sometimes obscure attitude of the Soviet state toward the issue of nationality. Authorities claimed, for instance, that all the Soviet nationalities were equal. Why, then, keep the nationality specification in the passport? For many decades the term "Soviet character" has been promoted by the official ideology, but another question arises: to whom does this "character" belong if there is no such nation as "Soviet"? Instead, the loose concept of "the Soviet people" was put into circulation, though no one could point out the distinguishing qualities of this "people."

The ambiguity of the nationality issue is all-encompassing and marks all the aspects of the Soviet nationality policy, past and present; the Soviets often claimed that there were over a hundred nationalities in the

USSR. But this statistic is misleading, for seventy-three of those nationalities form less than 3 percent of the population. This policy received a
name in Soviet political slang a long time ago—*uravnilovka* (unjustified
unification). It was one of the major tools of the Stalinist solution to the
nationality problem, and it survived until the first ethnic unrest in the
early years of perestroika. This policy did not bear any sign of chauvin-
ism. On the contrary, it had a perfectly democratic surface. All the nationalities are equal, it was declared, and so is the state's approach to all
of them.

Nonetheless, what this "democracy" meant in fact was the lack of
an individualized approach to nationalities and republics. All of them
have been measured with the standard yardstick, so the biggest surprise
brought by perestroika was that Armenians differ from Lithuanians
not only in temperament, but also in their demands and wishes. The
policy of uravnilovka was totalitarian by nature, since the Soviet state
was identified with the center—that is, Russia, and more specifically,
Moscow.

The Stalinist model of nationality development was almost humorously schematic and unrealistic. Stalin himself invented a three-stage
formula for the desired developmental sequence, well described by Michael Rywkin: "The first stage would bring the flourishing (*rastvet*) of
individual nationalities under socialist conditions, followed by a process
of rapprochement (*sbkuzgebue*) among nationalities as they developed
more commonalities. The final stage would bring a fusion (*sliianie*) of all
Soviet nationalities in the future communist society" (*Soviet Society
Today*, 197). The "fusion" meant nothing but "a Russian melting pot in
which non-Russian nationalities are to be dissolved" (ibid.).

Thus, in the childhood of the Soviet Union, Stalin, who called himself
"father of the peoples," named his favorite "kids," the Russians, "the big
brothers" to all other nationalities, and the process of Russification
began. This process primarily involved two closely connected attacks:
on the ethnic population and on the language. Large numbers of Russians, attracted by privileges in employment, housing, and other areas,
have been brought to the republics, providing a major increase in the
nonnative labor force, but also in a scientific and artistic intelligentsia
and party-state bureaucracy. As a result, in some republics' capitals such
as Riga, Latvia, by the beginning of perestroika, Russians outnumbered
natives.

The language problem has indeed become a stumbling block to progress on the nationality issue. The Russian language had been declared
"the language of internationality communication," which means that
while the Russian residents of the republics could easily survive without knowing the language of the country they lived in, the natives, in

contrast, had to learn Russian. In the "lucky" republics Russian was taught in all secondary and high schools, often to the detriment of the native language. Russian was the common language in the stores, hospitals, and police stations, so that sometimes the only place the natives could speak their own languages was at home with their families. In the "unlucky" republics, particularly in Asia, native languages have been almost completely abandoned and the alphabets changed, so postwar generations are not even able to use the languages of their ancestors.

The language problem is the initial and the strongest impulse for nationalistic and secession movements in such republics as the Baltics, Moldavia, Uzbekistan, and even the Slavic Belorussia and Ukraine, which are closest to Russia. We should consider how strongly the language issue, like Stalinist policies overall, has affected ethnic cultures and the arts.

Stalin, following his passion for doublethink formulas, invented a rule for ethnic cultures: "National in form, socialist in content." The obscure meaning of this openly anti-Marxist dogma (in Marxist aesthetics, form and content are inseparable) is simply that ethnic (nationalistic, religious) ideas were prohibited, while ethnic surfaces, such as folk costumes in dance, drama, and cinema, were encouraged. According to Stalin's formula, which was followed by Khrushchev and Brezhnev, costumed Georgian wine makers, Latvian fishermen, and Ukrainian cossacks were supposed to speak the unified Soviet language and promote the ideas of the Communist party. To review how different Soviet nations and ethnic groups reacted to this task, we turn now to the film cultures of the republics, some of which have become well known by giving up their ethnic names and being called "Soviet"—against their will.

THE TRANSCAUCASIAN MODEL

Georgia is a beautiful land in the southwest part of the Soviet Union on the coast of the Black Sea. Georgia is an ancient nation, with a strong Orthodox Christian tradition since the fourth century A.D., prouder of itself and of its noble cultural and historical past than any other nation in the USSR. Georgia is also a peasant nation, a nation of shepherds and wine makers. Georgians are considered remarkable cooks and no less remarkable eaters and drinkers. They can feed you to death with their boundless hospitality, but they can also kill you if you do not show enough respect for their traditions. Georgians are famous for their unrestrained tempers and for their polyphonic male choruses. And Georgians are famous for their elaborate and exuberant toasts, which may begin by celebrating the incredible hair of your late grandmother and in fifteen minutes come to the fabulous career of your grandson yet unborn.

One should visit Georgia, rest on the hill by the ancient temple of Djvari, and observe the tints of green in the mountains and trees, in the intersecting Kura and Aragvi rivers, in the rocks of the temple and the ground, to realize the vision and wisdom of the people born in this land. To comprehend why this country has produced such colorful arts, especially the "Georgian school," the best film movement in the Soviet Union, one should wander the quiet, labyrinthine alleys in Tbilisi, the Georgian capital.

The Georgian School: Legends that Became Life

Even though Georgian cinema is one of the oldest in the Soviet Union (the first filming was done in 1908), and despite the astounding growth of film after the Sovietization of Georgia in 1921, even despite the several brilliant debuts of the creators of the Georgian school during Khrushchev's thaw, the movement itself did not begin until Brezhnev's stagnation regime in the late 1960s.

The term "Georgian school" is relative. Most of the directors were graduates of the "Russian school"—the All-Union State Film School in Moscow. Besides, artistic credos differ not only among filmmakers but also within a filmmaker's own work. The heavy, black-and-white, static form and the abstract, nonnarrative subject matter of Tengiz Abuladze's *Supplication* (*Mol'ba*, 1968), a photographic counterpoint to the poetry of the classic Georgian poet, Vazha Pshavela, read on the sound track, is scarcely comparable to the painterly, "primitive" visual poetry of Georgy Shengelaya's *Pirosmani* (1970), an unconventional biography of the famous Georgian naive artist. But *Supplication* is even less related to Abuladze's next work, the lively and fast-paced comedy *The Necklace for My Beloved*. At the same time *Pirosmani*, slow and highly metaphysical, seems to belong to another director rather than to Shengelaya, who also made the musical *The Veri Quarter Tunes* (*Melodii Veriiskogo kvartala*, 1973), which might painlessly have competed with *The Sound of Music, Mary Poppins*, or *Oliver!*

Still, the creations of the Georgian school clearly have shared roots. These films are unquestionably Georgian. This quality goes far beyond the ethnic decoration, such as colorful folk costumes or the no less colorful Georgian temper, evident in the generous and expansive gestures and the family squabbles.

Beyond the ethnic surface, in the air and spirit of the Georgian school productions, there is a folk tradition in which all the narratives and characters are clothed. Both original scripts and adaptations of classic Georgian literature, such as Abuladze's *Supplication* and Eldar Shengelaya's 1978 *Stepmother Samanishvili* (*Machekha Samanishvili*), are deeply rooted in folklore, as is almost all Georgian culture. This fantastic, even absurd folklore, though never losing touch with the lives of common people, is odd, romantic, and humorous. The closest analogies to this artistic universe can be seen in Fellini's *Amarcord* and Latin America's literary magic realism as explored by Gabriel García Márquez.

The blend of irony and romanticism provides another shared trait: the movement's favorite genre—the sad comedy, or comic drama, or, as it is most commonly called by Soviets, tragicomedy. In some films, as in Abuladze's 1977 poetic tale *The Wishing Tree*, the accent is on the humorous aspects of the dramatic and even the tragic. In others, as in Eldar Shengelaya's *Extraordinary Exhibition* (*Neobyknovennaya vystavka*, 1969), pure comedy reveals its dramatic side. In any case, the Gordian knot of tears and laughter determines the narrative structure and the nature of the world created.

The genre of tragicomedy was described above as an almost universal model for the Soviet screen, since it covers both drama and comedy and reaches into melodrama. The elements of tragicomedy might be found in such contrasting Russian films as Eldar Ryazanov's satiric melodrama *A Forgotten Tune for the Flute* and Vasily Pichul's glasnost blockbuster drama *Little Vera*. Georgian tragicomedy, nonetheless, might never have been confused with its Russian relative. The mark distinguishing it from all other genre productions is the dimension of parable supplied by the folklore tradition and lacking in Russian films, which are mostly urban-oriented. Ryazanov, for instance, aiming at parable in *A Forgotten Tune*, exploits the cheap mysticism of life-after-death encounters. Directors of the Georgian school would never need such theatrics, since any miracle of their magic-realist world grows organically out of the same ground stepped on by diligent peasants, abandoned brides, and naughty children.

Everything in the parable dimension of the Georgian school evolves into a symbol, although these symbols are earthy. The theme of *Pirosmani* is not only the life and times of Niko Pirosmanashvili, but the destiny of an artist in the world of the blind. And the motifs of *Supplication*, *The Wishing Tree*, Nodar Managadze's 1977 fable *Legends That Became Life* (*Ozhivshiye legendy*), and many other Georgian films of the 1970s and early 1980s are no less than life and death, evil and good, love and intolerance, faith and betrayal.

But political and ideological subject matter can scarcely be found in the Georgian school productions. This explains the paradox of why the lustrous movement emerged during the darkest post-Stalinist years of stagnation. While many nonconformist filmmakers under Brezhnev were busy searching for opportunities to escape—some, such as Andrei Tarkovsky in *Solaris* (1972) and *The Mirror* (*Zerkalo*, 1975), into philosophy and the auteur style; others, such as Nikita Mikhalkov in *The Slave of Love* (*Raba liubvi*, 1976) and *Unfinished Piece for a Player Piano* (*Neokonchennaya piesa dlya mekhanicheskogo pianino*, 1977), into the stylized past; others, such as Vladimir Men'shov in *Moscow Does Not Believe in Tears* (1979), into genre—Georgian filmmakers found their own promised land for escapism: ethnic tradition, spirit, and character.

The relationship between Tbilisi and Moscow had been growing peacefully. Georgians were avoiding confrontation, and the authorities were promoting unique ethnic art all over the world as proof of their successful nationalities policy. Perestroika, however, disturbed the peace. Escapism went out of fashion while ideology came into fashion. Perestroika appeared on the Georgian screen in the shape of Tengiz Abuladze's celebrated epic *Repentance*. The film, which had been started in 1984 under Konstantin Chernenko, Gorbachev's mannequinlike predecessor, was supported by Eduard Shevardnadze, the leader of the Georgian Communist party at that time, and then briefly shelved. It was finally distributed nationally, and it shook up the public with its pioneering de-Stalinization. Abuladze's film was an important social event for the Soviet cinema and Soviet audiences. *Repentance*, on the other hand, affected Georgian cinema artistically.

It is still a Georgian school creation, although something has changed. Historical allusions substitute for what had been pure folkloric metaphor, rigidly turning a poetic parable into a political allegory. In one scene, a woman in white, blindfolded, carrying scales and displaying the manners of a call girl, portrays Justice under a tyrant. In another scene, two young, romantic protagonists find themselves buried alive in a plowed field while mounted guards led by the tyrant chase them. This latter example is particularly demonstrative, since the archetypical model for the sequence is obviously taken from a folk fairy tale, but the meaning attached to it must be unmistakably interpreted as contemporary and political.

If a metaphor relates to an allegory as a sign with multiple meanings relates to a sign with a singular meaning, then *Repentance* brought a metaphor raised by the Georgian school, and correspondingly the school itself, to a dead end. But even if *Repentance* did not cause the untimely though glorious death of the Georgian school, it certainly promised no good prognosis for romantic and symbolic language in the times of glasnost.

The attempts to revive the school in recent years looked more like a sad postscript. Georgy Shengelaya, creator of *Pirosmani* and *The Veri Quarter Tunes*, was the most persistent in these attempts. After a preperestroika road movie, *A Journey of the Young Composer (Puteshe-stviye molodogo kompozitora*, 1984), set in Georgia in 1909, Shengelaya returned to the beginning of the century to make a black-and-white film ballad, *Hareba and Gogi (Hareba i Gogi*, 1988). A Georgian version of *Butch Cassidy and the Sundance Kid*, Shengelaya's feature brings us into a small mountain peasant gang with two leads, Hareba and Gogi, who do almost exactly what the famous duo of Paul Newman and Robert Redford did, and end precisely the same way. The film with its all-male cast promotes the restoration of old-fashioned values, such as friendship and faithfulness, courage and the delights of living danger-ously, that were so often glorified by Georgian school productions. The way the story is told can be described as a "deromanticized romanti-cism" using a black-and-white purity of image.

Georgy Shengelaya has finished a new feature, *Khadzhi Murat*, an ad-aptation of Leo Tolstoy's Caucasian fable. It seems to be in the same stylistic and thematic vein as Shengelaya's previous productions. The new film's distribution will clearly not differ much from that of *Hareba and Gogi*. The latter did well in Georgia, for obvious nostalgic reasons, but passed away almost unnoticed nationally. The reason for that is also apparent: the film has nothing to do with current social and political issues. But what was a merit in the stagnant past has become a short-coming under perestroika and glasnost.

The New Wave: Against the Current

The challenge glasnost presented to the Georgian school was not the only one it met in the 1980s. The first, preperestroika dare came from inside—from the frontier of Georgian film. It should be remembered that the Georgian school itself was a strong (and informal) association of auteurs.

Georgia has also provided Soviet cinema with two of its most power-ful and unique directors, who belong neither to the Georgian school nor to any other film movement. Sergei Paradjanov and Otar Ioseliani have created film universes that are ultimately harmonious and hermetic. Both focus on "cinema for cinema's sake" rather than on narrative. Both need no words to express their cinematic ideas: the visual images in their films dominate the dialogue. Here the aesthetic similarities end and the extreme artistic oppositions begin, but Paradjanov and Ioseliani share one other trait: both have nothing, or almost nothing, to do with perestroika.

Sergei Paradjanov, a Tbilisian of Armeninan descent, who died in Au-gust 1990, made a name for himself in the 1960s with *Shadows of For-gotten Ancestors (Teni zabytykh predkov*, 1965) and *Pomegranate Blos-som (Tsvet granata*, 1969), and then spent roughly seventeen years in jail and exile for "homosexuality," which was a political action against this obstinate filmmaker. Paradjanov himself was allowed to say "Action" again only in the early 1980s. In *The Legend of Suram Fortress* (*Legenda o Suramskoi kreposti*, 1984), and most recently in *Ashik Kerib* (1988), he returned to his Eastern ornaments on historical or literary canvases, which continue to appeal as if neither the times nor the political order had changed.

Otar Ioseliani, the director of *Falling Leaves, There Lived a Thrush* (*Zhil pevchii drozd*, 1971) and *Pastoral* (1976), in which he created a mesmerizingly chaotic and inconstant world where people meet only to part and where no other meaning exists but motion itself, left for France right before perestroika. He made a later film, *Le Favoris de la Lune* (1984), in the country of his mentor, Robert Bresson, earning praise as an "authentically French" director.

Both Paradjanov and Ioseliani have strongly influenced Soviet film, opening new horizons for filmmaking, but neither of them begat disciples as their creative individuality developed. Furthermore, both Paradjanov and Ioseliani belong to the generation of the sixties, the generation of the Georgian school. The new wave of auteurs emerged from the generation of the 1970s, which grew up and looked down during the stagnation period while their artistic elders were creating whimsical ethnic patterns.

What first strikes an eye familiar with Georgian cinema in the works of the new-wave directors is the lack of ethnic surfaces: costumes, rites, and so forth. The debut film by Alexander Rekhviashvili, one of the leaders of the new wave's first flow, *Georgian Chronicle of the Nineteenth Century* (*Gruzinskaya hronika XIX veka*, 1979), places us in a Kafkaesque city where a lonely student goes through all the circles of bureaucratic hell to help the peasants of his home village win back their land from bourgeois industrialists. The distorted urban sets in the *Chronicle* remind one of German expressionism and *Caligari*. The horrifyingly circular structure of the narrative, the morose suspense of the slow-paced action, the atmosphere of silent torture in a vacuum, bring to mind Orson Welles's *Trial*. The long sequence in the forest where two assassins chase the student and finally eliminate him, leaving the rest of the film without a hero, is obviously influenced by Kurosawa's *Rashomon*. What is harder to find in *Georgian Chronicle* is the influence of Rekhviashvili's native predecessors in the Georgian school.

The *Chronicle* is Georgian, however, in title and in spirit as well. So is another chronicle by another leader of the new wave, Irakli Kvirikadze's *Swimmer*. In an ironically cheerful mode, this faked documentary, like Woody Allen's *Zelig*, follows an invented Georgian celebrity, a unique swimmer at the beginning of this century, and then turns to his offspring, who inherited their ancestor's gift. The playful mosaic of *The Swimmer* combines the historical panorama of almost a whole century in a political subplot, the wild humor of nearly obscene anecdotes, and shots of the filming of the movie itself.

Rekhviashvili made only three films after the *Chronicle*, and of these, *The Step* (*Stupen'*, 1986) and *Coming Closer* were made under glasnost; Kvirikadze has completed one, *The Voyage of Comrade Stalin to Africa* (*Puteshestviye tovarischa Stalina v Afriku*, 1991). Meanwhile, *Rosy-cheeked Don Juan Is Crying*, a project focused on Georgian immigrants in France and written by Kvirikadze, won the Grand Prix at the 1989 French national script contest, and the Georgian filmmaker was named the best French screenwriter of 1989.

In the nearly ten years between *The Swimmer* and *The Voyage of Comrade Stalin to Africa*, Kvirikadze wrote a script for his wife, Nana Djordjadze, to shoot as her first feature. *My English Granddad* (*Robinzonada, ili Moi angliiskii dedushka*, 1987) perfectly illustrates the caprices of Kvirikadze's fantasy as well as the trend the couple represents in the new Georgian cinema. The hero, a British telegraphist named Christopher Hughes (played by a Georgian actor, Zhanri Lolashvili), goes to a remote Georgian village in 1920 to build the London–Delhi telegraph line. Eventually he decides to stay, falling in love with a beautiful woman named Anna. Her brother, a local Soviet official, forbids her to see the foreigner, and finally throws Hughes out of the village. The sharp-witted Englishman, however, takes up residence right by the telegraph pole, claiming that Britain had bought the land for three yards around every pole all over the world. In this "new England," Anna continues seeing her Robinson until he, along with her Communist brother, is killed by the real landlord, who takes vengeance on the Soviets for depriving him of his land. "His name has never been mentioned in our house," says the grandson-narrator in a voice-over, "but the family always cherished it."

The blend of irony, oddity, and compassion makes the style of the Kvirikadze-Djordjadze duo that of "lyrical absurdism." This is also the couple's ideology, which survives the temptations of glasnsost and the social and political stresses of perestroika.

Rekhviashvili in *The Step* took a step in a different direction, and the distance he covered from *Georgian Chronicle* to the new film somehow reflects the way Soviet society developed between 1979 and 1986. Alexi, the hero of *The Step*, lives in a modern urban environment, much more realistic than the one in the surrealistic *Chronicle*. This world, however, is also surreal in essence. The same faces keep appearing in Alexi's apartment; the same words are being said day after day. All action takes place in interiors and employs, as Karen Rosenberg notes, a "slow camera moving through narrow rooms and corridors to build a suffocating atmosphere" ("Glasnost and Georgian Cinema," 25). Every character inhabiting this world is obsessed with something (growing mushrooms in the basement, placing a puppy on a revolving phonograph turntable, watering exuberant plants), which adds to the claustrophobic feeling the film provokes.

In the final shot, Alexi, a young biologist, whose life goal is to find a life goal, breaks out of this absurd existence, which has become routine. He rejects a career and the city (a motif essential to the film and to Georgian cinema overall) and leaves for a vague future in the mountains of the countryside. But while the camera, finally liberated from the interior vacuum, soars over the landscape, observing the retreating hero in a long shot, the director cuts short this optimistic coda with a final question mark. In the same frame we see another figure moving in the opposite direction—another Alexi leaving the countryside for the city.

Clearly, what makes *The Step* stand out against the background of traditional Georgian cinema and keeps it in tune with perestroika is that it presents a young hero before the first vital step in life, trying to come to grips with society and himself. Such a hero appeared in Otar Ioseliani's first features, *Falling Leaves* and *There Lived a Thrush*, but could scarcely be found in the Georgian school productions. Under glasnost, a young hero in a global quest has become a trademark of the cinema of the Georgian new wave.

Where *The Step* ends, *Anemia* begins. The switch to what happens after the escape marks the borderline between the first and the second flowings of the new wave. Vakhtang Kotetishvili, the director of *Anemia* (1988), brings his young hero Nika from Tbilisi to a godforsaken mountain village to teach in a local boarding school. While Rekhviashvili left the illusion that perhaps once out of the urban asylum, in the land of old values carried by old shepherds, one can find a key to the search, Kotetishvili presents a feast of disillusionment. Anemia—weakness and paleness of being—characterizes life in the movie, which is deliberately anemic, weakly slow-paced, and tonelessly beautiful itself. The principal of the school, a crazy Stalinist, a little dictator, leads the crew of eight monster teachers who teach seven students to be nobodies. Seasons pass, but nothing changes in this comatose "dead materialists' society." Nika's ideals slowly die, and then his soul does the same. The only rebellion allowed the hero is to simulate suicide. The only catharsis given in this world is the revealing of the cinematic game itself.

The teacher and friend who actually committed suicide in these mountains leaves a note for Nika: "Show the film from the closet to everybody, and you will be saved." What appears in this amateur film found by Nika in the closet where the busts of Stalin are stored is extra footage from *Anemia* itself: actors, sets, and the dead friend newly alive. Another illusion crowns disillusionment, but this does not cure the lethal disease diagnosed.

An earlier "second flow" feature, Alexander Tsabadze's *Spot* (*Pyatno*, 1985), is even less conformist and even more gloomy. This time we observe the city, Tbilisi, but not the scenic views of it *The Veri Quarter Tunes* might have shown. Rather we see the slums, the dark side of life. Never before had Georgian cinema presented its picturesque capital as an asphalt jungle, a realm of faceless apartment buildings and airless lower depths. Here Kisho, the protagonist, a rock and roll child, lives, a musician and poet who sings about human alienation. Kisho, a typical representative of the silent generation of the late 1970s and early 1980s, is Camus's perfect stranger in a world of boring coincidences, irresponsible encounters, and cruel games. *The Spot* tries him for this.

In a childish street game Kisho loses three thousand rubles, a sum he had never carried. The joke grows into a real threat when the winners demand the money. Kisho's friend Archi gives Kisho a hand and accompanies him to the sewers where payment must take place. The rest is absurdly tragic: a fight, a sudden gunshot, and Archi is killed, not the hero, but the only positive character in the film. The creators of *The Spot* ask who will pay for this accidental death, leaving Kisho leaning over the dead friend, the first one who did help someone else. Will the stranger be able to stay away from life as he used to? The questions are for us to answer.

The way Georgian cinema developed over two decades, from the Georgian school's naive patterns to *Repentance* to the nonconformist social features of the new wave, is even more dramatic than Russian cinema's path from stagnant films to *Little Vera*. The results in *Little Vera* and in *The Step, Anemia, The Spot*, and other Georgian new-wave productions, such as Teimuraz Babluani's *Migrating Sparrows* (*Perelet vorobyev*, 1979) and *The Sun of the Sleepless* (*Solntse nespyaschikh*, 1988), are about the same. They are open questions for those who cannot keep their eyes closed anymore.

However, the dramatic challenge that Georgian cinema meets (in contrast to that of Russian film) is to balance the new openness (as a new democratic country) with the ethnic tradition so masterfully developed by the Georgian school. Will Georgian cinema be able to withstand this challenge and preserve its ethnic uniqueness? Glasnost favors open-ended questions.

THE WESTERN MODEL: THE BALTICS

If 1989 will go down in world history as the year of Eastern Europe and the fall of the Berlin Wall, 1990 deserves to be remembered as the year of the Baltics. For the first time in the history of the Soviet Union a move toward actual political freedom was taken. On 11 March 1990, Lithuania declared its independence; Latvia and Estonia followed, in spite of notorious threats from Moscow, including a tank parade in the streets of Vilnius, the Lithuanian capital. Three tiny Baltic republics proved to the Soviet nations and to the whole world that real perestroika begins where the central party and government control ends—that perestroika comes from the people's will, not from decisions made from above.

In close-up, the three republics have much less in common than they seem to in a long shot from overseas. The "Baltic unit" itself is something of a Moscow invention. Lithuania and Latvia make up one of the smallest cultural and linguistic groups in the Western world, the Baltic group. But Lithuania, in contrast to Latvia, was strongly influenced by Poland, its neighbor, to which it once belonged and to which it has been linked as ally and enemy for centuries. Estonia, in turn, is much closer to the Scandinavian cultures, Finland and Sweden in particular, than to its Soviet confederates. (Estonia belongs to the Ugro-Finnish linguistic group, which unites it with Finland and Hungary.)

However, some similarities always distinguished the Baltics from the other Soviet republics. These distinctions will eventually lose their significance, as the Baltics have become independent countries, but they clearly influenced the Baltics' relationships with the Soviet Union and the rest of the world during the fifty years of Soviet rule there. Politically, the Baltics were the last to be included in the Soviet Union. Before that they were developed and sovereign democratic republics. No wonder the Baltics opened the secessionist movement, blazing the trail for Moldavia, Georgia, Armenia, Uzbekistan, the Ukraine, and others.

The peoples of the Baltics have never forgotten the arms that forced them to become the "Soviet people." But instead of starting hand-to-hand combat, as the southern and eastern republics did, Baltic democratic movements employed their lawyers to prove that the notorious 1940 Molotov-Ribbentrop treaty, which freed Stalin's hands to invade the three Baltic countries, was illegal. This is more than politics, however. This is the Baltic spirit, very different from the ethnic egos of other Soviet republics. The Baltic nations are composed, adamant, and rational, in contrast with the "ungovernable" Georgians or the "slovenly" Russians. Baltic emotions are usually hidden. In fine arts, for instance, Estonians are most successful in graphic design—computed and comfortable beauty. Lithuanians and Latvians have developed painting schools whose abstract expressionism is also rational in essence. This may explain why all three republics, not particularly outstanding in fiction film, are famous for the "marginal" film arts: documentary in Latvia and Lithuania, animation in Estonia.

Among the Soviet nations, the Baltics are considered the most civilized in ethnic character as well as in life-style. Living standards are relatively high there, and in comparison to the rest of the country they are closer to Western standards. The Baltics are referred to in Russia and the other republics as "the West," culturally as well as geographically. In many ways, this is true. Placed between the West and the East, but administratively forced to belong to the East, the Baltics have always gravitated culturally toward the West, and northwestern Europe in particular.

However, the Western quality of the Baltic film cultures appears to have mutated under the Communist regime. In the Brezhnev era, the Western influence produced a thirst for commercialism (vital for the tiny Baltic film industries) that undermined the health of Latvian cinema long before the hullabaloo about moneymaking in the film industry began in Moscow. During the 1970s and 1980s, the Riga Studio in the Latvian capital manufactured numerous detective films (some of them for television), having as much to do with Latvian culture and tradition as hamburgers have to do with Hamburg. Most of the movies were based on English and American novels, such as *Mirage* (*Mirazh*, 1983, based on a J. H. Chase novel). Perry Mason also once appeared on the Baltic screen in the 1987 Lithuanian film *All Against One* (*Vse protiv odnogo*). One of the most successful Soviet miniseries of the early 1980s was the Lithuanian-made, soap opera–like *Rich Man, Poor Man* (*Bogach, bednyak*, 1982, based on an Irwin Shaw novel). Although these films were relatively well done, especially compared to Eastern Russian and Soviet Asian productions, the major advantage they had was that Baltic actors and Latvian sets looked rather Western to Soviet audiences. Besides, Baltic actors, speaking their native languages, were being dubbed into Russian (the general rule for ethnic films that are to be distributed outside the producing republic), which created a certain "foreign" flavor for the Soviet viewer.

Another, deeper side of the same Western quality in the Baltic cinema is the existentialist theme and attitude, both in subject matter and in film form. Ingmar Bergman was apparently more important for Lithuanian and Estonian auteurs than were Eisenstein or more recent Russian directors. Consider several examples from different republics.

Kaljo Kiisk, the Estonian champion of the 1970s, made *Madness* (*Bezumiye*, 1969), a film that was shelved in Russia for almost two decades. *Madness* locks us up in a mental institution where a Hitchcockian plot is married to a slightly perverse Bergmanian intellectuality and pace. The time: World War II. The Nazi investigator, played by Yuri Yarvet, an Estonian star who was King Lear in Grigori Kozintsev's celebrated 1971 production, a little man with big, crazy eyes, goes to the institution in a small Estonian town. He pretends to be a new doctor, and his mission is to unmask a British spy who reportedly hides in the asylum as a patient. Not revealing the antagonist (who, as it turns out, does not exist at all), the film follows the gradual psychic decay of the protagonist, surrounding him with an atmosphere of total madness, external and internal as well.

The leading Latvian auteur, Janis Streich, also paid tribute to existential problems in his 1982 *To Remember or to Forget (Pomnit' ili zabyt')*. It is the story of an intelligent, childless young nurse who steals a baby from her hospital and then experiences a nightmare of guilty conscience. The film balances between melodrama and a deep existentialist inquiry into individuality. Melodrama wins, however, partly because of the restrictions the Soviets put on such a non-Russian angle.

Latvian cinema could legally celebrate a true feast of existentialism only under glasnost in Arvids Krievs's *Photo with a Woman and a Wild Boar (Fotografiya s zhenshchinoi i dikim kabanom,* 1987). As a kind of Latvian *Fatal Attraction*—and quite an attractive one—*The Photo with a Woman* was the first film in the Soviet Union to put down roots in the field of sensuality, though not in the sense of emotions: there were plenty of those released by the Soviet film industry in passionate scandals among workers and bosses in the so-called industrial movies. Focusing on a nice, ordinary Latvian woman who mysteriously ruins the lives of several men as a classic femme fatale, the film depicts sensuality as a particular secret reality parallel to the everyday open one. This reality had barely existed in Soviet film before, partly since the perspective is alien to the Russian tradition, while the West had almost completely squeezed it out, from early Buñuel to Adrian Lyne.

The Latvian experiment, however, also displayed shortcomings in treating this new subject. The innocent Soviet West, losing its innocence in one of the first R-rated Soviet movies, counted on the tradition of rationalism too much and lacked eroticism and irrationality, the means by which one could penetrate the story's consciousness. As *The Photo with a Woman* also shows, if glasnost has affected the Baltic fiction film, this influence seems rather minor when compared with the impact of openness on Baltic politics and the Baltic documentary. (Latvia has opened new horizons for the glasnost documentary in *Is It Easy to Be Young?, Higher Judgment, Poperechnaya Street,* and others, as discussed above.)

Lithuania's film culture is the strongest in the three Baltic states. Like both the Latvian and Estonian film industries, Lithuanian cinema from the late 1960s to the early 1980s was not outstanding, though like its neighbors it had a leading auteur, one more controversial than Kaljo Kiisk in Estonia or Janis Streich in Latvia. Vitautas Zhalakiavichius became famous nationally with one of his earliest and best films, *Nobody Wanted to Die* (*Nikto ne khotel umirat'*, 1965), a Westernized Eastern about the post–World War II Lithuanian countryside. The members of the Lokis family, farmers who live in the woods (the name in Lithuanian means "bear"), find themselves unintentionally involved in the secret war between the Soviets and the anti-Communist partisan army "The Wood Brothers," which in a Soviet film of 1965 was presented as a bandit gang. Everyone in this family faces a vital choice: which side to take, and ultimately, whether to live or to die. What is intended to be a well-mixed black-and-white action film becomes a sharp set of variations on the existential theme of choice.

Nobody Wanted to Die is unquestionably a Lithuanian production, with only a touch of Soviet (and not Russian) ideology. Zhalakiavichius's interest in the history of his land; the focus on a big peasant family in which each of the four brothers is precisely characterized; the wild and beautiful Baltic nature setting, and the director's attention to its nuances; the measured pace and deeply psychological tone of the film—all these traits distinguish the Lithuanian cinema.

Nobody Wanted to Die features a group of remarkable new actors, who formed what was soon known as the "Lithuanian acting school." It has won a leading place for Lithuanian film and theater in the Baltic region, and high marks throughout the country. These actors, including Juozas Budraitis, Regimantas Adomaitis, and Donatas Banionis, who easily conquered the national screen as well, were soloists in an ensemble of equals. Having different artistic credos and exploring different personal themes throughout their careers, the Lithuanian school actors have developed a specific Lithuanian style of acting: highly intellectual, introspective, and introverted, precise in detail, but concerned primarily with the general image of the world created by an actor.

But the short flourishing of Lithuanian cinema in the 1960s ceased. Zhalakiavichius left Lithuania for Moscow and in the 1970s made a series of Russian features on the Latin American liberation movement. *This Sweet Word—Liberty* (*Eto sladkoye slovo—svoboda*, 1973) and *Centaurs* (*Kentavry*, 1978) proved the director's interest in historic cataclysms but added little to Lithuanian cinema. When Zhalakiavichius went back to his homeland, this time as the head of a Lithuanian studio, he still made nothing equal to *Nobody Wanted to Die*. His 1987 feature *Weekend in Hell* (*Weekend v adu*) follows the trend of previous Moscow-made political productions. What happens in a regular Soviet war movie if its heroes, two escapees from a Nazi camp, find themselves naked at a Baltic resort beach in the company of German officers? The answer is easily predictable. Masquerade (successful to the point that one of the leads speaks German, while another simulates muteness); a duel of irreconcilable standpoints; exposure; another escape. Nothing else happens in *Weekend in Hell*, mixed professionally, performed in masterly fashion, but hardly made in a new Lithuania, which in 1987 was waking up to the struggle for independence.

The revival of Lithuanian film is connected with the name of a director from a different generation than Zhalakiavichius. Algimantas Puipa, born in 1951, started his film career in the mid-1970s and found success in the early 1980s with *The Daughter of a Horse Thief* (*Doch konokrada*, 1981) and *A Woman and Her Four Men* (*Zhenschina i chetvero ee muzhchin*, 1983). These two epic parables from the Lithuanian peasant past clearly reflect Puipa's durable style: a panoramic view of life; a focus on a family, essential for Lithuanian culture and film; an interest in the little, everyday history that confirms or conflicts with the big history in the background; an attraction to the ordinary and minute realism in depicting it, interwoven with a romantic attitude toward love and women; a severe visual poetry and a thoughtfully modulated rhythm.

In 1987, Puipa directed *The Eternal Light* (*Vechnoye siyaniye*), described by Ian Christie as "a period romance staged in the Nordic silent style to fine effect" ("Revolutionary Riga," 2). There is, however, little glasnost in this glasnost-era production. The period is the early 1950s, the first post-Stalinist years, colored with the somnolent harshness of life in those times. We see rainy and misty landscapes of the countryside, and eroded roads. Eternal yearning is the leitmotiv of this world. Says Puipa, "We wanted to depict the life at a slushy crossroads. There are no more gunshots in the woods. Stalinist ruthless collectivization, villages brought to naught, all of this is yesterday. And today—the lull and the anxious waiting: where and how will life go?" (Zorky, "Eternal Light," 1).

Against this background the unusual romance of the village groom, Anitsetas, and his enigmatic wife develops and comes to an unhappy end. The romance begins after Anitsetas marries the lonely and unsociable beauty Amelia, and ends before love has a chance to keep its promises. Eternal yearning leads Amelia away, leaving Anitsetas at the slushy crossroads. Puipa's world is sad, but not gloomy, and the film is not named *The Eternal Light* by accident. People in this world are unconsciously resistant to slush. Their faces are lit by the internal light of spiritual beauty and strength, which makes the director's individualist concept "pessimistically optimistic," and brings us back to Baltic existentialism, Lithuanian style.

Puipa, however, hardly idealizes individualism. His next feature, *The Day of Fish* (*Den' ryby*, 1990), portrays the crisis of individualism in soberly ironic terms as the urban communal locale, unusual for a Lithuanian film, squeezes out an individual in search of himself. Veronica, the protagonist of the drama, a writer, is an outsider by choice, constantly evaluating the world outside and inside herself. The world is lacking moral stability. Everything in this world, masterfully executed by Puipa and his longtime companion, cinematographer Rimantas Juodvalkis, seems liquid and floating: things, people, and values. Veronica's friends celebrate her birthday without her; her boozy girlfriend leaves her a lover whose name is unclear, saying, "If you don't like him, throw him away"; and Veronica establishes the new relationship this way: "No promises; if I say to you 'Leave,' you leave."

Puipa does not condemn; he diagnoses the problem and, along with his heroes, searches for a solution. One solution—motherhood for Veronica—looks like a compromise, but this does not cancel the anxiety of the search dictated by the director's belief in individualism. This search, however, is not a search for a new order of things. Puipa here is no more politically engaged than any other intellectual artist whose approach to society is purely moral. His 1991 feature, *Ticket to the Taj Mahal*, continues Puipa's themes while interspersing color fantasy sequences about the Taj Mahal "dreamed" by the protagonist, who lives in a crushing (black-and-white) squalor of oppression and poverty.

The same is true about the new Estonian cinema, most strongly represented by two glasnost-era features, Leida Laius's and Arvo Iho's *Games for Schoolchildren* and Arvo Iho's *Bird Watcher* ([*The Observer*], *Nablyudatel'*, 1987). The former is a harshly realistic tale about abandoned children growing up in orphanages. The latter is a down-to-earth love-hate romance between a Russian forester and poacher who lives on a tiny desert island and a young Estonian ornithologist who dies in the finale from the crossbow trap hidden in the woods by his lover.

Despite Leida Laius's conviction that "neither *Games for Schoolchildren*, nor its follow-up *The Stolen Date* [*Ukradennoye svidaniye*, 1988], could have been produced before [glasnost]" ("Glasnost and Perestroika," 87), her own features, as well as her cinematographer's directorial solo debut in *The Bird Watcher*, subordinate the social to the moral, not to the political. Against this Baltic background, the new Lithuanian feature *Awakening* (*Probuzhdeniye*, 1990) looks unusually political. Filmed by the excellent drama director Jonas Vaitkus as a screen adaptation of his stage production, *Awakening* is a political phantasmagoria made in extremely loud, Fassbinder-like colors and cut with black-and-white newsreels from the Stalinist era. The narrative focuses on a love triangle: former school friends meet again in 1940, when Lithuania was invaded by the Soviets, to discover that one of them, Piyus, had become a NKVD (KGB) interrogator killing people at random, while the other one, Pranas, married to Piyus's ex-girlfriend, had become the head of the anti-Soviet resistance movement, and the interrogator's victim.

All three of them face a vital choice, and all three of them die in the end since the moral human choice and the historical choice are incompatible in a time of ruthless terror. But the familiar existentialist perspective in Vaitkus's interpretation is expressed through openly political images, some of which are adopted from the aesthetics of a political cabaret. In one of the dream sequences, for instance, the NKVD agent Piyus commits suicide at the top of an enormous statue of Stalin. In another scene, the ghost of Stalin comes to talk to the agonized rebel, Pranas.

Nothing astounding awaits us here: it is the same desperate call for freedom of speech, familiar to us from many other Soviet pictures of the past five years. The voice, though, in contrast to the Soviet productions, does not speak Russian. The voice of the Baltics today knows its ethnic difference and independence on film as well as in politics.

"WILD KAZAKH BOYS": THE MODEL FOR THE FUTURE

Nobody in the Soviet Union has heard of the "Wild Kazakh boys." The name appeared first at the 1989 Sundance Film Festival in Salt Lake City, which has been turned by Robert Redford into a mecca for American independent cinema. The discovery of the new wave from the remote Soviet republic of Kazakhstan was no less sensational than the previous year's breakthrough, *sex, lies, and videotape*.

Kazakhstan, like the other Asian republics, has always been notorious in the Soviet Union for its artistic (and nonartistic) conservatism. Each of these republics might give birth to a creative filmmaker or a fresh movie, but the average film was depressingly faceless. From provincial Brezhnevian die-hardism to the miserable technical condition of the studios, everything seemed inimical to change even after change was declared an official policy. Yet the new word in glasnost filmmaking did not come from Moscow or Leningrad, from Georgia or the Baltics, but from the "spiritual swamp" of Kazakhstan, with only a little help from the center. The movement has emerged from the specialized ethnic (Kazakh) directing class at VGIK. Sergei Soloyev, the class mentor and the playful creator of *Assa* and *Black Rose Stands for Sorrow, Red Rose Stands for Love*, has done everything to facilitate his students' entrance into the industry, as well as to pass on to them his new perspective on film as a game. Never before in the Soviet Union (or, probably, in the world) have film students received the right to direct mainstream features. The first was Rashid Nugmanov, who, after a short semidocumentary, *Yakh-ha!*, made *The Needle*, which we described above as an offbeat, flippant thriller. What started with *The Needle* appeared to be a "new wave" in the precise sense of the term.

The origin of this new wave was exactly what it should be. Like the French new wave, which was a rebellious response to the older generation's "quality" films, and like the "new German cinema," which arose from the ruins of the film of the "new economic miracle" era, the Kazakh new wave was unexpected, but prepared for by boredom and stagnation. The "Wild Kazakh boys," Rashid Nugmanov, Alexander Baranov, Bakhyt Kilibayev, Abai Karpikov, and Serik Aprymov, became an association of accomplices. They share facilities and ideas. They help each other out while making movies, and support each other when their productions have trouble gaining official recognition or meet obstacles in release.

The cinema of the new wave is truly young at heart, while all the filmmakers are surprisingly young in age as well—below 35—which is rare by both Hollywood and Soviet standards (although Truffaut made his first feature at twenty-seven, Fassbinder his at twenty-three). The feeling a viewer gets from the new-wave productions is that they are made by friends and for friends, with an easy spirit and a lot of improvisation. These films are like messages sealed in bottles and thrown into the sea: those who fish out the message become members of the club and friends as well.

"You've said that The Needle really isn't about drugs at all. What do you mean by that?" Nugmanov, the director of the first new-wave film, was asked in an interview. "It's about friends who are trying to play in film, that's all. We just wanted to have fun," was the response (Horton, "Nomad from Kazakhstan," 35). The Needle (1988), like the films that followed, is permeated with the sense of excitement felt by a movie-making tyro. Furthermore, Nugmanov's flip-flop tale is an adopted child of Godard's 1959 A bout de souffle (Breathless), resembling the French new-wave film in the type of hero and the alienated mode of narration. It is also "poor cinema" in the Godardian sense, made on an extremely low budget with a lot of inventiveness, which, as the international mainstream experience shows, often dies out when money comes in.

The main trait of the Kazakh new wave, however, is unique and startling, particularly in the context of the ethnic problem in the Soviet Union. The cinema of the "Wild Kazakh Boys" is not Kazakh except in location. In a country overwhelmed with ethnic clashes, the young Asian filmmakers began to search for a universal model of film language, not caring much about their ethnic identity. In the interview cited above, Nugmanov noted, "Being Kazakh means I know my ancestors back to the seventeenth century, my tribe, that is, and its structure. We have always had the same language, the same Moslem culture" (36). But later on, when asked why The Needle was shot in Russian, Nugmanov confessed, "In our family we almost never speak Kazakh, but instead we used Russian. I don't feel strongly about speaking Kazakh, you see" (34).

The Needle is related to anything but Muslim culture. It is a cousin of the stereotypical Hollywood thriller, melodrama, and road movie, seen through the lens of a European film mentality, particularly that of the French new wave, which adored old Hollywood. Even on the sound track, The Needle is filled with different languages—Russian, Italian, French, German, English, and at last Kazakh—as a hallmark of its aesthetic mix.

The same ethnic vacuum pervades other Kazakh new-wave productions, such as The Three (Troye, 1988), written and directed by the authors of The Needle's script, Alexander Baranov and Bakhyt Kilibayev. The film originally was named Fofan, which to the Western ear sounds like Kazakh, but probably comes from a new-wave credo, transliterated from English: "For fun." The three leading characters of this hour-long "desert comedy" are bomzhs (homeless outcasts), the newly discovered social group favored by the glasnost screen's dark vision. They are freelancers in life, and earn their daily bread (vodka) digging ditches for an army squad located in the area. They are also gamblers in the game of life, and when the film crew arrives to shoot a thriller in the desert, the heroes volunteer to perform a risky stunt for decent money. After the stunt is done, it turns out that the whole thing was the drunken production manager's joke, and the camera was not rolling. However, the stunned stuntman pays the daredevil tramps a sum that they throw to the winds for pleasure, and they perform this deliverance from money quite artistically. They find a soldier who used to humiliate them, and pay him to return the humiliation. In the end the three "citizens of the world" take off for a new adventure in a metaphysiacally lit shot resembling the last shot of Jim Jarmusch's Down by Law.

Another feature in the Wenders-Jarmusch vein from Kazakhstan, Abai Karpikov's Little Fish in Love (Vliublennaya rybka, 1989), is even more influenced by the Western postmodern canon than The Three, and it is no less cosmopolitan.

"Little Fish" is a young man who is as wordless and cool as the real fish he stares at continually in the aquarium of a friend. A "midnight cowboy" from a Kazakh city, he does nothing (in his life and in the film) but wander around in search of something vague. The film is built from a series of seemingly unnecessary scenes and encounters that are strung on a mood instead of a narrative. As Forrest Ciesol, one of the first American discoverers of the new Kazakh film, notes, "While he clearly lacks Wenders' sense of character, Karpikov nevertheless succeeds in creating the sleek, minimalist atmosphere of a city that some residents claim has 'fallen into a deep sleep, dreaming of better times'" ("Kazakhstan Wave," 57).

A similar structure (filled with a different style and sense) is found in another new-wave feature, the most powerful to date, Serik Aprymov's *Last Stop* (*Poslednyaya ostanovka*, 1989). Once again, the hero, a young man named Erken who returns from the army to his godforsaken native village on the devastated Kazakh plains, is the only element tying the film into a narrative. The hero encounters there a wild chain of events, including a friend's party, a wedding, a fight, and a drunkard's cross fire with the police from a rooftop—all depicted chaotically. What the director presents to us is a picture of the world's and culture's decline, symbolized in the agony of Muslim patriarchal society in Asia. "The naturalism of these scenes," according to Ciesol, "is so startling that it borders on surrealism" (ibid.).

Director Serik Aprymov is a native of Aksuat, the village where the action of *The Last Stop* takes place. The whole cast is made up of the natives: the director's friends, relatives, and neighbors. Even before the production was finished, villagers complained to the studio about the way their lives were being depicted. Letters of complaint and objections went from the local Communist party to the Central Party Committee and other authorities, accusing "the prodigal son," Aprymov, of distorting rural reality and painting everything black. The film was shelved. However, Rashid Nugmanov, who by that time had become an official himself (while still a film student he was elected the head of the Kazakh filmmakers' Union), had no doubt that Aprymov will triumph. As he said in an interview, "It is now becoming more dangerous to try to stop the release of a controversial film than it is to make one" (Ciesol, "Many Hollywoods," 68).

The trend represented by *The Needle*, *The Three*, *Little Fish in Love*, and *The Last Stop* is not the only one in the new Kazakh cinema. Side by side with the postmodern formal games played by Nugmanov and his fellow filmmakers there are warm and simpleminded pictures about children and animals, more "Asiatic," and, alas, less exciting, such as Derezhan Omirbaev's short, *The Summer Heat* (*Letnyaya zhara*, 1988), or Talgat Temenov's *Toro* (1986) and *The Wolf Cub among People* (*Volchonok sredi liudei*, 1988). But the search for a universal film idiom should not be over soon, as indicated by the intensity of the new wave's beginning. Kazakhfilm Studio reports confirm this. Nugmanov shot his second feature, *Big Mac*, in Leningrad during late 1991, based on Shakespeare's *Macbeth*; possible coproductions with Hollywood are being explored. The codirectors of *The Three* made *Woman of the Day* (*Zhenschina dnya*, 1990), a stylized criminal melodrama, together, and then split up and finished solo features: Kilibayev made *Klish* (1990), an urban thriller, and Baranov made *He and She* (*On i ona*, 1990), a melodrama.

Furthermore, the wave seems to have spread out, passing over the borders of Kazakhstan. In the neighboring republic of Uzbekistan, which is considered to have the most feudal and brutal social life, which made the most melodramatic films under Brezhnev, now producing thousands of overideologized, perestroika-supporting feet of film, a few young filmmakers have emereged who obviously care for art and "for fun" more than anything else. In 1988, director Dzhahongir Faiziev and screenwriter Yuri Dashevsky made a short film in Moscow, strangely named *Kyadya* (in Korean, "dog soup"), a black comedy about seven workers hunting two stray dogs for the reason hidden in the title, on the eve of Communist Revolution Day. Their next joint venture, a 1989 feature no less strangely entitled *Siz Kim Siz?* (no translation is given, but in Uzbek it means "Who are you?"), develops the same subversively humorous trend, sparkling against the regular socialist-realist Asian background— "a socialist absurdity."

"Who are you?" the leads of this road movie ask each other—a driver and a hitchhiker, who seem to be a doctor and a college instructor. After they are stopped by the traffic police, it turns out that one of them is a KGB officer. He is eager to take vengeance on the "simple cops" who dared to cross his path. Then another road movie begins: that of the endless road through the local bureaucracy's offices. The result of this journey is unexpectedly effective: it turns out that the "college instructor" is also a KGB officer, only of a higher rank.

Does this world, divided into KGB agents and bureaucrats, look like the real Soviet Union today? Yes and no, as the creators' sarcasm belongs to the absurdist tradition in art rather than to "life as it is." Does this comedy, hilariously scary, fit the new wave that soon might change its name from "Kazakh" to "Central Asian"? It certainly does, as the freedom gained by the ethnic cinemas of the region appears more and more multifaceted, and the freedom to mock the KGB is married with the freedom to choose any artistic language.

"Today's young Central Asian filmmakers clearly have a dual mission," concludes Forrest Ciesol, and we join him in this optimistic coda. "It is to make films that reflect their culture, and to drag the bureaucratic Soviet film industry—most likely kicking and screaming—into the twenty-first century" ("Many Hollywoods," 70).

"Soviet cinema does not exist anymore," stated the Ukrainian director Yuri Ilienko after the Montreal screening of his Ukrainian-Canadian coproduction *Swan Lake: The Zone* (*Lebedinoye ozero: Zona*, 1990), a static parable, a variation on Robert Bresson's *Un condamné à mort c'est escapé* (*A Man Escaped*, 1956), only with a Soviet prison and Soviet symbolism. Whatever this statement means (it might mean, for instance, the unprecedented influx of Western money into the budgets of Ukrainian studios), and however premature this statement is, it sounds both like a warning and like a promise. The warning: if Soviet cinema does not exist, what has replaced it? In this chapter we have examined cinemas of five regions: Georgia, Estonia, Latvia, Lithuania, and Kazakhstan. By accident or not, these regions are the most progressive, and not only in a cinematic sense. Some of them already do not belong to the Soviet Union, and have to open a new page of their cultural and political history. This does not mean that we consider the other two-thirds of the Soviet Union negligible for film experts and viewers. Some of the ethnic cinemas not covered here for reasons of space, such as Armenian or Kirghis, undoubtedly deserve serious discussion. But some other republics' film industries are hardly ready to become the film industries of independent countries.

Take Moldavia, one of the most conservative republics under Brezhnev and one of the most revolutionary under Gorbachev. During the preglasnost years many Moldavian intellectuals were forced to "emigrate" to Moscow; the most famous ethnic playwright, Ion Drutse, and the most prominent ethnic filmmaker, Emil Lotyanu, were among them. As a result, Lotyanu began to film his Moldavian tales in Moscow, but soon switched to more cosmopolitan subjects. After the colorful (though Moscow-made) *Gypsies Take off to the Sky* (*Tabor uhodit v nebo*, 1976), Lotyanu made a Chekhov adaptation, *My Sweet and Tender Beast* (*Moi laskovyi i nezhnyi zver'*, 1978), and *Anna Pavlova* (1983), a biography of the famous Russian ballerina and "citizen of the world," coproduced with England. Meanwhile, the Moldavian cinema was specializing in cheap and nonethnic detective stories, easy for marketing in the center. Perhaps because of this inertia, Moldavian cinema in the past few years has not fully used glasnost, either in terms of its ethnic identity, or in terms of the search for a new language.

The same situation would meet us in some Asian republics, such as Tadzhikistan and Turkmenia. Rare courageous attempts to break through the routine of stagnant thinking in these republics have not yet created a film culture for the ethnic cinemas. What is worse, however, is that these republics still seem to think of themselves as Russian provinces. Even the vast and developed republics of the Ukraine and Belorussia, which have large and much more financially independent film industries than the Asian and even the Baltic republics, take one step toward glasnost and then two steps back. Both republics also fail to appreciate their most talented filmmakers. Roman Balayan (*Flights at Night and in Daydreams* [*Polioty vo sne i nayavu*], *Police Spy, Lady Macbeth of the Mtsensk District* [*Ledi Macbet Mtsenskogo uezda*]), one of the most promising Soviet directors of the early 1980s, left Kiev for the more liberal center. And Arkady Ruderman, one of the brightest glasnost documentarians, escaped the wrath of local Belorussian authorities by stealing the copy of his *Theater in the Times of Perestroika and Glasnost* from the studio shelf and moving to Leningrad. (The article by Marina Pork about this adventure in *Soviet Film* was ironically called "Kinosamizdat.") Some of the filmmakers who stay, such as the Ukrainian Ilienko, look to the West. Some do not know where to look.

What caused this situation in the majority of the Soviet republics was Communist Russia, which sacrificed its own ethnic identity to the ambiguous "Soviet" one, and the Stalinist hardliners in the Kremlin. The question is, how can this knot of old problems and new circumstances be undone? There is an answer, and that is what promising about Ilienko's claim that "Soviet cinema does not exist anymore." It is never too late to begin with the beginning. As in Eastern Europe, there is a "zero hour" in the history of the Soviet Union and Soviet film.

In Place of a Conclusion: The Zero Hour

HOW SHOULD WE conclude writing about a process of change that is still in transition? We have elected to end with an open dialogue. Our point of departure is the final part of the last chapter, in which the Ukrainian director Yuri Ilienko pronounced in 1990 that there is no more Soviet Union and no more Soviet cinema.

How do we react?

HORTON: Let's go back to our beginning and the Moscow joke that Gorbachev's perestroika has become a case of perestrelka—cross fire. That is actually only half the joke. The punchline is that the cross fire, perestrelka, will lead to pereklichka, or a roll call, as in a prison roll call. The cynical implication, of course, is that too much freedom leads to a return of Stalinist-style totalitarianism.

I think we can conclude that, since the prodemocratic events of August 1991, it has been virtually impossible to imagine a neo-Stalinist reimposing centralized rule with an iron hand again. Clearly this is what Ilienko was suggesting when he stated "the Soviet Union no longer exists," for in September 1991 it officially ceased to exist. What appears to be developing is a loose confederacy of social democrats or semidemocratic socialists, rather than a tight union under communism.

In terms of the end of Soviet cinema, I feel, to paraphrase Mark Twain's statement, "the reports of its death have been greatly exaggerated." Ilienko's words reflect the spirit of our title: the zero hour. Zero has a number of connotations, but one of the strongest for me is in the sense that Jean-Luc Godard used to say that his filmmaking was an effort to get back to zero, back to the basics of film language, back to a fresh chance to reinvent one's own cinema. (Ironically, we note that in Godard's case his zero included rediscovering the cinema of Dziga Vertov, as opposed to that of the better-known Sergei Eisenstein.)

Soviet cinema as it has been practiced for the past sixty years *is* rapidly ceasing to exist. No one can dispute that, as Valentin Tolstykh said in May 1990, in the Soviet Union today, "there is no longer a question of control over the arts" ("Sixth Congress," 25). We should contrast this with the disturbing trend in the opposite direction in the United States, as the forces associated with Jesse Helms continue to suggest the need for censorship in the arts in America.

The zero hour is the zone of transformation and redefinition, an area that acknowledges both perestroika and perestrelka, yet allows the freedom for filmmakers to go beyond these realities as well.

BRASHINSKY: I would like us to remember a few years back. When glasnost first exploded, many of us shared a highly charged air of excitement and enthusiasm. No matter what has happened during the last five years and what will happen, we have to begin with a full appreciation of this atmosphere and opportunity for change. However, having said this, I am not too optimistic about the chances for either the Soviet Union or for Soviet cinema. To this degree I sympathize with Ilienko's remarks while recognizing that he was exaggerating for dramatic effect.

The zero hour is not a negative term. It is neutral. Perestroika had not completely failed by 1991, but it had not had any serious economic or sociopolitical success either. We still have to admit that the Soviet Union as a whole remains at a zero hour from which it has not yet advanced. The independent countries emerging from the union might be entering a new hour, but this is another story.

HORTON: But given this overall situation, is it fair to say that the Soviet film industry itself has actually made rather remarkable progress toward perestroika, toward restructuring along a market-cinema model? In other words, is Soviet cinema perhaps one bright spot in the midst of the present confusion?

BRASHINSKY: It certainly is, yes. And that is, I think, because film is a unique product that is either sold or not, that is popular with audiences or not, and so with the development of cooperative (independent) production houses, of genre films, of coproductions, we have begun to see a variety of possibilities for a market-based industry. But there is still a long way to go. Take 1990, for instance, in which the Soviet "Film Market" offered over forty films for world sale, and yet only two were bought ("Everyone Should Pay His Way," 29). That's not exactly a winning season. But it is a zero hour.

Furthermore, let's remember that a market-modeled film industry does not just depend on reorganizing filmmaking, but on the development of a new film audience. Audiences need to get used to the new films as well, and in this light, the more Little Veras and Taxi Blues are made, the more Soviet audiences will be ready to "buy" the Soviet film industry's "product."

So the zero hour is, for me, the end and the beginning meeting each other at the crossroads. It is that neutral state in which the past still exists, but the possibilities for a new scale, for a new time count, are there.

HORTON: You are reminding me of something Lev Kuleshov wrote back in 1918: "The bases of cinema art are still unknown, its future paths still shrouded in mist, and cinema's innovators (of whom there are, unfortunately, few) grope their way uncertainly towards new achievements and new interpretations of cinema" (Taylor and Christie, *Film Factory*, 45).

BRASHINSKY: Well, remember that between 1918, when Kuleshov made these remarks, and 1925, when Eisenstein's *Potemkin* appeared, marking the birth of a truly revolutionary cinema, seven years had passed. And I suggest that the zero hour may also take years before the outlines of new approaches will be clear. In this sense Kuleshov's words are important to repeat: Soviet cinema (and the Soviet Union as well) must begin by saying "we are back to a beginning and we know nothing. We have to rediscover all." Only with such an understanding will Soviet cinema and the whole country survive and produce something new.

We have to be honest and say even considering those films we've discussed, such as *Little Vera* and *A Forgotten Tune for the Flute* or *The Cold Summer of '53*, which have been appreciated around the world, they have been recognized not so much for their development of a new universal film language, but in terms of the freedom of subject matter, the creation or representation of new truths about the Soviet Union, and a freer use of film language in a Soviet context. We are still waiting to see what contributions the new Soviet cinema will make to film as a worldwide art.

But let us be hopeful about the potential that exists within the zero hour, for, remembering the 1917 Revolution once more, no other nation has experienced such sweeping changes and turmoil on such a scale in the twentieth century as the Soviet Union has gone through. And based on that alone, the potential for further sweeping changes to grow out of the current turmoil is there. However, we know that the results of that 1917 zero hour could have been much brighter.

HORTON: I would like to move from the potential to the actual. Part of the pleasure of working on this project for me has been that of experiencing the zero hour personally. By this I mean that in deciding to write about the first five years of Soviet cinema under glasnost, we could have no preconceived notion of where we would end up. Now that we have reached the end of our five-year journey, I must say I have something of a double vision of the Soviet film situation.

On the one hand, 1990 brought an unprecedented five Soviet films into the Cannes Festival limelight: Pavel Loungine's gritty, realistic *Taxi Blues*, Stanislav Govorukhin's documentary *We Cannot Live This Way*, Vitaly Kanevsky's *Freeze, Die, Revive*, Yuri Ilienko's allegorical *Swan Lake: The Zone*, and Gleb Panfilov's *Mother*, a respected recasting of the Gorky novel, which itself, of course, had been turned into Pudovkin's fine film. I am struck, first of all, by the healthy diversity of this group. *Taxi Blues* and *Swan Lake: The Zone*, for instance, are both coproductions of one form or another, yet each film has maintained the integrity of the filmmaker, in part by being shot in Russian rather than English, and each has found an appreciative audience. Furthermore, *We Cannot Live This Way* suggests that the documentary movement in the Soviet Union is still very much a part of the ongoing national dialogue under perestroika.

And yet I have my fears for Soviet cinema as well. I believe that the new freedoms have also brought the freedom for American cinema to dominate the Soviet market as it has done in most countries around the world. The next few years should see a flood of American films, particularly action-adventure-comedy movies, and the growth of the video market in the Soviet Union. These factors will, initially at least, tend to work against any efforts made in any direction by any part of the emerging new Soviet film industry. But, I am predicting, after American films and videos reach a certain saturation point, Soviet audiences will begin to return to Soviet films and Soviet videos. This pattern has developed in country after country—I am thinking specifically of Greece and Yugoslavia, for instance—and I see no reason why the Soviet Union should differ widely from this phenomenon.

In sum, I feel the zero hour is one of both danger and creativity. But within this zero period, do you have a tinge of nostalgia for the golden years of subsidized cinema within which Tarkovskys and Paradjanovs could exist? Will the market model of cinema simply degenerate into sex, lies, violence, and videotapes?

BRASHINSKY: What one perhaps could be nostalgic about is not so much a subsidized cinema per se, but the quality of peace that existed in the past, which was conducive to creating quality films. But there is no turning back. A market-based cinema is an absolute necessity for the maturity of the medium. For if a culture cannot survive in some way in a market situation—each filmmaker finding his or her audience—then it is a very weak culture and deserves to die. This means that if a space does not exist within which to create "art" films in a market-based cinema, then those films do not deserve to be produced. Look at Kurosawa, for instance. He is one of the greatest directors in the world, but it is important to see that as such, he has a following: millions of people want to see his films. The same test should exist for Soviet directors as well. And if you do not want to make money and you want to heal your traumas by means of your art, help yourself. Everyone must have his or her own road.

Obviously at the moment life is so confused in the Soviet Union that the average person "cannot live this way," and does not yet have a "normal" basis from which to work in a factory, live with a family, or make a film. Without some sense of normality, great art will be difficult to create even if they have all the freedom in the world.

That is why, I think, a film like *Taxi Blues* is interesting, for it has its artistic, cinematic merits as well as its abilities—in a genre fashion in this case—to reach a large audience.

HORTON: Yes. I am particularly interested in those crossover films that are emerging that succeed in finding an enthusiastic audience, and yet that do have much to offer as films as well. I see *Little Vera, The Needle, The Cold Summer of '53, Zerograd,* and others in this light. I would add one more as we close out 1990. It would be Sergei Bodrov's *Card Player.* Just one year after winning awards with his *Freedom Is Paradise,* he returned with this genre picture that blends the American thief romance with Dostoevsky's *Gambler* and contemporary slice-of-life films. I feel the film works on all those levels without being pretentious. The tightly controlled script by Bodrov and Valeri Barakin and the fine casting of Valeri Garkavin as "the Greek," the protagonist "bad guy" with a pure heart, and Elena Safonova as the tortured female lead, all work together to offer a near-perfect blend of entertainment and realism (that is, a cinematic mediatation on present Soviet reality). Somewhere between an old Bogart film and Dostoevsky's stories of gamblers as losers, *The Card Player* satisfies a widely diversified audience. As we write this, the film is playing in a local Brooklyn movie house catering to Russian-speaking audiences; this is proof enough that Bodrov has gone beyond the film-festival circuit to reach a popular following.

BRASHINSKY: Right. The Bodrovs of the new Soviet cinema are not Tarkovskys or Paradjanovs, but neither are they hacks. They are regular professional filmmakers, something the Soviet cinema has needed for a long, long time. They are craftspeople. Every film culture needs to have a number of craftspeople like Bodrov in order for Tarkovskys to emerge. And maybe, who knows, the time of Tarkovskys has passed away, and the Bodrovs are those who are anticipated by the world's film culture.

1991

Filmography

ALL SOVIET FILMS mentioned in the text are listed below by title in English and Russian, date, and director ("dir."), with "doc." added for those that are documentaries.

A few films such as *Little Vera, Repentance,* and *Rasputin* have appeared in video stores in the United States; for other Soviet films, we refer the reader to several sources. IFEX maintains a list of contemporary Soviet films on videotape: IFEX (International Film Exchange), 201 West 52nd Street, New York, New York 10019. Phone: (212) 582-4318; Fax: (212) 956-2257.

Obtaining videotapes of recent films from the Soviet Union is still difficult. There may soon be several independent Soviet companies marketing NTSC (American-format) videotapes with subtitles. At the moment, the reader is advised to get in contact with Sovexportfilm, which itself may enter the field, for the latest information: Sovexportfilm, Kalashny pereulok 14, Moscow 103869. Phone: 290 5009; Telex: 411143 SEF SU.

The University of Wisconsin has a fine collection of Soviet cinema from the "stagnation" years of the 1970s on film (35 mm prints, for the most part): Dr. Vance Kepley, Jr., Department of Communication Arts, 6112 Vilas Hall, 821 University Avenue, Madison, Wisconsin 53706. Phone: (608) 262-2277.

Loyola University in New Orleans has started a Soviet and East European film and video collection which is available for research purposes on campus: Dr. Andrew Horton, English Department, Loyola University, New Orleans, Louisiana 70118. Phone: (504) 865-2260.

An organization that concerns itself specifically with Soviet and East European media studies can also help those wishing to know more about Soviet film: Working Group on Cinema and Television (USSR and Eastern Europe), Dr. Denise J. Youngblood, Chair, Department of History, University of Vermont, Wheeler House, 442 Main Street, Burlington, Vermont 05405. Phone: (802) 656-3180.

African Hunt (Afrikanskaya ohota, 1988). Doc., dir. Igor Alimpiev.
Against the Current (Protiv techeniya, 1988). Doc., dir. Dmitri Delov.
All Against One (Vse protiv odnogo, 1987). Dir. Arturas Pozdniakovas.
Andrei Rublev (1967). Dir. Andrei Tarkovsky.
And the Past Seems But a Dream (A proshloye kazhetsya snom, 1987). Dir. Sergei Miroshnichenko.

And What about You Guys? (*A u vas vo dvore?* [*In Our Courtyard*], 1987). Doc., dir. V. Kuzmina.

And What If It Is Love? (*A esli eto liubov'?*, 1962). Dir. Yuli Raizman.

Anemia (1988). Dir. Vakhtang Kotetishvili.

Angels with Broken Wings (*Podranki* [*Orphans*], 1976). Dir. Nikolai Gubenko.

Anna Pavlova (1983). Dir. Emil Lotyanu (Soviet-British coproduction).

The Arsonists (*Podzhigateli*, 1989). Dir. Alexander Surin.

The Ascent (*Voskhozhdeniye*, 1977). Dir. Larissa Shepitko.

Ashik Kerib (1988). Dir. Sergei Paradjanov.

Assa (1988). Dir. Sergei Solovyev.

Assuage My Sorrows (*Utoli moya pechali*, 1989). Dir. Alexander Alexandrov and Vladimir Prokhorov.

Asya's Happiness (*Asino schastye*, 1967). Dir. Andrei Konchalovsky.

At Home among Strangers, a Stranger at Home (*Svoi sredi chuzhikh, chuzhoi sredi svoikh*, 1974). Dir. Nikita Mikhalkov.

At the Bottom of Life: How Much Is Love . . . (*Na dne: Skol'ko stoit liubov' . . .*, 1988). Doc., dir. Yevgeny Katz.

Autumn Marathon (*Osennii marafon*, 1979). Dir. Georgi Danelia.

Awakening (*Probuzhdeniye*, 1990). Dir. Jonas Vaitkus.

Ballad of a Soldier (*Ballada o soldate*, 1959). Dir. Grigori Chukhrai.

Banya (1990). Dir. Chris Schmidt (U.S.-Soviet coproduction).

Battleship Potemkin (*Bronenosets "Potemkin,"* 1925). Dir. Sergei Eisenstein.

Bed and Sofa (*Tret'ya Meshchanskaya*, 1927). Dir. Abram Room.

Beware, Automobile! (*Beregis' avtomobilya*, 1966). Dir. Eldar Ryazanov.

The Bird Watcher (*Nablyudatel'* [*The Observer*], 1987). Dir. Arvo Iho.

Blackmailer (*Shantazhist*, 1988). Dir. Valeri Kurykin.

Black Rose Stands for Sorrow, Red Rose Stands for Love (*Chernaya roza—emblema pechali, krasnaya roza—emblema liubvi*, 1989). Dir. Sergei Solovyev.

Blue Mountains, or Improbable Story (*Golubye gory, ili Neobyknovennaya istoriya*, 1984). Dir. Eldar Shengelaya.

BOMZH (1988). Dir. Nikolai Skuibin.

The Bootleggers (*Samogonschiki*, 1961). Dir. Leonid Gaidai.

The Brick Flag (*Kirpichnyi flag*, 1988). Doc., dir. Saulius Berzhinis.

Brief Encounters (*Korotkiye vstrechi*, 1968). Dir. Kira Muratova.

The Burglar (*Vzlomschik*, 1987). Dir. Valery Ogorodnikov.

The Card Player (*Katala*, 1990). Dir. Sergei Bodrov and Alexander Bourovsky.

Carnival Night (*Karnaval'naya noch*, 1956). Dir. Eldar Ryazanov.

Centaurs (*Kentavry*, 1978). Dir. Vitautas Zhalakiavichius.

Chapayev (1934). Dir. Sergei Vasilyev and Georgi Vasilyev.

Chernobyl: Chronicle of Difficult Weeks (*Chernobyl: Hronika trudnykh nedel'*, 1986). Doc., dir. Vladimir Shevchenko.

Chronicle of a Parade (*Hronika demonstratsii*, 1989). Doc., dir. Dmitry Zhelkovsky.

Circus (*Tsirk*, 1936). Dir. Grigori Alexandrov.

The Cold Summer of '53 (*Holodnoye leto '53-go*, 1987). Dir. Alexander Proshkin.

Coma (*Koma*, 1989). Dir. Nijole Adomenaite and Boris Gorlov.

Coming Closer (*Priblizheniye*, 1991). Dir. Alexander Rekhviashvili.

Commissar (*Komissar*, 1967). Dir. Alexander Askoldov.

The Communist (1957). Dir. Yuli Raizman.

Computer Games (*Kompyuternye igry*, 1988). Doc., dir. Alexey Sidelnikov.

Confession: Chronicle of Alienation (*Ispoved': Hronika otchuzhdeniya*, 1988). Docudrama, dir. Georgi Gavrilov.

Conscience (*Sovest'*, 1968). Dir. Vladimir Denisenko.

Cosmogony (*Kosmogoniya*, 1988). Doc., dir. N. Mahmudov.

Counterclaim (*Vstrechnyi isk*, 1988). Dir. Arkady Ruderman and Yuri Haschevatsky.

The Cranes Are Flying (*Letyat zhuravli*, 1957). Dir. Mikhail Kalatozov.

The Crew (*Ekipazh*, 1980). Dir. Alexander Mitta.

Criminal Quartet (*Kriminal'nyi qvartet*, 1989). Dir. Alexander Muratov.

Dark Eyes (*Ochi chernyie*, 1987). Dir. Nikita Mikhalkov (Italy).

Dark Nights in Sochi (*V gorode Sochi tiomnye nochi*, 1989). Dir. Vasily Pichul.

The Daughter of a Horse Thief (*Doch konokrada*, 1981). Dir. Algimantas Puipa.

Daydreams (*Grezy*, 1987). Dir. Yevgeni Kondratiev.

The Day of Fish (*Den' ryby*, 1990). Dir. Algimantas Puipa.

The Day of Wrath (*Den' gneva*, 1987). Dir. Sulambek Mamilov.

Dear Elena Sergeevna (*Dorogaya Elena Sergeevna*, 1988). Dir. Eldar Ryazanov.

Death in Film (*Smert' v kino*, 1991). Dir. Valery Frid and Konstantin Khudyakov.

Defense Counsel Sedov (*Zaschitnik Sedov*, 1989). Dir. Yevgeny Tsymbal.

Demobilized (*Dembil'*, 1991). Doc., dir. Alexey Khaniatin.

The Diamond Hand (*Brilliantovaya ruka*, 1969). Dir. Leonid Gaidai.

Dignity, or The Mystery of a Smile (*Dostoinstvo, ili Taina ulybki*, 1987). Doc., dir. Sh. Mahmudov.

Dmitry Shostakovich: Sonata for Viola (*Dmitri Shostakovich: Al'tovaya sonata*, 1987). Doc., dir. Semen Aranovich and Alexander Sokurov.

The Dog's Feast (*Sobachii pir*, 1990). Dir. Leonid Menaker.

Early on Sunday (*V voskresenye rano*, 1987). Doc., dir. Murat Mamedov.

Earth (*Zemlya*, 1930). Dir. Alexander Dovzhenko.

The Eternal Light (*Vechnoye siyaniye*, 1987). Dir. Algimantas Puipa.

The Evening Sacrifice (*Zhertva vechernyaya*, 1987). Doc., dir. Alexander Sokurov.

Exhausted Towns (*Ustalye goroda*, 1988). Doc., dir. Igor Rodnyansky.

The Extraordinary Adventures of Mr. West in the Land of the Bolsheviks (*Neobychainye priklyucheniya mistera Vesta v strane bol'shevikov*, 1924). Dir. Lev Kuleshov.

Extraordinary Exhibition (*Neobyknovennaya vystavka*, 1969). Dir. Eldar Shengelaya.

Falling Leaves (*Listopad*, 1967). Dir. Otar Ioseliani.

The Fall of Otrar (*Padeniye Otrara*, 1990). Dir. Ardak Amirkulov.

The Fall of the House of Romanov (*Padeniye dinastii Romanovykh*, 1927). Dir. Esther Shub.

Farewell, Street Urchins (*Proschai, shpana zamoskvoretskaya*, 1988). Dir. Alexander Pankratov.

Le Favoris de la Lune (1984). Dir. Otar Ioseliani (France).

Flights at Night and in Daydreams (*Polioty vo sne i nayavu*, 1983). Dir. Roman Balayan.

The Flooding Zone (*Zona zatopleniya*, 1989). Doc., dir. Boris Shun'kov.

Fools Die on Friday (*Duraki umirayut po pyatnitsam*, 1991). Dir. Rudolf Frountov (Soviet-Bulgarian coproduction).

Forgive (*Prosti*, 1988). Dir. Ernest Yasan.

A Forgotten Tune for the Flute (*Zabytaya melodiya dlya fleity*, 1987). Dir. Eldar Ryazanov.

The Fountain (*Fontan*, 1988). Dir. Yuri Mamin.

The Fourth Dream of Anna Andreevna (*Chetvertyi son Anny Andreevny*, 1989). Doc., dir. Nikolai Obuhovich.

Fox Hunt (*Okhota na lis*, 1980). Dir. Vadim Abdrashitov.

Freedom Is Paradise (*SER*, 1989). Dir. Sergei Bodrov.

Freeze, Die, Revive (*Zamri, umri, voskresni*, 1990). Dir. Vitaly Kanevsky.

The Frozen Cherry (*Zimnyaya vishnya*, 1987). Dir. Igor Maslennikov.

Full Moon (*Polnoluniye*, 1989). Dir. Naana Chankova.

Games for Schoolchildren (*Igry dlya detei shkol'nogo vozrasta*, 1985). Dir. Leida Laius and Arvo Iho.

Garage (*Garazh*, 1980). Dir. Eldar Ryazanov.

Georgian Chronicle of the Nineteenth Century (*Gruzinskaya hronika XIX veka*, 1979). Dir. Alexander Rekhviashvili.

The Girl without an Address (*Devushka bez adresa*, 1957). Dir. Eldar Ryazanov.

The Glass Eye (*Steklyannyi glaz*, 1928). Dir. Lili Brik.

God's Tramp (*Bich bozhii*, 1989). Dir. Oleg Fialko.

The Green Fire of the Goat (*Zelyonyi ogon kozy*, 1989). Dir. Anatoly Mateshko.

Gypsies Take off to the Sky (*Tabor uhodit v nebo*, 1976). Dir. Emil Lotyanu.

Happiness (*Schastye*, 1935). Dir. Alexander Medvedkin.

Happiness Is Near (*Schastye blizko*, 1978). Dir. Margarita Kasimova.

The Happy Guys (*Veselye rebyata*, 1934). Dir. Grigori Alexandrov.

Hareba and Gogi (*Hareba i Gogi*, 1988). Dir. Georgy Shengelaya.

He and She (*On i ona*, 1990). Dir. Alexander Baranov.

Heiress Apparent (*Naslednitsa po pryamoi*, 1982). Dir. Sergei Solovyev.

Higher Judgment (*Vysshii sud*, 1987). Doc., dir. Hertz Frank.

His Excellency's Aide (*Adyutant ego prevoskhoditel'stva*, 1970). Dir. Yevgeny Tashkov.

Homecoming (*Vozvrascheniye*, 1987). Doc., dir. Tatyana Chubakova.

The Homeland of Electricity (*Rodina electrichestva*, 1957). Dir. Larissa Shepitko.

An Hour of Democracy (*Chas demokratii*, 1988). Doc., dir. Romuald Pipars.

How Do You Do (1988). Doc., dir. Sergei Baranov.

Hunting the Dragon (*Ohota na drakona*, 1988). Dir. Latif Faiziyev.

The Husband and Daughter of Tamara Alexandrovna (*Muzh i doch' Tamary Alexandrovny*, 1989). Dir. Olga Narutskaya.

The Incident on a Regional Scale (*ChePe raionnogo masshtaba*, 1988). Dir. Sergei Snezhkin.

Intergirl (*Interdevochka*, 1989). Dir. Pyotr Todorovsky (Soviet-Swedish coproduction).

The Irony of Fate, or Hope You Enjoyed Your Steambath (*Ironiya sud'by, ili S legkim parom*, 1975). Dir. Eldar Ryazanov.

Is It Easy to Be Young? (*Legko li byt' molodym?* 1987). Doc., dir. Juris Podnieks.

Is Stalin with Us? (*Stalin s nami?* 1989). Doc., dir. Tofik Shakhverdiev.

It (*Ono*, 1989). Dir. Sergei Ovcharov.

Ivan's Childhood (*Ivanovo detstvo*, 1962). Dir. Andrei Tarkovsky.

Ivan Vasilievich Changes His Profession (*Ivan Vasilievich menyayet professiyu*, 1973). Dir. Leonid Gaidai.

I Was on Service in the Guard of Stalin (*Ya sluzhil v okhrane Stalina*, 1989). Doc., dir. Semen Aranovich.

Jazzmen (*My iz djaza*, 1983). Dir. Karen Shakhnazarov.

A Journey of the Young Composer (*Puteshestviye molodogo kompozitora*, 1984). Dir. Georgy Shengelaya.

Kerosene Seller's Wife (*Zhena kerosinschika*, 1989). Dir. Alexander Kaidanovsky.

The Key Not to Be Passed On (*Kliuch bez prava peredachi*, 1976). Dir. Dinara Asanova.

Khadzhi Murat (1990). Dir. Georgy Shengelaya.

Kin Dza Dza (1987). Dir. Georgi Danelia.

Kinfolk (*Rodnya*, 1982). Dir. Nikita Mikhalkov.

The King of Crime (Vory v zakone [Thieves in Law], 1988). Dir. Yuri Kara.
Klish (1990). Dir. Bakhyt Kilibayev.
Kond (1987). Dir. A. Khachatrian.
Kyadya (1989). Short, dir. Dzhahongir Faiziev.
Lady Macbeth of the Mtsensk District (Ledi Macbet Mtsenskogo uezda, 1989). Dir. Roman Balayan.
The Last Stop (Poslednyaya ostanovka, 1989). Dir. Serik Aprymov.
The Left-hander (Levsha, 1988). Dir. Sergei Ovcharov.
The Legend of Suram Fortress (Legenda o Suramskoi kreposti, 1984). Dir. Sergei Paradjanov.
Legends That Became Life (Ozhivshiye legendy, 1977). Dir. Nodar Managadze.
The Lesson of Life (Urok zhizni, 1955). Dir. Yuli Raizman.
Let There Be Theater! (Tumbalalaika, 1987). Dir. Marina Goldovskaya.
Lifeguard (Spasatel', 1980). Dir. Sergei Solovyev.
A Life without . . . (Zhizn' bez . . . , 1987). Doc., dir. Mark Soosaar.
Limita, or The Fourth Dream (Limita, ili Chetvertyi son, 1988). Doc., dir. Yevgeny Golovnya.
Little Fish in Love (Vliublennaya rybka, 1989). Dir. Abai Karpikov.
Little Vera (Malen'kaya Vera, 1988). Dir. Vasily Pichul.
A Lonely Woman Looks for a Life Companion (Odinokaya zhenschina zhelaet paznakomitsya, 1987). Dir. Vyacheslav Krishtofovich.
The Long Farewell (Dolgiye provody, 1971). Dir. Kira Muratova.
The Look (Vzglyad, 1988). Dir. Valery Ahadov.
Madness (Bezumiye, 1969). Dir. Kaljo Kiisk.
Magdan's Donkey (Lurdja Magdany, 1955). Short, dir. Tengiz Abuladze and Revaz Chheidze.
The Man from Capuchins Boulevard (Chelovek s bul'vara Kaputsinov, 1987). Dir. Alla Surikova.
Man from Nowhere (Chelovek niotkuda, 1961). Dir. Eldar Ryazanov.
Mankurt (1990). Dir. Hodjakurly Narliev.
The Manservant (Sluga, 1989). Dir. Vadim Abdrashitov.
The Man Who Never Was (Chelovek, kotorogo ne bylo, 1990). Dir. Peeter Simm.
Man with a Movie Camera (Chelovek s kinoapparatom, 1929). Doc., dir. Dziga Vertov.
Maria (1988). Doc., dir. Alexander Sokurov.
Marshal Blucher: A Portrait against the Background of the Epoch (Marshal Blucher: Portret na fone epohi, 1988). Doc., dir. Vladimir Eisner.
Marshal Rokossovsky: Life and Times (Marshal Rokossovksy: Zhizn' i vremya, 1988). Doc., dir. Boris Golovnya.
Maxim Gorky: The Last Years (Maxim Gorky: Posledniye gody, 1987). Doc., dir. Semen Aranovich.

The Meeting Place Cannot Be Changed (*Mesto vstrechi izmenit' nel'zya*, 1979). Television, dir. Stanislav Govorukhin.

The Messenger Boy (*Kourier*, 1987). Dir. Karen Shakhnazarov.

Microphone (*Mikrofon*, 1989). Doc., dir. Georgi Shklyarevsky.

Migrating Sparrows (*Perelet vorobyev*, 1979). Short, dir. Teimuraz Babluani.

Mirages (*Miragy*, 1989). Dir. Igor Aleinikov and Gleb Aleinikov.

The Mirror (*Zerkalo*, 1975). Dir. Andrei Tarkovsky.

A Mirror for a Hero (*Zerkalo dlya geroya*, 1988). Dir. Vladimir Khotinenko.

Modern Times (*Novyie vremena*, 1988). Doc., dir. Georgi Negashev.

More Light (*Bol'she sveta*, 1988). Doc., dir. Marina Babak.

Moscow Does Not Believe in Tears (*Moskva slezam ne verit*, 1979). Dir. Vladimir Men'shov.

Mother (*Mat'*, 1926). Dir. Vsevolod Pudovkin.

Mother (*Mat'*, 1990). Dir. Gleb Panfilov.

Mr. Designer (*Gospodin oformitel'*, 1989). Dir. Oleg Teptsov.

My English Granddad (*Robinzonada, ili Moi angliiskii dedushka*, 1987). Dir. Nana Djordjadze.

My Friend Ivan Lapshin (*Moy droug Ivan Lapshin*, 1984). Dir. Alexei Gherman.

My Home in Green Hills (*Moi dom na zelenykh kholmakh*, 1985). Dir. Asya Suleeva.

My Name Is Arlekino (*Menya zovut Arlekino*, 1988). Dir. Valery Rybarev.

My Sweet and Tender Beast (*Moi laskovyi i nezhnyi zver'*, 1978). Dir. Emil Lotyanu.

The Name Day (*Den' angela* [*Day of Angel*], 1988). Dir. Nikolai Makarov and Sergei Selyanov.

The Necklace for My Beloved (*Ozherelye dlya moei liubimoi*, 1972). Dir. Tengiz Abuladze.

The Needle (*Igla*, 1988). Dir. Rashid Nugmanov.

The Neptune Feast (*Prazdnik Neptuna*, 1986). Short, dir. Yuri Mamin.

Nobody Wanted to Die (*Nikto ne khotel umirat'*, 1965). Dir. Vitautas Zhalakiavichius.

October (*Oktyabr'*, 1927). Dir. Sergei Eisenstein.

An Office Romance (*Sluzhebnyi roman*, 1978). Dir. Eldar Ryazanov.

The Old Walls (*Starye steny*, 1974). Dir. Victor Tregubovich.

One Hundred Days after Childhood (*Sto dnei posle detstva*, 1975). Dir. Sergei Solovyev.

The One with a Song (*Tot kto s pesnei*, 1989). Doc., dir. V. Tarik.

Ordinary Fascism (*Obyknovennyi fashism*, 1966). Doc., dir. Mikhail Romm.

Our Mother Is a Hero (*Nasha mama, geroi*, 1989). Doc., dir. Nikolai Obuhovich.

Pain (*Bol'*, 1988). Doc., dir. Sergei Lukyanchikov.

Pants (*Shtany*, 1989). Dir. Valery Priemykhov.

Parallel Movement (*Parallel'noye dvizheniye*, 1988). Short, dir. the Chepayev Group.

Passport (*Pasport*, 1991). Dir. Georgi Danelia (Soviet-French-Israeli coproduction).

Pastoral (1976). Dir. Otar Ioseliani.

The Peasant Women of Ryazan (*Baby Ryazanskiye*, 1927). Dir. Olga Preobrazhenskaya.

The Photo with a Woman and a Wild Boar (*Fotografiya s zhenshchinoi i dikim kabanom*, 1987). Dir. Arvids Krievs.

Piebald Dog Running along the Shore (*Pegii pes, beguschii kraem morya*, 1991). Dir. Karen Gevorkian.

Pirosmani (1970). Dir. Georgy Shengelaya.

Plumbum, or A Dangerous Game (*Pliumbum, ili Opasnaya igra*, 1987). Dir. Vadim Abdrashitov.

Police Spy (*Filior*, 1987). Dir. Roman Balayan.

Pomegranate Blossom (*Tsvet granata*, 1969). Dir. Sergei Paradjanov.

Poperechnaya Street {*Ulitsa Poperechnaya* [*Transverse Street*], 1988). Doc., dir. Ivar Seletskis.

Practical Joke (*Rozygrysh*, 1977). Dir. Vladimir Men'shov.

Prishvin's Paper Eyes (*Bumazhnye glaza Prishvina*, 1989). Dir. Valery Ogorodnikov.

Raisa Nemtchinskaya, Actress of the Circus (*Raisa Nemtchinskaya, actrisa tsirka*, 1970). Doc., dir. Marina Goldovskaya.

Repentance (*Pokayaniye*, 1984). Dir. Tengiz Abuladze.

Revolution Square (*Ploschad' Revolyutsii*, 1989). Doc., dir. Alexander Ivankin.

Risk (1988), and *Risk II*. Doc., dir. Dmitry Borshchevsky.

Risk Group (*Gruppa riska*, 1988). Doc., dir. Andrei Nikishin.

Road to Life (*Putyovka v zhizn'*, 1931). Dir. Nikolai Ekk.

Rock (*Rok*, 1988). Doc., dir. Alexei Uchitel.

Romance of the Lovers (*Romans o vliublennykh*, 1974). Dir. Andrei Konchalovsky.

The Rumyantsev Case (*Delo Rumyantseva*, 1955). Dir. Iosif Kheifits.

The Ruthless Romance (*Zhestokii romans*, 1984). Dir. Eldar Ryazanov.

Save and Protect (*Spasi i sohrani*, 1989). Dir. Alexander Sokurov.

Scarecrow (*Chuchelo* [*Weirdo*], 1984). Dir. Rolan Bykov.

Schors (1939). Dir. Alexander Dovzhenko.

Seryozha (1960). Dir. Georgi Danelia and Igor Talankin.

Seventeen Moments of Spring (*Semnadzat' mgnovenii vesny*, 1973). Television, dir. Tatyana Lioznova.

Shadows of Forgotten Ancestors (*Teni zabytykh predkov*, 1965). Dir. Sergei Paradjanov.

Siz Kim Siz? (1989). Dir. Dzhahongir Faiziev.

The Slave of Love (*Raba liubvi*, 1976). Dir. Nikita Mikhalkov.

Solaris (1972). Dir. Andrei Tarkovsky.

Solovki Regime (*Vlast' solovetskaya*, 1988). Doc., dir. Marina Goldovskaya.

Somebody Was Here (*Zdes' kto-to byl*, 1989). Dir. Igor Aleinikov and Gleb Aleinikov.

Someone Else's Children (*Chuzhyie deti*, 1958). Dir. Tengiz Abuladze.

The Spot (*Pyatno*, 1985). Dir. Alexander Tsabadze.

A Spring for the Thirsty (*Rodnik dlya zhazhduschikh*, 1965). Dir. Yuri Ilienko.

The Step (*Stupen'*, 1986). Dir. Alexander Rekhviashvili.

Stepmother Samanishvili (*Machekha Samanishvili*, 1978). Dir. Eldar Shengelaya.

The Stolen Date (*Ukradennoye svidaniye*, 1988). Dir. Leida Laius.

A Story of Marshal Konev (*Povest' o Marshale Koneve*, 1988). Doc., dir. Lev Danilov.

Strike (*Stachka*, 1924). Dir. Sergei Eisenstein.

The Struggle for a Fleet (*Bitva za flot*, 1989). Dir. the Che-payev Group.

Subway (*Metro*, 1986). Doc., dir. students at VGIK (the national film school).

Suicide Wild Boars (*Vepri suitsida*, 1988). Short, dir. Yevgeni Yufit.

The Summer Heat (*Letnyaya zhara*, 1988). Short, dir. Derezhan Omirbaev.

The Sun of the Sleepless (*Solntse nespyaschikh*, 1988). Dir. Teimuraz Babluani.

Supplication (*Mol'ba*, 1968). Dir. Tengiz Abuladze.

Swan Lake: The Zone (*Lebedinoye ozero: Zona*, 1990). Dir. Yuri Ilienko.

The Swimmer (*Plovets*, 1982). Dir. Irakli Kvirikadze.

The Swineherd and the Shepherd (*Svinarka i pastukh*, 1941). Dir. Ivan Pyryev.

The Tailor (*Portnoi*, 1988). Doc., dir. Vladislav Mirzoian.

Taxi Blues (1990). Dir. Pavel Loungine (French-Soviet coproduction).

The Temple (*Hram*, 1988). Doc., dir. Vladimir Dyakonov.

Ten Little Indians (*Desyat' negrityat*, 1987). Dir. Stanislav Govorukhin.

That's All the Love (*I vsya liubov'*, 1989). Dir. Anatoly Vasilyev.

Theater in the Times of Perestroika and Glasnost (*Teatr vremen perestroiki i glasnosti*, 1987). Doc., dir. Arkady Ruderman.

There Lived a Thrush (*Zhil pevchii drozd*, 1971). Dir. Otar Ioseliani.

This Is How We Live (*Tak i zhivem*, 1987). Doc., dir. Vladimir Oseledchik.

This Sweet Word—Liberty (*Eto sladkoye slovo—svoboda*, 1973). Dir. Vitautas Zhalakiavichius.

The Three (*Troye*, 1988). Dir. Alexander Baranov and Bakhyt Kilibayev.

Three Songs of Lenin (*Tri pesni o Lenine*, 1934). Dir. Dziga Vertov.

Ticket to the Taj Mahal (*Bilet do Taj Mahala*, 1991). Dir. Algimantas Puipa.

Today and Always (*Segodnya i vsegda*, 1982). Dir. Margarita Kasimova.

Tomorrow Is a Holiday (Zavtra prazdnik, 1987). Doc., dir. Sergei Bukovsky.
To Remember or to Forget (Pomnit' ili zabyt', 1982). Dir. Janis Streich.
Toro (1986). Short, dir. Talgat Temenov.
A Touch (Prikosnoveniye, 1987). Doc., dir. Algis Arlauskas.
Tough Kids (Patsany, 1983). Dir. Dinara Asanova.
Tractor Drivers (Traktoristy, 1939). Dir. Ivan Pyryev.
Tractors (1987). Short, dir. Igor Aleinikov and Gleb Aleinikov.
Tragedy in Rock (Tragediya v stile rok, 1988). Dir. Savva Kulish.
The Train Stopped (Ostanovilsya poezd, 1982). Dir. Vadim Abdrashitov.
Tread on the Soft Grass (Gulyanie po myagkoi trave, 1987). Dir. Naana
    Chankova.
The Trial (Protsess, 1987), and The Trial II. Doc., dir. Igor Belyayev.
The Trial of Mironov (Protsess Mironova, 1919). Dir. Dziga Vertov.
The Twelve Chairs (Dvenadsat' stulyev, 1971). Dir. Leonid Gaidai.
The Twist of Fate (Peremena uchasti, 1987). Dir. Kira Muratova.
Two Fyodors (Dva Fyodora, 1958). Dir. Marlen Khutsiev.
Unfinished Piece for a Player Piano (Neokonchennaya piesa dlya mekhani-
    cheskogo pianino, 1977). Dir. Nikita Mikhalkov.
The Unknown War (Velikaya Otechestvennaya, 1978). Television, dir.
    Roman Karmen and others.
The Veri Quarter Tunes (Melodii Veriiskogo kvartala, 1973). Dir. Georgy
    Shengelaya.
The Very Same Münchhausen (Tot samyi Myunhgauzen, 1983). Television,
    dir. Mark Zakharov.
The Villain (Merzavets, 1989). Dir. Vaghif Mustafayev.
Volga, Volga (1938). Dir. Grigori Alexandrov.
The Voyage of Comrade Stalin to Africa (Puteshestviye tovarischa Stalina
    v Afriku, 1991). Dir. Irakli Kvirikadze.
The Wartime Romance (Voenno-polevoi roman, 1984). Dir. Pyotr To-
    dorovsky.
The War Was Tomorrow (Zavtra byla voina, 1987). Dir. Yuri Kara.
The Weakness Syndrome (Astenicheskii sindrom, 1989). Dir. Kira Mura-
    tova.
We Cannot Live This Way (Tak zhit' nel'zya, 1990). Doc., dir. Stanislav
    Govorukhin.
Weekend in Hell (Weekend v adu, 1987). Dir. Vitautas Zhalakiavichius.
Weekend on the Caspian Sea (Weekend na Kaspii, 1989). Doc., dir. Valery
    Grunin.
We'll Survive Till Monday (Dozhivem do ponedel'nika, 1968). Dir. Stanis-
    lav Rostotsky.
Whiskers (Bakenbardy, 1990). Dir. Yuri Mamin.
White Sun of the Desert (Beloye solntse pustyni, 1970). Dir. Vladimir Motyl.
The Wild Pigeon (Chuzhaya belaya i Ryaboi, 1986). Dir. Sergei Solovyev.

Wings (*Krylya*, 1966). Dir. Larissa Shepitko.

The Wishing Tree (*Drevo zhelaniya*, 1977). Dir. Tengiz Abuladze.

Without Witnesses (*Bez svidetelei*, 1983). Dir. Nikita Mikhalkov.

The Wolf Cub among People (*Volchonok sredi liudei*, 1988). Dir. Talgat Temenov.

A Woman and Her Four Men (*Zhenschina i chetvero ee muzhchin*, 1983). Dir. Algimantas Puipa.

Woman of the Day (*Zhenschina dnya*, 1990). Dir. Alexander Baranov and Bakhyt Kilibayev.

The Wood Goblin (*Leshii*, 1987). Doc., dir. Boris Kustov.

Woodpeckers Don't Get Headaches (*Ne bolit golova u diatla*, 1974). Dir. Dinara Asanova.

"Wreck," the Cop's Daughter (*Avaria, doch menta*, 1989). Dir. Mikhail Tumanishvili.

Yakh-ha! (1987). Short docudrama, dir. Rashid Nugmanov.

You and I (*Ty i ya*, 1971). Dir. Larissa Shepitko.

Zerograd (*Gorod zero*, 1989). Dir. Karen Shakhnazarov.

Zigzag of Fortune (*Zigzag udachi*, 1969). Dir. Eldar Ryazanov.

Zone (*Zona*, 1987). Doc., dir. Murat Mamedov.

Zoya (1944). Dir. Lev Arnshtam.

Bibliography

IN ADDITION to "works cited," this list includes those works that influenced us even if they are not directly alluded to in the text. Several references are taken from an as yet unpublished collection of essays by Soviet critics on glasnost cinema, *The Russians Are Coming: Soviet Critics on Contemporary Soviet Cinema*, edited by Andrew Horton and Michael Brashinsky. Other sources of particular help in this project are the following:

1. Personal interviews, identified in the text by date, interviewer, and location.

2. Discussions held at "New Thinking and the Cinema of Today," the Soviet Filmmakers' Union symposium held at Dom Kino, Moscow, July 1989. The quotations and references in the text are to notes taken by Andrew Horton. The proceedings are available in edited form in Russian and English from the Soviet Filmmakers' Union, 13 Vasilyevskaya Street, Moscow 123825, USSR.

3. Talks given at the IREX–Film Arts Academy Conference on Media, in Moscow, 28 October to 7 November 1989.

4. Papers presented and discussions held between Soviet and American film scholars at "The Spirit of Soviet Film Satire," a conference held at Loyola University, New Orleans, 25–27 October 1990.

CINEMA

Abdullayeva, Zara. "Three, Seven, Zero" (in Russian). *Iskusstvo kino*, no. 9 (1989): 25–31.

Agisheva, Nina. "Intolerance Again?" *Moscow News*, no. 10 (1989): 3.

Aitmatov, Chingiz. *The Day Lasts More than a Hundred Years*. Bloomington: Indiana University Press, 1983.

Allen, Robert C., and Douglas Gomery. *Film History: Theory and Practice*. New York: Knopf, 1985.

Anninski, Lev. "Is It Easy to Be Grown-Up?" In Horton and Brashinsky, *The Russians Are Coming*. (Previously published in *Kino* [Riga], no. 4 [1987]: 7.)

———. "The Softness of *Plumbum*." In Horton and Brashinsky, *The Russians Are Coming*.

Arlitskaite, Grazhina. "The Unnecessary Notes on the Margins of the Completed Films" (in Russian). *Kino* (Vilnius), no. 2 (1990): 6–8.

Aufderheide, Pat. "Tiptoeing between the Party Line and the Bottom Line." *In These Times*, 5–18 August 1987, 18–20.

Aumont, Jacques. *Montage Eisenstein*. Translated by Lee Hildretch, Constance Penley, and Andrew Ross. Bloomington: Indiana University Press, 1987.

Babitsky, Paul, and John Rimberg. *The Soviet Film Industry*. New York: Praeger, 1955.

Barnouw, Erik. *Documentary: A History of the Non-fiction Film*. Oxford: Oxford University Press, 1983.

Barringer, Felicity. "Glasnost in Wide Screen: Hush, Hush, Old Stalinist." *New York Times*, 25 November 1988.

Bazin, André. "The Myth of Stalin in the Soviet Cinema." Translated by Alain Piette and Bert Cardullo. *New Orleans Review* 15, no. 3 (Fall 1988): 5–17.

Berman, Boris. "Satire Fed by Candour." *Moscow News*, no. 45 (1988): 12.

Birkos, Alexander S. *Soviet Cinema: Directors and Films*. Hamden, Conn.: Archon Books, 1976.

Bohlen, Celestine. "Out of the USSR, a Filmmakers' Revolution." *Washington Post*, 3 November 1986.

Boldyreva, Elena. "New Shelf for Old." *Soviet Film*, no. 10 (1990): 16–17.

Bordwell, David. *Making Meaning*. Cambridge, Mass.: Harvard University Press, 1989.

Bordwell, David, Janet Staiger, and Kristin Thompson. *The Classical Hollywood Cinema: Film Style and Mode of Production to 1960*. New York: Columbia University Press, 1985.

Boym, Svetlana. "Kitsch as Satire in Recent Soviet Cinema." Paper presented at "The Spirit of Soviet Film Satire," a conference held at Loyola University, New Orleans, 25–27 October 1990.

Bozhovich, Viktor. "Kira Muratova: 'I Make Films about What Is in Me.'" *Soviet Film*, no. 3 (1990): 17–19.

Brashinsky, Michael. "The Ant Hill in the Year of the Dragon." *New Orleans Review* 17, no. 1 (Spring 1990): 74–78.

———. "To Tell an Interesting Story: An Interview with Milos Forman" (in Russian). *Iskusstvo kino*, no. 8 (1988): 111–13.

Brashinsky, Michael, and Sergei Dobrotvorsky. "Through the Looking Glass." *Soviet Film*, no. 9 (1989): 21–22.

Brown, Georgia. "Bird Watching." *Village Voice*, 22 May 1990, 55–56.

Budiak, Liudmila M. "We Cannot Live This Way." *Film Quarterly* 44, no. 2 (Winter 1990–1991): 28–33.

Christensen, Julie. "Fathers and Sons at the Georgian Film Studio." *Wide Angle* 12, no. 4 (October 1990): 48–61.

Christie, Ian. "Revolutionary Riga." *American Film* 15, no. 5 (February 1990): 2.

Ciesol, Forrest. "After a Twenty-five Year Struggle with Censors, Uzbek Hero Tamerlane Rides Again." *Variety*, 13 June 1990.

———. "Kazakhstan Wave." *Sight and Sound* 59 (Winter 1989–1990): 56–58.

———. "The Many Hollywoods of Central Asia." *World Monitor* (February 1990): 66–70.

Cohen, Louis H. *The Cultural-Political Traditions and Developments of the Soviet Cinema, 1917–1972.* New York: Arno, 1974.

Danielou, Laurent. "Les films sovietiques à Cannes: Session de rattrapage." *Cahiers du cinéma*, no. 431–32 (May 1990): 55–56.

D'Arcy, David. "Finally, a Documented Documentary." *American Film* 15, no. 5 (February 1990): 14–15.

"Declaration of the Formation of the Filmmakers' Union on the Federation Basis" (in Russian). *Iskusstvo kino*, no. 8 (1990): 3–4.

de Lauretis, Teresa. *Alice Doesn't: Feminism, Semiotics, Cinema.* Bloomington: Indiana University Press, 1984.

———. *Technologies of Gender.* Bloomington: Indiana University Press, 1987.

Demin, Victor. "Shooting the Shot-down Targets" (in Russian). *Iskusstvo kino*, no. 9 (1989): 5–9.

Dickinson, Thorold, and Catherine de la Roche. *Soviet Cinema.* London, 1948. Reprint. New York: Arno, 1972.

Dmitriev, Vladimir. "Waiting for the Oscar, or Nanook of the East" (in Russian). *Iskusstvo kino*, no. 10 (1989): 16–21.

Dobrotvorsky, Sergei. "The Most Avant-Garde of All Parallel Ones." In Horton and Brashinsky, *The Russians Are Coming.* Translated by Ekaterina Dobrotvorskaya. (First published in a slightly different form in *New Orleans Review* 17, no. 1 [Spring 1990]: 84–87.)

Doherty, Thomas. *Teenagers and Teenpics: The Juvenilization of American Movies in the 1950s.* Boston: Unwin Hyman, 1988.

Dolmatovskaya, Galina, and Irina Shilova. *Who's Who in the Soviet Cinema.* Moscow: Progress Press, 1979.

Dondurey, Daniil. "Money Is Not All" (in Russian). *Iskusstvo kino*, no. 10 (1989): 3–12.

Drozdova, Marina. "A Dandy of the Postpunk Period, or Goodbye, America, Oh! . . ." In Horton and Brashinsky, *The Russians Are Coming.*

———. "Fofan." *Soviet Film*, no. 8 (1989): 18–19.

———. "Midseasonal Anarchists." In Horton and Brashinsky, *The Russians Are Coming.*

Eagle, Herbert. "The Indexicality of *Little Vera* and the End of Socialist Realism." *Wide Angle* 12, no. 4 (October 1990): 26–37.

———. "Soviet Cinema Today: On the Semantic Potential of a Discredited Canon." *Michigan Quarterly Review* (Fall 1989): 743–60.

Eidsvik, Charles. "Mock Realism: The Comedy of Futility in Eastern Europe." In *Comedy/Cinema/Theory*, edited by Andrew Horton, 91–105. Berkeley and Los Angeles: University of California Press, 1991.

Eisenstein, Sergei. *Film Form*. Translated by Jay Leyda. New York: Harcourt, Brace, and World, 1949.

———. *The Film Sense*. Translated by Jay Leyda. New York: Harcourt, Brace, and World, 1947.

———. *Immoral Memories*. Translated by Herbert Marshall. Boston: Houghton Mifflin, 1983.

———. *Notes of a Film Director*. Translated by Jay Leyda. New York: Dover, 1970.

Elsaesser, Thomas. *New German Cinema: A History*. New Brunswick, N.J.: Rutgers University Press, 1989.

"Everyone Should Pay His Way: A Look at the First Soviet Film Markets." *Soviet Film*, no. 4 (1990): 29–30.

Fenin, George M., and William K. Everson. *The Western: From Silents to the Seventies*. Rev. ed. New York: Penguin, 1977.

Festival des Films du Monde, 23 August–3 September 1990, Montreal. Program. Montreal, 1990.

"Film: Renovation of the Artistic Consciousness" (in Russian). *Iskusstvo kino*, no. 9 (1989).

"Film of the Totalitarian Epoch" (in Russian). *Iskusstvo kino*, no. 1 (1990): 111–20; no. 2 (1990): 109–17; no. 3 (1990): 100–112.

Fischer, Lucy. *Shot/Countershot: Film Tradition and Women's Cinema*. Princeton: Princeton University Press, 1989.

Galichenko, Nicholas. *Glasnost: Soviet Cinema Responds*. Edited by Robert Allington. Austin: University of Texas Press, 1991.

Gladilshchikov, Yuri. "Intergirls and Not Girls" (in Russian). *Iskusstvo kino*, no. 5 (1989): 85–90.

———. "Made in US(SR)A, or How We Make American Movies." *Literary Gazette International* 1, no. 6 (April 1990): 22–23.

"Glasnost and Perestroika Enable Estonia to Showcase Local Films." *Variety*, 5–11 July 1989.

Golovskoy, Val S., and John Rimberg. *Behind the Soviet Screen: The Motion Picture Industry in the USSR, 1972–1982*. Ann Arbor, Mich.: Ardis, 1986.

Goodman, Walter. "Ancient Omelet." Review of *The Legend of Suram Fortress*. *New York Times*, 18 February 1987.

———. "Class Differences in a Classless Society." Review of *A Forgotten Tune for the Flute*. *New York Times*, 18 December 1988.

———. "Rose Petals from Heaven." Review of *Ashik Kerib*. *New York Times*, 29 September 1988.

Goukassian, Frijeta. *Women in World Cinema*. Leningrad: KIWI, 1990.

Grant, Barry Keith, ed. *Film Genre Reader*. Austin: University of Texas Press, 1986.

Gulchenko, Victor. "Stockhom Does Not Believe in Tears" (in Russian). *Iskusstvo kino*, no. 1 (1990): 62–68.

Hecht, Leo. "Union of Soviet Socialist Republics." In *World Cinema Since 1945*, edited by William Luhr, 558–86. New York: Ungar, 1987.

Hoberman, J. "Suddenly, Last Summer: *Ghostbusters II.*" *Village Voice*, 27 June 1989, 65–66.

Holloway, Ron. "Soviet Cinema Special Report." *Hollywood Reporter*, 23 February 1988, 1–23.

———. "Tbilisi Hub a 'Socialist Cinecitta.'" *Hollywood Reporter*, 23 August 1988, 1–3.

Horton, Andrew. "*Little Vera.*" *Film Quarterly* 42, no. 4 (Summer 1989): 18–21.

———. "Nomad from Kazakhstan: An Interview with Rashid Nugmanov." *Film Criticism* 14, no. 2 (Summer 1990): 33–38.

———. "'Nothing Worth Living For': Soviet Youth and the Documentary Movement." *Wide Angle* 12, no. 4 (October 1990): 38–47.

———. "Soviet Cinema Comes of Age." *New Orleans Review* 17, no. 1 (Spring 1990): 73–74.

———. "Yugoslavia: Multi-Faceted Cinema." In *World Cinema Since 1945*, edited by William Luhr, 639–60. New York: Ungar, 1987.

Horton, Andrew, and Michael Brashinsky, eds. *The Russians Are Coming: Soviet Critics on Contemporary Soviet Cinema*. Manuscript.

Ibragimbekov, Rustam. "Free, But United" (in Russian). *Iskusstvo kino*, no. 3 (1989): 3–17.

Iensen, Tatyana. "Unhappy Guys" (in Russian). *Iskusstvo kino*, no. 9 (1990): 82–86.

Ilyenko, Yuri. "In Memory of Sergei Paradzhanov." *Moscow News*, no. 16 (1990): 6.

Izvolensky, Pyotr. "Siz Kim Siz?" *Soviet Film*, no. 2 (1990): 10.

Karakhan, Lev. "Jobless Prophets." In Horton and Brashinsky, *The Russians Are Coming*.

Karpinsky, Lev. "Is Stalin in Us?" (in Russian). *Sovetskii ekran*, no. 17 (1990): 4–6.

Keller, Bill. "Alcohol and Bigotry in a Soviet Film Test the Limits of the New Openness." *New York Times*, 29 August 1990.

Kepley, Vance, Jr. *In the Service of the State: The Cinema of Alexander Dovzhenko*. Madison: University of Wisconsin Press, 1986.

———. "The Workers' International Relief and the Cinema of the Left, 1921–1935." *Cinema Journal* 23, no. 1 (Fall 1983): 9–12.

Kimmel, Dan. "Yanks, Sovs Find Common Chord in *Banya.*" *Variety*, 15 August 1990.

Kiselev, Alexander. "From Euclides to Lobachevsky." In Horton and Brashinsky, *The Russians Are Coming*.

———. "A Highly Promising Crisis: Young Cinema." *Soviet Film*, no. 2 (1990): 5–7, 26.

———. "Wuthering Voids." In Horton and Brashinsky, *The Russians Are Coming*.

Kohler, Ingeborg. "Interview with Alexander Askoldov." *German Film Kino*, no. 28 (1988): 29–30.

Kuleshov, Lev V. *Essays and Materials* (in Russian). Moscow: Iskusstvo, 1979.

———. *Kuleshov on Film: Writings of Lev Kuleshov*. Translated and edited by Ronald Levaco. Berkeley and Los Angeles: University of California Press, 1974.

Kuzin, Vladilen. "Documentary—Concoction of Freedom" (in Russian). *Iskusstvo kino*, no. 2 (1990): 9–16.

Lardner, James. "A Moment We Had to Grasp" (in Russian). *Iskusstvo kino*, no. 5 (1989): 121–30.

Lary, N. M. *Dostoevsky and Soviet Film*. Ithaca: Cornell University Press, 1987.

Lawton, Anna. "Film Biz Shakeout Sweeps USSR." *Variety*, 2 May 1990.

———. "Happy Glasnost." *The World and I* (December 1989): 30–43.

———. "Rewriting History: A New Trend in the Documentary Film." *Soviet Observer*, 29 September 1988, 14.

———. "Soviet Cinema Four Years Later." *Wide Angle* 12, no. 4 (October 1990): 8–25.

———. "Soviet Filmmakers Create Federation While Trying to Avert 'Katastroika.'" *Variety*, 13 June 1990.

———. "Toward a New Openness in Soviet Cinema, 1976–1987." In *Post New Wave Cinema in the Soviet Union and Eastern Europe*, edited by Daniel J. Goulding, 1–50. Bloomington: Indiana University Press, 1989.

Le Fanu, Mark. *The Cinema of Andrei Tarkovsky*. London: British Film Institute, 1987.

Leyda, Jay. *Kino: A History of the Russian and Soviet Film*. Rev. ed. Princeton: Princeton University Press, 1983.

Liehm, Mira, and Antonin Liehm. *The Most Important Art: Soviet and East European Film after 1945*. Berkeley and Los Angeles: University of California Press, 1977.

Listov, Victor. "History on the Screen." Manuscript.

Livshin, Semyon. "Film-Money-Film." *Soviet Film*, no. 4 (1990): 36–37.

Mamin, Yuri. Remarks at the American premiere of *Whiskers*, at "The Spirit of Soviet Film Satire," a conference held at Loyola University, New Orleans, 25–27 October 1990.

———. "39 Degrees C." *Soviet Film*, no. 11 (1990): 14–17.

Marshall, Herbert. *Masters of Soviet Cinema.* New York: Routledge, 1983.

Maslin, Janet. "Harshness of Soviet Life in 'Taxi Blues.'" *New York Times,* 18 January 1991.

————. "Satire." Review of *Repentance. New York Times,* 4 December 1987.

Mast, Gerald. *The Comic Mind: Comedy and the Movies.* 2d ed. Chicago: University of Chicago Press, 1979.

Mayne, Judith. *Kino and the Woman Question: Feminism and Soviet Silent Film.* Columbus: Ohio State University Press, 1989.

Menashe, Louis. "Glasnost in the Soviet Cinema." *Cineaste* 16, no. 1–2 (1987–1988): 28–33.

————. "*Repentance.*" *Cineaste* 16, no. 3 (1988): 47–49.

Michelson, Annette, ed. *Kino-Eye: The Writings of Dziga Vertov.* Translated by Kevin O'Brien. Berkeley and Los Angeles: University of California Press, 1984.

Mitchell, W.J.T. *Iconology: Image, Text, Ideology.* Chicago: University of Chicago Press, 1986.

Moskvina, Tatyana. " 'Global Cinema' of the Petrograd District" (in Russian). *Iskusstvo kino,* no. 7 (1990): 70–80.

Moss, Kevin. "A Russian Münchhausen: Aesopian Translation." Talk given at "The Spirit of Soviet Film Satire," a conference held at Loyola University, New Orleans, 25–27 October 1990.

Mulvey, Laura. *Visual and Other Pleasures.* Bloomington: Indiana University Press, 1989.

Muratov, Sergei. "Restored Vision." *The Glasnost Film Festival.* Catalogue. Oakland, Calif.: The Video Project, 1989.

Muratov, Sergei, and Marina Topaz. "The Screen of the Perestroika Era." *Sputnik,* no. 2 (1990): 32–35.

Muratova, Kira. "I Make Films about What Is in Me." *Soviet Film,* no. 2 (1990): 19.

Musser, Charles. "Festivals." Review of the Glasnost Documentary Film Festival distributed by the Museum of Modern Art, 1988–1989. *Cineaste* 17, no. 2 (1989): 27–30.

"New Thinking and the Cinema of Today." Soviet Filmmakers' Union Symposium held at Dom Kino, Moscow, July 1989.

Nichols, Bill. *Ideology and the Image.* Bloomington: Indiana University Press, 1981.

Nugmanov, Rashid, and Tolomush Okeev. "One Thousand and One Concerns" (in Russian). *Iskusstvo kino,* no. 4 (1990): 36–40.

Ochirova, Tatyana. "Russian National Cinema: Project, Hypothesis, Reality?" *Soviet Film,* no. 9 (1990): 4–5.

Palmer, Jerry. *The Logic of the Absurd: On Film and Television Comedy.* London: British Film Institute, 1988.

Paul, William. "Bill Murray, King of Animal Comedy: Reaganite Comedy in a Kinder, Gentler Nation." *Film Criticism* 13, no. 1 (Fall 1988): 4–19. Special issue on American comedy, edited by Andrew Horton.

Petric, Vlada. "A Subtextual Reading of Kuleshov's Satire, *The Extraordinary Adventures of Mr. West in the Land of the Bolsheviks.*" Talk given at "The Spirit of Soviet Film Satire," a conference held at Loyola University, New Orleans, 25–27 October 1990.

Pichul, Vasily. "Independent Film" (in Russian). *Iskusstvo kino*, no. 3 (1989): 24–26.

Plakhov, Andrei. "Soviet Cinema into the Nineties." *Sight and Sound* 58 (Spring 1989): 23–24.

Polan, Dana. *Power and Paranoia: History, Narrative, and the American Cinema, 1940–1950.* New York: Columbia University Press, 1986.

Pork, Marina. "Kinosamizdat." *Soviet Film*, no. 5 (1990): 16–17.

Pudovkin, V. I. *Film Technique and Film Acting.* Translated by Ivor Montagu. New York: Bonanza Books, 1949.

Quart, Barbara. "Between Materialism and Mysticism: The Films of Larissa Shepitko." *Cineaste* 16, no. 3 (1988): 4–11.

"Releases: *Taxi Blues.*" *Moving Pictures International*, 18 October 1990, 17.

Robinson, Marc. "Zero City: Man—Zero." Talk given at the Florida State University Conference on Film and Literature, Tallahassee, Fla., January 1991.

Rosenberg, Karen. "Glasnost and Georgian Cinema." *Independent* (April 1988): 23–27.

Schatz, Thomas. *Hollywood Genres: Formulas, Filmmaking, and the Studio System.* New York: Random House, 1981.

Schnitzer, Juda, et al., eds. *Cinema in Revolution: The Heroic Era of the Soviet Film.* New York: Hill and Wang, 1973.

"The Screen in the Times of Perestroika and Glasnost: A Discussion at *Iskusstvo kino* Headquarters" (in Russian). *Iskusstvo kino*, no. 2 (1989): 3–32.

Seifer, Donna. "What Is Women's Cinema?" Paper presented at the AAASS Conference, Chicago, November 1989.

Seletskis, Ivar. "On the Federalization of the Union" (in Russian). *Iskusstvo kino*, no. 3 (1990): 20–21.

Shepotinnik, Peter. "With Perestroika, Without Tarkovsky." *New Orleans Review* 17, no. 1 (Spring 1990): 79–83.

Shmyrov, Vyacheslav. "A Generation without Freedom." *Soviet Film*, no. 10 (1990): 8–9.

Shumakov, Sergei. "Are the Russians Coming?" (in Russian). *Sovetskii ekran*, no. 4 (1990): 10–12.

Silverman, Kaja. *The Subject of Semiotics.* New York: Oxford University Press, 1983.

Simanovich, Grigori. "With What Shall We Lure the Viewer?" *Soviet Film*, no. 10 (1989): 24–25.

Sipe, Jeff. "In Competition: *Taxi Blues.*" *Moving Pictures International*, 11 May 1990, 32.

Smirnov, Pyotr. "What Next?" *Soviet Film*, no. 9 (1989): 14–15.

Smirnova, Avdotya. "The Discreet Charm of One Film." In Horton and Brashinsky, *The Russians Are Coming.*

Sovexportfilm annual film catalogues. Moscow: Sovexportfilm, 1983–1990.

"Soviets Struggle for Rights." *The Business of Film at Cannes*, no. 8 (17 May 1990): 1–2.

Span, Paula. "The Bare Facts about Glasnost: Soviet Actress Natalya Negoda's American Premiere." *Washington Post*, 1 April 1989.

Strat. "*The Weakness Syndrome.*" Review. *Variety*, 28 February 1990.

Sullivan, Rob. "Hollywood Peaceniks." *Nuclear Times* (May–June 1988): 16–24.

Tapinas, Laimonas. *Lithuanian Film Makers*. Vilnius: Mintis, 1988.

Tarkovsky, Andrei. *Sculpting in Time.* Austin: University Texas Press, 1989.

Taylor, Richard, ed. and trans., and Ian Christie, ed. *The Film Factory: Russian and Soviet Cinema in Documents.* Cambridge, Mass.: Harvard University Press, 1988.

"That Glasnost Girl: Natalya Negoda." *Playboy* (May 1989): 140–49.

Timofeevsky, Alexander. "In the Tenderest Shroud." In Horton and Brashinsky, *The Russians Are Coming.*

Tolstykh, Valentin. "The Sixth Congress . . . What Then?" *Soviet Film*, no. 5 (1990): 24–25.

Tsivian, Yuri. *Silent Witness: Russian Films, 1908–1919*, edited by Paolo Cherchi Usai et al. Bloomington: Indiana University Press, 1990.

Tsyrkun, Nina. "Youth Cinema Today in the USSR." Talk given at the IREX–Film Arts Academy Conference on Media, held in Moscow, 28 October–7 November 1989.

Turovskaya, Maya. "Behind the Scenes on the Making of *Volga, Volga.*" Talk given at "The Spirit of Soviet Film Satire," a conference held at Loyola University, New Orleans, 25–27 October 1990.

———. "*Commissar.*" In Horton and Brashinsky, *The Russians Are Coming.*

Valiulis, Skirmantas. "Venturing into a Taboo Area." Review of *The Brick Flag. Soviet Film*, no. 11 (1989): 28–29.

Vardunas, Vladimir. "*The Fountain*: An Interview Yuri Mamin Might Have Given to a Person Who Hasn't Seen the Film." *Soviet Film*, no. 4 (1989): 15–17.

Vasilyev, Andrei. "Untapped Bonanza." *Soviet Film*, no. 4 (1990): 14–16.

Vazsky, Michael. "Soviet Film Audiences." Talk given at "New Thinking and the Cinema of Today," the Soviet Filmmakers' Union symposium held at Dom Kino, Moscow, July 1989.

Verdon-Roe, Vivienne. "Introduction." *The Glasnost Film Festival*. Catalogue. Oakland, Calif.: The Video Project, 1989.

Vorontsov, Yuri, and Igor Rachuk. *The Phenomenon of the Soviet Cinema*. Moscow: Progress, 1980.

Warshow, Robert. *The Immediate Experience*. Garden City, N.Y.: Doubleday, 1962.

Williams, Mark. *Road Movies*. New York: Proteus Books, 1982.

Williamson, Anne. "In the Soviet Orbit: Prisoner—The Essential Paradjanov." *Film Comment* (April 1989): 57–63.

Wood, Robin. *Hollywood from Vietnam to Reagan*. New York: Columbia University Press, 1986.

Wright, Will. *Six-guns and Society: A Structural Study of the Western*. Berkeley and Los Angeles: University of California Press, 1975.

Yampolsky, Mikhail. "Cinema without Cinema." In Horton and Brashinsky, *The Russians Are Coming*.

———. "The Dignity of a Soviet Cowboy." *Soviet Film*, no. 6 (1990): 25.

———. "The Emergence of Faces." *Soviet Film*, no. 9 (1989): 29.

———. "The Trauma of Silence." *Soviet Film*, no. 12 (1990): 5.

Zarkhi, Nina. "Another Cinema" (in Russian). *Iskusstvo kino*, no. 9 (1990): 72–75.

Zorkaya, Neya. *The Illustrated History of the Soviet Cinema*. New York: Hippocrene Books, 1989.

Zorky, Andrei. "The Eternal Light" (in Russian). *Novye Filmy* (January 1989): 1–2.

LITERATURE, CULTURE, POLITICS

Aksyonov, Vassily. "Not Quite a Sentimental Journey." *New Republic*, 16 April 1990, 21–25.

Andrew, Joe. *Women in Russian Literature, 1780–1863*. New York: St. Martin's Press, 1988.

Attwood, Lynne. *The New Soviet Man and Woman: Sex Role Socialization in the USSR*. Bloomington: Indiana University Press, 1990.

Bakhtin, Mikhail. *Art and Answerability*. Translated by Vadim Liapunov, edited by Michael Holquist and Vadim Liapunov. Austin: University of Texas Press, 1990.

———. *The Dialogic Imagination: Four Essays*. Translated by Caryl Emerson and Michael Holquist. Austin: University of Texas Press, 1981.

———. *Problems of Dostoevsky's Poetics*. Edited and translated by Caryl Emerson. Minneapolis: University of Minnesota Press, 1984.

———. *Rabelais and His World*. Translated by Helen Irwolsky. Bloomington: University of Indiana Press.

Belyaeva, Nina. "The Unmarked Road to Soviet Feminism." *In These Times*, 21–27 March 1990, 12–13.

Blos, Peter. *Son and Father: Before and beyond the Oedipus Complex*. New York: Macmillan, 1985.

Brown, Edward J. *Russian Literature since the Revolution*. Cambridge, Mass.: Harvard University Press, 1982.

Bulgakov, Mikhail. *The Master and Margarita*. New York: Harper and Row, 1967.

Chua-Eoan, Howard G. "My Wife Is a Very Independent Lady." *Time*, 8 June 1988, 38–43.

Clark, Katerina. *The Soviet Novel: History as Ritual*. Rev. ed. Chicago: University of Chicago Press, 1985.

DeCurtis, Anthony. "Anarchy in the USSR." *Rolling Stone*, 12–16 July 1990, 67–70.

Derrida, Jacques. *Positions*. Translated by Alan Bass. Chicago: University of Chicago Press, 1981.

Desai, Padma. *Perestroika in Perspective: The Design and Dilemmas of Soviet Reform*. Princeton: Princeton University Press, 1989.

du Plessix Gray, Francine. "Soviet Women." *New Yorker*, 19 February 1990, 48–81.

———. *Soviet Women: Walking the Tightrope*. New York: Doubleday, 1990.

Echoes of Glasnost in Soviet Ukraine. North York, Ontario: York University Press, 1990.

Edmondson, Linda Harriet. *Feminism in Russia, 1900–1917*. Stanford: Stanford University Press, 1984.

Eklof, Ben. *Soviet Briefing: Gorbachev and the Reform Period*. Boulder, Colo.: Westview Press, 1989.

Friedberg, Maurice, and Heyward Isham, eds. *Soviet Society under Gorbachev: Current Trends and the Prospects for Reform*. Armonk, N.Y.: M. E. Sharpe, 1987.

Gerzon, Mark. *A Choice of Heroes: The Changing Face of American Manhood*. Boston: Houghton Mifflin, 1982.

Gorbachev, Mikhail. *Perestroika: New Thinking for Our Country and the World*. New York: Harper and Row, 1987.

Hayward, Max. *Writers in Russia, 1917–1978*. New York: Harcourt Brace Jovanovich, 1983.

Hingley, Ronald. *Russian Writers and Soviet Society, 1917–1978*. London: Weidenfeld and Nicolson, 1979.

Hosking, Geoffrey. *The Awakening of the Soviet Union*. Cambridge, Mass.: Harvard University Press, 1990.

Hubbs, Joanna. *Mother Russia: The Feminine Myth in Russian Culture*. Bloomington: Indiana University Press, 1988.

Jameson, Fredric. *The Ideologies of Theory: Essays, 1971–1986.* Vol. 2. Minneapolis: University of Minnesota Press, 1988.

Keller, Bill. "Mr. President: Democracy, Gorbachev's Way." *New York Times,* 18 March 1990.

Kraminova, Natalya. "Politics Not for Women?" *Moscow News,* no. 10 (1989): 14.

Krivorotov, Victor, and Sergey Chernyshov. "The Myths of Our Revolution." *Literary Gazette International* 1, no. 7 (May 1990): 4–5; no. 8 (June 1990): 10–11.

Kyzlasova, Irina. *Russian Icons: Fourteenth to Sixteenth Centuries.* Translated by Sergei Volynets. Leningrad: Aurora Art, 1988.

McCuaig, Kerry. "Effects of Perestroika and Glasnost on Women." *Canadian Women's Studies* 10, no. 4 (Winter 1989): 11–14.

Mann, Judy. "Vox Populi Sovietskaya." *Washington Post,* 22 March 1989.

Mickiewicz, Ellen Propper. *Media and the Russian Public.* New York: Praeger, 1981.

Moroz, Oleg. "Vilnius: A Night in Spring." *Literary Gazette International* 1, no. 7 (May 1990): 16–17.

Nelson, Cary, and Lawrence Grossberg, eds. *Marxism and the Interpretation of Culture.* Urbana: University of Illinois Press, 1988.

O'Toole, Michael J. *Structure, Style, and Interpretation in the Russian Short Story.* New Haven: Yale University Press, 1982.

Pierce, Charles Sanders. *Collected Papers.* Edited by Charles Hartshorne and Paul Weiss. Vols. 1–8. Cambridge, Mass.: Harvard University Press, 1931.

Popov, Gavriil. "Dangers of Democracy." Translated by Antonina W. Bouis. *New York Review of Books,* 16 August 1990, 27–28.

Propp, Vladimir. *Theory and History of Folklore.* Vol. 5. Minneapolis: University of Minnesota Press, 1984.

Ratushinskaya, Irina. *Grey Is the Color of Hope.* Translated by Alyona Kojevnikov. New York: Knopf, 1988.

Remnick, David. "The Communist Party Cut-Up." *New York Review of Books,* 17 May 1990, 3–5.

———. "Soviets Await Benefits of Gorbachev Reforms." *Washington Post,* 8 August 1988.

Rishina, Irinia. ". . . For Many Shall Come in My Name: Interview with Svetlana Aleksiyevich, Author of *Sealed Coffin Boys.*" *Literary Gazette International* 1, no. 8 (June 1990): 3–5.

Ryan, Michael. *Marxism and Deconstruction: A Critical Articulation.* Baltimore: Johns Hopkins University Press, 1982.

Rywkin, Michael. *Soviet Society Today.* Armonk, N.Y.: M. E. Sharpe, 1989.

Segel, Harold B. *Twentieth-Century Russian Drama: From Gorky to the Present.* New York: Columbia University Press, 1979.

Shipler, David K. *Russia: Broken Idols, Solemn Dreams.* New York: Penguin, 1983.

Smolowe, Jill. "Heroines of Soviet Labor." *Time,* 8 June 1988, 28–37.

Snitow, Alan. "A New Generation: An Interview with Elena Zelinskaya." *In These Times,* 28 March–3 April 1990, 12–13.

Solzhenitsyn, Aleksandr. *One Day in the Life of Ivan Denisovich.* New York: E. P. Dutton, 1963.

Starr, S. Frederick. *Red and Hot: The Fate of Jazz in the Soviet Union.* New York: Oxford University Press, 1983.

Stites, Richard. *The Women's Liberation Movement in Russia: Feminism, Nihilism, and Bolshevism, 1860–1930.* Princeton: Princeton University Press, 1978.

Stulova, Marina. "Time for Change." Translated by Andrei Stulov. *Canadian Women's Studies* 10, no. 4 (Winter 1989): 96–98.

Taubman, William, and Jane Taubman. *Moscow Spring.* New York: Summit, 1989.

Tolstaya, Tatyana. "Notes from Underground." *New York Review of Books,* 31 May 1990, 3–7.

Traver, Nancy. *Kife: The Lives and Dreams of Soviet Youth.* New York: St. Martin's Press, 1990.

Trimble, Jeff. "Gorbachev a Failure? What Soviet Citizens Think of Their Leader." *Connoisseur* (June 1989): 76–79.

Troitsky, Artemy. *Back in the USSR: The True Story of Rock in Russia.* Boston: Faber and Faber, 1987.

Troy, Carol. "Moscow's Women." *Ms.* (April 1988): 54–63.

Vasilkova, Inna. "Thirty-three Women and One Man." *Moscow News,* no. 52 (1988): 6.

Voinovich, Vladimir. *The Life and Extraordinary Adventures of Private Ivan Chonkin.* New York: Farrar, Strauss, and Giroux, 1976.

Voznesensky, Andrei. "Prophecies of a Greedy Observer." *New York Times Book Review,* 27 November 1988.

Welsh, David J. *Russian Comedy, 1765–1823.* The Hague: Mouton, 1966.

Whitney, Craig J. "The Revolution Is Today; Bureaucracy Is Forever." *New York Times,* 15 April 1990.

Yershov, Peter. *Comedy in the Soviet Theater.* New York: Praeger, 1956.

Index